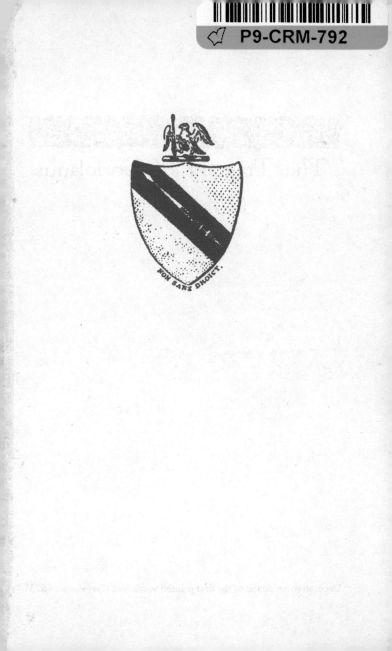

The Tragedy of Coriolanus:

Decorative headband of the first printed version of *Coriolanus*, 1623.

William Shakespeare

Coriolanus

With New and Updated Critical Essays and a Revised Bibliography

Edited by Reuben Brower

THE SIGNET CLASSIC SHAKESPEARE
General Editor: Sylvan Barnet

A SIGNET CLASSIC

SIGNET CLASSIC
Published by New American Library, a division of
Penguin Group (USA) Inc., 375 Hudson Street,
New York, New York 10014, USA
Penguin Group (Canada), 10 Alcorn Avenue, Toronto,
Ontario M4V 3B2, Canada (a division of Pearson Penguin Canada Inc.)
Penguin Books Ltd., 80 Strand, London WC2R 0RL, England
Penguin Ireland, 25 St. Stephen's Green, Dublin 2,
Ireland (a division of Penguin Books Ltd.)
Penguin Group (Australia), 250 Camberwell Road, Camberwell, Victoria 3124,
Australia (a division of Pearson Australia Group Pty. Ltd.)
Penguin Books India Pvt. Ltd., 11 Community Centre, Panchsheel Park,
New Delhi - 110 017, India
Penguin Group (NZ), cnr Airborne and Rosedale Roads, Albany,
Auckland 1310, New Zealand (a division of Pearson New Zealand Ltd.)
Penguin Books (South Africa) (Pty.) Ltd., 24 Sturdee Avenue,
Rosebank, Johannesburg 2196, South Africa

Penguin Books Ltd., Registered Offices:
80 Strand, London WC2R 0RL, England

Published by Signet Classic, an imprint of New American Library,
a division of Penguin Group (USA) Inc.

First Signet Classic Printing (Second Revised Edition), July 2002

10 9 8 7

Library of Congress Catalog Card Number: 2001055137

Printed in the United States of America

Contents

Shakespeare: An Overview

Biographical Sketch

Between the record of his baptism in Stratford on 26 April 1564 and the record of his burial in Stratford on 25 April 1616, some forty official documents name Shakespeare, and many others name his parents, his children, and his grandchildren. Further, there are at least fifty literary references to him in the works of his contemporaries. More facts are known about William Shakespeare than about any other playwright of the period except Ben Jonson. The facts should, however, be distinguished from the legends. The latter, inevitably more engaging and better known, tell us that the Stratford boy killed a calf in high style, poached deer and rabbits, and was forced to flee to London, where he held horses outside a playhouse. These traditions are only traditions; they may be true, but no evidence supports them, and it is well to stick to the facts.

Mary Arden, the dramatist's mother, was the daughter of a substantial landowner; about 1557 she married John Shakespeare, a tanner, glove-maker, and trader in wool, grain, and other farm commodities. In 1557 John Shakespeare was a member of the council (the governing body of Stratford), in 1558 a constable of the borough, in 1561 one of the two town chamberlains, in 1565 an alderman (entitling him to the appellation of "Mr."), in 1568 high bailiff—the town's highest political office, equivalent to mayor. After 1577, for an unknown reason he drops out of local politics. What *is* known is that he had to mortgage his wife's property, and that he was involved in serious litigation.

The birthday of William Shakespeare, the third child and the eldest son of this locally prominent man, is unrecorded, but the Stratford parish register records that the infant was baptized on 26 April 1564. (It is quite possible that he was born on 23 April, but this date has probably been assigned by tradition because it is the date on which, fifty-two years later, he died, and perhaps because it is the feast day of St. George, patron saint of England.) The attendance records of the Stratford grammar school of the period are not extant, but it is reasonable to assume that the son of a prominent local official attended the free school—it had been established for the purpose of educating males precisely of his class—and received substantial training in Latin. The masters of the school from Shakespeare's seventh to fifteenth years held Oxford degrees; the Elizabethan curriculum excluded mathematics and the natural sciences but taught a good deal of Latin rhetoric, logic, and literature, including plays by Plautus, Terence, and Seneca.

On 27 November 1582 a marriage license was issued for the marriage of Shakespeare and Anne Hathaway, eight years his senior. The couple had a daughter, Susanna, in May 1583. Perhaps the marriage was necessary, but perhaps the couple had earlier engaged, in the presence of witnesses, in a formal "troth plight" which would render their children legitimate even if no further ceremony were performed. In February 1585, Anne Hathaway bore Shakespeare twins, Hamnet and Judith.

That Shakespeare was born is excellent; that he married and had children is pleasant; but that we know nothing about his departure from Stratford to London or about the beginning of his theatrical career is lamentable and must be admitted. We would gladly sacrifice details about his children's baptism for details about his earliest days in the theater. Perhaps the poaching episode is true (but it is first reported almost a century after Shakespeare's death), or perhaps he left Stratford to be a schoolmaster, as another tradition holds; perhaps he was moved (like Petruchio in *The Taming of the Shrew*) by

> Such wind as scatters young men through the world,
> To seek their fortunes farther than at home
> Where small experience grows.   (1.2.49–51)

In 1592, thanks to the cantankerousness of Robert Greene, we have our first reference, a snarling one, to Shakespeare as an actor and playwright. Greene, a graduate of St. John's College, Cambridge, had become a playwright and a pamphleteer in London, and in one of his pamphlets he warns three university-educated playwrights against an actor who has presumed to turn playwright:

> There is an upstart crow, beautified with our feathers, that with his *tiger's heart wrapped in a player's hide* supposes he is as well able to bombast out a blank verse as the best of you, and being an absolute Johannes-factotum [i.e., jack-of-all-trades] is in his own conceit the only Shake-scene in a country.

The reference to the player, as well as the allusion to Aesop's crow (who strutted in borrowed plumage, as an actor struts in fine words not his own), makes it clear that by this date Shakespeare had both acted and written. That Shakespeare is meant is indicated not only by *Shake-scene* but also by the parody of a line from one of Shakespeare's plays, *3 Henry VI*: "O, tiger's heart wrapped in a woman's hide" (1.4.137). If in 1592 Shakespeare was prominent enough to be attacked by an envious dramatist, he probably had served an apprenticeship in the theater for at least a few years.

In any case, although there are no extant references to Shakespeare between the record of the baptism of his twins in 1585 and Greene's hostile comment about "Shake-scene" in 1592, it is evident that during some of these "dark years" or "lost years" Shakespeare had acted and written. There are a number of subsequent references to him as an actor. Documents indicate that in 1598 he is a "principal comedian," in 1603 a "principal tragedian," in 1608 he is one of the "men players." (We do not have, however, any solid information about which roles he may have played; later traditions say he played Adam in *As You Like It* and the ghost in *Hamlet*, but nothing supports the assertions. Probably his role as dramatist came to supersede his role as actor.) The profession of actor was not for a gentleman, and it occasionally drew the scorn of university men like Greene who resented writing speeches for persons less educated than themselves, but it was respectable enough; players, if prosperous, were in effect members of the bourgeoisie, and there is nothing to suggest that Stratford considered William Shakespeare less than a solid citizen. When, in 1596, the Shakespeares were granted a coat of arms—i.e., the right to be considered gentlemen—the grant was made to Shakespeare's father, but probably William Shakespeare had arranged the matter on his own behalf. In subsequent transactions he is occasionally styled a gentleman.

Although in 1593 and 1594 Shakespeare published two narrative poems dedicated to the Earl of Southampton, *Venus and Adonis* and *The Rape of Lucrece*, and may well have written most or all of his sonnets in the middle nineties, Shakespeare's literary activity seems to have been almost entirely devoted to the theater. (It may be significant that the two narrative poems were written in years when the plague closed the theaters for several months.) In 1594 he was a charter member of a theatrical company called the Chamberlain's Men, which in 1603 became the royal company, the King's Men, making Shakespeare the king's playwright. Until he retired to Stratford (about 1611, apparently), he was with this remarkably stable company. From 1599 the company acted primarily at the Globe theater, in which Shakespeare held a one-tenth interest. Other Elizabethan dramatists are known to have acted, but no other is known also to have been entitled to a share of the profits.

Shakespeare's first eight published plays did not have his name on them, but this is not remarkable; the most popular play of the period, Thomas Kyd's *The Spanish Tragedy*, went through many editions without naming Kyd, and Kyd's authorship is known only because a book on the profession of acting happens to quote (and attribute to Kyd) some lines on the interest of Roman emperors in the drama. What is remarkable is that after 1598 Shakespeare's name commonly appears on printed plays—some of which are not his. Presumably his name was a drawing card, and publishers used it to attract potential buyers. Another indication of his popularity comes from Francis Meres, author of *Palladis Tamia: Wit's Treasury* (1598). In this anthology of snippets accompanied by an essay on literature, many playwrights are mentioned, but Shakespeare's name occurs more often than any other, and Shakespeare is the only play-wright whose plays are listed.

From his acting, his play writing, and his share in a playhouse, Shakespeare seems to have made considerable money. He put it to work, making substantial investments in Stratford real estate. As early as 1597 he bought New Place, the second-largest house in Stratford. His family moved in soon afterward, and the house remained in the family until a granddaughter died in 1670. When Shakespeare made his will in 1616, less than a month before he died, he sought to leave his property intact to his descendants. Of small bequests to relatives and to friends (including three actors, Richard Burbage, John Heminges, and Henry Condell), that to his wife of the second-best bed has provoked the most comment. It has sometimes been taken as a sign of an unhappy marriage (other supposed signs are the appar-ently hasty marriage, his wife's seniority of eight years, and his residence in London without his family). Perhaps the second-best bed was the bed the couple had slept in, the best bed being reserved for visitors. In any case, had Shakespeare not excepted it, the bed would have gone (with the rest of his household possessions) to his daughter and her husband.

On 25 April 1616 Shakespeare was buried within the chancel of the church at Stratford. An unattractive monu-ment to his memory, placed on a wall near the grave, says that he died on 23 April. Over the grave itself are the lines, perhaps by Shakespeare, that (more than his literary fame) have kept his bones undisturbed in the crowded burial ground where old bones were often dislodged to make way for new:

> Good friend, for Jesus' sake forbear
> To dig the dust enclosed here.
> Blessed be the man that spares these stones
> And cursed be he that moves my bones.

A Note on the Anti-Stratfordians, Especially Baconians and Oxfordians

Not until 1769—more than a hundred and fifty years after Shakespeare's death—is there any record of anyone expressing doubt about Shakespeare's authorship of the plays and poems. In 1769, however, Herbert Lawrence nominated Francis Bacon (1561–1626) in *The Life and Adventures of Common Sense*. Since then, at least two dozen other nominees have been offered, including Christopher Marlowe, Sir Walter Raleigh, Queen Elizabeth I, and Edward de Vere, 17th earl of Oxford. The impulse behind all anti-Stratfordian movements is the scarcely concealed snobbish opinion that "the man from Stratford" simply could not have written the plays because he was a country fellow without a university education and without access to high society. Anyone, the argument goes, who used so many legal terms, medical terms, nautical terms, and so forth, and who showed some familiarity with classical writing, must have attended a university, and anyone who knew so much about courtly elegance and courtly deceit must himself have moved among courtiers. The plays do indeed reveal an author whose interests were exceptionally broad, but specialists in any given field—law, medicine, arms and armor, and so on—soon find that the plays do not reveal deep knowledge in specialized matters; indeed, the playwright often gets technical details wrong.

The claim on behalf of Bacon, forgotten almost as soon as it was put forth in 1769, was independently reasserted by Joseph C. Hart in 1848. In 1856 it was reaffirmed by W. H. Smith in a book, and also by Delia Bacon in an article; in 1857 Delia Bacon published a book, arguing that Francis Bacon had directed a group of intellectuals who wrote the plays.

Francis Bacon's claim has largely faded, perhaps because it was advanced with such evident craziness by Ignatius Donnelly, who in *The Great Cryptogram* (1888) claimed to break a code in the plays that proved Bacon had written not only the plays attributed to Shakespeare but also other Renaissance works, for instance the plays of Christopher Marlowe and the essays of Montaigne.

Consider the last two lines of the Epilogue in *The Tempest*:

As you from crimes would pardoned be,
Let your indulgence set me free.

What was Shakespeare—sorry, Francis Bacon, Baron Verulam—*really* saying in these two lines? According to Baconians, the lines are an anagram reading, "Tempest of Francis Bacon, Lord Verulam; do ye ne'er divulge me, ye words." Ingenious, and it is a pity that in the quotation the letter *a* appears only twice in the cryptogram, whereas in the deciphered message it appears three times. Oh, no problem; just alter "Verulam" to "Verul'm" and it works out very nicely.

Most people understand that with sufficient ingenuity one can torture any text and find in it what one wishes. For instance: Did Shakespeare have a hand in the King James Version of the Bible? It was nearing completion in 1610, when Shakespeare was forty-six years old. If you look at the 46th Psalm and count forward for forty-six words, you will find the word *shake*. Now if you go to the end of the psalm and count backward forty-six words, you will find the word *spear*. Clear evidence, according to some, that Shakespeare slyly left his mark in the book.

Bacon's candidacy has largely been replaced in the twentieth century by the candidacy of Edward de Vere (1550–1604), 17th earl of Oxford. The basic ideas behind the Oxford theory, advanced at greatest length by Dorothy and Charlton Ogburn in *This Star of England* (1952, rev. 1955), a book of 1297 pages, and by Charlton Ogburn in *The Mysterious William Shakespeare* (1984), a book of 892 pages, are these: (1) The man from Stratford could not possibly have had the mental equipment and the experience to have written the plays—only a courtier could have written them; (2) Oxford had the requisite background (social position, education, years at Queen Elizabeth's court); (3) Oxford did not wish his authorship to be known for two basic reasons: writing for the public theater was a vulgar pursuit, and the plays show so much courtly and royal disreputable behavior that they would have compromised Oxford's position at court. Oxfordians offer countless details to support the claim. For example, Hamlet's phrase "that ever I was born to set it right" (1.5.89) barely conceals "E. Ver, I was born to set it right," an unambiguous announcement of de Vere's authorship, according to *This Star of England* (p. 654). A second example: Consider Ben

Jonson's poem entitled "To the Memory of My Beloved Master William Shakespeare," prefixed to the first collected edition of Shakespeare's plays in 1623. According to Oxfordians, when Jonson in this poem speaks of the author of the plays as the "swan of Avon," he is alluding not to William Shakespeare, who was born and died in Stratford-on-Avon and who throughout his adult life owned property there; rather, he is alluding to Oxford, who, the Ogburns say, used "William Shakespeare" as his pen name, and whose manor at Bilton was on the Avon River. Oxfordians do not offer any evidence that Oxford took a pen name, and they do not care that Oxford had sold the manor in 1581, forty-two years before Jonson wrote his poem. Surely a reference to the Shakespeare who was born in Stratford, who had returned to Stratford, and who had died there only seven years before Jonson wrote the poem is more plausible. And exactly why Jonson, who elsewhere also spoke of Shakespeare as a playwright, and why Heminges and Condell, who had acted with Shakespeare for about twenty years, should speak of Shakespeare as the author in their dedication in the 1623 volume of collected plays is never adequately explained by Oxfordians. Either Jonson, Heminges and Condell, and numerous others were in on the conspiracy, or they were all duped—equally unlikely alternatives. Another difficulty in the Oxford theory is that Oxford died in 1604, and some of the plays are clearly indebted to works and events later than 1604. Among the Oxfordian responses are: At his death Oxford left some plays, and in later years these were touched up by hacks, who added the material that points to later dates. *The Tempest*, almost universally regarded as one of Shakespeare's greatest plays and pretty clearly dated to 1611, does indeed date from a period after the death of Oxford, but it is a crude piece of work that should not be included in the canon of works by Oxford.

The anti-Stratfordians, in addition to assuming that the author must have been a man of rank and a university man, usually assume two conspiracies: (1) a conspiracy in Elizabethan and Jacobean times, in which a surprisingly large number of persons connected with the theater knew that the actor Shakespeare did not write the plays attributed to him but for some reason or other pretended that he did; (2) a conspiracy of today's Stratfordians, the professors who teach Shakespeare in the colleges and universities, who are said to have a vested interest in preserving Shakespeare as the author of the plays they teach. In fact, (1) it is inconceivable that the secret of Shakespeare's non-authorship could have been preserved by all of the people who supposedly were in on the conspiracy, and (2) academic fame awaits any scholar today who can disprove Shakespeare's authorship.

The Stratfordian case is convincing not only because hundreds or even thousands of anti-Stratford arguments—of the sort that say "ever I was born" has the secret double meaning "E. Ver, I was born"—add up to nothing at all but also because irrefutable evidence connects the man from Stratford with the London theater and with the authorship of particular plays. The anti-Stratfordians do not seem to understand that it is not enough to dismiss the Stratford case by saying that a fellow from the provinces simply couldn't have written the plays. Nor do they understand that it is not enough to dismiss all of the evidence connecting Shakespeare with the plays by asserting that it is perjured.

The Shakespeare Canon

We return to William Shakespeare. Thirty-seven plays as well as some nondramatic poems are generally held to constitute the Shakespeare canon, the body of authentic works. The exact dates of composition of most of the works are highly uncertain, but evidence of a starting point and/or of a final limiting point often provides a framework for informed guessing. For example, *Richard II* cannot be earlier than 1595, the publication date of some material to which it is indebted; *The Merchant of Venice* cannot be later than 1598, the year Francis Meres mentioned it. Sometimes arguments for a date hang on an alleged topical allusion, such as the lines about the unseasonable weather in *A Midsummer Night's Dream*, 2.1.81–117, but such an allusion, if indeed it is an allusion to an event in the real world, can be variously interpreted, and in any case there is always the possibility that a topical allusion was inserted years later, to bring the play up to date. (The issue of alterations in a text between the time that Shakespeare drafted it and the time that it was printed—alterations due to censorship or playhouse practice or Shakespeare's own second thoughts—will be discussed in "The Play Text as a Collaboration" later in this overview.) Dates are often attributed on the basis of style, and although conjectures about style usually rest on other conjectures (such as Shakespeare's development as a playwright, or the appropriateness of lines to character), sooner or later one must rely on one's literary sense. There is no documentary proof, for example, that *Othello* is not as early as *Romeo and Juliet*, but one feels that *Othello* is a later, more mature work, and because the first record of its performance is 1604, one is glad enough to set its composition at that date and not push it back into Shakespeare's early years. (*Romeo and Juliet* was first published in 1597, but evidence suggests that it was written a little earlier.) The following chronology, then, is indebted not only to facts but also to informed guesswork and sensitivity. The dates, necessarily imprecise for some works, indicate something like a scholarly consensus concerning the time of original composition. Some plays show evidence of later revision.

Plays. The first collected edition of Shakespeare, published in 1623, included thirty-six plays. These are all accepted as Shakespeare's, though for one of them, *Henry VIII*, he is thought to have had a collaborator. A thirty-seventh play, *Pericles*, published in 1609 and attributed to Shakespeare on the title page, is also widely accepted as being partly by Shakespeare even though it is not included in the 1623 volume. Still another play not in the 1623 volume, *The Two Noble Kinsmen*, was first published in 1634, with a title page attributing it to John Fletcher and Shakespeare. Probably most students of the subject now believe that Shakespeare did indeed have a hand in it. Of the remaining plays attributed at one time or another to Shakespeare, only one, *Edward III*, anonymously published in 1596, is now regarded by some scholars as a serious candidate. The prevailing opinion, however, is that this rather simple-minded play is not Shakespeare's; at most he may have revised some passages, chiefly scenes with the Countess of

Salisbury. We include *The Two Noble Kinsmen* but do not include *Edward III* in the following list.

1588–94	*The Comedy of Errors*
1588–94	*Love's Labor's Lost*
1589–91	*2 Henry VI*
1590–91	*3 Henry VI*
1589–92	*1 Henry VI*
1592–93	*Richard III*
1589–94	*Titus Andronicus*
1593–94	*The Taming of the Shrew*
1592–94	*The Two Gentlemen of Verona*
1594–96	*Romeo and Juliet*
1595	*Richard II*
1595–96	*A Midsummer Night's Dream*
1596–97	*King John*
1594–96	*The Merchant of Venice*
1596–97	*1 Henry IV*
1597	*The Merry Wives of Windsor*
1597–98	*2 Henry IV*
1598–99	*Much Ado About Nothing*
1598–99	*Henry V*
1599	*Julius Caesar*
1599–1600	*As You Like It*
1599–1600	*Twelfth Night*
1600–1601	*Hamlet*
1601–1602	*Troilus and Cressida*
1602–1604	*All's Well That Ends Well*
1603–1604	*Othello*
1604	*Measure for Measure*
1605–1606	*King Lear*
1605–1606	*Macbeth*
1606–1607	*Antony and Cleopatra*
1605–1608	*Timon of Athens*
1607–1608	*Coriolanus*
1607–1608	*Pericles*
1609–10	*Cymbeline*
1610–11	*The Winter's Tale*
1611	*The Tempest*

1612–13	*Henry VIII*
1613	*The Two Noble Kinsmen*

Poems. In 1989 Donald W. Foster published a book in which he argued that "A Funeral Elegy for Master William Peter," published in 1612, ascribed only to the initials W.S., *may* be by Shakespeare. Foster later published an article in a scholarly journal, *PMLA* 111 (1996), in which he asserted the claim more positively. The evidence begins with the initials, and includes the fact that the publisher and the printer of the elegy had published Shakespeare's *Sonnets* in 1609. But such facts add up to rather little, especially because no one has found any connection between Shakespeare and William Peter (an Oxford graduate about whom little is known, who was murdered at the age of twenty-nine). The argument is based chiefly on statistical examinations of word patterns, which are said to correlate with Shakespeare's known work. Despite such correlations, however, many readers feel that the poem does not sound like Shakespeare. True, Shakespeare has a great range of styles, but his work is consistently imaginative and interesting. Many readers find neither of these qualities in "A Funeral Elegy."

1592–93	*Venus and Adonis*
1593–94	*The Rape of Lucrece*
1593–1600	*Sonnets*
1600–1601	*The Phoenix and the Turtle*

Shakespeare's English

1. Spelling and Pronunciation. From the philologist's point of view, Shakespeare's English is modern English. It requires footnotes, but the inexperienced reader can comprehend substantial passages with very little help, whereas for the same reader Chaucer's Middle English is a foreign language. By the beginning of the fifteenth century the chief grammatical changes in English had taken place, and the final unaccented -*e* of Middle English had been lost (though it survives even today in spelling, as in *name*); during the fifteenth century the dialect of London, the commercial and political center, gradually displaced the provincial dialects, at least in writing; by the end of the century, printing had helped to regularize and stabilize the language, especially spelling. Elizabethan spelling may seem erratic to us (there were dozens of spellings of *Shakespeare*, and a simple word like *been* was also spelled *beene* and *bin*), but it had much in common with our spelling. Elizabethan spelling was conservative in that for the most part it reflected an older pronunciation (Middle English) rather than the sound of the language as it was then spoken, just as our spelling continues to reflect medieval pronunciation—most obviously in the now silent but formerly pronounced letters in a word such as *knight*. Elizabethan pronunciation, though not identical with ours, was much closer to ours than to that of the Middle Ages. Incidentally, though no one can be certain about what Elizabethan English sounded like, specialists tend to believe it was rather like the speech of a modern stage Irishman (*time* apparently was pronounced *toime*, *old* pronounced *awld*, *day* pronounced *die*, and *join* pronounced *jine*) and not at all like the Oxford speech that most of us think it was.

An awareness of the difference between our pronunciation and Shakespeare's is crucial in three areas—in accent, or number of syllables (many metrically regular lines may look irregular to us); in rhymes (which may not look like rhymes); and in puns (which may not look like puns). Examples will be useful. Some words that were at least on occasion stressed differently from today are *aspèct*, *còmplete*, *fòrlorn*, *revènue*, and *sepùlcher*. Words that sometimes had an additional syllable are *emp[e]ress*, *Hen[e]ry*, *mon[e]th*, and *villain* (three syllables, *vil-lay-in*). An additional syllable is often found in possessives, like *moon*'s (pronounced *moones*) and in words ending in *-tion* or *-sion*. Words that had one less syllable than they now have are *needle* (pronounced *neel*) and *violet* (pronounced *vilet*). Among rhymes now lost are *one* with *loan*, *love* with *prove*, *beast* with *jest*, *eat* with *great*. (In reading, trust your sense of metrics and your ear, more than your eye.) An example of a pun that has become obliterated by a change in pronunciation is Falstaff's reply to Prince Hal's "Come, tell us your reason" in *1 Henry IV*: "Give you a reason on compulsion? If reasons were as plentiful as blackberries, I would give no man a reason upon compulsion, I" (2.4.237–40). The *ea* in *reason* was pronounced rather like a long *a*, like the *ai* in *raisin*, hence the comparison with blackberries.

Puns are not merely attempts to be funny; like metaphors they often involve bringing into a meaningful relationship areas of experience normally seen as remote. In *2 Henry IV*, when Feeble is conscripted, he stoically says, "I care not. A man can die but once. We owe God a death" (3.2.242–43), punning on *debt*, which was the way *death* was pronounced. Here an enormously significant fact of life is put into simple commercial imagery, suggesting its commonplace quality. Shakespeare used the same pun earlier in *1 Henry IV*, when Prince Hal says to Falstaff, "Why, thou owest God a death," and Falstaff replies, " 'Tis not due yet: I would be loath to pay him before his day. What need I be so forward with him that calls not on me?" (5.1.126–29).

Sometimes the puns reveal a delightful playfulness; sometimes they reveal aggressiveness, as when, replying to Claudius's "But now, my cousin Hamlet, and my son," Hamlet says, "A little more than kin, and less than kind!" (1.2.64–65). These are Hamlet's first words in the play, and we already hear him warring verbally against Claudius. Hamlet's "less than kind" probably means (1) Hamlet is not of Claudius's family or nature, *kind* having the sense it still has in our word *mankind*; (2) Hamlet is not kindly (affectionately) disposed toward Claudius; (3) Claudius is not naturally (but rather unnaturally, in a legal sense incestuously) Hamlet's father. The puns evidently were not put in as sops to the groundlings; they are an important way of communicating a complex meaning.

2. Vocabulary. A conspicuous difficulty in reading Shakespeare is rooted in the fact that some of his words are no longer in common use—for example, words concerned with armor, astrology, clothing, coinage, hawking, horsemanship, law, medicine, sailing, and war. Shakespeare had a large vocabulary—something near thirty thousand words—but it was not so much a vocabulary of big words as a vocabulary drawn from a wide range of life, and it is partly his ability to call upon a great body of concrete language that gives his plays the sense of being in close contact with life. When the right word did not already exist, he made it up. Among words thought to be his coinages are *accommodation, all-knowing, amazement, bare-faced, countless, dexterously, dislocate, dwindle, fancy-free, frugal, indistinguishable, lackluster, laughable, overawe, premeditated, sea change, star-crossed.* Among those that have not survived are the verb *convive,* meaning to feast together, and *smilet,* a little smile.

Less overtly troublesome than the technical words but more treacherous are the words that seem readily intelligible to us but whose Elizabethan meanings differ from their modern ones. When Horatio describes the Ghost as an "erring spirit," he is saying not that the ghost has sinned or made an error but that it is wandering. Here is a short list of some of the most common words in Shakespeare's plays that often (but not always) have a meaning other than their most usual modern meaning:

'a	he
abuse	deceive
accident	occurrence
advertise	inform
an, and	if
annoy	harm
appeal	accuse
artificial	skillful
brave	fine, splendid
censure	opinion
cheer	(1) face (2) frame of mind
chorus	a single person who comments on the events
closet	small private room
competitor	partner
conceit	idea, imagination
cousin	kinsman
cunning	skillful
disaster	evil astrological influence
doom	judgment
entertain	receive into service

envy	malice
event	outcome
excrement	outgrowth (of hair)
fact	evil deed
fancy	(1) love (2) imagination
fell	cruel
fellow	(1) companion (2) low person (often an insulting term if addressed to someone of approximately equal rank)
fond	foolish
free	(1) innocent (2) generous
glass	mirror
hap, haply	chance, by chance
head	army
humor	(1) mood (2) bodily fluid thought to control one's psychology
imp	child
intelligence	news
kind	natural, acting according to nature
let	hinder
lewd	base
mere(ly)	utter(ly)
modern	commonplace
natural	a fool, an idiot
naughty	(1) wicked (2) worthless
next	nearest
nice	(1) trivial (2) fussy
noise	music
policy	(1) prudence (2) stratagem
presently	immediately
prevent	anticipate
proper	handsome
prove	test
quick	alive
sad	serious
saw	proverb
secure	without care, incautious
silly	innocent

sensible	capable of being perceived by the senses
shrewd	sharp
so	provided that
starve	die
still	always
success	that which follows
tall	brave
tell	count
tonight	last night
wanton	playful, careless
watch	keep awake
will	lust
wink	close both eyes
wit	mind, intelligence

All glosses, of course, are mere approximations; sometimes one of Shakespeare's words may hover between an older meaning and a modern one, and as we have seen, his words often have multiple meanings.

3. Grammar. A few matters of grammar may be surveyed, though it should be noted at the outset that Shakespeare sometimes made up his own grammar. As E.A. Abbott says in *A Shakespearian Grammar,* "Almost any part of speech can be used as any other part of speech": a noun as a verb ("he childed as I fathered"); a verb as a noun ("She hath made compare"); or an adverb as an adjective ("a seldom pleasure"). There are hundreds, perhaps thousands, of such instances in the plays, many of which at first glance would not seem at all irregular and would trouble only a pedant. Here are a few broad matters.

Nouns: The Elizabethans thought the *-s* genitive ending for nouns (as in *man's*) derived from *his*; thus the line " 'gainst the count his galleys I did some service," for "the count's galleys."

Adjectives: By Shakespeare's time adjectives had lost the endings that once indicated gender, number, and case. About the only difference between Shakespeare's adjectives and ours is the use of the now redundant *more* or *most* with the comparative ("some more fitter place") or superlative

("This was the most unkindest cut of all"). Like double comparatives and double superlatives, double negatives were acceptable; Mercutio "will not budge for no man's pleasure."

Pronouns: The greatest change was in pronouns. In Middle English *thou, thy,* and *thee* were used among familiars and in speaking to children and inferiors; *ye, your,* and *you* were used in speaking to superiors (servants to masters, nobles to the king) or to equals with whom the speaker was not familiar. Increasingly the "polite" forms were used in all direct address, regardless of rank, and the accusative *you* displaced the nominative *ye.* Shakespeare sometimes uses *ye* instead of *you,* but even in Shakespeare's day *ye* was archaic, and it occurs mostly in rhetorical appeals.

Thou, thy, and *thee* were not completely displaced, however, and Shakespeare occasionally makes significant use of them, sometimes to connote familiarity or intimacy and sometimes to connote contempt. In *Twelfth Night* Sir Toby advises Sir Andrew to insult Cesario by addressing him as *thou:* "If thou thou'st him some thrice, it shall not be amiss" (3.2.46–47). In *Othello* when Brabantio is addressing an unidentified voice in the dark he says, "What are you?" (1.1.91), but when the voice identifies itself as the foolish suitor Roderigo, Brabantio uses the contemptuous form, saying, "I have charged thee not to haunt about my doors" (93). He uses this form for a while, but later in the scene, when he comes to regard Roderigo as an ally, he shifts back to the polite *you,* beginning in line 163, "What said she to you?" and on to the end of the scene. For reasons not yet satisfactorily explained, Elizabethans used *thou* in addresses to God—"O God, thy arm was here," the king says in *Henry V* (4.8.108)—and to supernatural characters such as ghosts and witches. A subtle variation occurs in *Hamlet.* When Hamlet first talks with the Ghost in 1.5, he uses *thou,* but when he sees the Ghost in his mother's room, in 3.4, he uses *you,* presumably because he is now convinced that the Ghost is not a counterfeit but is his father.

Perhaps the most unusual use of pronouns, from our point of view, is the neuter singular. In place of our *its, his* was often used, as in "How far that little candle throws *his* beams." But the use of a masculine pronoun for a neuter noun came to seem unnatural, and so *it* was used for the possessive as well as the nominative: "The hedge-sparrow fed the cuckoo so long / That it had it head bit off by it young." In the late sixteenth century the possessive form *its* developed, apparently by analogy with the *-s* ending used to indicate a genitive noun, as in *book*'s, but *its* was not yet common usage in Shakespeare's day. He seems to have used *its* only ten times, mostly in his later plays. Other usages, such as "you have seen Cassio and she together" or the substitution of *who* for *whom,* cause little problem even when noticed.

Verbs, Adverbs, and Prepositions: Verbs cause almost no difficulty: The third person singular present form commonly ends in *-s*, as in modern English (e.g., "He blesses"), but sometimes in *-eth* (Portia explains to Shylock that mercy "blesseth him that gives and him that takes"). Broadly speaking, the *-eth* ending was old-fashioned or dignified or "literary" rather than colloquial, except for the words *doth, hath,* and *saith.* The *-eth* ending (regularly used in the King James Bible, 1611) is very rare in Shakespeare's dramatic prose, though not surprisingly it occurs twice in the rather formal prose summary of the narrative poem *Lucrece.* Sometimes a plural subject, especially if it has collective force, takes a verb ending in *-s*, as in "My old bones aches." Some of our strong or irregular preterites (such as *broke*) have a different form in Shakespeare (*brake*); some verbs that now have a weak or regular preterite (such as *helped*) in Shakespeare have a strong or irregular preterite (*holp*). Some adverbs that today end in *-ly* were not inflected: "grievous sick," "wondrous strange." Finally, prepositions often are not the ones we expect: "We are such stuff as dreams are made on," "I have a king here to my flatterer."

Again, none of the differences (except meanings that have substantially changed or been lost) will cause much difficulty. But it must be confessed that for some elliptical passages there is no widespread agreement on meaning. Wise editors resist saying more than they know, and when they are uncertain they add a question mark to their gloss.

Shakespeare's Theater

In Shakespeare's infancy, Elizabethan actors performed wherever they could—in great halls, at court, in the courtyards of inns. These venues implied not only different audiences but also different playing conditions. The innyards must have made rather unsatisfactory theaters: on some days they were unavailable because carters bringing goods to London used them as depots; when available, they had to be rented from the innkeeper. In 1567, presumably to avoid such difficulties, and also to avoid regulation by the Common Council of London, which was not well disposed toward theatricals, one John Brayne, brother-in-law of the carpenter turned actor James Burbage, built the Red Lion in an eastern suburb of London. We know nothing about its shape or its capacity; we can say only that it may have been the first building in Europe constructed for the purpose of giving plays since the end of antiquity, a thousand years earlier. Even after the building of the Red Lion theatrical activity continued in London in makeshift circumstances, in marketplaces and inns, and always uneasily. In 1574 the Common Council required that plays and playing places in London be licensed because

> sundry great disorders and inconveniences have been found to ensue to this city by the inordinate haunting of great multitudes of people, specially youth, to plays, interludes, and shows, namely occasion of frays and quarrels, evil practices of incontinency in great inns having chambers and secret places adjoining to their open stages and galleries.

The Common Council ordered that innkeepers who wished licenses to hold performance put up a bond and make contributions to the poor.

The requirement that plays and innyard theaters be licensed, along with the other drawbacks of playing at inns and presumably along with the success of the Red Lion, led James Burbage to rent a plot of land northeast of the city walls, on property outside the jurisdiction of the city. Here he built England's second playhouse, called simply the Theatre. About all that is known of its construction is that it was wood. It soon had imitators, the most famous being the Globe (1599), essentially an amphitheater built across the Thames (again outside the city's jurisdiction), constructed with timbers of the Theatre, which had been dismantled when Burbage's lease ran out.

Admission to the theater was one penny, which allowed spectators to stand at the sides and front of the stage that jutted into the yard. An additional penny bought a seat in a covered part of the theater, and a third penny bought a more comfortable seat and a better location. It is notoriously difficult to translate prices into today's money, since some things that are inexpensive today would have been expensive in the past and vice versa—a pipeful of tobacco (imported, of course) cost a lot of money, about three pennies, and an orange (also imported) cost two or three times what a chicken cost—but perhaps we can get some idea of the low cost of the penny admission when we realize that a penny could also buy a pot of ale. An unskilled laborer made about five or sixpence a day, an artisan about twelve pence a day, and the hired actors (as opposed to the sharers in the company, such as Shakespeare) made about ten pence a performance. A printed play cost five or sixpence. Of course a visit to the theater (like a visit to a baseball game today) usually cost more than the admission since the spectator probably would also buy food and drink. Still, the low entrance fee meant that the theater was available to all except the very poorest people, rather as movies and most athletic events are today. Evidence indicates that the audience ranged from apprentices who somehow managed to scrape together the minimum entrance fee and to escape from their masters for a few hours, to prosperous members of the middle class and aristocrats who paid the additional fee for admission to the galleries. The exact proportion of men to women cannot be determined, but women of all classes certainly were present. Theaters were open every afternoon but Sundays for much of the year, except in times of plague, when they were closed because of fear of infection. By the way, no evidence suggests the presence of toilet facilities. Presumably the patrons relieved themselves by making a quick trip to the fields surrounding the playhouses.

There are four important sources of information about the

structure of Elizabethan public playhouses—drawings, a contract, recent excavations, and stage directions in the plays. Of drawings, only the so-called de Witt drawing (c. 1596) of the Swan—really his friend Aernout van Buchell's copy of Johannes de Witt's drawing—is of much significance. The drawing, the only extant representation of the interior of an Elizabethan theater, shows an amphitheater of three tiers, with a stage jutting from a wall into the yard or

Johannes de Witt, a Continental visitor to London, made a drawing of the Swan theater in about the year 1596. The original drawing is lost; this is Aernout van Buchell's copy of it.

center of the building. The tiers are roofed, and part of the stage is covered by a roof that projects from the rear and is supported at its front on two posts, but the groundlings, who paid a penny to stand in front of the stage or at its sides, were exposed to the sky. (Performances in such a playhouse were held only in the daytime; artificial illumination was not used.) At the rear of the stage are two massive doors; above the stage is a gallery.

The second major source of information, the contract for the Fortune (built in 1600), specifies that although the Globe (built in 1599) is to be the model, the Fortune is to be square, eighty feet outside and fifty-five inside. The stage is to be forty-three feet broad, and is to extend into the middle of the yard, i.e., it is twenty-seven and a half feet deep.

The third source of information, the 1989 excavations of the Rose (built in 1587), indicate that the Rose was fourteen-sided, about seventy-two feet in diameter with an inner yard almost fifty feet in diameter. The stage at the Rose was about sixteen feet deep, thirty-seven feet wide at the rear, and twenty-seven feet wide downstage. The relatively small dimensions and the tapering stage, in contrast to the rectangular stage in the Swan drawing, surprised theater historians and have made them more cautious in generalizing about the Elizabethan theater. Excavations at the Globe have not yielded much information, though some historians believe that the fragmentary evidence suggests a larger theater, perhaps one hundred feet in diameter.

From the fourth chief source, stage directions in the plays, one learns that entrance to the stage was by the doors at the rear (*"Enter one citizen at one door, and another at the other"*). A curtain hanging across the doorway—or a curtain hanging between the two doorways—could provide a place where a character could conceal himself, as Polonius does, when he wishes to overhear the conversation between Hamlet and Gertrude. Similarly, withdrawing a curtain from the doorway could "discover" (reveal) a character or two. Such discovery scenes are very rare in Elizabethan drama, but a good example occurs in *The Tempest* (5.1.171), where a stage direction tells us, *"Here Prospero discovers Ferdinand and Miranda playing at chess."* There was also some sort of playing space "aloft" or "above" to represent, for instance, the top of a city's walls or a room above the street. Doubtless each theater had its own peculiarities, but perhaps we can talk about a "typical" Elizabethan theater if we realize that no theater need exactly fit the description, just as no mother is the average mother with 2.7 children.

This hypothetical theater is wooden, round, or polygonal (in *Henry V* Shakespeare calls it a "wooden *O*") capable of holding some eight hundred spectators who stood in the yard around the projecting elevated stage—these spectators were the "groundlings"—and some fifteen hundred additional spectators who sat in the three roofed galleries. The stage, protected by a "shadow" or "heavens" or roof, is entered from two doors; behind the doors is the "tiring house" (attiring house, i.e., dressing room), and above the stage is some sort of gallery that may sometimes hold spectators but can be used (for example) as the bedroom from which Romeo—according to a stage direction in one text—"goeth down." Some evidence suggests that a throne can be lowered onto the platform stage, perhaps from the "shadow"; certainly characters can descend from the stage through a trap or traps into the cellar or "hell." Sometimes this space beneath the stage accommodates a sound-effects man or musician (in *Antony and Cleopatra* "*music of the hautboys* [oboes] *is under the stage*") or an actor (in *Hamlet* the "*Ghost cries under the stage*"). Most characters simply walk on and off through the doors, but because there is no curtain in front of the platform, corpses will have to be carried off (Hamlet obligingly clears the stage of Polonius's corpse, when he says, "I'll lug the guts into the neighbor room"). Other characters may have fallen at the rear, where a curtain on a doorway could be drawn to conceal them.

Such may have been the "public theater," so called because its inexpensive admission made it available to a wide range of the populace. Another kind of theater has been called the "private theater" because its much greater admission charge (sixpence versus the penny for general admission at the public theater) limited its audience to the wealthy or the prodigal. The private theater was basically a large room, entirely roofed and therefore artificially illuminated, with a stage at one end. The theaters thus were distinct in two ways: One was essentially an amphitheater that catered to the general public; the other was a hall that catered to the wealthy. In 1576 a hall theater was established in Blackfriars, a Dominican priory in London that had been suppressed in 1538 and confiscated by the Crown and thus was not under the city's jurisdiction. All the actors in this Blackfriars theater were boys about eight to thirteen years old (in the public theaters similar boys played female parts; a boy Lady Macbeth played to a man Macbeth). Near the end of this section on Shakespeare's theater we will talk at some length about possible implications in this convention of using boys to play female roles, but for the moment we should say that it doubtless accounts for the relative lack of female roles in Elizabethan drama. Thus, in *A Midsummer Night's Dream*, out of twenty-one named roles, only four are female; in *Hamlet*, out of twenty-four, only two (Gertrude and Ophelia) are female. Many of Shakespeare's characters have fathers but no mothers—for instance, King Lear's daughters. We need not bring in Freud to explain the disparity; a dramatic company had only a few boys in it.

To return to the private theaters, in some of which all of the performers were children—the "eyrie of . . . little eyases" (nest of unfledged hawks—2.2.347–48) which Rosencrantz mentions when he and Guildenstern talk with Hamlet. The theater in Blackfriars had a precarious existence, and ceased operations in 1584. In 1596 James Burbage, who had already made theatrical history by building the Theatre, began to construct a second Blackfriars theater. He died in 1597, and for several years this second Blackfriars theater was used by a troupe of boys, but in 1608 two of Burbage's sons and five other actors (including Shakespeare) became joint operators of the theater, using it in the winter when the open-air Globe was unsuitable. Perhaps such a smaller theater, roofed, artificially illuminated, and with a tradition of a wealthy audience, exerted an influence in Shakespeare's late plays.

Performances in the private theaters may well have had intermissions during which music was played, but in the public theaters the action was probably uninterrupted, flowing from scene to scene almost without a break. Actors would enter, speak, exit, and others would immediately enter and establish (if necessary) the new locale by a few properties and by words and gestures. To indicate that the scene took place at night, a player or two would carry a torch. Here are some samples of Shakespeare establishing the scene:

This is Illyria, lady.   (*Twelfth Night*, 1.2.2)

Well, this is the Forest of Arden.   (*As You Like It*, 2.4.14)

This castle has a pleasant seat; the air
Nimbly and sweetly recommends itself
Unto our gentle senses.   (*Macbeth*, 1.6.1–3)

The west yet glimmers with some streaks of day.
                                         (*Macbeth*, 3.3.5)

Sometimes a speech will go far beyond evoking the minimal setting of place and time, and will, so to speak, evoke the social world in which the characters move. For instance, early in the first scene of *The Merchant of Venice* Salerio suggests an explanation for Antonio's melancholy. (In the following passage, *pageants* are decorated wagons, floats, and *cursy* is the verb "to curtsy," or "to bow.")

Your mind is tossing on the ocean,
There where your argosies with portly sail—
Like signiors and rich burghers on the flood,
Or as it were the pageants of the sea—
Do overpeer the petty traffickers
That cursy to them, do them reverence,
As they fly by them with their woven wings.   (1.1.8–14)

Late in the nineteenth century, when Henry Irving produced the play with elaborate illusionistic sets, the first scene showed a ship moored in the harbor, with fruit vendors and dock laborers, in an effort to evoke the bustling and exotic life of Venice. But Shakespeare's words give us this exotic, rich world of commerce in his highly descriptive language when Salerio speaks of "argosies with portly sail" that fly with "woven wings"; equally important, through Salerio Shakespeare conveys a sense of the orderly, hierarchical

society in which the lesser ships, "the petty traffickers," curtsy and thereby "do . . . reverence" to their superiors, the merchant prince's ships, which are "Like signiors and rich burghers."

On the other hand, it is a mistake to think that except for verbal pictures the Elizabethan stage was bare. Although Shakespeare's Chorus in *Henry V* calls the stage an "unworthy scaffold" (Prologue 1.10) and urges the spectators to "eke out our performance with your mind" (Prologue 3.35), there was considerable spectacle. The last act of *Macbeth*, for instance, has five stage directions calling for *"drum and colors,"* and another sort of appeal to the eye is indicated by the stage direction *"Enter Macduff, with Macbeth's head."* Some scenery and properties may have been substantial; doubtless a throne was used, but the pillars supporting the roof would have served for the trees on which Orlando pins his poems in *As You Like It.*

Having talked about the public theater—"this wooden *O*"—at some length, we should mention again that Shakespeare's plays were performed also in other locales. Alvin Kernan, in *Shakespeare, the King's Playwright: Theater in the Stuart Court 1603–1613* (1995) points out that "several of [Shakespeare's] plays contain brief theatrical performances, set always in a court or some noble house. When Shakespeare portrayed a theater, he did not, except for the choruses in *Henry V*, imagine a public theater" (p. 195). (Examples include episodes in *The Taming of the Shrew, A Midsummer Night's Dream, Hamlet,* and *The Tempest.*)

A Note on the Use of Boy Actors in Female Roles

Until fairly recently, scholars were content to mention that the convention existed; they sometimes also mentioned that it continued the medieval practice of using males in female roles, and that other theaters, notably in ancient Greece and in China and Japan, also used males in female roles. (In classical Noh drama in Japan, males still play the female roles.) Prudery may have been at the root of the academic failure to talk much about the use of boy actors, or maybe there really is not much more to say than that it was a convention of a male-centered culture (Stephen Green-

blatt's view, in *Shakespearean Negotiations* [1988]). Further, the very nature of a convention is that it is not thought about: Hamlet is a Dane and Julius Caesar is a Roman, but in Shakespeare's plays they speak English, and we in the audience never give this odd fact a thought. Similarly, a character may speak in the presence of others and we understand, again without thinking about it, that he or she is not heard by the figures on the stage (the aside); a character alone on the stage may speak (the soliloquy), and we do not take the character to be unhinged; in a realistic (box) set, the fourth wall, which allows us to see what is going on, is miraculously missing. The no-nonsense view, then, is that the boy actor was an accepted convention, accepted unthinkingly—just as today we know that Kenneth Branagh is not Hamlet, Al Pacino is not Richard III, and Denzel Washington is not the Prince of Aragon. In this view, the audience takes the performer for the role, and that is that; such is the argument we now make for race-free casting, in which African-Americans and Asians can play roles of persons who lived in medieval Denmark and ancient Rome. But gender perhaps is different, at least today. It is a matter of abundant academic study: The Elizabethan theater is now sometimes called a transvestite theater, and we hear much about cross-dressing.

Shakespeare himself in a very few passages calls attention to the use of boys in female roles. At the end of *As You Like It* the boy who played Rosalind addresses the audience, and says, "O men, . . . if I were a woman, I would kiss as many of you as had beards that pleased me." But this is in the Epilogue; the plot is over, and the actor is stepping out of the play and into the audience's everyday world. A second reference to the practice of boys playing female roles occurs in *Antony and Cleopatra*, when Cleopatra imagines that she and Antony will be the subject of crude plays, her role being performed by a boy:

> The quick comedians
> Extemporally will stage us, and present
> Our Alexandrian revels: Antony
> Shall be brought drunken forth, and I shall see
> Some squeaking Cleopatra boy my greatness.   (5.2.216–20)

In a few other passages, Shakespeare is more indirect. For instance, in *Twelfth Night* Viola, played of course by a boy, disguises herself as a young man and seeks service in the house of a lord. She enlists the help of a Captain, and (by way of explaining away her voice and her beardlessness) says,

> I'll serve this duke
> Thou shalt present me as an eunuch to him.   (1.2.55–56)

In *Hamlet*, when the players arrive in 2.2, Hamlet jokes with the boy who plays a female role. The boy has grown since Hamlet last saw him: "By'r Lady, your ladyship is nearer to heaven than when I saw you last by the altitude of a chopine" (a lady's thick-soled shoe). He goes on: "Pray God your voice . . . be not cracked" (434–38).

Exactly how sexual, how erotic, this material was and is, is now much disputed. Again, the use of boys may have been unnoticed, or rather not thought about—an unexamined convention—by most or all spectators most of the time, perhaps *all* of the time, except when Shakespeare calls the convention to the attention of the audience, as in the passages just quoted. Still, an occasional bit seems to invite erotic thoughts. The clearest example is the name that Rosalind takes in *As You Like It*, Ganymede—the beautiful youth whom Zeus abducted. Did boys dressed to play female roles carry homoerotic appeal for straight men (Lisa Jardine's view, in *Still Harping on Daughters* [1983]), or for gay men, or for some or all women in the audience? Further, when the boy actor played a woman who (for the purposes of the plot) disguised herself as a male, as Rosalind, Viola, and Portia do—so we get a boy playing a woman playing a man—what sort of appeal was generated, and for what sort of spectator?

Some scholars have argued that the convention empowered women by letting female characters display a freedom unavailable in Renaissance patriarchal society; the convention, it is said, undermined rigid gender distinctions. In this view, the convention (along with plots in which female characters for a while disguised themselves as young men) allowed Shakespeare to say what some modern gender

critics say: Gender is a constructed role rather than a bio-
logical given, something we make, rather than a fixed binary
opposition of male and female (see Juliet Dusinberre, in
Shakespeare and the Nature of Women [1975]). On the other
hand, some scholars have maintained that the male disguise
assumed by some female characters serves only to reaffirm
traditional social distinctions since female characters who
don male garb (notably Portia in *The Merchant of Venice*
and Rosalind in *As You Like It*) return to their female garb
and at least implicitly (these critics say) reaffirm the status
quo. (For this last view, see Clara Claiborne Park, in an
essay in *The Woman's Part*, ed. Carolyn Ruth Swift Lenz et
al. [1980].) Perhaps no one answer is right for all plays; in
As You Like It cross-dressing empowers Rosalind, but in
Twelfth Night cross-dressing comically traps Viola.

Shakespeare's Dramatic Language: Costumes, Gestures and Silences; Prose and Poetry

Because Shakespeare was a dramatist, not merely a poet,
he worked not only with language but also with costume,
sound effects, gestures, and even silences. We have already
discussed some kinds of spectacle in the preceding section,
and now we will begin with other aspects of visual language;
a theater, after all, is literally a "place for seeing." Consider
the opening stage direction in *The Tempest*, the first play in
the first published collection of Shakespeare's plays: *"A
tempestuous noise of thunder and Lightning heard: Enter a
Ship-master, and a Boteswain."*

Costumes: What did that shipmaster and that boatswain
wear? Doubtless they wore something that identified them
as men of the sea. Not much is known about the costumes
that Elizabethan actors wore, but at least three points are
clear: (1) many of the costumes were splendid versions of
contemporary Elizabethan dress; (2) some attempts were
made to approximate the dress of certain occupations and of
antique or exotic characters such as Romans, Turks, and
Jews; (3) some costumes indicated that the wearer was

supernatural. Evidence for elaborate Elizabethan clothing can be found in the plays themselves and in contemporary comments about the "sumptuous" players who wore the discarded clothing of noblemen, as well as in account books that itemize such things as "a scarlet cloak with two broad gold laces, with gold buttons down the sides."

The attempts at approximation of the dress of certain occupations and nationalities also can be documented from the plays themselves, and it derives additional confirmation from a drawing of the first scene of Shakespeare's *Titus Andronicus*—the only extant Elizabethan picture of an identifiable episode in a play. (See pp. xxxviii–xxxix.) The drawing, probably done in 1594 or 1595, shows Queen Tamora pleading for mercy. She wears a somewhat medieval-looking robe and a crown; Titus wears a toga and a wreath, but two soldiers behind him wear costumes fairly close to Elizabethan dress. We do not know, however, if the drawing represents an actual stage production in the public theater, or perhaps a private production, or maybe only a reader's visualization of an episode. Further, there is some conflicting evidence: In *Julius Caesar* a reference is made to Caesar's doublet (a close-fitting jacket), which, if taken literally, suggests that even the protagonist did not wear Roman clothing; and certainly the lesser characters, who are said to wear hats, did not wear Roman garb.

It should be mentioned, too, that even ordinary clothing can be symbolic: Hamlet's "inky cloak," for example, sets him apart from the brightly dressed members of Claudius's court and symbolizes his mourning; the fresh clothes that are put on King Lear partly symbolize his return to sanity. Consider, too, the removal of disguises near the end of some plays. For instance, Rosalind in *As You Like It* and Portia and Nerissa in *The Merchant of Venice* remove their male attire, thus again becoming fully themselves.

Gestures and Silences: Gestures are an important part of a dramatist's language. King Lear kneels before his daughter Cordelia for a benediction (4.7.57–59), an act of humility that contrasts with his earlier speeches banishing her and that contrasts also with a comparable gesture, his ironic

kneeling before Regan (2.4.153–55). Northumberland's failure to kneel before King Richard II (3.3.71–72) speaks volumes. As for silences, consider a moment in *Coriolanus*: Before the protagonist yields to his mother's entreaties (5.3.182), there is this stage direction: *"Holds her by the hand, silent."* Another example of "speech in dumbness" occurs in *Macbeth*, when Macduff learns that his wife and children have been murdered. He is silent at first, as Malcolm's speech indicates: "What, man! Ne'er pull your hat upon your brows. Give sorrow words" (4.3.208–09). (For a discussion of such moments, see Philip C. McGuire's *Speechless Dialect: Shakespeare's Open Silences* [1985].)

Of course when we think of Shakespeare's work, we think primarily of his language, both the poetry and the prose.

Prose: Although two of his plays (*Richard II* and *King John*) have no prose at all, about half the others have at least one quarter of the dialogue in prose, and some have notably more: *1 Henry IV* and *2 Henry IV*, about half; *As You Like It*

and *Twelfth Night*, a little more than half; *Much Ado About Nothing*, more than three quarters; and *The Merry Wives of Windsor*, a little more than five sixths. We should remember that despite Molière's joke about M. Jourdain, who was amazed to learn that he spoke prose, most of us do not speak prose. Rather, we normally utter repetitive, shapeless, and often ungrammatical torrents; prose is something very different—a sort of literary imitation of speech at its most coherent.

Today we may think of prose as "natural" for drama; or even if we think that poetry is appropriate for high tragedy we may still think that prose is the right medium for comedy. Greek, Roman, and early English comedies, however, were written in verse. In fact, prose was not generally considered a literary medium in England until the late fifteenth century; Chaucer tells even his bawdy stories in verse. By the end of the 1580s, however, prose had established itself on the English comic stage. In tragedy, Marlowe made some use of prose, not simply in the speeches of clownish servants but even in the speech of a tragic hero, Doctor Faustus. Still, before Shakespeare, prose normally was used in the theater only for special circumstances: (1) letters and proclamations, to set them off from the poetic dialogue; (2) mad characters, to indicate that normal thinking has become disordered; and (3) low comedy, or speeches uttered by clowns even when they are not being comic. Shakespeare made use of these conventions, but he also went far beyond them. Sometimes he begins a scene in prose and then shifts into verse as the emotion is heightened; or conversely, he may shift from verse to prose when a speaker is lowering the emotional level, as when Brutus speaks in the Forum.

Shakespeare's prose usually is not prosaic. Hamlet's prose includes not only small talk with Rosencrantz and Guildenstern but also princely reflections on "What a piece of work is a man" (2.2.312). In conversation with Ophelia, he shifts from light talk in verse to a passionate prose denunciation of women (3.1.103), though the shift to prose here is perhaps also intended to suggest the possibility of madness. (Consult Brian Vickers, *The Artistry of Shakespeare's Prose* [1968].)

Poetry: Drama in rhyme in England goes back to the Middle Ages, but by Shakespeare's day rhyme no longer dominated poetic drama; a finer medium, blank verse (strictly speaking, unrhymed lines of ten syllables, with the stress on every second syllable) had been adopted. But before looking at unrhymed poetry, a few things should be said about the chief uses of rhyme in Shakespeare's plays. (1) A couplet (a pair of rhyming lines) is sometimes used to convey emotional heightening at the end of a blank verse speech; (2) characters sometimes speak a couplet as they leave the stage, suggesting closure; (3) except in the latest plays, scenes fairly often conclude with a couplet, and sometimes, as in *Richard II*, 2.1.145–46, the entrance of a new character within a scene is preceded by a couplet, which wraps up the earlier portion of that scene; (4) speeches of two characters occasionally are linked by rhyme, most notably in *Romeo and Juliet*, 1.5.95–108, where the lovers speak a sonnet between them; elsewhere a taunting reply occasionally rhymes with the previous speaker's last line; (5) speeches with sententious or gnomic remarks are sometimes in rhyme, as in the duke's speech in *Othello* (1.3.199–206); (6) speeches of sardonic mockery are sometimes in rhyme—for example, Iago's speech on women in *Othello* (2.1.146–58)—and they sometimes conclude with an emphatic couplet, as in Bolingbroke's speech on comforting words in *Richard II* (1.3.301–2); (7) some characters are associated with rhyme, such as the fairies in *A Midsummer Night's Dream*; (8) in the early plays, especially *The Comedy of Errors* and *The Taming of the Shrew*, comic scenes that in later plays would be in prose are in jingling rhymes; (9) prologues, choruses, plays-within-the-play, inscriptions, vows, epilogues, and so on are often in rhyme, and the songs in the plays are rhymed.

Neither prose nor rhyme immediately comes to mind when we first think of Shakespeare's medium: It is blank verse, unrhymed iambic pentameter. (In a mechanically exact line there are five iambic feet. An iambic foot consists of two syllables, the second accented, as in *away*; five feet make a pentameter line. Thus, a strict line of iambic pentameter contains ten syllables, the even syllables being stressed more heavily than the odd syllables. Fortunately, Shakespeare usually varies the line somewhat.) The first speech in *A Midsummer Night's Dream*, spoken by Duke Theseus to his betrothed, is an example of blank verse:

> Now, fair Hippolyta, our nuptial hour
> Draws on apace. Four happy days bring in
> Another moon; but, O, methinks, how slow
> This old moon wanes! She lingers my desires,
> Like to a stepdame, or a dowager,
> Long withering out a young man's revenue. (1.1.1–6)

As this passage shows, Shakespeare's blank verse is not mechanically unvarying. Though the predominant foot is the iamb (as in *apace* or *desires*), there are numerous variations. In the first line the stress can be placed on "fair," as the regular metrical pattern suggests, but it is likely that "Now" gets almost as much emphasis; probably in the second line "Draws" is more heavily emphasized than "on," giving us a trochee (a stressed syllable followed by an unstressed one); and in the fourth line each word in the phrase "This old moon wanes" is probably stressed fairly heavily, conveying by two spondees (two feet, each of two stresses) the oppressive tedium that Theseus feels.

In Shakespeare's early plays much of the blank verse is end-stopped (that is, it has a heavy pause at the end of each line), but he later developed the ability to write iambic pentameter verse paragraphs (rather than lines) that give the illusion of speech. His chief techniques are (1) enjambing, i.e., running the thought beyond the single line, as in the first three lines of the speech just quoted; (2) occasionally replacing an iamb with another foot; (3) varying the position of the chief pause (the caesura) within a line; (4) adding an occasional unstressed syllable at the end of a line, traditionally called a feminine ending; (5) and beginning or ending a speech with a half line.

Shakespeare's mature blank verse has much of the rhythmic flexibility of his prose; both the language, though richly figurative and sometimes dense, and the syntax seem natural. It is also often highly appropriate to a particular character. Consider, for instance, this speech from *Hamlet*, in which Claudius, King of Denmark ("the Dane"), speaks to Laertes:

> And now, Laertes, what's the news with you?
> You told us of some suit. What is't, Laertes?
> You cannot speak of reason to the Dane
> And lose your voice. What wouldst thou beg, Laertes,
> That shall not be my offer, not thy asking?   (1.2.42–46)

Notice the short sentences and the repetition of the name "Laertes," to whom the speech is addressed. Notice, too, the shift from the royal "us" in the second line to the more intimate "my" in the last line, and from "you" in the first three lines to the more intimate "thou" and "thy" in the last two lines. Claudius knows how to ingratiate himself with Laertes.

For a second example of the flexibility of Shakespeare's blank verse, consider a passage from *Macbeth*. Distressed by the doctor's inability to cure Lady Macbeth and by the imminent battle, Macbeth addresses some of his remarks to the doctor and others to the servant who is arming him. The entire speech, with its pauses, interruptions, and irresolution (in "Pull't off, I say," Macbeth orders the servant to remove the armor that the servant has been putting on him), catches Macbeth's disintegration. (In the first line, *physic* means "medicine," and in the fourth and fifth lines, *cast the water* means "analyze the urine.")

> Throw physic to the dogs, I'll none of it.
> Come, put mine armor on. Give me my staff.
> Seyton, send out.——Doctor, the thanes fly from me.——
> Come, sir, dispatch. If thou couldst, doctor, cast
> The water of my land, find her disease
> And purge it to a sound and pristine health,
> I would applaud thee to the very echo,
> That should applaud again.——Pull't off, I say.——
> What rhubarb, senna, or what purgative drug,
> Would scour these English hence? Hear'st thou of them?
> (5.3.47–56)

Blank verse, then, can be much more than unrhymed iambic pentameter, and even within a single play Shakespeare's blank verse often consists of several styles, depending on the speaker and on the speaker's emotion at the moment.

The Play Text as a Collaboration

Shakespeare's fellow dramatist Ben Jonson reported that the actors said of Shakespeare, "In his writing, whatsoever he penned, he never blotted out line," i.e., never crossed out material and revised his work while composing. None of Shakespeare's plays survives in manuscript (with the possible exception of a scene in *Sir Thomas More*), so we cannot fully evaluate the comment, but in a few instances the published work clearly shows that he revised his manuscript. Consider the following passage (shown here in facsimile) from the best early text of *Romeo and Juliet*, the Second Quarto (1599):

Ro. Would I were sleepe and peace so sweet to rest
The grey eyde morne smiles on the frowning night,
Checkring the Easterne Clouds with streaks of light,
And darknesse fleckted like a drunkard reeles,
From forth daies pathway, made by *Tytans* wheeles.
Hence will I to my ghostly Friers close cell,
His helpe to craue, and my deare hap to tell.

                                            Exit.

Enter Frier alone with a basket.   (night,
Fri. The grey-eyed morne smiles on the frowning
Checking the Easterne clowdes with streaks of light:
And fleckeld darknesse like a drunkard reeles,
From forth daies path, and *Titans* burning wheeles:
Now erethe sun aduance his burning eie,

Romeo rather elaborately tells us that the sun at dawn is dispelling the night (morning is smiling, the eastern clouds are checked with light, and the sun's chariot—Titan's wheels—advances), and he will seek out his spiritual father, the Friar. He exits and, oddly, the Friar enters and says pretty much the same thing about the sun. Both speakers say that "the gray-eyed morn smiles on the frowning night," but there are small differences, perhaps having more to do with the business of printing the book than with the author's composition: For Romeo's "checkring," "fleckted," and "pathway," we get the Friar's "checking," "fleckeld," and "path." (Notice, by the way, the inconsistency in Elizabethan spelling: Romeo's "clouds" become the Friar's "clowdes.")

Both versions must have been in the printer's copy, and it seems safe to assume that both were in Shakespeare's manuscript. He must have written one version—let's say he first wrote Romeo's closing lines for this scene—and then he decided, no, it's better to give this lyrical passage to the Friar, as the opening of a new scene, but he neglected to delete the first version. Editors must make a choice, and they may feel that the reasonable thing to do is to print the text as Shakespeare intended it. But how can we know what he intended? Almost all modern editors delete the lines from

Romeo's speech, and retain the Friar's lines. They don't do this because they know Shakespeare's intention, however. They give the lines to the Friar because the first published version (1597) of *Romeo and Juliet* gives only the Friar's version, and this text (though in many ways inferior to the 1599 text) is thought to derive from the memory of some actors, that is, it is thought to represent a performance, not just a script. Maybe during the course of rehearsals Shakespeare—an actor as well as an author—unilaterally decided that the Friar should speak the lines; if so (remember that we don't know this to be a fact) his final intention was to give the speech to the Friar. Maybe, however, the actors talked it over and settled on the Friar, with or without Shakespeare's approval. On the other hand, despite the 1597 version, one might argue (if only weakly) on behalf of giving the lines to Romeo rather than to the Friar, thus: (1) Romeo's comment on the coming of the daylight emphasizes his separation from Juliet, and (2) the figurative language seems more appropriate to Romeo than to the Friar. Having said this, in the Signet edition we have decided in this instance to draw on the evidence provided by earlier text and to give the lines to the Friar, on the grounds that since Q1 reflects a production, in the theater (at least on one occasion) the lines were spoken by the Friar.

A playwright sold a script to a theatrical company. The script thus belonged to the company, not the author, and author and company alike must have regarded this script not as a literary work but as the basis for a play that the actors would create on the stage. We speak of Shakespeare as the author of the plays, but readers should bear in mind that the texts they read, even when derived from a single text, such as the First Folio (1623), are inevitably the collaborative work not simply of Shakespeare with his company—doubtless during rehearsals the actors would suggest alterations—but also with other forces of the age. One force was governmental censorship. In 1606 parliament passed "an Act to restrain abuses of players," prohibiting the utterance of oaths and the name of God. So where the earliest text of *Othello* gives us "By heaven" (3.3.106), the first Folio gives "Alas," presumably reflecting the compliance of stage practice with the law. Similarly, the 1623 version of *King Lear* omits the oath "Fut" (probably from "By God's foot") at 1.2.142, again presumably reflecting the line as it was spoken on the stage. Editors who seek to give the reader the play that Shakespeare initially conceived—the "authentic" play conceived by the solitary Shakespeare—probably will restore the missing oaths and references to God. Other editors, who see the play as a collaborative work, a construction made not only by Shakespeare but also by actors and compositors and even government censors, may claim that what counts is the play as it was actually performed. Such editors regard the censored text as legitimate, since it is the play that was (presumably) finally put on. A performed text, they argue, has more historical reality than a text produced by an editor who has sought to get at what Shakespeare initially wrote. In this view, the text of a play is rather like the script of a film; the script is not the film, and the play text is not the performed play. Even if we want to talk about the play that Shakespeare "intended," we will find ourselves talking about a script that he handed over to a company with the intention that it be implemented by actors. The "intended" play is the one that the actors—we might almost say "society"—would help to construct.

Further, it is now widely held that a play is also the work of readers and spectators, who do not simply receive meaning, but who create it when they respond to the play. This idea is fully in accord with contemporary post-structuralist critical thinking, notably Roland Barthes's "The Death of the Author," in *Image-Music-Text* (1977) and Michel Foucault's "What Is an Author?," in *The Foucault Reader* (1984). The gist of the idea is that an author is not an isolated genius; rather, authors are subject to the politics and other social structures of their age. A dramatist especially is a worker in a collaborative project, working most obviously with actors—parts may be written for particular actors—but working also with the audience. Consider the words of Samuel Johnson, written to be spoken by the actor David Garrick at the opening of a theater in 1747:

> The stage but echoes back the public voice;
> The drama's laws, the drama's patrons give,
> For we that live to please, must please to live.

The audience—the public taste as understood by the playwright—helps to determine what the play is. Moreover, even members of the public who are not part of the playwright's immediate audience may exert an influence through censorship. We have already glanced at governmental censorship, but there are also other kinds. Take one of Shakespeare's most beloved characters, Falstaff, who appears in three of Shakespeare's plays, the two parts of *Henry IV* and *The Merry Wives of Windsor*. He appears with this name in the earliest printed version of the first of these plays, *1 Henry IV*, but we know that Shakespeare originally called him (after an historical figure) Sir John Oldcastle. Oldcastle appears in Shakespeare's source (partly reprinted in the Signet edition of *1 Henry IV*), and a trace of the name survives in Shakespeare's play, 1.2.43–44, where Prince Hal punningly addresses Falstaff as "my old lad of the castle." But for some reason—perhaps because the family of the historical Oldcastle complained—Shakespeare had to change the name. In short, the play as we have it was (at least in this detail) subject to some sort of censorship. If we think that a text should present what we take to be the author's intention, we probably will want to replace *Falstaff* with *Oldcastle*. But if we recognize that a play is a collaboration, we may welcome the change, even if it was forced on Shakespeare. Somehow *Falstaff*, with its hint of *false-staff*, i.e., inadequate prop, seems just right for this fat knight who, to our delight, entertains the young prince with untruths. We can go as far as saying that, at least so far as a play is concerned, an insistence on the author's original intention (even if we could know it) can sometimes impoverish the text.

The tiny example of Falstaff's name illustrates the point that the text we read is inevitably only a version—something in effect produced by the collaboration of the playwright with his actors, audiences, compositors, and editors—of a fluid text that Shakespeare once wrote, just as the *Hamlet* that we see on the screen starring Kenneth Branagh is not the *Hamlet* that Shakespeare saw in an open-air playhouse starring Richard Burbage. *Hamlet* itself, as we shall note in a moment, also exists in several versions. It is not surprising that there is now much talk about the *instability* of Shakespeare's texts.

Because he was not only a playwright but was also an actor and a shareholder in a theatrical company, Shakespeare probably was much involved with the translation of the play from a manuscript to a stage production. He may or may not have done some rewriting during rehearsals, and he may or may not have been happy with cuts that were made. Some plays, notably *Hamlet* and *King Lear*, are so long that it is most unlikely that the texts we read were acted in their entirety. Further, for both of these plays we have more than one early text that demands consideration. In *Hamlet*, the Second Quarto (1604) includes some two hundred lines not found in the Folio (1623). Among the passages missing from the Folio are two of Hamlet's reflective speeches, the "dram of evil" speech (1.4.13–38) and "How all occasions do inform against me" (4.4.32–66). Since the Folio has more numerous and often fuller stage directions, it certainly looks as though in the Folio we get a theatrical version of the play, a text whose cuts were probably made—this is only a hunch, of course—not because Shakespeare was changing his conception of Hamlet but because the playhouse demanded a modified play. (The problem is complicated, since the Folio not only cuts some of the Quarto but adds some material. Various explanations have been offered.)

Or take an example from *King Lear*. In the First and Second Quarto (1608, 1619), the final speech of the play is given to Albany, Lear's surviving son-in-law, but in the First Folio version (1623), the speech is given to Edgar. The Quarto version is in accord with tradition—usually the highest-ranking character in a tragedy speaks the final words. Why does the Folio give the speech to Edgar? One possible answer is this: The Folio version omits some of Albany's speeches in earlier scenes, so perhaps it was decided (by Shakespeare? by the players?) not to give the final lines to so pale a character. In fact, the discrepancies are so many between the two texts, that some scholars argue we do not simply have texts showing different theatrical productions. Rather, these scholars say, Shakespeare substantially revised the play, and we really have two versions of *King Lear* (and of *Othello* also, say some)—two different plays—not simply two texts, each of which is in some ways imperfect.

In this view, the 1608 version of *Lear* may derive from Shakespeare's manuscript, and the 1623 version may derive from his later revision. The Quartos have almost three hundred lines not in the Folio, and the Folio has about a hundred lines not in the Quartos. It used to be held that all the texts were imperfect in various ways and from various causes— some passages in the Quartos were thought to have been set from a manuscript that was not entirely legible, other passages were thought to have been set by a compositor who was new to setting plays, and still other passages were thought to have been provided by an actor who misremembered some of the lines. This traditional view held that an editor must draw on the Quartos and the Folio in order to get Shakespeare's "real" play. The new argument holds (although not without considerable strain) that we have two authentic plays, Shakespeare's early version (in the Quarto) and Shakespeare's—or his theatrical company's—revised version (in the Folio). Not only theatrical demands but also Shakespeare's own artistic sense, it is argued, called for extensive revisions. Even the titles vary: Q1 is called *True Chronicle Historie of the life and death of King Lear and his three Daughters*, whereas the Folio text is called *The Tragedie of King Lear*. To combine the two texts in order to produce what the editor thinks is the play that Shakespeare intended to write is, according to this view, to produce a text that is false to the history of the play. If the new view is correct, and we do have texts of two distinct versions of *Lear* rather than two imperfect versions of one play, it supports in a textual way the post-structuralist view that we cannot possibly have an unmediated vision of (in this case) a play by Shakespeare; we can only recognize a plurality of visions.

Editing Texts

Though eighteen of his plays were published during his lifetime, Shakespeare seems never to have supervised their publication. There is nothing unusual here; when a playwright sold a play to a theatrical company he surrendered his ownership to it. Normally a company would not publish the play, because to publish it meant to allow competitors to acquire the piece. Some plays did get published: Apparently hard-up actors sometimes pieced together a play for a publisher; sometimes a company in need of money sold a play; and sometimes a company allowed publication of a play that no longer drew audiences. That Shakespeare did not concern himself with publication is not remarkable; of his contemporaries, only Ben Jonson carefully supervised the publication of his own plays.

In 1623, seven years after Shakespeare's death, John Heminges and Henry Condell (two senior members of Shakespeare's company, who had worked with him for about twenty years) collected his plays—published and unpublished—into a large volume, of a kind called a folio. (A folio is a volume consisting of large sheets that have been folded once, each sheet thus making two leaves, or four pages. The size of the page of course depends on the size of the sheet—a folio can range in height from twelve to sixteen inches, and in width from eight to eleven; the pages in the 1623 edition of Shakespeare, commonly called the First Folio, are approximately thirteen inches tall and eight inches wide.) The eighteen plays published during Shakespeare's lifetime had been issued one play per volume in small formats called quartos. (Each sheet in a quarto has been folded twice, making four leaves, or eight pages, each page being about nine inches tall and seven inches wide, roughly the size of a large paperback.)

Heminges and Condell suggest in an address "To the great variety of readers" that the republished plays are presented in better form than in the quartos:

> Before you were abused with diverse stolen and surreptitious copies, maimed and deformed by the frauds and stealths of injurious impostors that exposed them; even those, are now offered to your view cured and perfect of their limbs, and all the rest absolute in their numbers, as he [i.e., Shakespeare] conceived them.

There is a good deal of truth to this statement, but some of the quarto versions are better than others; some are in fact preferable to the Folio text.

Whoever was assigned to prepare the texts for publication

in the first Folio seems to have taken the job seriously and yet not to have performed it with uniform care. The sources of the texts seem to have been, in general, good unpublished copies or the best published copies. The first play in the collection, *The Tempest*, is divided into acts and scenes, has unusually full stage directions and descriptions of spectacle, and concludes with a list of the characters, but the editor was not able (or willing) to present all of the succeeding texts so fully dressed. Later texts occasionally show signs of carelessness: in one scene of *Much Ado About Nothing* the names of actors, instead of characters, appear as speech prefixes, as they had in the Quarto, which the Folio reprints; proofreading throughout the Folio is spotty and apparently was done without reference to the printer's copy; the pagination of *Hamlet* jumps from 156 to 257. Further, the proofreading was done while the presses continued to print, so that each play in each volume contains a mix of corrected and uncorrected pages.

Modern editors of Shakespeare must first select their copy; no problem if the play exists only in the Folio, but a considerable problem if the relationship between a Quarto and the Folio—or an early Quarto and a later one—is unclear. In the case of *Romeo and Juliet*, the First Quarto (Q1), published in 1597, is vastly inferior to the Second (Q2), published in 1599. The basis of Q1 apparently is a version put together from memory by some actors. Not surprisingly, it garbles many passages and is much shorter than Q2. On the other hand, occasionally Q1 makes better sense than Q2. For instance, near the end of the play, when the parents have assembled and learned of the deaths of Romeo and Juliet, in Q2 the Prince says (5.3.208–9),

> Come, *Montague;* for thou art early vp
> To see thy sonne and heire, now earling downe.

The last three words of this speech surely do not make sense, and many editors turn to Q1, which instead of "now earling downe" has "more early downe." Some modern editors take only "early" from Q1, and print "now early down"; others take "more early," and print "more early down." Further, Q1 (though, again, quite clearly a garbled and abbreviated text) includes some stage directions that are not found in Q2, and today many editors who base their text on Q2 are glad to add these stage directions, because the directions help to give us a sense of what the play looked like on Shakespeare's stage. Thus, in 4.3.58, after Juliet drinks the potion, Q1 gives us this stage direction, not in Q2: *"She falls upon her bed within the curtains."*

In short, an editor's decisions do not end with the choice of a single copy text. First of all, editors must reckon with Elizabethan spelling. If they are not producing a facsimile, they probably modernize the spelling, but ought they to preserve the old forms of words that apparently were pronounced quite unlike their modern forms—*lanthorn, alablaster*? If they preserve these forms are they really preserving Shakespeare's forms or perhaps those of a compositor in the printing house? What is one to do when one finds *lanthorn* and *lantern* in adjacent lines? (The editors of this series in general, but not invariably, assume that words should be spelled in their modern form, unless, for instance, a rhyme is involved.) Elizabethan punctuation, too, presents problems. For example, in the First Folio, the only text for the play, Macbeth rejects his wife's idea that he can wash the blood from his hand (2.2.60–62):

> No: this my Hand will rather
> The multitudinous Seas incarnardine,
> Making the Greene one, Red.

Obviously an editor will remove the superfluous capitals, and will probably alter the spelling to "incarnadine," but what about the comma before "Red"? If we retain the comma, Macbeth is calling the sea "the green one." If we drop the comma, Macbeth is saying that his bloody hand will make the sea ("the Green") *uniformly* red.

An editor will sometimes have to change more than spelling and punctuation. Macbeth says to his wife (1.7.46–47):

> I dare do all that may become a man,
> Who dares no more, is none.

For two centuries editors have agreed that the second line is unsatisfactory, and have emended "no" to "do": "Who dares do more is none." But when in the same play (4.2.21–22) Ross says that fearful persons

> Floate vpon a wilde and violent Sea
> Each way, and moue,

need we emend the passage? On the assumption that the compositor misread the manuscript, some editors emend "each way, and move" to "and move each way"; others emend "move" to "none" (i.e., "Each way and none"). Other editors, however, let the passage stand as in the original. The editors of the Signet Classic Shakespeare have restrained themselves from making abundant emendations. In their minds they hear Samuel Johnson on the dangers of emendation: "I have adopted the Roman sentiment, that it is more honorable to save a citizen than to kill an enemy." Some departures (in addition to spelling, punctuation, and lineation) from the copy text have of course been made, but the original readings are listed in a note following the play, so that readers can evaluate the changes for themselves.

Following tradition, the editors of the Signet Classic Shakespeare have prefaced each play with a list of characters, and throughout the play have regularized the names of the speakers. Thus, in our text of *Romeo and Juliet*, all speeches by Juliet's mother are prefixed "Lady Capulet," although the 1599 Quarto of the play, which provides our copy text, uses at various points seven speech tags for this one character: *Capu. Wi.* (i.e., Capulet's wife), *Ca. Wi., Wi., Wife, Old La.* (i.e., Old Lady), *La.,* and *Mo.* (i.e., Mother). Similarly, in *All's Well That Ends Well*, the character whom we regularly call "Countess" is in the Folio (the copy text) variously identified as *Mother, Countess, Old Countess, Lady,* and *Old Lady*. Admittedly there is some loss in regularizing, since the various prefixes may give us a hint of the way Shakespeare (or a scribe who copied Shakespeare's manuscript) was thinking of the character in a particular scene—for instance, as a mother, or as an old lady. But too much can be made of these differing prefixes, since the social relationships implied are *not* always relevant to the given scene.

We have also added line numbers and in many cases act and scene divisions as well as indications of locale at the beginning of scenes. The Folio divided most of the plays into acts and some into scenes. Early eighteenth-century editors increased the divisions. These divisions, which provide a convenient way of referring to passages in the plays, have been retained, but when not in the text chosen as the basis for the Signet Classic text they are enclosed within square brackets, [ ], to indicate that they are editorial additions. Similarly, though no play of Shakespeare's was equipped with indications of the locale at the heads of scene divisions, locales have here been added in square brackets for the convenience of readers, who lack the information that costumes, properties, gestures, and scenery afford to spectators. Spectators can tell at a glance they are in the throne room, but without an editorial indication the reader may be puzzled for a while. It should be mentioned, incidentally, that there are a few authentic stage directions—perhaps Shakespeare's, perhaps a prompter's—that suggest locales, such as *"Enter Brutus in his orchard,"* and *"They go up into the Senate house."* It is hoped that the bracketed additions in the Signet text will provide readers with the sort of help provided by these two authentic directions, but it is equally hoped that the reader will remember that the stage was not loaded with scenery.

Shakespeare on the Stage

Each volume in the Signet Classic Shakespeare includes a brief stage (and sometimes film) history of the play. When we read about earlier productions, we are likely to find them eccentric, obviously wrongheaded—for instance, Nahum Tate's version of *King Lear*, with a happy ending, which held the stage for about a century and a half, from the late seventeenth century until the end of the first quarter of the nineteenth. We see engravings of David Garrick, the greatest actor of the eighteenth century, in eighteenth-century garb as King Lear, and we smile, thinking how absurd the production must have been. If we are more thoughtful, we say, with the English novelist L. P. Hartley, "The past is a foreign country: they do things differently there." But if the eighteenth-century staging is a foreign country, what of the plays of the late sixteenth and seventeenth centuries? A foreign language, a foreign theater, a foreign audience.

Probably all viewers of Shakespeare's plays, beginning with Shakespeare himself, at times have been unhappy with the plays on the stage. Consider three comments about production that we find in the plays themselves, which suggest Shakespeare's concerns. The Chorus in *Henry V* complains that the heroic story cannot possibly be adequately staged:

> But pardon, gentles all,
> The flat unraisèd spirits that hath dared
> On this unworthy scaffold to bring forth
> So great an object. Can this cockpit hold
> The vasty fields of France? Or may we cram
> Within this wooden *O* the very casques
> That did affright the air at Agincourt?
>
> . . . .
>
> Piece out our imperfections with your thoughts.
>
> (Prologue 1.8–14,23)

Second, here are a few sentences (which may or may not represent Shakespeare's own views) from Hamlet's longish lecture to the players:

> Speak the speech, I pray you, as I pronounced it to you, trippingly on the tongue. But if you mouth it, as many of our players do, I had as lief the town crier spoke my lines. . . . O, it offends me to the soul to hear a robustious periwig-pated fellow tear a passion to tatters, to very rags, to split the ears of the groundlings. . . . And let those that play your clowns speak no more than is set down for them, for there be of them that will themselves laugh, to set on some quantity of barren spectators to laugh too, though in the meantime some necessary question of the play be then to be considered. That's villainous and shows a most pitiful ambition in the fool that uses it. (3.2.1–47)

Finally, we can quote again from the passage cited earlier in this introduction, concerning the boy actors who played the female roles. Cleopatra imagines with horror a theatrical version of her activities with Antony:

> The quick comedians
> Extemporally will stage us, and present
> Our Alexandrian revels: Antony
> Shall be brought drunken forth, and I shall see
> Some squeaking Cleopatra boy my greatness
> I' th' posture of a whore.
>   (5.2.216–21)

It is impossible to know how much weight to put on such passages—perhaps Shakespeare was just being modest about his theater's abilities—but it is easy enough to think that he was unhappy with some aspects of Elizabethan production. Probably no production can fully satisfy a playwright, and for that matter, few productions can fully satisfy *us;* we regret this or that cut, this or that way of costuming the play, this or that bit of business.

One's first thought may be this: Why don't they just do "authentic" Shakespeare, "straight" Shakespeare, the play as Shakespeare wrote it? But as we read the plays—words written to be performed—it sometimes becomes clear that we do not know *how* to perform them. For instance, in *Antony and Cleopatra* Antony, the Roman general who has succumbed to Cleopatra and to Egyptian ways, says, "The nobleness of life / Is to do thus" (1.1.36–37). But what is "thus"? Does Antony at this point embrace Cleopatra? Does he embrace and kiss her? (There are, by the way, very few scenes of kissing on Shakespeare's stage, possibly because boys played the female roles.) Or does he make a sweeping gesture, indicating the Egyptian way of life?

This is not an isolated example; the plays are filled with lines that call for gestures, but we are not sure what the gestures should be. *Interpretation* is inevitable. Consider a passage in *Hamlet.* In 3.1, Polonius persuades his daughter, Ophelia, to talk to Hamlet while Polonius and Claudius eavesdrop. The two men conceal themselves, and Hamlet encounters Ophelia. At 3.1.131 Hamlet suddenly says to her, "Where's your father?" Why does Hamlet, apparently out of nowhere—they have not been talking about Polonius—ask this question? Is this an example of the "antic disposition" (fantastic behavior) that Hamlet earlier (1.5.172) had told Horatio and others—including us—he would display? That is, is the question about the whereabouts of her father a seemingly irrational one, like his earlier question (3.1.103) to Ophelia, "Ha, ha! Are you honest?" Or, on the other hand, has Hamlet (as in many productions) suddenly glimpsed Polonius's foot protruding from beneath a drapery at the rear? That is, does Hamlet ask the question because he has suddenly seen something suspicious and now is testing Ophelia? (By the way, in productions that do give Hamlet a physical cue, it is almost always Polonius rather than Claudius who provides the clue. This itself is an act of interpretation on the part of the director.) Or (a third possibility) does Hamlet get a clue from Ophelia, who inadvertently betrays the spies by nervously glancing at their place of hiding? This is the interpretation used in the BBC television version, where Ophelia glances in fear toward the hiding place just after Hamlet says "Why wouldst thou be a breeder of sinners?" (121–22). Hamlet, realizing that he is being observed, glances here and there *before* he asks "Where's your father?" The question thus is a climax to what he has been doing while speaking the preceding lines. Or (a fourth interpretation) does Hamlet suddenly, without the aid of any clue whatsoever, intuitively (insightfully, mysteriously, wonderfully) sense that someone is spying? Directors must decide, of course—and so must readers.

Recall, too, the preceding discussion of the texts of the plays, which argued that the texts—though they seem to be before us in permanent black on white—are unstable. The Signet text of *Hamlet*, which draws on the Second Quarto (1604) and the First Folio (1623) is considerably longer than any version staged in Shakespeare's time. Our version, even if spoken very briskly and played without any intermission, would take close to four hours, far beyond "the two hours' traffic of our stage" mentioned in the Prologue to *Romeo and Juliet*. (There are a few contemporary references to the duration of a play, but none mentions more than three hours.) Of Shakespeare's plays, only *The Comedy of Errors*, *Macbeth*, and *The Tempest* can be done in less than three hours without cutting. And even if we take a play that exists only in a short text, *Macbeth*, we cannot claim that we are experiencing the very play that Shakespeare conceived, partly because some of the Witches' songs almost surely are non-Shakespearean additions, and partly because we are not willing to watch the play performed without an intermission and with boys in the female roles.

Further, as the earlier discussion of costumes mentioned, the plays apparently were given chiefly in contemporary, that is, in Elizabethan dress. If today we give them in the costumes that Shakespeare probably saw, the plays seem not contemporary but curiously dated. Yet if we use our own dress, we find lines of dialogue that are at odds with what we see; we may feel that the language, so clearly not our own, is inappropriate coming out of people in today's dress. A common solution, incidentally, has been to set the plays in the nineteenth century, on the grounds that this attractively distances the plays (gives them a degree of foreignness, allowing for interesting costumes) and yet doesn't put them into a museum world of Elizabethan England.

Inevitably our productions are adaptations, *our* adaptations, and inevitably they will look dated, not in a century but in twenty years, or perhaps even in a decade. Still, we cannot escape from our own conceptions. As the director Peter Brook has said, in *The Empty Space* (1968):

> It is not only the hair-styles, costumes and make-ups that look dated. All the different elements of staging—the shorthands of behavior that stand for emotions; gestures, gesticulations and tones of voice—are all fluctuating on an invisible stock exchange all the time. . . . A living theatre that thinks it can stand aloof from anything as trivial as fashion will wilt. (p. 16)

As Brook indicates, it is through today's hairstyles, costumes, makeup, gestures, gesticulations, tones of voice—this includes our *conception* of earlier hairstyles, costumes, and so forth if we stage the play in a period other than our own—that we inevitably stage the plays.

It is a truism that every age invents its own Shakespeare, just as, for instance, every age has invented its own classical world. Our view of ancient Greece, a slave-holding society in which even free Athenian women were severely circum-scribed, does not much resemble the Victorians' view of ancient Greece as a glorious democracy, just as, perhaps, our view of Victorianism itself does not much resemble theirs. We cannot claim that the Shakespeare on our stage is the true Shakespeare, but in our stage productions we find a Shakespeare that speaks to us, a Shakespeare that our ancestors doubtless did not know but one that seems to us to be the true Shakespeare—at least for a while.

Our age is remarkable for the wide variety of kinds of staging that it uses for Shakespeare, but one development deserves special mention. This is the now common practice of race-blind or color-blind or nontraditional casting, which allows persons who are not white to play in Shakespeare. Previously blacks performing in Shakespeare were limited to a mere three roles, Othello, Aaron (in *Titus Andronicus*), and the Prince of Morocco (in *The Merchant of Venice*), and there were no roles at all for Asians. Indeed, African-Americans rarely could play even one of these three roles, since they were not welcome in white companies. Ira Aldridge (c.1806–1867), a black actor of undoubted talent, was forced to make his living by performing Shakespeare in England and in Europe, where he could play not only Othello but also—in whiteface—other tragic roles such as King Lear. Paul Robeson (1898–1976) made theatrical history when he played Othello in London in 1930, and there was some talk about bringing the production to the United States, but there was more talk about whether American audiences would tolerate the sight of a black man—a real black man, not a white man in blackface—kissing and then killing a white woman. The idea was tried out in summer stock in 1942, the reviews were enthusiastic, and in the following year Robeson opened on Broadway in a production that ran an astounding 296 performances. An occasional all-black company sometimes performed Shakespeare's plays, but otherwise blacks (and other minority members) were in effect shut out from performing Shakespeare. Only since about 1970 has it been common for nonwhites to play major roles along with whites. Thus, in a 1996–97 production of *Antony and Cleopatra*, a white Cleopatra, Vanessa Red-grave, played opposite a black Antony, David Harewood.

Multiracial casting is now especially common at the New York Shakespeare Festival, founded in 1954 by Joseph Papp, and in England, where even siblings such as Claudio and Isabella in *Measure for Measure* or Lear's three daughters may be of different races. Probably most viewers today soon stop worrying about the lack of realism, and move beyond the color of the performers' skin to the quality of the performance.

Nontraditional casting is not only a matter of color or race; it includes sex. In the past, occasionally a distinguished woman of the theater has taken on a male role—Sarah Bernhardt (1844–1923) as Hamlet is perhaps the most famous example—but such performances were widely regarded as eccentric. Although today there have been some performances involving cross-dressing (a drag *As You Like It* staged by the National Theatre in England in 1966 and in the United States in 1974 has achieved considerable fame in the annals of stage history), what is more interesting is the casting of women in roles that traditionally are male but that need not be. Thus, a 1993–94 English production of *Henry V* used a woman—*not* cross-dressed—in the role of the governor of Harfleur. According to Peter Holland, who reviewed the production in *Shakespeare Survey* 48 (1995), "having a female Governor of Harfleur feminized the city and provided a direct response to the horrendous threat of rape and murder that Henry had offered, his language and her body in direct connection and opposition" (p. 210). Ten years from now the device may not play so effectively, but today it speaks to us. Shakespeare, born in the Elizabethan Age, has been dead nearly four hundred years, yet he is, as Ben Jonson said, "not of an age but for all time." We must understand, however, that he is "for all time" precisely because each age finds in his abundance something for itself and something of itself.

And here we come back to two issues discussed earlier in this introduction—the instability of the text and, curiously, the Bacon/Oxford heresy concerning the authorship of the plays. *Of course* Shakespeare wrote the plays, and we should daily fall on our knees to thank him for them—and yet there is something to the idea that he is not their only author. Every editor, every director and actor, and every reader to some degree shapes them, too, for when we edit, direct, act, or read, we inevitably become Shakespeare's collaborator and re-create the plays. The plays, one might say, are so cunningly contrived that they guide our responses, tell us how we ought to feel, and make a mark on us, but (for better or for worse) we also make a mark on them.

—SYLVAN BARNET
Tufts University

Introduction

The closing speech of *Coriolanus* reminds us of similar speeches at the end of other plays by Shakespeare:

> Take him up.
> Help, three o' th' chiefest soldiers; I'll be one.
> Beat thou the drum, that it speak mournfully;
> Trail your steel pikes. Though in this city he
> Hath widowed and unchilded many a one,
> Which to this hour bewail the injury,
> Yet he shall have a noble memory.
> *Exeunt, bearing the body of Marcius.*
> *A dead march sounded.*

So *Julius Caesar*:

> According to his virtue, let us use him
> With all respect and rites of burial.
> Within my tent his bones tonight shall lie,
> Most like a soldier, ordered honorably. . . .

And *Hamlet*:

> Let four captains
> Bear Hamlet like a soldier to the stage,
> For he was likely, had he been put on,
> To have proved most royal; and for his passage
> The soldiers' music and the rite of war
> Speak loudly for him. . . .

Though we recognize in all these endings the convention by which the curtainless Elizabethan stage was cleared of its actors, yet we can easily imagine that the convention might have been expressed in different language, and without this special emphasis on the protagonist—borne from the scene "like a soldier," with "music and the rite of war"— particularly when he happened to be Hamlet. It seems certain that the gesture so expressed was more than a stage-convention, or rather that it represented another and deeper convention about the nature of the chief actor in a tragedy. The modern reader certainly feels some strain in speaking of *The* Tragedy *of Coriolanus,* particularly if he has just been reading *King Lear* or *Antony and Cleopatra,* plays that most of us regard as prime examples of that ever debatable term. George Bernard Shaw has called *Coriolanus* Shakespeare's "finest comedy"; one critic has described it as a satire; another, as a debate rather than a tragedy. Most of us will agree that when we speak of *Coriolanus* as a "tragedy," we mean something rather peculiar. But those who admire the play will rejoice in that "peculiarity." The aim of this introductory essay is to give some clue to its essence, to its rare and special value. (The editor assumes that the reader will have read the play at least once before turning to the Introduction.)

　　The more alert and more literate members of Shakespeare's audience—not to be identified with any one social class—would have recognized that the three processional speeches above marked the death of a hero in a more than modern conventional sense. Even if they were relatively unread, they were literate in a most relevant respect, through hearing in the theater the language of dying heroes in these and in many other plays. They would have sensed much by way of implication in "virtue," "like a soldier," and "a noble memory," just as they would have appreciated the special force of "deeds" in the great speech of Cominius:

> *Cominius.* I shall lack voice: the deeds of Coriolanus
> 　　Should not be uttered feebly. It is held
> 85　That valor is the chiefest virtue and
> 　　Most dignifies the haver. If it be,
> 　　The man I speak of cannot in the world
> 　　Be singly counterpoised. At sixteen years,
> 　　When Tarquin made a head for Rome, he fought
> 90　Beyond the mark of others. Our then dictator,

Whom with all praise I point at, saw him fight,
When with his Amazonian chin he drove
The bristled lips before him. He bestrid
An o'erpressed Roman, and i' th' consul's view
Slew three opposers; Tarquin's self he met,   95
And struck him on his knee. In that day's feats,
When he might act the woman in the scene,
He proved best man i' th' field, and for his meed
Was brow-bound with the oak. His pupil age
Man-ent'red thus, he waxèd like a sea;   100
And, in the brunt of seventeen battles since,
He lurched all swords of the garland. For this last,
Before and in Corioles, let me say,
I cannot speak him home. He stopped the fliers,
And by his rare example made the coward   105
Turn terror into sport; as weeds before
A vessel under sail, so men obeyed
And fell below his stem. His sword, death's stamp,
Where it did mark, it took; from face to foot
He was a thing of blood, whose every motion   110
Was timed with dying cries. Alone he ent'red
The mortal gate of th' city, which he painted
With shunless destiny; aidless came off,
And with a sudden reinforcement struck
Corioles like a planet. Now all's his,   115
When by and by the din of war 'gan pierce
His ready sense, then straight his doubled spirit
Requick'ned what in flesh was fatigate,
And to the battle came he; where he did
Run reeking o'er the lives of men, as if   120
'Twere a perpetual spoil; and till we called
Both field and city ours, he never stood
To ease his breast with panting.

Menenius.   Worthy man! ....

Cominius.   Our spoils he kicked at,   125
And looked upon things precious as they were
The common muck of the world. He covets less
Than misery itself would give, rewards
His deeds with doing them, and is content
To spend the time to end it.

130 Menenius.   He's right noble.
    Let him be called for.   (2.2.83–123; 125–31)

Consider the growth of the picture of Coriolanus in this
speech and, in particular, certain words and phrases important for defining the special character of his tragedy.
Menenius' comment at the end, "right noble," is the key to
the speech, and also one of the more important thematic
expressions for interpreting Coriolanus' whole career. The
meaning of "noble"—like "worthy," it is often equivalent in
Shakespeare to "heroic"—is summed up in this tremendous
survey of the "deeds of Coriolanus." The theme is anticipated at the start by direct statement: "It is held/That *valor* is
the chiefest virtue . . ." (line 85), "valor" being defined here
as the ancient Roman "virtue," the Latin *virtus*.

As Cominius' story begins, the stress falls first on Coriolanus as wonder boy ("At sixteen years," line 88), as the
beardless youth with "Amazonian chin" (line 92)—a description that reminds us oddly of his potent mother,
Volumnia. We next see him crowned, "brow-bound with the
oak" (line 99); then we get an impression of boyhood swiftly
thrust into manhood: "His pupil age/Man-ent'red thus"
(lines 99–100). The brusque compound renews the physical
energy of "ent'red" ("initiated into"), especially as it is
linked at once with "waxèd like a sea" (line 100), an image
that turns the "man" into a vast natural force. Again Coriolanus is crowned: "He lurched all swords of the garland"
(line 102); but how oddly this is put, as if men were swords
and swords wore garlands, as if the man himself now wore
the ornament of "swords." He stands a "rare example" (line
105) against the "fliers," who appear as mere "weeds
before/A vessel" (lines 106–7). With "below his stem" (line
108), the man becomes the "stem," the bow, of a ship. From
pointed bow, the image glides in true Shakespearean fashion
to "sword," to "stamp" (line 108), a die for stamping a coin
or a medal. Where the "stamp" made its "mark," its cutting
edge "took" (line 109): it killed. The sword is seen now as a
sword-machine coming down on its victims, quite literally
"impressing" them. Then Coriolanus himself is dehuman-
ized, turned into a mere blood-thing (line 110), with "every

motion . . . timed" (lines 110–11), working with mechanical regularity, yet incongruously dripping with blood.

"Alone"—once more the "rare example"—he entered the "mortal," the fatal, gate by which death comes (lines 111–12). He "painted [it]/With shunless destiny" (lines 112–13): the bloody instrument smeared it with the gore of dying men, made it one with the death of men who could not escape their fate. The abstractness of idiom fits in with the whole style of Shakespeare's vision in the speech and in the play, imparting to the hero the added impersonality of a divine power. We may recall Volumnia's awesome image:

> Death, that dark spirit, in's nervy arm doth lie,
> Which, being advanced, declines, and then men die.
>
> (2.1.166–67)

She too sees Coriolanus as the great sword-sweeping arm of Death.

He "struck/Corioles like a planet" (lines 114–15). Now Coriolanus is a more terrifying force of nature, "striking" with fatal disease as the planets were believed to do, by the death-ray of the Elizabethan cosmos. There is a final impression of swift action and "reeking" gore before Cominius' summing up (lines 125–30). Coriolanus' reward for his "deeds" lies in the pure doing, in "living it up in action." Heroic violence, it is suggested, is self-destructive: in killing time, the hero is killing himself.

Shakespeare's audience—that better part of which we have spoken—would have recognized more quickly and more certainly than a twenty-first-century audience that the core of this speech was an epic, or rather, heroic, narrative in the Greco-Roman tradition. Many would have already seen other "noble Roman histories," plays on similar Roman or Greek subjects; and many would have had in grammar school some direct contact with Latin epic and with Greek epic story in Latin versions. They would have caught in "noble" and the "deeds of Coriolanus" an echo of phrases like Homer's *klea andron,* "the glorious deeds of great heroës dead," as Chapman translates it. In "The man I speak of," they would have heard Virgil's *arma virumque cano,* in which *virum* is related to *virtus,* to "valor" as described by Cominius. (Stanyhurst's translation of Virgil [1582] renders *virum* as "manhood," a word that shows the identification, frequent in Shakespeare, of "man" with "hero.") To appreciate more fully the "nobility" of Coriolanus' career and what Shakespeare made of it, we need to have some notion of the heroic ideal implied by Cominius' speech and by Coriolanus' further history in the play.

Shakespeare himself was familiar with the ancient heroic tradition in various forms. If he knew little Greek, he had access to Latin and French translations of Homer, to Virgil, Ovid, and Seneca in the original and translation, and to the early books of Chapman's *Iliad,* of which he had made use in *Troilus and Cressida* (1601–02). Although Chapman considerably revised his earlier version before publishing his complete *Iliad* in 1611, his translation may serve as a relevant example of the Renaissance remaking of the ancient heroic ideal. Back of Chapman stands the Homeric hero as he is presented in the *Iliad:* he is the man who "goes forward" in battle to display his excellence in fighting, who faces death with clear-eyed awareness and with very human fears, knowing that his lot or *moira* is unchangeable, that his every act is related to divine if only partially understood powers. The greatest of heroes, Achilles, goes well beyond the typical heroic norms, both in the excesses of his wrath and in the assertion of an absolute superheroism that aims at being "godlike" indeed, and that makes him finally a deeply tragic figure. In asserting his own will, Achilles ironically brings on himself the death of Patroclus, and in living out the violence of wrath, he comes to recognize the uselessness and the inevitability of all violence. In the scene with Priam near the close of the *Iliad,* he sees that both the hero and his victim are acting parts within a pattern controlled by the gods.

The Renaissance image of the ancient hero, though ultimately inherited from Homer, had been much affected by the two great Roman transformations of Virgil and Seneca, and by the reshaping of the Greco-Roman tradition in the medieval romances. These various traditions were complexly blended in the Renaissance theory of the Heroic Poem, an ideal pattern that attempted to strike a compromise between Romance and ancient epic. (*The Faerie Queene* is the unclassic example of what happened when traditions so opposed were combined in a single work.) But the theory itself was much more classical than romantic and much more Virgilian than Homeric. The true heroic poem was like the *Aeneid,* required to have an abstract subject, preferably Christian and explicitly moral, and a hero who equaled and surpassed Aeneas as an exemplar of virtue.

There are many signs in Chapman's *Iliad* of his response to this Renaissance theory: for example, his view that the *Iliad* is "the true image of all virtues and humane government." Homer embodies all truth, and the highest truth is "learning," learning in a very special sense:

> . . . this is learning; to have skill to throw
> Reins on your body's powers that nothing know,
> And fill the soul's powers so with act and art
> That she can curb the body's angry part,
> All perturbations; all affects that stray
> From this one object, which is to obey
> Her sovereign empire. . . .
>
> *The Tears of Peace* (1609)

In the first word of the *Iliad*—"wrath"—Homer "contracts" his "Proposition," his subject: "predominant perturbation," that is, "the body's fervor and fashion of outward fortitude, to all possible height of heroical action." The "affects," the passions when "predominant," do not obey the rule of "the soul," or "reason," as Chapman says elsewhere. We have in Chapman the translator a heroic poet who distrusts heroic passion—since it leads almost inevitably to a failure of "learning"—but who has the wisdom to admit that this same passion offers the greatest occasions for the exercise of moral control.

Consider now Chapman's version (1611) of the scene in the *Iliad,* Book I, in which Achilles is tempted to draw his sword, but on Athena's advice decides not to:

> Thetis' son at this stood vext. His heart
> Bristled his bosom and two ways drew his discursive part—

If, from his thigh his sharp sword drawn, he should make room
   about
Atrides' person, slaught'ring him, or sit his anger out
And curb his spirit. While these thoughts strived in his blood
   and mind
And he his sword drew, down from heaven Athenia stooped
   and shined . . .
He, turning back his eye, amaze struck every faculty,
Yet straight he knew her by her eyes, so terrible they were
Sparkling with ardor, and thus spoke: "Thou seed of Jupiter,
Why com'st thou? To behold his pride, that boasts our
   empery?
Then witness, with it, my revenge, and see that insolence die
That lives to wrong me." She replied: "I come from heaven to
   see
Thy anger settled, if thy soul will use her sovereignty
In fit reflection. I am sent from Juno, whose affects
Stand heartily inclined to both. Come, give both respects
And cease contention. Draw no sword. Use words, and such as
   may
Be bitter to his pride, but just. For, trust in what I say,
A time shall come when thrice the worth of that he forceth now
He shall propose for recompense of these wrongs. Therefore
   throw
Reins on thy passions, and serve us."

Chapman, we see, has turned the episode into one of
"learning" in his sense. First, the inner action is given much
greater importance than in the original. This Achilles is
more of a meditator than Homer's: "His heart . . . two ways
drew his *discursive* part," that is, the part that reasons. In
Homer we have simply a very physical heart in a "shaggy
chest," whereas in Chapman we find Hamlet's contrast of
man and "beast that wants discourse of reason." The process
by which Chapman's Achilles "curbs his spirit" is a good
example of how Chapman takes over an elementary form of
thought from Homer and gives it a new and complex interpretation. So we hear of various powers of mind: "amaze
struck every faculty. . . ." More significant is Athena's
advice on the right way to settle anger. Homer's goddess

says merely, "Stop quarreling; don't draw your sword." But Chapman's says:

> "Therefore throw
> Reins on thy passions, and serve us."

This Athena adds another note; like Hamlet, Achilles is to "speak daggers," but use none: "Draw no sword. Use words . . . but *just*" ones. The addition is important, since Chapman is in fact eager to make Achilles' wrath moral by substituting controlled anger for mere passion. Achilles' reply to Athena is another example of "learning":

> "Though my heart
> Burn in anger, yet my soul must conquer th' angry part
> And yield you conquest. Who subdues his earthly part
> for heaven,
> Heaven to his prayers subdues his wish."

The basic opposition of passions and soul may be either Platonic or Christian, but Chapman's language is so emphatically Christian that we may wonder whether we are listening to a hero or a saint. (At other points in Chapman's *Iliad,* Achilles is as bloodthirsty and cruel as Homer's hero at his worst.) Whatever Chapman's intention may have been, his true hero seems more often to be Hector, who displays the self-control, the self-knowledge, that Achilles aspires to but rarely achieves.

Although Chapman has so completely reinterpreted the ancient heroic image in Renaissance terms, we can still trace in his heroes the main outlines of the heroic role as it appears in the *Iliad.* But it is the Renaissance transformation of the ancient ideal that is most instructive if we are to understand the heroes of Shakespeare: in particular, Chapman's tendency to regard the heroic career as moral education or as a tragic failure to live up to a moral ideal. Modern readers, it should be added, are in general too prone to see the meditativeness of the Renaissance hero and to miss the complete heroic image as Shakespeare and Chapman understood it.

For a practicing dramatist, this ideal, a blend of the ancient and modern, pagan and Christian, held important possibilities. A Renaissance Achilles or Hector who faced the irony of his situation, who clearly recognized the conflict of allegiances, would be tragic in the fullest sense. He would be, for example, the Antony of *Antony and Cleopatra*. The ideal that Shakespeare had encountered in Chapman's *Iliad* and elsewhere was wonderfully renewed for him by his reading of another ancient classic, one that he read with the closest attention, Plutarch's *Lives of the Noble Grecians and Romans* in North's translation. (See pages 159–95.) It is worth noting here that twice in the *Life of Coriolanus* Plutarch illustrates his point by quoting Homer, and especially interesting that in defending Homer's allowance for "our own free will and reason" he quotes, in a fairly lax version, the lines on Achilles' "angry heart."

The concept of the true hero implied in the North-Plutarch *Life,* on which Shakespeare's play is largely based, is very close to Chapman's, as may be seen from some of the more general comments on the hero's character:

> ... this Martius' natural wit and great heart did marvelously stir up his courage to do and attempt notable acts. But on the other side, for lack of education, he was so choleric and impatient, that he would yield to no living creature, which made him churlish, uncivil, and altogether unfit for any man's conversation. Yet men marveling much at his constancy, that he was never overcome with pleasure nor money and how he would endure easily all manner of pains and travails, thereupon they well liked and commended his stoutness and temperancy. But for all that, they could not be acquainted with him, as one citizen useth to be with another in the city. His behavior was so unpleasant to them by reason of a certain insolent and stern manner he had, which, because he was too lordly, was disliked. And to say truly, the greatest benefit that learning bringeth unto men is this: that it teacheth men that be rude and rough of nature, by compass and rule of reason, to be civil and courteous, and to like better the mean state than the higher. Now in those days, valiantness was honored in Rome above all other virtues, which they call *virtus*, by the name of virtue itself, as including in that general name all other special virtues besides. So that *virtus* in the Latin was as much as valiantness.
>
> (Plutarch's *Life of Coriolanus*, p. 160)

Note first the high praise of Martius' "great heart" and "notable acts" and more especially what follows: *"But on the other side"*—here North sounds exactly like Chapman—"for lack of education, he was so choleric and impatient, that he would yield to no living creature . . ." North reinforces this with a remark showing clearly that "education" means "learning" in Chapman's sense of the word: "And to say truly, the greatest benefit that learning bringeth unto men is this: that it teacheth men that be rude and rough of nature, by compass and rule of reason, to be civil and courteous. . . ." But in the next sentence we are reminded that Coriolanus was the pattern of *virtus*. Yet according to North's view—and it would be Chapman's, too—Coriolanus was not fit to be "a prince" or "governor," because he "lacked the gravity and affability that is gotten with judgment of learning and reason . . ." (p. 172). He has another characteristic that is connected with his "choler" and his "self-will and opinion" (we should say, "pride"): "[he] remembered not how willfulness is the thing of the world, which a governor of a commonwealth, for pleasing should shun, being that which Plato called 'solitariness'" (p. 172). Note how Coriolanus' obstinacy and pride are described as "solitariness," the uncivil "aloneness" of men "who will never yield to others' reason. . . ."

Bearing in mind Plutarch's picture of heroic Coriolanus, and this brief sketch of the ancient hero in Renaissance guise, let us return to the "deeds of Coriolanus" in Shakespeare's play. We can now appreciate more fully certain features of Cominius' narrative: the august and at times coldly Latin style, the *nobility* of this display of *virtue*, the terrifying energy of a hero who is a lone instrument of death and destiny. We see in Coriolanus a figure like Achilles in his most vengeful phase, hurrying for slaughter, who "did/Run reeking o'er the lives of men. . . ." We recall, too, how in earlier scenes Shakespeare has stressed by imagery and stage business the "bloodiness," "aloneness," and other nonhuman qualities underlined also in Cominius' portrait. Coriolanus has been pictured as "mantled," "painted," "smeared," and "masqued" in blood; heard cannonlike with "thunderlike percussion" of sounds; seen swordlike "outdaring his senseless sword" and acting alone, apart from his plebeian followers—both impressions being vividly merged in the very scene when his men *"wave their swords"* and *"take him up in their arms"*:

O me alone! Make you a sword of me?

Whether these cries are to be read as questions or as exclamations—and there is no certainty—it is clear that in uttering them Coriolanus sees himself in splendid isolation, like a sword swung aloft in battle.

But this very emphasis on a nonhuman aloneness is a sign that Shakespeare was not writing an ancient heroic tragedy, not even of the Renaissance type of *Antony and Cleopatra*. He had seen in Plutarch's "solitariness" another subject and another possible treatment. "Suppose we set Achilles down in the Roman forum—what then?" There are subtle hints in Cominius' speech of this other subject and attitude: "It is *held*/That valor is the chiefest virtue . . . *if it be.* . . ." Then Menenius' "He's right noble./Let him be called for" is just, but also offhand and curt in Coriolanus' own manner. "Enough of that," Menenius seems to say—and irony breaks in. "Say more," he implies, "and you may remind people of this hero's immense pride," "his haughty obstinate mind," as North puts it, a quality that Shakespeare stresses much more than Plutarch. But Shakespeare does not limit himself, as some critics suppose, to portraying a flawed proud and angry man. He had grasped in the *Lives* and in the Roman historians the importance of the forum, of the Roman state, which he viewed with his contemporaries as an example both of "the mischiefs of discord and civil dissention" and of the well-ordered society, a model of a true commonwealth. Shakespeare sets the "deeds of Coriolanus" against the great parable of Menenius, "the body's members" and their revolt "against the Belly" (1.1.97–155). There are many contemporary documents that show a familiarity with this figure and with the related metaphor of the "disease" and "health" of the body politic. To the Elizabethan mind, the state, in more than a modern figurative sense, embodies a natural order: the parts receive from the governing center "that

natural competency/Whereby they live. . . ." The dramatic
point of the brilliantly comic scene in which this fable is presented does not lie in the fable itself, but in the way it is acted
out by Menenius in cooperation with the citizens. The good-
natured insolence and sturdy candor, the tough repartee of
the exchanges, belong to a game played between patrician
and people. The "Belly-smile" of the patrician, and the
"great toe" of the plebeian, both help to impart the feeling of
healthy relatedness in a civil society. To that, *Enter Caius
Marcius*—followed by Menenius' greeting:

> Hail, noble Marcius!

with the answer:

> Thanks. What's the matter, you dissentious rogues
> That, rubbing the poor itch of your opinion,
> Make yourselves scabs?   (164–67)

The "nature" of the state is henceforth counterpoised by the
"nature" of Coriolanus: "What he cannot help is his nature,"
one citizen says to another in the beginning of this same
scene, "you account a vice in him." From here to the end of
the play Shakespeare keeps dramatizing this clash of natures
until Coriolanus, still protesting, hears "Great Nature" cry
" 'Deny not.' " and

> He bowed his nature, never known before
> But to be rough, unswayable, and free   (5.6.25–26)

In North's version of the climactic scene where Coriolanus
gives in to his mother's pleas (5.3), there is considerable
emphasis on the claims of "nature" and the "natural" in
various senses. But there is nothing in the *Life* as a whole
like Shakespeare's interweaving throughout his drama of
variations on this central theme. The opposition of "natures"
in *Coriolanus* produces a continuous play of irony, as every
protestation of the hero, or of his friends and enemies, is
heard against a suppressed negation.

Again taking a hint from Plutarch—which he develops fully and explicitly—Shakespeare introduces one further strand of ironic ambiguity into his picture of Coriolanus, the link between his heroic energy and his love of his mother. "There's no man in the world," she explains near the end of the play, "More bound to's mother" (5.3.158–59)(Such is the stuff of heroes: Achilles must have his guardian Thetis.) "[W]hat he hath done famously . . ." a citizen says, "though soft-conscienced men can be content to say it was for his country, he did it to please his mother and to be partly proud, which he is, even to the altitude of his virtue" (1.1.36–41). More curious still, war-making, love, and marriage are closely related and almost identified in the minds of Volumnia and her son. Coriolanus has a way of embracing generals as if they were brides of war:

> *Marcius. [To Cominius]* O, let me clip ye
> In arms as sound as when I wooed; in heart
> As merry as when our nuptial day was done,
> And tapers burned to bedward! (1.6.29–32)

Much later—with the inevitably ironic echo—Aufidius answers him in kind:

> that I see thee here,
> Thou noble thing, more dances my rapt heart
> Than when I first my wedded mistress saw
> Bestride my threshold. (4.5.119–22)

If we keep in mind these many contrasts in the nature of Coriolanus, and the heroic image that his role evokes by similarity and by contrast, and if we remember, too, the vision of society symbolized by Menenius' fable, we shall appreciate better the Shakespearean complexity of the climactic scenes of the play. We shall also reach a truer measure of its peculiar flavor as tragedy. Consider first the scene where Coriolanus, about to be made consul, makes his magnificent attack on the tribunes and their officers. To him, the advice to abolish the tribuneship is a call to a godlike "noble life":

> Therefore, beseech you—
> You that will be less fearful than discreet;
> That love the fundamental part of state
> More than you doubt the change on't; that prefer
> A noble life before a long, and wish
> To jump a body with a dangerous physic
> That's sure of death without it—at once pluck out
> The multitudinous tongue; let them not lick
> The sweet which is their poison. Your dishonor
> Mangles true judgment, and bereaves the state
> Of that integrity which should become't;
> Not having the power to do the good it would,
> For th' ill which doth control't.   (3.1.149–61)

By this point in the play the noble life is not only being equated with the "deeds of Coriolanus," but with the ironic qualifications of his pride. "A 'noble' life" on his lips can be taken by the tribunes and people simply as "the life of the nobles, the senate." Coriolanus' plea for the "fundamental part of state," his concern for the "integrity" of the body politic seemingly echoes Menenius' fable; but "to pluck out/The multitudinous tongue," to eliminate the tribunes, is effectively to deny the people any part in the government. Coriolanus does not want a "blended" voice, but only one. He alone, he half implies, is the proper voice of the state. He is making this plea, he says, in the interest of avoiding "confusion." The hero who pleads for order, who fears revolution, speaks revolutionary doctrines and nearly starts one. He of course intends a counterrevolution; but he very nearly sets a true popular revolution under way.

The metaphor that runs through Coriolanus' speech is the familiar medical one of the play (used once, but only once, by Plutarch): he offers "a dangerous physic," and in his view he is the health of the state. But to the tribune Sicinius "He's a disease that must be cut away" (293). Menenius accepts the implication, but proposes "a cure" rather than "surgery." He would proceed by "the humane way" of compromise; that is, by Chapman's (and Plutarch's) way of "humane government." But the fatality of Coriolanus' nature—his pride and "choler," his lack of temperance—carries him on to destroy what he thinks he is saving. "His nature is too noble for the world," says Menenius,

> He would not flatter Neptune for his trident,
> Or Jove for's power to thunder. His heart's his mouth:
> What his breast forges, that his tongue must vent;
> And, being angry, does forget that ever
> He heard the name of death.   (255–59)

Here is the man who will equal the gods, the forgelike machine of war and death, deafened by wrath.

Coriolanus' insistence on being true to his heroic nature is constantly to the fore from this point to the end of the play. So in the next scene with the nobles and Volumnia, a scene that has no parallel in Plutarch, he asks with boyish puzzlement,

> Why did you wish me milder—Would you have me
> False to my nature? Rather say I play
> The man I am.   (3.2.14–16)

Her sensible advice fits—up to a point—Chapman's and North's concept of "education":

> I have a heart as little apt as yours,
> But yet a brain that leads my use of anger
> To better vantage.   (29–31)

And Menenius comments, "Well said, noble woman!" But this is not Coriolanus' nobility; his is of the pure Homeric type, absolute and without compromise. "You are too absolute," Volumnia well says,

> Though therein you can never be too noble
> But when extremities speak.   (40–41)

But Volumnia does not altogether understand her son: it is exactly in "extremities" that the hero must be "too noble," that his nature clearly cries out. Coriolanus faces a dilemma similar to Antony's—how to be both noble and politic.

Volumnia attempts to make him feel that the politic can be identified at one and the same time with nobility, with loyalty to the better part of the state and to the family, and most significantly, with loyalty to herself:

> I am in this
> Your wife, your son, these senators, the nobles. . . .
>
> (64–65)

Her despairing

> Do as thou list.
> Thy valiantness was mine, thou suck'st it from me,
> But owe thy pride thyself. (128–30)

only increases the sense of their likeness, of the physical bond between them: they are one flesh and one blood.

But the physical intensity of the appeal is persuasive for the moment, and for the first time in the scene, Coriolanus calls her "mother":

> Mother, I am going to the marketplace. . . . (131)

What this curbing of his nature costs him comes out earlier in the same scene, when like Othello he says farewell to arms:

> Away, my disposition, and possess me
> Some harlot's spirit! My throat of war be turned,
> Which quired with my drum, into a pipe
> Small as an eunuch. . . . (111–14)

And when he suddenly reverses himself:

> I will not do't;
> Lest I surcease to honor mine own truth,
> And by my body's action teach my mind
> A most inherent baseness. (120–23)

Though the words Coriolanus uses are very like Chapman's, his actions have really turned the ideal upside down. While everyone is urging him to "curb the body's angry part" by exercise of "spirit," he sees only a betrayal of spirit by flesh.

He will seek "a world elsewhere," outside state and family, out of the ordered nature he had known in Rome, and fight, now truly "alone,/Like to a lonely dragon, that his fen/Makes feared and talked of more than seen. . ." (4.1.29–31). With splendid irony he asserts that though outside society he will still be the same noble hero: "you shall/Hear . . . never of me aught/But what is like me formerly" (51–53). In the flattering talk of the Volscians he seems to recover his old nobility, "as if he were son and heir to Mars," but this newfound independence is an illusion, as Aufidius' ominous hints make clear. Aufidius' explanation of why Coriolanus was "hated" and "banished"—though it neglects some reasons, and though it is not Shakespeare's "last word" on his hero—does offer one important hypothesis borne out by much of the play:

> whether ['twas] *nature*,
> Not to be other than one thing, not moving
> From th' casque to th' cushion, but commanding peace
> Even with the same austerity and garb
> As he controlled the war. . . .   (4.7.41–45)

In this last phase of Coriolanus' career there is, as in Achilles' last battles, something much more frightening about his pride and his wrath. "He was," says Cominius

> a kind of nothing, titleless,
> Till he had forged himself a name o' th' fire
> Of burning Rome.   (5.1.13–15)

He harshly rejects his "old father," Menenius,

> Away! . . .
> Wife, mother, child, I know not. . . .   (5.2.81, 83)

The Second Watch gives one final impression of Coriolanus' dehumanization just before the women come to beg him to save the city: "He's the rock, the oak not to be windshaken" (111–12). What then will happen to the man who supposes he is "author of himself," the absolute hero detached from humanity?

As when Menenius pleads with him earlier, he will attempt to separate personal allegiance from allegiance to country. When the women approach, his eye moves quickly from his wife to his mother, who claims and receives his attention during most of the scene. He speaks to her first in the strange impersonal style that others have used of him: "the honored mold/Wherein this trunk was framed ..." (5.3.22–23); but at once he is stressing the close physical bond of mother and son: "and in her hand/The grandchild to her blood" (23–24). With a typical turn, he at once denies this and all similar bonds: "All bond and privilege of nature, break!" (25). He will be deliberately unnatural; but when he sees those "doves' " eyes, he "melts"—and how wonderfully the imagery recalls the hard godlike self he has tried to be: "I melt, and am not/Of stronger earth ..." (28–29)—he is not the metallic machine man of earlier scenes. When his "mother bows," it is indeed a "perturbation" in Nature, and "Great Nature" cries out against it (33). He denies "instinct," innate impulse, and, with consummate irony, declares that he is "author of himself," as it were, self-born!

But soon he is yielding to Nature in the sense of family affection, as he gives his wife "a kiss/Long as my exile" (44–45) while still insisting that he is not yielding to Nature in the sense of allegiance to his country. When he sees his mother kneeling he comes out with great hyperbolic oaths in the best heroic vein:

> Then let the pebbles on the hungry beach
> Fillip the stars! Then let the mutinous winds
> Strike the proud cedars 'gainst the fiery sun. ...
>
> (58–60)

Like Othello and Lear, Coriolanus invokes the very disorder he fears, the disorder of which he is the unconscious instrument. Like Hector he sees his sons as the reincarnation of his own heroism, his words recalling his own nobility and his lonely strength and inhumanity. He prays that the boy may prove

> To shame unvulnerable, and stick i' th' wars
> Like a great sea-mark, standing every flaw. . . .
>
> (73–74)

But he is still trying to hold off the claims of wife and mother: "Tell me not," he shouts, "Wherein I seem unnatural," (82–83).

Then come Volumnia's two great appeals in answer to his poignantly absurd assertion. The keynote of the first is struck in

> thy sight, which should
> Make our eyes flow with joy, hearts dance with comforts,
> Constrains them weep and shake with fear and sorrow,
> Making the mother, wife, and child, to see
> The son, the husband, and the father, tearing
> His country's bowels out.
>
> (98–103)

The body of the state, here realized with such physical vividness, is equated with mother, wife, and child, as if to say "tearing that body is tearing us." During the rest of the speech, Volumnia's language intensifies this identification until the climax,

> thou shalt no sooner
> March to assault thy country than to tread
> (Trust to't, thou shalt not) on thy mother's womb
> That brought thee to this world.
>
> (122–25)

This violent image is Plutarch's, and the identification of the mother with the body of the state is suggested by one of his comments; but the comment shows also the relative simplicity of his analysis, and his unawareness of the emotional confusion that Volumnia is exploiting so successfully:

> yet he had no reason for the love of his mother to pardon his country, but rather he should in pardoning his country, have spared his mother, because his mother and wife were members of the body of his country and city, which he did besiege.
> (Plutarch: *The Comparison of Alcibiades with*
> *Marcius Coriolanus*)

Volumnia's second appeal falls into three distinct phases. First she urges him to reconcile the Romans and the Volsces, offering the same kind of sensible advice she had given earlier when begging him to be "mild" to the tribunes. Next she makes a masterly attack on the very nobility that stands in the way of compromise, pointing out that the only practical "benefit" of being so absolutely noble is to destroy his country and gain a "name . . ./To th' ensuing age abhorred." She enforces her argument with a satirical picture of the Jove-like role Coriolanus has aimed at, seeking "To imitate the graces of the gods . . ." as if he were to "thunder" like Jove, and yet to "charge" his lightning with a "bolt" that would only split "an oak" (140–53). Something, yes, but hardly a cosmic catastrophe. She keeps reminding him that she speaks for wife, son, and mother; and in her final stroke she reinforces all three claims:

> This fellow had a Volscian to his mother:
> His wife is in Corioles, and his child
> Like him by chance.   (178–80)

Again she identifies personal and social bonds, as she reads him out of family, Rome, and humanity. His reply is one of the great speaking silences in Shakespeare:

> *Holds her by the hand, silent.*
>   O mother, mother!
> What have you done? Behold, the heavens do ope,
> The gods look down, and this unnatural scene
> They laugh at.   (182–85)

"Unnatural"—just when he is responding to all these most natural claims. For a moment he seems to see his dilemma more clearly, and to understand that in giving in to his mother he is responding to the demands of his native country and state. But he soon is talking as if all can be well: he can give in to his mother, be false to the Volscians, and "frame convenient peace."

The last scene of the play begins as an ironic repetition of the scene in which he had "mildly" given in to his mother's advice. At that time he had not been able to sustain the part, but now he "bows his nature" and comes "marching" in, *"the commoners being with him."* In contrast to the usual isolation of his figure from the plebeians, Coriolanus is seen *with* the people, and we catch another ironic reflection from the past: Menenius' easy companionship with the lower orders. Coriolanus seems for once to "belong," and he cries happily, "I am returned your soldier;/No more infected with my country's love . . ." (5.6.71–72). What was once his health is now disease, and loyalty to the enemies of Rome is his "cure." He is so terribly unaware of what he has been doing that he responds with dreamlike deafness to Aufidius' cry of "traitor"—the exact echo of the Tribunes' earlier "Has spoken like a traitor . . ." (3.1.162).

When he finally takes in Aufidius' cruel caricature of how he had given in to his mother, he can hardly speak: "Hear'st thou, Mars?" His incoherent cry, reminding us of the godlike soldier he had been, is inadequate, but dramatically concentrated in the highest degree. Shakespeare was never more successful than in this brief dialogue in focusing the rich meanings of a whole play in the slightest verbal gestures. To Aufidius' slanderous "boy of tears," he cries:

> Cut me to pieces, Volsces, men and lads,
> Stain all your edges on me. "Boy"! False hound!
> If you have writ your annals true, 'tis there,
> That, like an eagle in a dovecote, I
> Fluttered your Volscians in Corioles.
> Alone I did it. "Boy"?   (112–17)

"Alone" and " 'Boy'?" carry the weight of his whole dramatic career. In "Alone" we recall his cult of independence, his integrity, his insistence on being Coriolanus. But we hear also the opposite theme in a play in which wholeness of the state is the public ideal, in which metaphors of the body politic keep reminding us that the great natural order is realized in a whole of which the single man is only a part. This is his final denial of nature's bond, making only clearer his real dependence on Rome, his mother, Menenius, and now on the Volscians. "Boy?" in its scornful tone is Coriolanus' way of saying "*man*-hero." But the hero cannot act in this setting; he can only utter frustrated cries. He is in part behaving like a boy, and he had responded to his mother. The single word recalls too a long history of boyish irresponsibility and lack of control.

But there is another view, as always in this play: "The man is noble," one of the Volscians says, "and his fame folds in/This orb o' th' earth" (125–26). The "deeds of Coriolanus" cannot be forgotten any more than "the impatience" that North finds so dangerous in the "governor of a state." The closing processional speech, with which we began, marks the death of a hero: "Yet he shall have a noble memory" (154).

If we now compare Coriolanus with the model of all Greek and Roman literary heroes, Achilles, and with the Renaissance counterpart in Chapman and North, and finally with the chief characters of other Shakespearean tragedies, we can define more clearly the character of the play—surely the most original of Shakespeare's heroic dramas, whatever we choose to call it. Throughout *Coriolanus* Shakespeare is continually recalling the ancient model in imagery associating his hero with divinities and "shunless destiny." Like Menenius, Shakespeare has "godded him indeed." Perhaps Coriolanus is most like Achilles in his passionate pride, in his "choler," in his shifting from "rage to sorrow," emotions that lie very close together, as Plutarch had noted. But he comes nearest to the essence of Homer's hero in his absoluteness, in his determination to imitate "the graces of the gods," in his will to push the heroic to the limit until he destroys his own society along with his enemy's. In reducing all virtues to *virtus,* he is the Greek hero Romanized, while in his assertion of his own nature in the face of "Great Nature," he betrays the Senecan ancestry of the Elizabethan hero. Though many read him lessons in patience, he is incapable of true "learning."

But there is no moment when, like Achilles, he sees his anger and curses it, nothing to correspond to the scene with Priam, no vision of himself and a higher order within which his action and suffering are placed and made more comprehensible. His last gesture is like his first, to "use his lawful sword." He knows little of what Chapman calls the soul's "sovereignty in fit reflection," not to mention "subduing his earthly part for heaven." He is the most Roman, the least Christian, of Shakespeare's major heroes.

This Roman-ness is felt in the austerity of a style that lends itself so well to irony, and that is the best index to the quality of the play. In *Coriolanus,* Shakespeare seems to turn his back on the richness of language in *Antony and Cleopatra,* with the deliberate intention of creating a protagonist who will deny much that is common to his own and the Renaissance heroic ideal. And yet there are in Coriolanus the makings of a tragedy in Shakespeare's more typical manner: he is a man nobly conscious of his role, a "governor" like Lear or Macbeth on whom the health of society depends, a person like Lear and Othello of immense impatience in a situation calling for utmost patience, a man like Antony whose action is godlike and connected with dimly perceived supernatural forces. Both are instruments of the mighty Roman state, for Romans a prime symbol of the directing power of fate.

But there is of course an obvious defect that makes even Macbeth tragic in a sense of the word that does not fit Coriolanus: the lack of the troubled conscience that separates Macbeth from the tyrant he seems to be to his enemies. In the final scene with his mother, Coriolanus is barely conscious that he is betraying the Volscians, just as in his last entrance he does not realize that he has been "infected by his country's love." His whole career is based on an illusion of *aloneness,* the belief that a man, a general, a statesman can act alone. Hence the bafflement and humiliation when he must bow to others—feelings he can express only in rotelike speeches. It is the spectator, not Coriolanus, who feels the poignancy of this betrayal of others and himself. Like a "dull actor," as he says, he performs dully, and when out of his part, he is completely "out."

For Coriolanus has only one way of meeting the world—assertion of simple soldierly nobility. In this he has much in common with Othello, who also lives by absolutes, whose world collapses at any suggestion that he is *not* a soldier. But there is no terrible recognition by the hero, as there is in the final scenes of *Othello,* that simple soldiery and simple justice have not been enough, that they have indeed brought chaos again. Damnation, which Othello calls on himself, and which presupposes a sense of sin, is incomprehensible to this noble Roman. He is equally incapable of "noble" Antony's "I am so lated in the world that I/Have lost my way for ever."

One last comparison with Achilles is to the point. In comparison with Shakespeare's "men," these two are great boys. Both are strangely allied with their mothers, both produce "confusion" by their overdeveloped sense of self and their disregard of the claims of society. The difference in the end result depends on the difference noted earlier: Shakespeare sets his hero in a much more complex social world. The noble voice that calls to battle may no longer sound noble in the Capitol. Though it calls for order, it becomes indistinguishable from the voice of tyrant and traitor. The man who fears innovation, who has no gift for making compromises and dealing "mildly," may prove the most violent of innovators, worse than a mere mob. Shakespeare's picture of the people is not flattering, but not unintelligent: one cannot build an orderly society by following the whims of the many-headed monster. But fixity of principle in a prince can be as dangerous to the state as the fickleness of a mob.

Shakespeare's state is necessarily not that of the Roman republic, since both society and cosmos have been translated in Elizabethan-Jacobean terms. His subject—apart from the peculiar character of Coriolanus—is implicit in the "degree" speech of Troilus and Cressida (1.3.75). It should be remembered that Ulysses' speech was occasioned by Achilles' revolt and that Ulysses later tried to show Achilles the evils resulting from his loss of heroic nobility. Shakespeare returns in Coriolanus to the subject implied in these scenes of Troilus and Cressida, but with a new Achilles and a new certainty of aim, and with a resultant concentration lacking in the earlier play. In Troilus, Achilles was an ambiguous creature, a lover and a gangster, and the drama of disunity in the state was crossed by a drama of disunity in love. The end appropriately is sound and fury signifying nothing. But in Coriolanus, Shakespeare limits the social subject more severely, and though his picture of the social order is highly particularized, it does not lose a large clarity. As in *Antony and Cleopatra,* the "wide arch/Of the ranged" Roman state is never lost from view.

Against that ordered complexity the simple extremism of Coriolanus stands out in all its nobility and absurdity. The noble simplicity of the hero and the certainty with which issues are expressed and arguments are presented by Coriolanus and by his enemies, the high decorum of the rather chill oratorical style take us in the direction of French classical drama. This is, after *Julius Caesar,* Shakespeare's most *Latin* play.

It was "all in Plutarch," we may be tempted to say. (See pp. 159–95.) But when we read Plutarch we discover what Shakespeare was capable of learning—how wonderfully he selected and how skillfully he concentrated on his themes, embodying them in particular dramatic expressions. We can almost feel Shakespeare's excitement as he read; his recognition that here was a subject he had wanted to handle as early as when he was writing *Julius Caesar* and *Troilus.* What a discovery—after reading late medieval versions of the ancient heroic in which the hero is reduced to a chivalric lover or worse, to find that the hero is a man who has never ceased loving his mother, a man for whom marriage is second to war, whose true love is his own heroic image. Hints of these and other traits of Shakespeare's hero—his nobility and heroic virtue, his obstinate pride and lack of self-control—can be found in the *Life of Coriolanus.* Other basic features of Shakespeare's drama—the picture of the Roman state and society, the debate over the claims of nature, great and small—can also be traced to Plutarch's text. But though many separate elements of Shakespeare's grand design are Plutarchan, it is Shakespeare who has "put them together," and the "putting together" is a dramatic and poetic feat. The imagery of Volumnia's appeal, for example, is resonant with the sense of the state and society that Shakespeare had presented early in the play. In reporting Coriolanus' death, Plutarch merely says the conspirators "all fell upon him, and killed him in the marketplace, none of the people once offering to rescue him." There is no speech from Aufidius, and more notable, none from Coriolanus, nothing to correspond to "Alone I did it. 'Boy'?" Those few words show that Shakespeare had combined perfectly an intense and rich understanding of the hero-boy, mother's son, and noble Roman with his sharply outlined picture of the social and political world, in a total vision that makes the cry so large in reference, so poignantly absurd, so tragic in a curiously ironic sense.

—REUBEN BROWER
Harvard University

The Tragedy of
Coriolanus

The Tragedy of
Coriolanus

ACT 1

[*Scene 1. Rome. A street.*]

Enter a company of mutinous Citizens, with staves,
clubs, and other weapons.

First Citizen. Before we proceed any further, hear me
speak.

All. Speak, speak.

First Citizen. You are all resolved rather to die than
to famish?   5

All. Resolved, resolved.

First Citizen. First you know, Caius Marcius is chief
enemy to the people.

All. We know't, we know't.

First Citizen. Let us kill him, and we'll have corn°¹ at   *10*
our own price. Is't a verdict?

All. No more talking on't; let it be done. Away,
away!

1 The degree sign (°) indicates a footnote, which is keyed to the text by
line number. Text references are printed in **boldface** type; the annotation
follows in roman type. 1.1.10 **corn** grain (wheat, barley, etc., not
Indian corn)

3

Second Citizen. One word, good citizens.

15 *First Citizen.* We are accounted poor citizens, the
patricians good.° What authority surfeits on would
relieve us. If they would yield us but the superfluity
while it were wholesome, we might guess° they
relieved us humanely; but they think we are too
20 dear;° the leanness that afflicts us, the object° of
our misery, is as an inventory to particularize their
abundance;° our sufferance is a gain to them. Let
us revenge this with our pikes° ere we become
rakes.° For the gods know I speak this in hunger
25 for bread, not in thirst for revenge.

Second Citizen. Would you proceed especially against
Caius Marcius?

First Citizen. Against him first: he's a very dog to the
commonalty.°

30 *Second Citizen.* Consider you what services he has
done for his country?

First Citizen. Very well, and could be content to give
him good report for't, but that he pays himself with
being proud.

35 *Second Citizen.* Nay, but speak not maliciously.

First Citizen. I say unto you, what he hath done
famously he did it to that end; though soft-
conscienced men can be content to say it was for his
country, he did it to please his mother and to be
40 partly proud,° which he is, even to the altitude of
his virtue.°

Second Citizen. What he cannot help in his nature you
account a vice in him. You must in no way say he
is covetous.

16 **good** well-off 18 **guess** think 20 **dear** expensive 20 **object** sight
21–22 **inventory to particularize their abundance** list in which to read
a detailed account of their wealth as compared with our poverty 23
pikes pitchforks 24 **rakes** cf. "lean as a rake" 29 **commonalty**
common people 39–40 **to be partly proud** in part from pride 41
virtue valor (Latin sense)

First Citizen. If I must not, I need not be barren of 45
accusations. He hath faults (with surplus) to tire in
repetition. (*Shouts within.*) What shouts are these?
The other side o' th' city is risen. Why stay we
prating here? To th' Capitol!°

All. Come, come. 50

First Citizen. Soft,° who comes here?

Enter Menenius Agrippa.

Second Citizen. Worthy Menenius Agrippa, one that
hath always loved the people.

First Citizen. He's one honest enough; would all the
rest were so! 55

Menenius. What work's, my countrymen, in hand?
Where go you
With bats and clubs? The matter? Speak, I pray
you.

First Citizen. Our business is not unknown to th'
Senate; they have had inkling this fortnight what
we intend to do, which now we'll show 'em in 60
deeds. They say poor suitors have strong breaths;
they shall know we have strong arms too.

Menenius. Why, masters, my good friends, mine
honest neighbors,
Will you undo yourselves?

First Citizen. We cannot, sir; we are undone already. 65

Menenius. I tell you, friends, most charitable care
Have the patricians of you. For your wants,
Your suffering in this dearth,° you may as well
Strike at the heaven with your staves as lift them
Against the Roman state, whose course will on 70
The way it takes, cracking ten thousand curbs°
Of more strong link asunder than can ever

---

49 **Capitol** Capitoline Hill, on which the Temple of Jupiter stood (here
and often, for the Senate House nearby)   51 **Soft** stop (an interjection)
68 **dearth** famine   71 **curbs** restraints

Appear in your impediment.° For the dearth,
The gods, not the patricians, make it, and
75 Your knees to them (not arms) must help. Alack,
You are transported° by calamity
Thither where more attends you; and you slander
The helms° o' th' state, who care for you like
     fathers,
When you curse them as enemies.

80 *First Citizen.* Care for us! True, indeed! They ne'er
cared for us yet. Suffer us to famish, and their store-
houses crammed with grain; make edicts for usury,
to support usurers; repeal daily any wholesome act
established against the rich, and provide more
85 piercing statutes daily to chain up and restrain the
poor. If the wars eat us not up, they will; and
there's all the love they bear us.

Menenius. Either you must
Confess yourselves wondrous malicious,
90 Or be accused of folly. I shall tell you
A pretty tale; it may be you have heard it;
But since it serves my purpose, I will venture
To stale't° a little more.

First Citizen. Well, I'll hear it, sir. Yet you must not
95 think to fob off° our disgrace° with a tale. But,
and't° please you, deliver.

Menenius. There was a time when all the body's mem-
     bers
Rebelled against the Belly; thus accused it:
That only like a gulf° it did remain
100 I' th' midst o' th' body, idle and unactive,
Still cupboarding the viand,° never bearing
Like labor with the rest; where th' other instru-
     ments°

---

73 **in your impediment** in any hindrance you make   76 **transported**
carried out of your minds   78 **helms** helmsmen   93 **stale't** make it
stale   95 **fob off** set aside with a trick   95 **disgrace** misfortune   96
and't if it   99 **gulf** whirlpool   101 **viand** food   102 **instruments**
organs

Did see and hear, devise, instruct, walk, feel,
And, mutually participate,° did minister
Unto the appetite and affection° common   *105*
Of the whole body. The Belly answered—

First Citizen. Well, sir, what answer made the Belly?

Menenius. Sir, I shall tell you. With a kind of smile,
Which ne'er came from the lungs, but even thus—
For, look you, I may make the Belly smile   *110*
As well as speak—it tauntingly replied
To th' discontented members, the mutinous parts
That envied his receipt;° even so most fitly
As you malign our senators for that
They are not such as you.

First Citizen.   Your Belly's answer—What? *115*
The kingly crownèd head, the vigilant eye,
The counselor heart, the arm our soldier,
Our steed the leg, the tongue our trumpeter,
With other muniments° and petty helps
In this our fabric, if that they—

Menenius.   What then?   *120*
'Fore me,° this fellow speaks! What then? What
then?

First Citizen. Should by the cormorant Belly be restrained,
Who is the sink° o' th' body—

Menenius.   Well, what then?

First Citizen. The former agents, if they did complain,
What could the Belly answer?

Menenius.   I will tell you;   *125*
If you'll bestow a small (of what you have little)
Patience awhile, you'st° hear the Belly's answer.

First Citizen. Y'are° long about it.

104 **mutually participate** taking part in common   105 **affection** inclination   113 **his receipt** what he received   119 **muniments** furnish-
ings (fortifications)   121 **'Fore me** by my soul   123 **sink** sewer   127
you'st you'll (for "you shalt")   128 **Y'are** you're

Menenius.   Note me this, good friend;
Your most grave Belly° was deliberate,
130 Not rash like his accusers, and thus answered:
"True is it, my incorporate friends," quoth he,
"That I receive the general food at first,
Which you do live upon; and fit it is,
Because I am the storehouse and the shop°
135 Of the whole body. But, if you do remember,
I send it through the rivers of your blood,
Even to the court, the heart, to th' seat o' th' brain;
And, through the cranks° and offices° of man,
The strongest nerves° and small inferior veins
140 From me receive that natural competency°
Whereby they live; and though that all at once"—
You, my good friends, this says the Belly, mark
me—

First Citizen. Ay, sir; well, well.

Menenius.   "Though all at once cannot
See what I do deliver out to each,
145 Yet I can make my audit up, that all
From me do back receive the flour of all,
And leave me but the bran." What say you to't?

First Citizen. It was an answer. How apply you this?

Menenius. The senators of Rome are this good Belly,
150 And you the mutinous members. For examine
Their counsels and their cares, disgest° things rightly
Touching the weal o' th' common,° you shall find
No public benefit which you receive
But it proceeds or comes from them to you,
155 And no way from yourselves. What do you think,
You, the great toe of this assembly?

---

129 **Your most grave Belly** this most grave belly we speak of   134
shop factory   138 **cranks** winding paths   138 **offices** parts of a house
where household work is done, e.g., kitchen   139 **nerves** tendons   140
natural competency supply adequate to their nature   151 **disgest**
digest   152 **weal o' th' common** welfare of the people

First Citizen. I the great toe! Why the great toe?

Menenius. For that, being one o' th' lowest, basest, poorest,
Of this most wise rebellion, thou goest foremost.
Thou rascal,° that are worst in blood° to run,   160
Lead'st first to win some vantage.°
But make you ready your stiff° bats and clubs;
Rome and her rats are at the point of battle;
The one side must have bale.°

Enter Caius Marcius.

Hail, noble Marcius!

Marcius. Thanks. What's the matter, you dissentious rogues   165
That, rubbing the poor itch of your opinion,
Make yourselves scabs?°

First Citizen.   We have ever your good word.

Marcius. He that will give good words to thee will flatter
Beneath abhorring. What would you have, you curs,
That like nor peace nor war? The one affrights you,   170
The other makes you proud. He that trusts to you,
Where he should find you lions, finds you hares;
Where foxes, geese. You are no surer, no,
Than is the coal of fire upon the ice,
Or hailstone in the sun. Your virtue is   175
To make him worthy whose offense subdues him°
And curse that justice did it.° Who deserves greatness
Deserves your hate; and your affections° are
A sick man's appetite, who desires most that
Which would increase his evil. He that depends   180
Upon your favors swims with fins of lead

---

160 **rascal** a lean deer, or a hound   160 **blood** condition   161 **vantage** advantage   162 **stiff** stout   164 **bale** harm   167 **Make yourselves scabs** make scabs for yourselves (also, "make yourselves into loathsome fellows")   176 **subdues him** lays him low   177 **that justice did it** the justice that punished him   178 **affections** desires

And hews down oaks with rushes. Hang ye! Trust
    ye?
With every minute you do change a mind,
And call him noble that was now your hate,
185   Him vile that was your garland. What's the matter
That in these several places of the city
You cry against the noble Senate, who
(Under the gods) keep you in awe, which else
Would feed on one another? What's their seeking?

Menenius. For corn at their own rates, whereof they
190   say
The city is well stored.

Marcius.   Hang 'em! They say!
They'll sit by th' fire, and presume to know
What's done i' th' Capitol: who's like to rise,
Who thrives and who declines; side factions° and
    give out
195   Conjectural marriages, making parties strong,
And feebling° such as stand not in their liking
Below their cobbled shoes. They say there's grain
    enough!
Would the nobility lay aside their ruth,°
And let me use my sword, I'd make a quarry°
200   With thousands of these quartered slaves, as high
As I could pick my lance.

Menenius. Nay, these are almost thoroughly per-
    suaded;
For though abundantly they lack discretion,
Yet are they passing° cowardly. But, I beseech you,
What says the other troop?

205 *Marcius.*   They are dissolved. Hang 'em!
They said they were an-hungry;° sighed forth
    proverbs°—

---

194 **side factions** take sides (form parties)   196 **feebling** weakening
(bringing down)   198 **ruth** compassion   199 **quarry** heap of dead
(usually of game animals)   204 **passing** exceedingly   206 **an-hungry**
hungry   206 **sighed forth proverbs** (implying that they talk like
rustics)

That hunger broke stone walls, that dogs must eat,
That meat was made for mouths, that the gods sent
  not
Corn for the rich men only. With these shreds
They vented their complainings, which being an-
  swered,   210
And a petition granted them, a strange one,
To break the heart of generosity°
And make bold power look pale, they threw their
  caps
As they would hang them on the horns o' th' moon,
Shouting their emulation.°

Menenius.   What is granted them? 215

Marcius. Five tribunes to defend their vulgar° wisdoms,
Of their own choice. One's Junius Brutus—
Sicinius Velutus, and—I know not. 'Sdeath!
The rabble should have first unroofed the city,
Ere so prevailed with me; it will in time   220
Win upon power° and throw forth greater themes
For insurrection's arguing.°

Menenius.   This is strange.

Marcius. Go, get you home, you fragments!

Enter a Messenger, hastily.

Messenger. Where's Caius Marcius?

Marcius.   Here: what's the matter?

Messenger. The news is, sir, the Volsces are in arms. 225

Marcius. I am glad on't: then we shall ha' means to
  vent°
Our musty superfluity. See, our best elders.

---

212 **break the heart of generosity** give the deathblow to the nobility
215 **Shouting their emulation** expressing envious joy   216 **vulgar**
common, plebeian   221 **Win upon power** get the better of authority
222 **For insurrection's arguing** for rebels to debate in action (abstract
for concrete, as often in *Coriolanus*)   226 **vent** get rid of

Enter Sicinius Velutus, Junius Brutus, Cominius,
Titus Lartius, with other Senators.

First Senator. Marcius, 'tis true that you have lately
    told us;
The Volsces are in arms.

Marcius.   They have a leader,
230   Tullus Aufidius, that will put you to't.°
I sin in envying his nobility;
And were I anything but what I am,
I would wish me only he.

Cominius.   You have fought together.

Marcius. Were half to half the world by th' ears, and
    he
235   Upon my party, I'd revolt, to make
Only my wars with him. He is a lion
That I am proud to hunt.

First Senator.   Then, worthy Marcius,
Attend upon Cominius to these wars.

Cominius. It is your former promise.

Marcius.   Sir, it is,
240   And I am constant.° Titus Lartius, thou
Shalt see me once more strike at Tullus' face.
What, art thou stiff?° Stand'st out?°

Titus.   No, Caius Marcius;
I'll lean upon one crutch and fight with t'other
Ere stay behind this business.

Menenius.   O, true-bred!

First Senator. Your company to th' Capitol; where
245   I know
Our greatest friends attend us.

Titus.   [*To Cominius*] Lead you on.

---

230 **put you to't** test you severely   240 **constant** faithful   242 **stiff**
obstinate, set (on not fighting)   242 **Stand'st out** you're staying out of
it?

    [*To Marcius*] Follow Cominius; we must follow
      you;
    Right worthy you priority.°

Cominius.   Noble Marcius!

First Senator. [*To the Citizens*] Hence to your homes;
    begone!

Marcius.   Nay, let them follow.
    The Volsces have much corn; take these rats
      thither   250
    To gnaw their garners. Worshipful mutineers,
    Your valor puts well forth.° Pray, follow.   *Exeunt.*

      Citizens steal away. Manet° Sicinius and Brutus.

Sicinius. Was ever man so proud as is this Marcius?

Brutus. He has no equal.

Sicinius. When we were chosen tribunes for the people— 255

Brutus. Marked you his lip and eyes?

Sicinius.   Nay, but his taunts.

Brutus. Being moved, he will not spare to gird° the
    gods.

Sicinius. Bemock the modest moon.

Brutus. The present wars devour him; he is grown
    Too proud to be so valiant.°

Sicinius.   Such a nature,   260
    Tickled with good success,° disdains the shadow
    Which he treads on at noon. But I do wonder
    His insolence can brook to be commanded
    Under Cominius.

---

248 **Right worthy you priority** you well deserve first place   252 **puts
well forth** gives fair promise (literally, buds)   252 s.d. **Manet** remains
(Latin; although the subject is plural, this form, the third person singular,
commonly appears in Elizabethan stage directions)   257 **gird** taunt
259–60 **grown/Too proud to be so valiant** i.e., such pride is not permissible in one so warlike (because dangerous)   261 **success** outcome

Brutus.   Fame, at the which he aims,
265 In whom already he's well graced, can not
    Better be held, nor more attained, than by
    A place below the first. For what miscarries
    Shall be the general's fault, though he perform
    To th' utmost of a man; and giddy censure
270 Will then cry out of Marcius "O, if he
    Had borne the business!"

Sicinius.   Besides, if things go well,
    Opinion, that so sticks on Marcius, shall
    Of his demerits° rob Cominius.

Brutus.   Come:
    Half all Cominius' honors are to Marcius,
275 Though Marcius earned them not; and all his faults
    To Marcius shall be honors, though indeed
    In aught he merit not.

Sicinius.   Let's hence, and hear
    How the dispatch° is made; and in what fashion,
    More than his singularity,° he goes
    Upon this present action.

280 *Brutus.*   Let's along.   *Exeunt.*

[Scene 2. *Corioli. The Senate House.*]

Enter Tullus Aufidius, with Senators of Corioles.

First Senator. So, your opinion is, Aufidius,
    That they of Rome are ent'red in° our counsels,
    And know how we proceed.

Aufidius.   Is it not yours?

---

273 **demerits** deserts   278 **dispatch** execution of the business   279
More than his singularity apart from his usual peculiarity of manner
1.2.2 **ent'red in** initiated into (familiar with)

What° ever have been thought on in this state
That could be brought to bodily act ere Rome   5
Had circumvention?° 'Tis not four days gone
Since I heard thence—these are the words—I think
I have the letter here. Yes, here it is:
"They have pressed a power,° but it is not known
Whether for east or west. The dearth is great;   10
The people mutinous; and it is rumored,
Cominius, Marcius your old enemy
(Who is of Rome worse hated than of you),
And Titus Lartius, a most valiant Roman,
These three lead on this preparation°   15
Whither 'tis bent—most likely 'tis for you.
Consider of it."

First Senator.   Our army's in the field.
We never yet made doubt but Rome was ready
To answer us.

Aufidius.   Nor did you think it folly
To keep your great pretenses° veiled till when   20
They needs must show themselves; which in the
    hatching,
It seemed, appeared to Rome. By the discovery
We shall be short'ned in our aim, which was
To take in° many towns ere almost Rome
Should know we were afoot.

Second Senator.   Noble Aufidius,   25
Take your commission; hie you to your bands:
Let us alone to guard Corioles.
If they set down before's,° for the remove°
Bring up your army; but I think you'll find
They've not prepared for us.

Aufidius.   O, doubt not that;   30
I speak from certainties. Nay, more,

---

4 **What** (plural, i.e., "counsels," line 2) 6 **circumvention** means to
circumvent 9 **pressed a power** collected troops 15 **preparation**
force that has been prepared 20 **great pretenses** main intentions (cf.
"grand design") 24 **take in** capture 28 **set down before's** lay siege
to us 28 **remove** raising of the siege

Some parcels° of their power are forth already,
And only hitherward.° I leave your honors.
If we and Caius Marcius chance to meet,
35   'Tis sworn between us we shall ever strike
Till one can do no more.

All.   The gods assist you!

Aufidius. And keep your honors safe!

First Senator.   Farewell.

Second Senator.   Farewell.

All. Farewell.   *Exeunt omnes.°*

[Scene 3. *Rome. A room in Marcius' house.*]

*Enter Volumnia and Virgilia, mother and wife to
Marcius. They set them down on two low stools,
and sew.*

Volumnia. I pray you, daughter, sing, or express yourself in a more comfortable° sort. If my son were
my husband, I should freelier rejoice in that absence wherein he won honor than in the embrace-
5   ments of his bed where he would show most love.
When yet he was but tender-bodied, and the only
son of my womb; when youth with comeliness
plucked all gaze° his way; when, for a day of kings'
entreaties, a mother should not sell him an hour
10   from her beholding; I, considering how honor
would become such a person°—that it was no
better than picture-like to hang by th' wall, if renown made it not stir—was pleased to let him seek
danger where he was like to find fame. To a cruel

32 **parcels** portions 33 **hitherward** i.e., to attack Rome 38 s.d.
omnes all (Latin) 1.3.2 **comfortable** cheerful 8 **plucked all gaze**
drew the eyes of all 11 **person** handsome figure

war I sent him, from whence he returned, his brows
bound with oak.° I tell thee, daughter, I sprang not   15
more in joy at first hearing he was a man-child than
now in first seeing he had proved himself a man.

Virgilia. But had he died in the business, madam,
how then?   20

Volumnia. Then his good report should have been my
son; I therein would have found issue. Hear me
profess° sincerely: had I a dozen sons, each in my
love alike, and none less dear than thine and my
good Marcius, I had rather had eleven die nobly
for their country than one voluptuously surfeit out   25
of action.

                    Enter a Gentlewoman.

Gentlewoman. Madam, the Lady Valeria is come to
visit you.

Virgilia. Beseech° you give me leave to retire myself.

Volumnia. Indeed, you shall not.   30
Methinks I hear hither your husband's drum;
See him pluck Aufidius down by th' hair;
As children from a bear, the Volsces shunning him.
Methinks I see him stamp thus, and call thus: 35
"Come on, you cowards, you were got° in fear,
Though you were born in Rome." His bloody brow
With his mailed hand then wiping, forth he goes,
Like to a harvest-man that's tasked to mow
Or° all or lose his hire.   40

Virgilia. His bloody brow? O Jupiter, no blood!

Volumnia. Away, you fool! It more becomes a man
Than gilt his trophy.° The breasts of Hecuba,°
When she did suckle Hector, looked not lovelier
Than Hector's forehead when it spit forth blood   45

16 **oak** ("garland" of honor for saving a fellow Roman in battle)   23
profess declare   30 **Beseech** I beg   36 **got** begotten   40 **Or** either
43 **trophy** monument   43 **Hecuba** (Queen of Troy and mother of
Hector, who defended the city from the Greeks)

At Grecian sword, contemning.° Tell Valeria
We are fit° to bid her welcome. *Exit Gentlewoman.*

Virgilia. Heavens bless° my lord from fell° Aufidius!

Volumnia. He'll beat Aufidius' head below his knee,
50   And tread upon his neck.

Enter Valeria with an Usher° and a Gentlewoman.

Valeria. My ladies both, good day to you.

Volumnia. Sweet madam!

Virgilia. I am glad to see your ladyship.

Valeria. How do you both? You are manifest house-
55   keepers.° What are you sewing here? A fine spot,°
in good faith. How does your little son?

Virgilia. I thank your ladyship; well, good madam.

Volumnia. He had rather see the swords and hear a
drum than look upon his schoolmaster.

60 *Valeria.* O' my word, the father's son! I'll swear 'tis
a very pretty boy. O' my troth, I looked upon him
o' Wednesday half an hour together; has such a
confirmed° countenance! I saw him run after a
gilded butterfly; and when he caught it, he let it go
65   again; and after it again; and over and over he
comes, and up again; catched it again; or whether
his fall enraged him, or how 'twas, he did so set
his teeth, and tear it. O, I warrant, how he mam-
mocked° it!

70 *Volumnia.* One on's° father's moods.

Valeria. Indeed, la, 'tis a noble child.

Virgilia. A crack,° madam.

---

46 contemning in scorn **47 fit** ready **48 bless** guard **48 fell** sav-
age **50 s.d. Usher** servant accompanying a lady **54–55 manifest
housekeepers** clearly stay-at-homes **55 spot** pattern in embroidery
63 confirmed determined **68–69 mammocked** tore to pieces **70
on's** of his **72 crack** rascal

Valeria. Come, lay aside your stitchery; I must have
you play the idle huswife with me this afternoon.

Virgilia. No, good madam; I will not out of doors.   75

Valeria. Not out of doors!

Volumnia. She shall, she shall.

Virgilia. Indeed, no, by your patience;° I'll not over
the threshold till my lord return from the wars.

Valeria. Fie, you confine yourself most unreasonably;   80
come, you must go visit the good lady that lies in.

Virgilia. I will wish her speedy strength, and visit her
with my prayers; but I cannot go thither.

Volumnia. Why I pray you?

Virgilia. 'Tis not to save labor, nor that I want° love.   85

Valeria. You would be another Penelope;° yet, they
say, all the yarn she spun in Ulysses' absence did
but fill Ithaca° full of moths. Come; I would your
cambric were sensible° as your finger, that you
might leave pricking it for pity. Come, you shall go   90
with us.

Virgilia. No, good madam, pardon me; indeed, I will
not forth.

Valeria. In truth, la, go with me, and I'll tell you excellent news of your husband.   95

Virgilia. O, good madam, there can be none yet.

Valeria. Verily, I do not jest with you; there came
news from him last night.

Virgilia. Indeed, madam?

Valeria. In earnest, it's true; I heard a senator speak   100
it. Thus it is: the Volsces have an army forth;

78 **patience** leave   85 **want** am lacking in   86 **Penelope** (Ulysses'
faithful wife, who by using her weaving as an excuse, postponed her
answer to offers of marriage)   88 **Ithaca** (Ulysses' home city)   89
sensible sensitive

against whom Cominius the general is gone, with
one part of our Roman power. Your lord and Titus
Lartius are set down before their city Corioles; they
105 nothing doubt prevailing, and to make it brief wars.
This is true, on mine honor; and so, I pray, go
with us.

Virgilia. Give me excuse, good madam; I will obey
you in everything hereafter.

110 *Volumnia.* Let her alone, lady; as she is now, she will
but disease our better mirth.°

Valeria. In troth, I think she would. Fare you well,
then. Come, good sweet lady. Prithee, Virgilia, turn
thy solemness out o' door, and go along with us.

115 *Virgilia.* No, at a word,° madam; indeed, I must not.
I wish you much mirth.

Valeria. Well then, farewell.

Exeunt Ladies.

[Scene 4. *Before Corioli.*]

*Enter Marcius, Titus Lartius, with drum and colors,
with Captains and Soldiers, as before the city Corioles.
To them a Messenger.*

Marcius. Yonder comes news: a wager they have met.

Lartius. My horse to yours, no.

Marcius.   'Tis done.

Lartius.   Agreed.

Marcius. Say, has our general met the enemy?

111 **disease our better mirth** spoil our fun, which would be better
(without her) 115 **at a word** to put it briefly

Messenger. They lie in view, but have not spoke° as
　　yet.

Lartius. So, the good horse is mine.

Marcius.　　　　　　　　　I'll buy him of you.　5

Lartius. No, I'll nor sell nor give him; lend you him
　　I will
For half a hundred years. Summon the town.

Marcius. How far off lie these armies?

Messenger.　　　　　　　Within this mile and half.

Marcius. Then shall we hear their 'larum,° and they
　　ours.
Now, Mars, I prithee, make us quick in work,　10
That we with smoking° swords may march from
　　hence
To help our fielded° friends! Come, blow thy blast.

　　　　They sound a parley. Enter two Senators
　　　　with others, on the walls of Corioles.

Tullus Aufidius, is he within your walls?

First Senator. No, nor a man that fears you less than
　　he;
That's lesser than a little. (*Drum afar off.*) Hark,
　　our drums　15
Are bringing forth our youth. We'll break our walls
Rather than they shall pound us up.° Our gates,
Which yet seem shut, we have but pinned with
　　rushes;
They'll open of themselves. (*Alarum far off.*) Hark
　　you, far off!
There is Aufidius. List what work he makes　20
Amongst your cloven° army.

Marcius.　　　　　　　O, they are at it!

1.4.4 **spoke** engaged　9 **'larum** alarum, call to arms　11 **smoking**
reeking (with blood)　12 **fielded** in the field of battle　17 **pound us up**
shut us in (cf. "dog pound")　21 **cloven** divided

Lartius. Their noise be our instruction.° Ladders, ho!

Enter the Army of the Volsces.

Marcius. They fear us not, but issue forth their city.
Now put your shields before your hearts, and fight
With hearts more proof° than shields. Advance,
25   brave Titus.
They do disdain us much beyond our thoughts,
Which makes me sweat with wrath. Come on, my
    fellows.
He that retires, I'll take him for a Volsce,
And he shall feel mine edge.

*Alarum. The Romans are beat back
to their trenches. Enter Marcius, cursing.*

30 *Marcius.* All the contagion of the south° light on you,
You shames of Rome! You herd of—boils and
    plagues
Plaster you o'er, that you may be abhorred
Farther than seen, and one infect another
Against the wind a mile!° You souls of geese
35   That bear the shapes of men, how have you run
From slaves that apes would beat! Pluto and hell!
All hurt behind, backs red, and faces pale
With flight and agued° fear! Mend° and charge
    home,°
Or, by the fires of heaven, I'll leave the foe,
40   And make my wars on you. Look to't. Come on;
If you'll stand fast, we'll beat them to their wives,
As they us to our trenches. Follow's.°

---

22 **be our instruction** be a lesson to us   25 **proof** tested (and so impenetrable)   30 **south** south wind (pestilential)   34 **Against the wind a mile** i.e., the infection carrying a mile in the face of a contrary wind   38 **agued** i.e., shaking as if from an ague-fit (*ague* = malarial fever)   38 **Mend** do better (pun on the hygienic sense)   38 **home** i.e., into the heart of the enemy's forces   42 **Follow's** follow us, i.e., follow me (the Folio gives "trenches followes." The adopted reading makes sense out of the Folio reading, but it is ugly and anticlimactic. Perhaps "followes" is a misplaced stage direction)

Another alarum; and Marcius follows them to
[the] gates and is shut in.°

So, now the gates are ope. Now prove good sec-
 onds!°
'Tis for the followers° Fortune widens them,
Not for the fliers. Mark me, and do the like.   *45*
       Enters the gates.

First Soldier. Foolhardiness; not I.

Second Soldier. Nor I.

First Soldier. See, they have shut him in.
       Alarum continues.

All.   To th' pot,° I warrant him.

Enter Titus Lartius.

Lartius. What is become of Marcius?

All.   Slain, sir, doubtless.

First Soldier. Following the fliers at the very heels, *50*
With them he enters; who, upon the sudden,
Clapped to their gates. He is himself alone,
To answer all the city.

Lartius.   O noble fellow!
Who sensibly° outdares his senseless sword,
And when it bows stand'st up! Thou art left,
 Marcius!   *55*
A carbuncle° entire, as big as thou art,
Were not so rich a jewel. Thou wast a soldier
Even to Cato's° wish, not fierce and terrible
Only in strokes; but with thy grim looks and
The thunder-like percussion of thy sounds   *60*
Thou mad'st thine enemies shake, as if the world
Were feverous and did tremble.

42 s.d. **is shut in** i.e., at the end of this speech Marcius enters the gates and is shut in 43 **seconds** helpers 44 **followers** pursuers 48 **To th' pot** to destruction (cf. "gone to pot") 54 **sensibly** though subject to feeling 56 **A carbuncle** a red precious stone 58 **Cato** (the Censor, stern upholder of old Roman virtues; see North, below, p. 165)

*Enter Marcius, bleeding, assaulted
by the enemy.*

First Soldier.   Look, sir.

Lartius.   O, 'tis Marcius!
  Let's fetch him off, or make remain alike.°
                    They fight, and all enter the city.

[Scene 5. *Within Corioli.*]

Enter certain Romans, with spoils.

First Roman. This will I carry to Rome.

Second Roman. And I this.

Third Roman. A murrain on't!° I took this for silver.
                    Exeunt.
                    Alarum continues still afar off.

*Enter Marcius and Titus Lartius
with a Trumpet.*°

Marcius. See here these movers° that do prize their
    hours
5   At a cracked drachma!° Cushions, leaden spoons,
    Irons of a doit,° doublets that hangmen would
    Bury with those that wore them, these base slaves,
    Ere yet the fight be done, pack up. Down with
        them!
    And hark, what noise the general makes! To him!
10 There is the man of my soul's hate, Aufidius,
    Piercing our Romans. Then, valiant Titus, take
    Convenient numbers to make good° the city;

---

63 **make remain alike** stay like him (*remain*, a noun, means "a stay")
1.5.3 **murrain on't** plague on it 3 s.d. **Trumpet** trumpeter 4
movers active fellows (ironical) 5 **drachma** Greek coin 6 **of a doit**
worth a doit (coin of little value) 12 **make good** make sure of

    Whilst I, with those that have the spirit, will haste
    To help Cominius.

Lartius.   Worthy sir, thou bleed'st;
    Thy exercise hath been too violent   *15*
    For a second course° of fight.

Marcius.   Sir, praise me not;
    My work hath yet not warmed me. Fare you well.
    The blood I drop is rather physical°
    Than dangerous to me. To Aufidius thus
    I will appear, and fight.

Lartius.   Now the fair goddess, Fortune,   *20*
    Fall deep in love with thee; and her great charms
    Misguide thy opposers' swords! Bold gentleman,
    Prosperity be thy page!°

Marcius.   Thy friend no less
    Than those she placeth highest! So farewell.

Lartius. Thou worthiest Marcius!

                                [*Exit Marcius.*]   *25*
    Go, sound thy trumpet in the marketplace;
    Call thither all the officers o' th' town,
    Where they shall know our mind. Away!   *Exeunt.*

    [Scene 6. *Near the camp of Cominius.*]

    Enter Cominius, as it were in retire, with soldiers.

Cominius. Breathe° you, my friends; well fought; we
        are come off°
    Like Romans, neither foolish in our stands
    Nor cowardly in retire.° Believe me, sirs,
    We shall be charged again. Whiles we have struck,

---

16 **course** bout 18 **physical** beneficial 23 **page** attendant 1.6.1
Breathe rest 1 **are come off** leave the field 3 **retire** retreat

5   By interims and conveying gusts° we have heard
     The charges of our friends. The Roman gods,
     Lead their successes° as we wish our own,
     That both our powers, with smiling fronts° encoun-
        t'ring,
     May give you thankful sacrifice!

                     Enter a Messenger.

                                          Thy news?

10   *Messenger.* The citizens of Corioles have issued,
     And given to Lartius and to Marcius battle.
     I saw our party to their trenches driven,
     And then I came away.

     Cominius.   Though thou speakest truth,
     Methinks thou speak'st not well. How long is't
        since?

15   *Messenger.* Above an hour, my lord.

     Cominius. 'Tis not a mile; briefly° we heard their
        drums.
     How couldst thou in a mile confound° an hour,
     And bring thy news so late?

     Messenger.   Spies of the Volsces
     Held me in chase, that I was forced to wheel
20   Three or four miles about; else had I, sir,
     Half an hour since brought my report.

                     Enter Marcius.

     Cominius.   Who's yonder
     That does appear as he were flayed? O gods!
     He has the stamp° of Marcius, and I have
     Before-time seen him thus.

     Marcius.   Come I too late?

     ---

     5 **By interims and conveying gusts** at intervals, by gusts of wind car-
     rying (the sound) 7 **successes** outcomes 8 **fronts** first lines (also,
     "faces") 16 **briefly** a short time ago 17 **confound** waste 23 **stamp**
     characteristic features (metaphor from coining)

Cominius. The shepherd knows not thunder from a
    tabor°   25
    More than I know the sound of Marcius' tongue
    From every meaner man.

Marcius.   Come I too late?

Cominius. Ay, if you come not in the blood of others,
    But mantled in your own.

Marcius.   O, let me clip° ye
    In arms as sound as when I wooed; in heart   30
    As merry as when our nuptial day was done,
    And tapers burned to bedward!°

Cominius.   Flower of warriors!
    How is't with Titus Lartius?

Marcius. As with a man busied about decrees:
    Condemning some to death and some to exile;   35
    Ransoming him, or pitying, threat'ning th' other;
    Holding Corioles in the name of Rome,
    Even like a fawning greyhound in the leash,
    To let him slip° at will.

Cominius.   Where is that slave
    Which told me they had beat you to your trenches?   40
    Where is he? Call him hither.

Marcius.   Let him alone;
    He did inform° the truth. But for our gentlemen,°
    The common file°—a plague! tribunes for them!—
    The mouse ne'er shunned the cat as they did budge
    From rascals worse than they.

Cominius.   But how prevailed you?   45

Marcius. Will the time serve to tell? I do not think.
    Where is the enemy? Are you lords o' th' field?
    If not, why cease you till you are so?

Cominius.   Marcius,

25 **tabor** small drum   29 **clip** embrace   32 **burned to bedward**
burned low, announcing the time for bed   39 **let him slip** unleash him
42 **inform** report   42 **gentlemen** (ironically)   43 **common file** i.e.,
the plebeian soldiers

We have at disadvantage fought and did
50   Retire to win our purpose.

Marcius. How lies their battle? Know you on which
    side
    They have placed their men of trust?

Cominius.   As I guess, Marcius,
    Their bands i' th' vaward° are the Antiates,
    Of their best trust; o'er them Aufidius,
    Their very heart of hope.

55 *Marcius.*   I do beseech you,
    By all the battles wherein we have fought,
    By th' blood we have shed together, by th' vows
    We have made to endure friends, that you directly
    Set me against Aufidius and his Antiates;
60   And that you not delay the present,° but,
    Filling the air with swords advanced and darts,
    We prove° this very hour.

Cominius.   Though I could wish
    You were conducted to a gentle bath,
    And balms applied to you, yet dare I never
65   Deny your asking. Take your choice of those
    That best can aid your action.

Marcius.   Those are they
    That most are willing. If any such be here—
    As it were sin to doubt—that love this painting
    Wherein you see me smeared; if any fear
70   Lesser his person° than an ill report;
    If any think brave death outweighs bad life,
    And that his country's dearer than himself;
    Let him alone, or so many so minded,
    Wave thus, to express his disposition,°
75   And follow Marcius.

                They all shout, and wave their swords; take
                him up in their arms, and cast up their caps.

---

53 **vaward** vanguard, advance troops 60 **delay the present** put off the
present occasion 62 **prove** make trial of 69–70 **fear/Lesser his
person** fear less for his body 74 **disposition** inclination

O me alone! Make you a sword of me?
If these shows be not outward, which of you
But is four Volsces? None of you but is
Able to bear against the great Aufidius
A shield as hard as his. A certain number,   80
Though thanks to all, must I select from all. The
    rest
Shall bear the business in some other fight,
As cause will be obeyed.° Please you to march;
And four shall quickly draw out my command,
Which men are best inclined.

Cominius.   March on, my fellows: 85
Make good this ostentation,° and you shall
Divide in all with us.   *Exeunt.*

[Scene 7. *The gates of Corioli.*]

*Titus Lartius, having set a guard upon Corioles, going
with drum and trumpet toward Cominius and Caius
Marcius, enters with a Lieutenant, other Soldiers, and
a Scout.*

Lartius. So, let the ports° be guarded; keep your
    duties
As I have set them down. If I do send, dispatch
Those centuries° to our aid; the rest will serve
For a short holding. If we lose the field,
We cannot keep the town.

Lieutenant.   Fear not our care, sir.   5

Lartius. Hence, and shut your gates upon's.
Our guider, come; to th' Roman camp conduct us.
                    Exit [*with the rest*].

___

83 **cause will be obeyed** occasion shall demand 86 **ostentation** display 1.7.1 **ports** gates 3 **centuries** companies (smallest units of Roman legion)

[Scene 8. *A field of battle.*]

Alarum as in battle. Enter Marcius and Aufidius,
at several doors.°

Marcius. I'll fight with none but thee, for I do hate
    thee
Worse than a promise-breaker.

Aufidius.   We hate alike:
Not Afric° owns a serpent I abhor
More than thy fame and envy. Fix thy foot.

5 *Marcius.* Let the first budger° die the other's slave,
And the gods doom him after!

Aufidius.   If I fly, Marcius,
Holloa° me like a hare.

Marcius.   Within these hours, Tullus,
Alone I fought in your Corioles walls,
And made what work I pleased. 'Tis not my blood
10 Wherein thou seest me masked. For thy revenge
Wrench up thy power to th' highest.

Aufidius.   Wert thou the Hector
That was the whip of your bragged progeny,°
Thou shouldst not scape me here.
        Here they fight, and certain Volsces come in
        the aid of Aufidius. Marcius fights till they
        be driven in breathless.
Officious, and not valiant, you have shamed me
15 In your condemnèd seconds.°

1.8.s.d. **at several doors** from different entrances 3 **Afric** Africa 5
budger one who moves 7 **Holloa** shout "halloo" after (in hunting)
12 **whip of your bragged progeny** the whip used by your boasted
ancestors, the Trojans, against the Greeks 15 **In your condemnèd sec-**
onds by your damnable help (cf. 1.4.43)

[Scene 9. *The Roman camp.*]

Flourish. Alarum. A retreat is sounded. Enter at one
door, Cominius with the Romans; at another door,
Marcius, with his arm in a scarf.

Cominius. If I should tell thee o'er this thy day's work,
Thou't° not believe thy deeds. But I'll report it
Where senators shall mingle tears with smiles;
Where great patricians shall attend, and shrug,°
I' th' end admire; where ladies shall be frighted,   5
And, gladly quaked,° hear more; where the dull
    tribunes,
That with the fusty° plebeians hate thine honors,
Shall say against their hearts "We thank the gods
Our Rome hath such a soldier."
Yet cam'st thou to a morsel of this feast,°   10
Having fully dined before.

Enter Titus [Lartius], with his power,
from the pursuit.

Lartius.   O general,
Here is the steed, we the caparison!°
Hadst thou beheld—

Marcius.   Pray now, no more. My mother,
Who has a charter° to extol her blood,
When she does praise me grieves me. I have done   15
As you have done, that's what I can; induced
As you have been, that's for my country.

1.9.2 **Thou't** thou wouldst   4 **shrug** i.e., in disbelief   6 **quaked** made
to shake   7 **fusty** moldy   10 **cam'st thou to a morsel of this feast**
(refers to Marcius' coming to support Cominius in the latter part of the
battle just ended)   12 **caparison** the (mere) trappings   14 **charter**
privilege granted her

He that has but effected his good will°
Hath overta'en° mine act.

Cominius.   You shall not be
20   The grave of your deserving; Rome must know
The value of her own. 'Twere a concealment
Worse than a theft, no less than a traducement,°
To hide your doings; and to silence that
Which, to the spire and top of praises vouched,°
25   Would seem but modest. Therefore, I beseech you,
In sign of what you are, not to reward
What you have done, before our army hear me.

Marcius. I have some wounds upon me, and they
        smart
To hear themselves rememb'red.

Cominius.   Should they not,
30   Well might they fester 'gainst° ingratitude,
And tent themselves° with death.° Of all the
        horses—
Whereof we have ta'en good, and good store°—
        of all
The treasure in this field achieved and city,
We render you the tenth; to be ta'en forth
35   Before the common distribution at
Your only choice.

Marcius.   I thank you, general;
But cannot make my heart consent to take
A bribe to pay my sword. I do refuse it,
And stand upon my common part with those
40   That have beheld the doing.
                    A long flourish. They all cry "Marcius!
                    Marcius!" cast up their caps and lances.
                    Cominius and Lartius stand bare.

___

. 18 **good will** firm intention   19 **overta'en** surpassed   22 **traducement** slander   24 **to the spire and top of praises vouched** though
attested in the highest terms of praise   30 **'gainst** against, in the face
of   31 **tent themselves** be cleansed (refers to cleaning a wound with a
linen roll, a "tent")   31 **death** (the "tent" being "death," the wounds
would prove fatal)   32 **good store** plenty

Marcius. May these same instruments, which you
    profane,
    Never sound more! When drums and trumpets shall
    I' th' field prove flatterers, let courts and cities be
    Made all of false-faced soothing!°
    When steel grows soft as the parasite's silk,   *45*
    Let him be made a coverture° for th' wars!
    No more, I say! For that° I have not washed
    My nose that bled, or foiled° some debile° wretch,
    Which without note here's many else have done,
    You shout me forth   *50*
    In acclamations hyperbolical;
    As if I loved my little should be dieted
    In° praises sauced with lies.

Cominius.   Too modest are you;
    More cruel to your good report than grateful
    To us that give° you truly. By your patience,   *55*
    If 'gainst yourself you be incensed, we'll put you
    (Like one that means his proper° harm) in
      manacles,
    Then reason safely with you. Therefore, be it
      known,
    As to us, to all the world, that Caius Marcius
    Wears this war's garland: in token of the which,   *60*
    My noble steed, known to the camp, I give him,
    With all his trim belonging;° and from this time,
    For what he did before Corioles, call him,
    With all th' applause and clamor of the host,
    Caius Marcius Coriolanus.   *65*
    Bear th' addition° nobly ever!
               Flourish. Trumpets sound, and drums.

Omnes.° Caius Marcius Coriolanus!

Coriolanus. I will go wash:
    And when my face is fair, you shall perceive
    Whether I blush, or no. Howbeit, I thank you.   *70*

---

44 **soothing** flattery 46 **coverture** clothing 47 **For that** because
48 **foiled** defeated 48 **debile** weak 52–53 **dieted/In** fed by 55
give report 57 **proper** own 62 **his trim belonging** the equipment
that goes with it 66 **addition** title 67 **Omnes** all (Latin)

I mean to stride your steed, and at all times
To undercrest your good addition°
To th' fairness° of my power.

Cominius.   So, to our tent;
Where, ere we do repose us, we will write
75 To Rome of our success. You, Titus Lartius,
Must to Corioles back; send us to Rome
The best,° with whom we may articulate°
For their own good and ours.

Lartius.   I shall, my lord.

Coriolanus. The gods begin to mock me. I, that now
80 Refused most princely gifts, am bound to beg
Of my lord general.

Cominius.   Take't; 'tis yours. What is't?

Coriolanus. I sometime lay here in Corioles
At a poor man's house; he used me kindly.
He cried to me; I saw him prisoner;
85 But then Aufidius was within my view,
And wrath o'erwhelmed my pity. I request you
To give my poor host freedom.

Cominius.   O, well begged!
Were he the butcher of my son, he should
Be free as is the wind. Deliver him, Titus.

Lartius. Marcius, his name?

90 *Coriolanus.*   By Jupiter, forgot!
I am weary; yea, my memory is tired.
Have we no wine here?

Cominius.   Go we to our tent.
The blood upon your visage dries; 'tis time
It should be looked to. Come.   *Exeunt.*

---

72 **undercrest your good addition** support the fine title you give (a
"crest" in heraldry is a figure above a shield; the suggested image is of a
shield with a man on horseback [line 71], beneath a crest [the "addition"])   73 **To th' fairness** to the exact measure   77 **best** chief men
77 **articulate** make terms

[Scene 10. *The camp of the Volsces.*]

*A flourish. Cornets. Enter Tullus Aufidius,
bloody, with two or three soldiers.*

Aufidius. The town is ta'en!

First Soldier. 'Twill be delivered back on good condition.°

Aufidius. Condition!
  I would I were a Roman; for I cannot,
  Being a Volsce, be that I am. Condition!   5
  What good condition° can a treaty find
  I' th' part that is at mercy?° Five times, Marcius,
  I have fought with thee; so often hast thou beat me;
  And wouldst do so, I think, should we encounter
  As often as we eat. By th' elements,   10
  If e'er again I meet him beard to beard,
  He's mine or I am his. Mine emulation
  Hath not that honor in't it had; for where
  I thought to crush him in an equal force,
  True sword to sword, I'll potch° at him some way,   15
  Or wrath or craft may get him.

First Soldier.   He's the devil.

Aufidius. Bolder, though not so subtle. My valor's
  poisoned
  With only suff'ring stain° by him; for him
  Shall fly out of itself.° Nor sleep nor sanctuary,
  Being naked,° sick, nor fane° nor Capitol,   20
  The prayers of priests nor times of sacrifice,

1.10.2 **condition** terms   6 **condition** (with pun on sense of "quality")
7 **I' th' part that is at mercy** on the side that is vanquished (at the
mercy of the victor)   15 **potch** poke (thrust, in fencing)   18 **stain**
darkening   19 **fly out of itself** go out of its natural course   20 **naked**
unarmed   20 **fane** shrine

Embarquements° all of fury, shall lift up
Their rotten privilege and custom 'gainst
My hate to Marcius. Where I find him, were it
25   At home, upon my brother's guard,° even there,
Against the hospitable canon,° would I
Wash my fierce hand in's heart. Go you to th' city;
Learn how 'tis held, and what they are that must
Be hostages for Rome.

First Soldier.   Will not you go?

Aufidius. I am attended° at the cypress grove. I pray
30   you—
'Tis south the city mills—bring me word thither
How the world goes, that to the pace of it
I may spur on my journey.

First Soldier.   I shall, sir.   *[Exeunt.]*

---

22 **Embarquements** restraints   25 **upon my brother's guard** with my
brother on guard (over him)   26 **hospitable canon** law of hospitality
30 **attended** awaited

ACT 2

[Scene 1. *Rome. A public place.*]

*Enter Menenius, with the two Tribunes of the
people, Sicinius, and Brutus.*

Menenius. The augurer° tells me we shall have news
tonight.

Brutus. Good or bad?

Menenius. Not according to the prayer of the people,
for they love not Marcius.   5

Sicinius. Nature teaches beasts to know their friends.

Menenius. Pray you, who does the wolf love?

Sicinius. The lamb.

Menenius. Ay, to devour him, as the hungry plebeians
would the noble Marcius.   10

Brutus. He's a lamb indeed, that baas like a bear.

Menenius. He's a bear indeed, that lives like a lamb.
You two are old men: tell me one thing that I shall
ask you.

Both. Well, sir.   15

Menenius. In what enormity° is Marcius poor in, that
you two have not in abundance?

2.1.1 **augurer** (more correctly "augur," Roman official who foretold the
future)   16 **enormity** fault

37

Brutus. He's poor in no one fault, but stored with all.

Sicinius. Especially in pride.

20 *Brutus.* And topping all others in boasting.

Menenius. This is strange now. Do you two know how
you are censured° here in the city—I mean of us
o' th' right-hand file?° Do you?

Both. Why, how are we censured?

25 *Menenius.* Because you talk of pride now—will you
not be angry?

Both. Well, well, sir, well.

Menenius. Why 'tis no great matter; for a very little
thief of occasion° will rob you of a great deal of
30 patience. Give your dispositions the reins, and be
angry at your pleasures; at the least, if you take it
as a pleasure to you in being so. You blame
Marcius for being proud?

Brutus. We do it not alone, sir.

35 *Menenius.* I know you can do very little alone; for
your helps are many, or else your actions would
grow wondrous single:° your abilities are too infant-
like for doing much alone. You talk of pride:
O that you could turn your eyes toward the napes of
40 your necks, and make but an interior survey of
your good selves! O that you could!

Both. What then, sir?

Menenius. Why, then you should discover a brace of
unmeriting, proud, violent, testy° magistrates (alias
45 fools) as any in Rome.

Sicinius. Menenius, you are known well enough° too.

21–22 **how you are censured** the opinion held of you   23 **o' th' right-
hand file** of the upper classes, patricians   28–29 **a very little thief of
occasion** i.e., a very little occasion is a thief who   37 **single** weak,
slight   44 **testy** snappish   46 **known well enough** i.e., notorious

Menenius. I am known to be a humorous° patrician,
and one that loves a cup of hot wine with not a
drop of allaying° Tiber in't; said to be something
imperfect in favoring the first complaint,° hasty and   50
tinderlike upon too trivial motion;° one that con-
verses° more with the buttock of the night than
with the forehead of the morning. What I think I
utter, and spend my malice in my breath. Meeting
two such wealsmen° as you are—I cannot call   55
you Lycurguses°—if the drink you give me touch
my palate adversely, I make a crooked face at it.
I cannot say your worships have delivered the
matter well, when I find the ass in compound with
the major part of your syllables;° and though I   60
must be content to bear with those that say you
are reverend grave men, yet they lie deadly that
tell you you have good faces. If you see this in the
map° of my microcosm,° follows it that I am
known well enough too? What harm can your   65
bisson conspectuities° glean out of this character,
if I be known well enough too?

Brutus. Come, sir, come, we know you well enough.

Menenius. You know neither me, yourselves, nor any
thing. You are ambitious for poor knaves' caps and   70
legs.° You wear out a good wholesome forenoon in
hearing a cause° between an orange-wife and a
forset-seller,° and then rejourn° the controversy of
threepence to a second day of audience. When you
are hearing a matter between party and party, if   75
you chance to be pinched with the colic, you make

47 **humorous** whimsical   49 **allaying** diluting   49–50 **something
imperfect in favoring the first complaint** somewhat at fault in siding
with the party who first puts his case   51 **motion** impulse   51–52 **con-
verses** associates   55 **wealsmen** statesmen   56 **Lycurgus** (a Greek
lawgiver)   59–60 **ass in compound with the major part of your syllables** (pun on overuse of "as-es" in legal expressions, e.g., "whereas")
64 **map** i.e., face   64 **microcosm** little world, i.e., body   66 **bisson
conspectuities** blind visual powers   70–71 **caps and legs** salutes and
bows   72 **cause** case   73 **forset-seller** seller of taps for wine kegs
73 **rejourn** adjourn

faces like mummers,° set up the bloody flag°
against all patience, and, in roaring for a chamber
pot, dismiss the controversy bleeding, the more en-
80 tangled by your hearing. All the peace you make
in their cause is calling both the parties knaves.
You are a pair of strange ones.

Brutus. Come, come, you are well understood to be
a perfecter giber° for the table than a necessary
85 bencher in the Capitol.°

Menenius. Our very priests must become mockers, if
they shall encounter such ridiculous subjects as you
are. When you speak best unto the purpose, it is
not worth the wagging of your beards; and your
90 beards deserve not so honorable a grave as to stuff
a botcher's° cushion or to be entombed in an ass's
packsaddle. Yet you must be saying Marcius is
proud; who, in a cheap estimation, is worth all
your predecessors since Deucalion;° though per-
95 adventure some of the best of 'em were hereditary
hangmen. Good-e'en to your worships. More of
your conversation° would infect my brain, being
the herdsmen of the beastly plebeians. I will be
bold to take my leave of you.

                    Brutus and Sicinius [step] aside.

                    Enter Volumnia, Virgilia, and Valeria.

100 How now, my as fair as noble ladies—and the
moon, were she earthly, no nobler—whither do
you follow your eyes so fast?

Volumnia. Honorable Menenius, my boy Marcius approaches; for the love of Juno, let's go.

105 *Menenius.* Ha? Marcius coming home?

---

77 **mummers** Christmas masquers, who act impromptu plays 77
bloody flag war flag 84 **giber** joker 84–85 **necessary bencher in
the Capitol** indispensable judge in the Senate (cf. "the bench" for
"court") 91 **botcher** mender of old clothes 94 **Deucalion** (the Noah
of Greek myth) 97 **conversation** cf. lines 51–52

Volumnia. Ay, worthy Menenius; and with most prosperous approbation.°

Menenius. Take my cap, Jupiter,° and I thank thee.
Hoo! Marcius coming home!

Two Ladies. Nay, 'tis true.   *110*

Volumnia. Look, here's a letter from him; the state
hath another, his wife another; and, I think, there's
one at home for you.

Menenius. I will make my very house reel tonight.
A letter for me?   *115*

Virgilia. Yes, certain, there's a letter for you; I saw't.

Menenius. A letter for me? It gives me an estate° of
seven years' health; in which time I will make a
lip° at the physician. The most sovereign prescrip-
tion in Galen° is but empiricutic,° and, to this pre-   *120*
servative, of no better report° than a horse-drench.°
Is he not wounded? He was wont to come home
wounded.

Virgilia. O, no, no, no.

Volumnia. O, he is wounded; I thank the gods for't.   *125*

Menenius. So do I too, if it be not too much. Brings
'a° victory in his pocket? The wounds become him.

Volumnia. On's brows, Menenius. He comes the third
time home with the oaken garland.

Menenius. Has he disciplined Aufidius soundly?   *130*

Volumnia. Titus Lartius writes they fought together,
but Aufidius got off.

Menenius. And 'twas time for him too, I'll warrant
him that. And° he had stayed by him, I would

106–7 **with most prosperous approbation** with signs of the greatest
success 108 **Jupiter** (god of the sky and upper air) 117 **estate**
state (fortune?) 118–19 **make a lip** make a face 120 **Galen** Greek
physician 120 **empiricutic** quackish 121 **report** reputation 121
horse-drench drink of horse-medicine 127 **'a** he 134 **And** if

135   not have been so fidiused° for all the chests in
       Corioles, and the gold that's in them. Is the Senate
       possessed° of this?

Volumnia. Good ladies, let's go. Yes, yes, yes. The
       Senate has letters from the General, wherein he
140   gives my son the whole name of° the war. He hath
       in this action outdone his former deeds doubly.

Valeria. In troth, there's wondrous things spoke of
       him.

Menenius. Wondrous! Ay, I warrant you, and not
145   without his true purchasing.°

Virgilia. The gods grant them true!

Volumnia. True? Pow waw!°

Menenius. True! I'll be sworn they are true. Where
       is he wounded?—[*To the Tribunes*] God save your
150   good worships! Marcius is coming home. He has
       more cause to be proud.—Where is he wounded?

Volumnia. I' th' shoulder and i' th' left arm. There
       will be large cicatrices° to show the people, when
       he shall stand for his place.° He received in the
155   repulse of Tarquin seven hurts i' th' body.

Menenius. One i' th' neck, and two i' th' thigh—
       there's nine that I know.

Volumnia. He had before this last expedition twenty-
       five wounds upon him.

160 *Menenius.* Now it's twenty-seven: every gash was an
       enemy's grave. (*A shout and flourish.*) Hark! the
       trumpets.

Volumnia. These are the ushers of Marcius. Before

---

135 **fidiused** "Aufidius-ed" (cf. line 130 "disciplined Aufidius soundly")
137 **possessed** duly informed   140 **name of** credit for   145 **true purchasing** really earning (the praise)   147 **Pow waw** (a Volumnian
"pooh-pooh")   153 **cicatrices** scars (Latin)   154 **place** i.e., the consulship

him he carries noise, and behind him he leaves
tears.　　　　　　　　　　　　　　　　　　　165
Death, that dark spirit, in's nervy° arm doth lie,
Which, being advanced, declines, and then men die.

*A sennet.° Trumpets sound. Enter Cominius the
general and Titus Lartius; between them, Coriolanus, crowned with an oaken garland; with
Captains and Soldiers, and a Herald.*

Herald. Know, Rome, that all alone Marcius did fight
Within Corioles gates, where he hath won,
With fame, a name to Caius Marcius; these　　　170
In honor follows Coriolanus.
Welcome to Rome, renownèd Coriolanus!

　　　　　　　　　　　　　　　　Sound. Flourish.

All. Welcome to Rome, renownèd Coriolanus!

Coriolanus. No more of this, it does offend my heart;
Pray now, no more.

Cominius.　　　　　Look, sir, your mother!

Coriolanus.　　　　　　　　　　　O,　175
You have, I know, petitioned all the gods
For my prosperity!
　　　　　　　　　　　　　　　Kneels.

Volumnia.　　　　Nay, my good soldier, up;
My gentle Marcius, worthy Caius, and
By deed-achieving° honor newly named—
What is it?—Coriolanus must I call thee?—　180
But, O, thy wife!

Coriolanus.　　　My gracious silence, hail!
Wouldst thou have laughed had I come coffined
home,
That weep'st to see me triumph? Ah, my dear,
Such eyes the widows in Corioles wear,
And mothers that lack sons.

---

166 **nervy** sinewy　167 s.d. **sennet** (set of notes for trumpet or cornet to
herald an important person, differing from a "flourish" or "fanfare"; cf.
s.d. line 161)　179 **deed-achieving** achieved by deeds (cf. "the deeds of
Coriolanus," 2.2.83)

185 *Menenius.*   Now, the gods crown thee!

Coriolanus. And live you yet? [*To Valeria*] O my
    sweet lady, pardon.

Volumnia. I know not where to turn. O, welcome
    home!
    And welcome, General: and y'are welcome all.

Menenius. A hundred thousand welcomes. I could
    weep,
    And I could laugh, I am light and heavy.° Wel-
190   come!
    A curse begin at very root on's heart
    That is not glad to see thee! You are three
    That Rome should dote on. Yet, by the faith of
    men,
    We have some old crab-trees here at home that
    will not
195   Be grafted° to your relish. Yet welcome, warriors.
    We call a nettle but a nettle, and
    The faults of fools but folly.

Cominius.   Ever right.

Coriolanus. Menenius, ever, ever.

Herald. Give way there, and go on.

Coriolanus. [*To Volumnia and Virgilia*] Your hand,
200   and yours!
    Ere in our own house I do shade my head,
    The good patricians must be visited;
    From whom I have received not only greetings,
    But with them change of honors.°

Volumnia.   I have lived
205   To see inherited° my very wishes
    And the buildings of my fancy. Only
    There's one thing wanting, which I doubt not but
    Our Rome will cast upon thee.

190 **light and heavy** both merry and sad   195 **grafted** i.e., improved
204 **change of honors** fresh honors   205 **inherited** in my possession

Coriolanus.   Know, good mother,
   I had rather be their servant in my way
   Than sway with them in theirs.

Cominius.   On, to the Capitol!   210
     Flourish. Cornets. Exeunt in state, as before.
         Brutus and Sicinius [come forward].

Brutus. All tongues speak of him, and the bleared
     sights
   Are spectacled to see him. Your prattling nurse
   Into a rapture° lets her baby cry
   While she chats° him; the kitchen malkin° pins
   Her richest lockram° 'bout her reechy° neck,   215
   Clamb'ring the walls to eye him. Stalls, bulks,°
     windows,
   Are smothered up, leads° filled and ridges horsed°
   With variable complexions,° all agreeing
   In earnestness to see him. Seld-shown flamens°
   Do press among the popular throngs, and puff   220
   To win a vulgar station.° Our veiled dames
   Commit the war of white and damask in
   Their nicely gawded° cheeks to th' wanton spoil
   Of Phoebus'° burning kisses. Such a pother,°
   As if that whatsoever god who leads him   225
   Were slyly crept into his human powers,
   And gave him graceful posture.

Sicinius.   On the sudden,
   I warrant him consul.

Brutus.   Then our office may,
   During his power, go sleep.

Sicinius. He cannot temp'rately transport his honors   230

---

213 **rapture** fit   214 **chats** gossips about   214 **malkin** slut   215 **lockram** coarse linen   215 **reechy** dirty   216 **bulks** stalls (stands for goods to be sold)   217 **leads** roofs (leaded)   217 **horsed** "ridden" by viewers   218 **variable complexions** different physical types   219 **Seld-shown flamens** priests rarely seen in public (each flamen was in charge of the cult of a particular deity)   221 **vulgar station** place with the common people   223 **gawded** adorned   224 **Phoebus** sun-god   224 **pother** commotion

From where he should begin and end,° but will
Lose those he hath won.

Brutus.   In that there's comfort.

Sicinius.   Doubt not
The commoners, for whom we stand, but they
Upon° their ancient malice will forget
235   With the least cause these his new honors; which°
That he will give them make I as little question
As° he is proud to do't.

Brutus.   I heard him swear,
Were he to stand for consul, never would he
Appear i' th' marketplace, nor on him put
240   The napless° vesture of humility;
Nor, showing, as the manner is, his wounds
To th' people, beg their stinking breaths.

Sicinius.   'Tis right.

Brutus. It was his word. O, he would miss it rather
Than carry° it but by the suit of the gentry to him
And the desire of the nobles.

245 *Sicinius.*   I wish no better
Than have him hold that purpose and to put it
In execution.

Brutus.   'Tis most like he will.

Sicinius. It shall be to him then as our good wills:°
A sure destruction.

Brutus.   So it must fall out
250   To him or our authorities. For an end,°
We must suggest° the people in what hatred
He still° hath held them; that to's power he would
Have made them mules, silenced their pleaders and

231 **and end** i.e., to where he should end   234 **Upon** on account
of   235 **which** i.e., "cause"   237 **As** as that   240 **napless** threadbare
244 **carry** win   248 **as our good wills** as we strongly desire   250 **For
an end** to force the issue (?) finally (?)   251 **suggest** insinuate into the
minds of   252 **still** ever

Dispropertied° their freedoms; holding them,
In human action and capacity,   255
Of no more soul nor fitness for the world
Than camels in their war, who have their provand°
Only for bearing burdens, and sore blows
For sinking under them.

Sicinius.   This, as you say, suggested
At some time when his soaring insolence   260
Shall touch the people—which time shall not want,°
If he be put upon't,° and that's as easy
As to set dogs on sheep—will be his fire
To kindle their dry stubble; and their blaze
Shall darken him forever.

                    Enter a Messenger.

Brutus.   What's the matter?   265

Messenger. You are sent for to the Capitol. 'Tis
    thought
That Marcius shall be consul.
I have seen the dumb men throng to see him and
The blind to hear him speak. Matrons flung gloves,
Ladies and maids their scarfs and handkerchers,   270
Upon him as he passed; the nobles bended,
As to Jove's statue, and the commons made
A shower and thunder with their caps and shouts.
I never saw the like.

Brutus.   Let's to the Capitol,
And carry with us ears and eyes for th' time,   275
But hearts for the event.°

Sicinius.   Have with you.° *Exeunt.*

254 **Dispropertied** dispossessed them of   257 **provand** provisions
261 **want** be lacking   262 **put upon't** provoked to it   276 **event** outcome   276 **Have with you** coming with you!

[Scene 2. *Rome. The Senate House.*]

*Enter two Officers, to lay cushions,° as it were,
in the Capitol.*

First Officer. Come, come, they are almost here. How
many stand for consulships?

Second Officer. Three, they say; but 'tis thought of
everyone Coriolanus will carry it.

5   *First Officer.* That's a brave fellow; but he's ven-
geance° proud, and loves not the common people.

Second Officer. Faith, there hath been many great
men that have flattered the people, who ne'er loved
them; and there be many that they have loved,
10   they know not wherefore; so that, if they love they
know not why, they hate upon no better a ground.
Therefore, for Coriolanus neither to care whether
they love or hate him manifests the true knowledge
he has in their disposition,° and out of his noble
15   carelessness lets them plainly see't.

First Officer. If he did not care whether he had their
love or no, he waved° indifferently 'twixt doing
them neither good nor harm. But he seeks their
hate with greater devotion than they can render it
20   him, and leaves nothing undone that may fully dis-
cover° him their opposite.° Now, to seem to affect°
the malice° and displeasure of the people is as bad
as that which he dislikes, to flatter them for their
love.

2.2.s.d. **cushions** i.e., seats for dignitaries   5–6 **vengeance** frightfully
(cf. "with a vengeance")   14 **in their disposition** of their mood   17
waved would waver   20–21 **discover** show   21 **opposite** opponent
21 **affect** aim at   22 **malice** ill will

Second Officer. He hath deserved worthily of his
country; and his ascent is not by such easy degrees
as those who, having been supple and courteous
to the people, bonneted,° without any further deed
to have them at all into their estimation and report.° But he hath so planted his honors in their   30
eyes and his actions in their hearts that for their
tongues to be silent and not confess so much were
a kind of ingrateful injury; to report otherwise were
a malice° that, giving itself the lie, would pluck
reproof and rebuke from every ear that heard it.   35

First Officer. No more of him; he's a worthy man.
Make way, they are coming.

*A sennet. Enter the Patricians and the Tribunes of the
People, Lictors° before them; Coriolanus, Menenius,
Cominius the Consul. Sicinius and Brutus take their
places by themselves. Coriolanus stands.*

Menenius. Having determined of° the Volsces, and
To send for Titus Lartius, it remains,
As the main point of this our after-meeting,   40
To gratify° his noble service that
Hath thus stood for° his country. Therefore, please
     you
Most reverend and grave elders, to desire
The present consul and last° general
In our well-found° successes, to report   45
A little of that worthy work performed
By Caius Marcius Coriolanus; whom
We met here both to thank and to remember°
With honors like himself.

First Senator.   Speak, good Cominius:

28 **bonneted** took off their caps (in flattery)   29–30 **to have them at
all into their estimation and report** to get themselves at all into,
win their way into, their esteem   34 **malice** act of ill will   37 s.d. **Lic-
tors** (attendants who preceded Roman officials to announce their
approach)   38 **determined of** decided concerning   41 **gratify** reward
42 **stood for** defended   44 **last** late   45 **well-found** fortunately met
with   48 **remember** distinguish

50   Leave nothing out for length, and make us think
        Rather our state's defective for requital
        Than we to stretch it out.° [*To the Tribunes*] Mas-
           ters o' th' people,
        We do request your kindest ears; and, after,
        Your loving motion toward the common body,°
        To yield° what passes here.

55 *Sicinius.*   We are convented°
        Upon a pleasing treaty,° and have hearts
        Inclinable to honor and advance
        The theme of our assembly.

    Brutus.   Which the rather°
        We shall be blessed° to do, if he remember
60   A kinder value° of the people than
        He hath hereto prized them at.

    Menenius.   That's off,° that's off;
        I would you rather had been silent. Please you
        To hear Cominius speak?

    Brutus.   Most willingly.
        But yet my caution was more pertinent
        Than the rebuke you give it.

65 *Menenius.*   He loves your people;
        But tie him not to be their bedfellow.
        Worthy Cominius, speak.
           Coriolanus rises and offers to go away.
                    Nay, keep your place.

    First Senator. Sit, Coriolanus; never shame to hear
        What you have nobly done.

    Coriolanus.   Your honors' pardon:
70   I had rather have my wounds to heal again
        Than hear say how I got them.

51–52 **our state's ... out** our government (the Senate) is lacking in
the resources for reward rather than we in our effort to extend it 54
motion toward the common body influence with the common
people 55 **yield** approve 55 **convented** convened 56 **treaty** proposal for discussion 58 **rather** sooner 59 **blessed** happy 60 **value**
estimate 61 **off** not to the point

Brutus.   Sir, I hope
My words disbenched° you not.

Coriolanus.   No, sir. Yet oft,
When blows have made me stay, I fled from words.
You soothed° not, therefore hurt not; but your
    people,
I love them as they weigh—

Menenius.   Pray now, sit down.   75

Coriolanus. I had rather have one scratch my head
    i' th' sun
When the alarum were struck than idly sit
To hear my nothings monstered.°   *Exit Coriolanus.*

Menenius.   Masters of the people,
Your multiplying spawn how can he flatter—
That's thousand to one good one—when you now
    see   80
He had rather venture all his limbs for honor
Than one on's ears° to hear it? Proceed, Cominius.

Cominius. I shall lack voice: the deeds of Coriolanus
Should not be uttered feebly. It is held
That valor is the chiefest virtue° and   85
Most dignifies the haver. If it be,
The man I speak of cannot in the world
Be singly counterpoised.° At sixteen years,
When Tarquin° made a head for° Rome, he fought
Beyond the mark of others. Our then dictator,   90
Whom with all praise I point at, saw him fight,
When with his Amazonian° chin he drove
The bristled lips before him. He bestrid
An o'erpressed Roman, and i' th' consul's view
Slew three opposers; Tarquin's self he met,   95

---

72 **disbenched** unseated   74 **soothed** flattered   78 **monstered** turned
into marvels   82 **Than one on's ears** than venture one of his ears   85
virtue (cf. Latin *virtus*, manly strength; on this speech, see Introduction
pp. lxiv–vii)   88 **singly counterpoised** matched in value (literally, in
weight) by one man   89 **Tarquin** (early king of Rome, expelled from
the city)   89 **made a head for** raised a force against   92 **Amazonian**
i.e., beardless

And struck him on his knee.° In that day's feats,
When he might act the woman in the scene,°
He proved best man i' th' field, and for his meed°
Was brow-bound with the oak. His pupil age°
100 Man-ent'red° thus, he waxèd like a sea;
And, in the brunt of seventeen battles since,
He lurched° all swords of the garland. For this last,
Before and in Corioles, let me say,
I cannot speak him home.° He stopped the fliers,
105 And by his rare example made the coward
Turn terror into sport; as weeds before
A vessel under sail, so men obeyed
And fell below his stem.° His sword, death's
    stamp,°
Where it did mark, it took;° from face to foot
110 He was a thing of blood, whose every motion
Was timed with dying cries. Alone he ent'red
The mortal gate of th' city, which he painted
With shunless destiny;° aidless came off,
And with a sudden reinforcement struck
115 Corioles like a planet.° Now all's his,
When by and by the din of war 'gan° pierce
His ready° sense, then straight his doubled° spirit
Requick'ned what in flesh was fatigate,°
And to the battle came he; where he did
120 Run reeking o'er the lives of men, as if
'Twere a perpetual spoil;° and till we called
Both field and city ours, he never stood
To ease his breast with panting.

Menenius.   Worthy man!

96 **on his knee** to his knees   97 **in the scene** on that stage   98 **meed**
reward   99 **His pupil age** the years when he was learning (the art of
war)   100 **Man-ent'red** having been initiated into manhood   102
lurched robbed   104 **speak him home** find words to match his merit
108 **stem** bow   108 **stamp** a die for stamping a coin or medal   109
took made its mark; killed (perhaps also, "infected fatally," cf. "struck,"
line 114)   112–13 **painted/With shunless destiny** smeared with blood
of dying men, who could not shun their fate   114–15 **struck/Corioles
like a planet** (planets supposedly had power to "strike," i.e., infect with
disease)   116 **'gan** began to   117 **ready** responsive   117 **doubled**
renewed   118 **fatigate** fatigued   121 **spoil** slaughter

2.2.

First Senator. He cannot but with measure fit° the honors
    Which we devise him.

Cominius.   Our spoils he kicked at,   *125*
    And looked upon things precious as they were
    The common muck of the world. He covets less
    Than misery° itself would give, rewards
    His deeds with doing them, and is content
    To spend the time to end it.°

Menenius.   He's right noble.   *130*
    Let him be called for.

First Senator.   Call Coriolanus.

Officer. He doth appear.

Enter Coriolanus.

Menenius. The Senate, Coriolanus, are well pleased
    To make thee consul.

Coriolanus.   I do owe them still°
    My life and services.

Menenius.   It then remains   *135*
    That you do speak to the people.

Coriolanus.   I do beseech you
    Let me o'erleap that custom, for I cannot
    Put on the gown,° stand naked,° and entreat them,
    For my wounds' sake, to give their suffrage. Please
      you
    That I may pass° this doing.

Sicinius.   Sir, the people   *140*
    Must have their voices;° neither will they bate°
    One jot of ceremony.

---

124 **with measure fit** measure up to; or, "bear with self-control"(?)
128 **misery** poverty   130 **To spend the time to end it** to kill it in
action ("to live it up in action")   134 **still** always   138 **gown** "vesture
of humility" (cf.2.1.240)   138 **naked** i.e., "without any coat underneath" (North)   140 **pass** pass over   141 **voices** votes   141 **bate**
deduct

Menenius.   Put them not to't.°
Pray you, go fit you to the custom, and
Take to you, as your predecessors have,
Your honor with your form.°

145 *Coriolanus.*   It is a part
That I shall blush in acting, and might well
Be taken from the people.

Brutus. [*To Sicinius*]   Mark you that.

Coriolanus. To brag unto them, "Thus I did, and
    thus!"
Show them th' unaching scars which I should hide,
150 As if I had received them for the hire
Of their breath only!

Menenius.   Do not stand upon't.°
We recommend to you, tribunes of the people,
Our purpose° to them; and to our noble consul
Wish we all joy and honor.

155 *Senators.* To Coriolanus come all joy and honor!
                    Flourish cornets. Then exeunt. Manet
                    Sicinius and Brutus.

Brutus. You see how he intends to use the people.

Sicinius. May they perceive's intent! He will require°
    them,
As if he did contemn what he requested
Should be in them to give.

Brutus.   Come, we'll inform them
160 Of our proceedings here. On th' marketplace,
I know, they do attend us.   [*Exeunt.*]

142 **Put them not to't** don't test them (by omitting any part of the ceremony) 145 **Your honor with your form** the honor with the ceremony
it imposes on you 151 **stand upon't** make an issue of it 153 **purpose** proposal 157 **require** ask

[Scene 3. *Rome. The Forum.*]

Enter seven or eight Citizens.

First Citizen. Once if he° do require our voices, we
ought not to deny him.

Second Citizen. We may, sir, if we will.

Third Citizen. We have power in ourselves to do it,
but it is a power that we have no power to do; for   5
if he show us his wounds and tell us his deeds, we
are to put our tongues into those wounds and speak
for them; so, if he tell us his noble deeds, we must
also tell him our noble acceptance of them. Ingratitude is monstrous; and for the multitude to be   10
ingrateful, were to make a monster of the multitude; of the which we being members, should bring
ourselves to be monstrous members.

First Citizen. And to make us no better thought of, a
little help will serve; for once we stood up° about   15
the corn, he himself stuck not to call us the many-
headed multitude.

Third Citizen. We have been called so of many; not
that our heads are some brown, some black, some
abram,° some bald, but that our wits are so di-   20
versely colored. And truly I think, if all our wits
were to issue out of one skull, they would fly east,
west, north, south, and their consent of° one direct
way should be at once to all the points o' th'
compass.   25

Second Citizen. Think you so? Which way do you
judge my wit would fly?

2.3.1 **Once if he** if he once   15 **once we stood up** when we took a
stand   20 **abram** auburn   23 **consent of** agreement on

Third Citizen. Nay, your wit will not so soon out as
another man's will; 'tis strongly wedged up in a
30   blockhead; but if it were at liberty, 'twould, sure,
southward.

Second Citizen. Why that way?

Third Citizen. To lose itself in a fog; where being
three parts melted away with rotten° dews, the
35   fourth would return for conscience sake, to help
to get thee a wife.°

Second Citizen. You are never without your tricks.
You may, you may.°

Third Citizen. Are you all resolved to give your
40   voices? But that's no matter, the greater part° carries it. I say, if he would incline to the people, there
was never a worthier man.

*Enter Coriolanus in a gown of humility,
with Menenius.*

Here he comes, and in the gown of humility. Mark
his behavior. We are not to stay all together, but to
45   come by him where he stands, by ones, by twos,
and by threes. He's to make his requests by particulars;° wherein every one of us has a single
honor, in giving him our own voices with our own
tongues. Therefore follow me, and I'll direct you
50   how you shall go by him.

All. Content, content.   [*Exeunt Citizens.*]

Menenius. O sir, you are not right. Have you not
known
The worthiest men have done't?

Coriolanus.   What must I say?—
"I pray, sir"—Plague upon't! I cannot bring
55   My tongue to such a pace. "Look, sir, my wounds!

34 **rotten** unhealthy 35–36 **for conscience ... wife** i.e., because of
the bastards he had fathered (?) 38 **You may, you may** cf. "O.K.,
O.K." 40 **greater part** majority 46–47 **by particulars** to each in
turn

I got them in my country's service, when
Some certain of your brethren roared and ran
From th' noise of our own drums."

Menenius.   O me, the gods!
You must not speak of that. You must desire them
To think upon° you.

Coriolanus.   Think upon me! Hang 'em!   60
I would they would forget me, like the virtues
Which our divines lose by 'em.°

Menenius.   You'll mar all.
I'll leave you. Pray you, speak to 'em, I pray you,
In wholesome° manner.   *Exit.*

Enter three of the Citizens.

Coriolanus.   Bid them wash their faces,
And keep their teeth clean. So, here comes a
     brace.°   65
You know the cause, sir, of my standing here.

Third Citizen. We do, sir; tell us what hath brought
you to't.

Coriolanus. Mine own desert.

Second Citizen. Your own desert?   70

Coriolanus. Ay, not mine own desire.

Third Citizen. How not your own desire?

Coriolanus. No, sir, 'twas never my desire yet to
trouble the poor with begging.

Third Citizen. You must think, if we give you any-   75
thing, we hope to gain by you.

Coriolanus. Well then, I pray, your price o' th' consulship?

First Citizen. The price is, to ask it kindly.

60 **think upon** think well of 62 **lose by 'em** waste on them in
preaching ("pearls before swine") 64 **wholesome** reasonable 65
brace pair (of dogs)

80   *Coriolanus.* Kindly sir, I pray let me ha't. I have
        wounds to show you, which shall be yours in pri-
        vate. Your good voice, sir; what say you?

      Second Citizen. You shall ha't, worthy sir.

      Coriolanus. A match,° sir. There's in all two worthy
85   voices begged. I have your alms. Adieu.

      Third Citizen. But this is something° odd.

      Second Citizen. And 'twere to give again—but 'tis no
        matter.   *Exeunt.*

                Enter two other Citizens.

      Coriolanus. Pray you now, if it may stand° with the
90   tune of your voices that I may be consul, I have
        here the customary gown.

      First Citizen. You have deserved nobly of your coun-
        try, and you have not deserved nobly.

      Coriolanus. Your enigma?

95   *First Citizen.* You have been a scourge to her enemies,
        you have been a rod to her friends. You have not
        indeed loved the common people.

      Coriolanus. You should account me the more virtuous,
        that I have not been common in my love. I will, sir,
100   flatter my sworn brother, the people, to earn a
        dearer estimation of° them; 'tis a condition° they
        account gentle; and since the wisdom of their choice
        is rather to have my hat than my heart, I will prac-
        tice the insinuating nod, and be off° to them most
105   counterfeitly; that is, sir, I will counterfeit the be-
        witchment of some popular man,° and give it boun-
        tiful to the desirers. Therefore, beseech you I may
        be consul.

---

84 **A match** agreed 86 **something** somewhat 89 **stand** agree
101 **dearer estimation of** higher valuation from 101 **condition**
quality 104 **be off** take my hat off 106 **popular man** ("friend of
the people")

Second Citizen. We hope to find you our friend; and
therefore give you our voices heartily.   *110*

First Citizen. You have received many wounds for
your country.

Coriolanus. I will not seal° your knowledge with
showing them. I will make much of your voices
and so trouble you no farther.   *115*

Both. The gods give you joy, sir, heartily!   [*Exeunt.*]

Coriolanus. Most sweet voices!
  Better it is to die, better to starve,
  Than crave the hire which first we do deserve.
  Why in this woolvish toge° should I stand here,   *120*
  To beg of Hob° and Dick that does appear°
  Their needless vouches?° Custom calls me to't.
  What custom wills, in all things should we do't,
  The dust on antique time would lie unswept,
  And mountainous error be too highly heaped   *125*
  For truth to o'erpeer.° Rather than fool it so,
  Let the high office and the honor go
  To one that would do thus. I am half through:
  The one part suffered, the other will I do.

          Enter three Citizens more.

  Here come moe° voices.   *130*
  Your voices! For your voices I have fought;
  Watched° for your voices; for your voices bear
  Of wounds two dozen odd; battles thrice six
  I have seen, and heard of; for your voices have
  Done many things, some less, some more. Your
    voices!   *135*
  Indeed, I would be consul.

---

113 **seal** make authentic (legal sense)   120 **in this woolvish toge** i.e.,
disguising myself (a backhand reference to "wolf in sheep's clothing";
note that Coriolanus "lives like a lamb," according to 2.1.12)   121 **Hob**
(nickname of "Robert," a country fellow)   121 **that does appear** i.e., as
they come, one by one   122 **vouches** confirmations   126 **o'erpeer**
rise above   130 **moe** more   132 **Watched** kept watch

First Citizen. He has done nobly, and cannot go without any honest man's voice.

Second Citizen. Therefore let him be consul. The gods
140 give him joy, and make him good friend to the
people!

All. Amen, amen. God save thee, noble consul!
                                   [*Exeunt Citizens.*]

Coriolanus. Worthy voices!

        Enter Menenius, with Brutus and Sicinius.

Menenius. You have stood your limitation;° and the
tribunes
145 Endue you with the people's voice. Remains
That in th' official marks° invested you
Anon do meet the Senate.

Coriolanus.   Is this done?

Sicinius. The custom of request you have discharged:
The people do admit you, and are summoned
150 To meet anon upon your approbation.°

Coriolanus. Where? At the Senate House?

Sicinius.   There, Coriolanus.

Coriolanus. May I change these garments?

Sicinius.   You may, sir.

Coriolanus. That I'll straight do, and, knowing myself again,
Repair° to th' Senate House.

155 *Menenius.* I'll keep you company. Will you along?°

Brutus. We stay here for the people.

Sicinius.   Fare you well.
                      Exeunt Coriolanus and Menenius.

144 **limitation** time set for requesting votes 146 **marks** insignia 150
anon upon your approbation at once to confirm your appointment (as
consul) 154 **Repair** return 155 **along** come too

He has it° now; and, by his looks, methinks
'Tis warm at's° heart.

Brutus.　　　　　　　With a proud heart he wore
His humble weeds. Will you dismiss the people?

Enter the Plebeians.

Sicinius. How now, my masters,° have you chose this
man?　　　　　　　　　　　　　　　　　　160

First Citizen. He has our voices, sir.

Brutus. We pray the gods he may deserve your loves.

Second Citizen. Amen, sir. To my poor unworthy
notice,
He mocked us when he begged our voices.

Third Citizen.　　　　　　　　　Certainly;
He flouted us downright.　　　　　　　　165

First Citizen. No, 'tis his kind of speech—he did not
mock us.

Second Citizen. Not one amongst us, save yourself,
but says
He used us scornfully. He should have showed us
His marks of merit, wounds received for's country.

Sicinius. Why, so he did, I am sure.　　　　　170

All. No, no; no man saw 'em.

Third Citizen. He said he had wounds which he could
show in private;
And with his hat, thus waving it in scorn,
"I would be consul," says he. "Aged custom,
But by your voices, will not so permit me;　　　175
Your voices therefore." When we granted that,
Here was "I thank you for your voices. Thank you,
Your most sweet voices. Now you have left your
voices,

157 **it** (the emotion that "warms his heart," either the satisfaction of success, or the irritation of offended pride; cf. "his fire," 2.1.263)　158 **at's**
at his　160 **my masters** gentlemen

I have no further° with you." Was not this mock-
     ery?

180 *Sicinius.* Why either were you ignorant° to see't,
     Or, seeing it, of such childish friendliness
     To yield° your voices?

Brutus.   Could you not have told him
     As you were lessoned:° when he had no power,
     But was a petty servant to the state,
185 He was your enemy, ever spake against
     Your liberties and the charters° that you bear
     I' th' body of the weal;° and now, arriving
     A place° of potency and sway o' th' state,°
     If he should still malignantly remain
190 Fast foe to th' plebeii,° your voices might
     Be curses to yourselves? You should have said
     That as his worthy deeds did claim no less
     Than what he stood for,° so his gracious nature
     Would think upon you° for your voices, and
195 Translate° his malice towards you into love,
     Standing your friendly lord.

Sicinius.   Thus to have said,
     As you were fore-advised, had touched° his spirit
     And tried his inclination; from him plucked
     Either his gracious promise, which you might,
200 As cause had called you up,° have held him to;
     Or else it would have galled his surly nature,
     Which easily endures not article°
     Tying him to aught. So, putting him to rage,
     You should have ta'en th' advantage of his choler,°
     And passed him unelected.

205 *Brutus.*   Did you perceive
     He did solicit you in free° contempt

179 **no further** no more to do   180 **ignorant** too dull   182 **yield**
give   183 **lessoned** instructed   186 **charters** privileges   187 **weal**
commonwealth   188 **A place** (direct object of "arriving," i.e., "reach-
ing")   188 **potency and sway o' th' state** power in managing the
state   190 **plebeii** (Latin for "plebeians")   193 **what he stood for** the
office he ran for   194 **think upon you** think well of you   195 **Translate** transform   197 **touched** tested   200 **As cause had called you up**
as an occasion (emergency) would have roused you   202 **article** condition   204 **choler** anger   206 **free** open

When he did need your loves; and do you think
That his contempt shall not be bruising to you
When he hath power to crush? Why, had your
    bodies
No heart° among you? Or had you tongues to cry°   *210*
Against the rectorship° of judgment?

Sicinius.   Have you
Ere now denied the asker, and now again,
Of° him that did not ask but mock, bestow
Your sued-for tongues?

Third Citizen. He's not confirmed; we may deny him
    yet.   *215*

Second Citizen. And will deny him.
I'll have five hundred voices of that sound.

First Citizen. I twice five hundred, and their friends
    to piece 'em.°

Brutus. Get you hence instantly, and tell those friends
They have chose a consul that will from them take   *220*
Their liberties, make them of no more voice
Than dogs that are as often beat for barking
As therefor° kept to do so.

Sicinius.   Let them assemble;
And, on a safer° judgment, all revoke
Your ignorant election.° Enforce° his pride   *225*
And his old hate unto you; besides, forget not
With what contempt he wore the humble weed,
How in his suit he scorned you; but your loves,
Thinking upon his services, took from you
Th' apprehension° of his present portance,°   *230*
Which most gibingly, ungravely, he did fashion
After the inveterate hate he bears you.

Brutus.   Lay

---

210 **heart** spirit 210 **cry** give your voices 211 **rectorship** rule
213 **Of** on 218 **piece 'em** add to them (cf. "piece out") 223
therefor for that reason 224 **safer** sounder 225 **ignorant election**
choice made in ignorance 225 **Enforce** urge, insist on 230 **apprehension** perception 230 **portance** bearing

A fault on us, your tribunes, that we labored,
No impediment between,° but that you must
Cast your election on him.

235 *Sicinius.*   Say you chose him
More after° our commandment than as guided
By your own true affections;° and that your minds,
Preoccupied with what you rather must do
Than what you should, made you against the grain
240 To voice him consul.° Lay the fault on us.

Brutus. Ay, spare us not. Say we read lectures to you,
How youngly he began to serve his country,
How long continued; and what stock he springs of,
The noble house o' th' Marcians, from whence came
245 That Ancus Marcius, Numa's° daughter's son,
Who after great Hostilius here was king;
Of the same house Publius and Quintus were,
That our best water brought by conduits hither;
[And Censorinus that was so surnamed]°
250 And nobly namèd so, twice being censor,
Was his great ancestor.

Sicinius.   One thus descended,
That hath beside well in his person wrought
To be set high in place, we did commend
To your remembrances: but you have found,
255 Scaling° his present bearing with his past,
That he's your fixèd enemy, and revoke
Your sudden° approbation.

Brutus.   Say you ne'er had done't
(Harp on that still) but by our putting on;°
And presently, when you have drawn your number,°
Repair to th' Capitol.

234 **No impediment between** putting no obstacle in your way (i.e.,
we have made the way free for you to choose him) 236 **after** following 237 **affections** desires 240 **voice him consul** make him
consul by your votes 245 **Numa** (second king of Rome) 249 **And
... surnamed** (see Textual Note, p. 151) 255 **Scaling** weighing 257
sudden hasty 258 **putting on** urging 259 **drawn your number**
gathered your crowd (of supporters)

Citizens.   We will so. Almost all   260
Repent in their election.   *Exeunt Plebeians.*

Brutus.   Let them go on;
This mutiny were better put in hazard°
Than stay, past doubt, for greater.
If, as his nature is, he fall in rage
With their refusal, both observe and answer   265
The vantage of his anger.°

Sicinius.   To th' Capitol, come.
We will be there before the stream o' th' people;
And this shall seem, as partly 'tis, their own,
Which we have goaded onward.   *Exeunt.*

---

262 This ... hazard i.e., it would be better to run the risk of this minor
disorder   **265–66 answer/The vantage of his anger** take advantage of
the opportunity his anger affords

ACT 3

[Scene 1. *Rome. A street.*]

*Cornets. Enter Coriolanus, Menenius, all the Gentry,
Cominius, Titus Lartius, and other Senators.*

Coriolanus. Tullus Aufidius then had made new
head?°

Lartius. He had, my lord; and that it was which caused
Our swifter composition.°

Coriolanus. So then the Volsces stand but as at first;
5   Ready, when time shall prompt them, to make road
Upon's° again.

Cominius.   They are worn,° Lord Consul, so
That we shall hardly in our ages° see
Their banners wave again.

Coriolanus.   Saw you Aufidius?

Lartius. On safeguard° he came to me; and did curse
10   Against the Volsces, for they had so vilely
Yielded the town. He is retired to Antium.

Coriolanus. Spoke he of me?

Lartius.   He did, my lord.

3.1.1 **made new head** raised a new force   3 **swifter composition**
coming to terms sooner   5–6 **make road/Upon's** invade us   6 **worn**
worn out   7 **ages** lifetime   9 **On safeguard** under safe-conduct

Coriolanus.   How? What?

Lartius. How often he had met you, sword to sword;
That of all things upon the earth he hated
Your person most; that he would pawn his fortunes   *15*
To hopeless restitution,° so he might
Be called your vanquisher.

Coriolanus.   At Antium lives he?

Lartius. At Antium.

Coriolanus. I wish I had a cause to seek him there,
To oppose his hatred fully. Welcome home.   *20*

        Enter Sicinius and Brutus.

Behold, these are the tribunes of the people,
The tongues o' th' common mouth. I do despise
   them;
For they do prank them° in authority,
Against all noble sufferance.°

Sicinius.   Pass no further.

Coriolanus. Ha? What is that?   *25*

Brutus. It will be dangerous to go on—no further.

Coriolanus. What makes this change?

Menenius. The matter?

Cominius. Hath he not passed the noble and the
   common?°

Brutus. Cominius, no.

Coriolanus.   Have I had children's voices?   *30*

First Senator. Tribunes, give way; he shall to th'
   marketplace.

Brutus. The people are incensed against him.

16 **To hopeless restitution** without hope of their being redeemed   23
prank them dress themselves up   24 **Against all noble sufferance** so
that no noble can endure it   29 **the noble and the common** the patricians and the plebeians

Sicinius.   Stop,
   Or all will fall in broil.°

Coriolanus.   Are these your herd?
   Must these have voices, that can yield them now,°
   And straight disclaim° their tongues? What are
35   your offices?
   You being their mouths, why rule you not their
    teeth?
   Have you not set them on?

Menenius.   Be calm, be calm.

Coriolanus. It is a purposed thing,° and grows by plot,
   To curb the will of the nobility.
40   Suffer't, and live with such as cannot rule,
   Nor ever will be ruled.

Brutus.   Call't not a plot.
   The people cry you mocked them; and of late,
   When corn was given them gratis, you repined,°
   Scandaled° the suppliants for the people, called
    them
45   Time-pleasers, flatterers, foes to nobleness.

Coriolanus. Why, this was known before.

Brutus.   Not to them all.

Coriolanus. Have you informed° them sithence?°

Brutus.   How! I inform them!

Coriolanus. You are like to do such business.

Brutus.   Not unlike
   Each way to better yours.°

Coriolanus. Why then should I be consul? By yond
50   clouds,

---

33 **in broil** into a riot 34 **now** at one time 35 **disclaim** disown 38 **purposed thing** premeditated affair 43 **repined** regretted it 44 **Scandaled** slandered 47 **informed** instructed 47 **sithence** since 48–49 **Not unlike/Each way to better yours** likely in every way to do your business better

Let me deserve so ill as you, and make me
Your fellow tribune.

Sicinius.   You show too much of that
For which the people stir.° If you will pass
To where you are bound, you must inquire your
    way,
Which you are out of,° with a gentler spirit,   55
Or never be so noble as a consul,
Nor yoke with him for° tribune.

Menenius.   Let's be calm.

Cominius. The people are abused;° set on.° This
    palt'ring°
Becomes not Rome; nor has Coriolanus
Deserved this so dishonored rub,° laid falsely°   60
I' th' plain way of his merit.

Coriolanus.   Tell me of corn!
This was my speech, and I will speak't again—

Menenius. Not now, not now.

First Senator.   Not in this heat, sir, now.

Coriolanus. Now, as I live, I will.
My nobler friends, I crave their pardons.   65
For the mutable, rank-scented meiny,° let them
Regard me as I do not flatter, and
Therein behold themselves. I say again,
In soothing them, we nourish 'gainst our Senate
The cockle° of rebellion, insolence, sedition,   70
Which we ourselves have ploughed for, sowed,
    and scattered,
By mingling them with us, the honored number;
Who lack not virtue, no, nor power, but that
Which they have given to beggars.

Menenius.   Well, no more.

---

53 **stir** are rebelling   55 **are out of** are straying from   57 **for** as   58
abused deceived   58 **set on** incited   58 **palt'ring** cheating   60 **rub**
hindrance (in bowling on the green, any roughness of ground)   60
falsely treacherously   66 **meiny** crowd   70 **cockle** weed

First Senator. No more words, we beseech you.

75 *Coriolanus.*   How! No more!
　　As for my country I have shed my blood,
　　Not fearing outward force, so shall my lungs
　　Coin words till their decay° against those measles,°
　　Which we disdain should tetter° us, yet sought
　　The very way to catch them.

80 *Brutus.*   You speak o' th' people,
　　As if you were a god, to punish, not
　　A man of their infirmity.°

Sicinius.   'Twere well
　　We let the people know't.

Menenius.   What, what? His choler?

Coriolanus. Choler?
85 　　Were I as patient as the midnight sleep,
　　By Jove, 'twould be my mind!

Sicinius.   It is a mind
　　That shall remain a poison where it is,
　　Not poison any further.

Coriolanus.   Shall remain!
　　Hear you this Triton° of the minnows? Mark you
　　His absolute "shall"?

Cominius.   'Twas from the canon.°

90 *Coriolanus.*   "Shall"!
　　O good but most unwise patricians! Why,
　　You grave but reckless senators, have you thus
　　Given Hydra here° to choose an officer,
　　That with his peremptory "shall," being but
95 　　The horn and noise o' th' monster's, wants not spirit
　　To say he'll turn your current in° a ditch,

---

78 **decay** death   78 **measles** (the disease; and "foul wretches," from
mesel, "leper")   79 **tetter** infect with leprous eruption   82 **of their
infirmity** having the same weaknesses as they   89 **Triton** sea-god,
trumpeter of Neptune (cf. "horn," line 95)   90 **from the canon** against
the law   93 **Given Hydra here** permitted this many-headed beast   96
in (aside) into

     And make your channel his? If he have power,
     Then vail your ignorance;° if none, awake
     Your dangerous lenity. If you are learned,°
     Be not as common fools; if you are not,   100
     Let them have cushions° by you. You are plebeians,
     If they be senators; and they are no less,°
     When, both your voices blended, the great'st taste
     Most palates theirs.° They choose their magistrate;
     And such a one as he, who puts his "shall,"   105
     His popular "shall," against a graver bench°
     Than ever frowned in Greece. By Jove himself,
     It makes the consuls base; and my soul aches
     To know, when two authorities are up,°
     Neither supreme, how soon confusion°   110
     May enter 'twixt the gap of both and take
     The one by th' other.°

Cominius.   Well, on to th' marketplace.

Coriolanus. Whoever gave that counsel to give forth
     The corn o' th' storehouse gratis, as 'twas used
     Sometime in Greece—

Menenius.   Well, well, no more of that.   115

Coriolanus. Though there the people had more abso-
          lute pow'r,
     I say they nourished disobedience, fed
     The ruin of the state.

Brutus.   Why shall the people give
     One that speaks thus their voice?

Coriolanus.   I'll give my reasons,
     More worthier than their voices. They know the
          corn   120

98 **vail your ignorance** let your ignorance (that gave the power) bow (to
him) 99 **learned** wise 101 **cushions** (symbol of senatorial rank; cf.
2.2 s.d.) 102 **no less** i.e., no less than senators 103–4 **the great'st
taste/Most palates theirs** the dominant flavor tastes most of them (they
have the most votes) 106 **bench** court 109 **up** active 110 **confusion** violent disorder (in a revolution) 111–12 **take/The one by th'
other** seize and overthrow one by means of the other

Was not our recompense,° resting well assured
They ne'er did service for't. Being pressed to° th'
   war,
Even when the navel° of the state was touched,
They would not thread° the gates; this kind of
   service

125 Did not deserve corn gratis. Being i' th' war,
Their mutinies and revolts, wherein they showed
Most valor, spoke not for them. Th' accusation
Which they have often made against the Senate,
All cause unborn,° could never be the native°

130 Of our so frank° donation. Well, what then?
How shall this bosom multiplied° digest°
The Senate's courtesy? Let deeds express
What's like to be their words: "We did request it;
We are the greater poll,° and in true fear

135 They gave us our demands." Thus we debase
The nature of our seats, and make the rabble
Call our cares° fears; which will in time
Break ope the locks o' th' Senate and bring in
The crows to peck the eagles.

Menenius.   Come, enough.

Brutus. Enough, with over measure.

140 *Coriolanus.*   No, take more.
What may be sworn by, both divine and human,
Seal what I end withal!° This double worship,
Where one part does disdain with cause, the other
Insult without° all reason; where gentry,° title,
   wisdom,

145 Cannot conclude° but by the yea and no

---

121 **recompense** reward for past services 122 **pressed to** conscripted
for 123 **navel** center (cf. Menenius' fable, 1.1) 124 **thread** pass
through 129 **All cause unborn** with no cause in existence 129
native original, parent (i.e., their accusation not the origin of our gift)
130 **frank** unsolicited 131 **bosom multiplied** many-bosomed beast
("Hydra," line 93) 131 **digest** (1) digest (2) understand ("bosom" can
mean both "cavity of the stomach" and "heart," i.e., "mind") 134 **poll**
number 137 **cares** (concern for the state) 142 **withal** with 144
without beyond 144 **gentry** gentle birth 145 **conclude** decide

Of general ignorance—it must omit°
Real necessities, and give way the while
To unstable slightness.° Purpose so barred,° it follows
Nothing is done to purpose. Therefore, beseech you—
You that will be less fearful than discreet;°   *150*
That love the fundamental part of state°
More than you doubt° the change on't; that prefer
A noble life before a long, and wish
To jump° a body with a dangerous physic°
That's sure of death without it—at once pluck out   *155*
The multitudinous tongue;° let them not lick
The sweet which is their poison. Your dishonor
Mangles true judgment, and bereaves the state
Of that integrity° which should become't;
Not having the power to do the good it would,   *160*
For th' ill which doth control't.°

Brutus.   'Has said enough.

Sicinius. Has spoken like a traitor and shall answer°
As traitors do.

Coriolanus.   Thou wretch, despite o'erwhelm thee!
What should the people do with these bald° tribunes,
On whom depending, their obedience fails   *165*
To th' greater bench?° In a rebellion,
When what's not meet, but what must be, was law,
Then were they chosen; in a better hour

146 **omit** overlook   148 **unstable slightness** unsteady trifling   148 **Purpose so barred** when the intention (of charting a policy in advance) is so thwarted   150 **less fearful than discreet** i.e., more prudent than fearful (on lines 150–161, see Introduction, p. lxxvii)   151 **fundamental part of state** basic constitution of the government   152 **doubt** fear   154 **jump** risk harming   154 **physic** medicine, treatment   156 **multitudinous tongue** (the voice of the "Hydra," the tribuneship)   159 **integrity** wholeness   161 **control't** overpower it   162 **answer** i.e., in court, be brought to trial; cf. lines 176, 323   164 **bald** trivial (pun)   166 **th' greater bench** i.e., the senate

Let what is meet be said it must be meet,°
170   And throw their power i' th' dust.

Brutus. Manifest treason!

Sicinius.   This a consul? No.

Brutus. The aediles,° ho!

                    Enter an Aedile.

                    Let him be apprehended.

Sicinius. Go, call the people, [*exit Aedile*] in whose
    name myself
Attach° thee as a traitorous innovator,
175   A foe to th' public weal. Obey, I charge thee,
And follow to thine answer.°

Coriolanus.   Hence, old goat!°

All [*Patricians*]. We'll surety° him.

Cominius.   Aged sir, hands off.

Coriolanus. Hence, rotten thing, or I shall shake thy
    bones
Out of thy garments.

Sicinius.   Help, ye citizens!

    ✳ *Enter a rabble of Plebeians, with the Aediles.*

180 *Menenius.* On both sides more respect.

Sicinius. Here's he that would take from you all your
    power.

Brutus. Seize him, aediles!

All [*Citizens*]. Down with him, down with him!

Second Senator. Weapons, weapons, weapons!
                    They all bustle about Coriolanus.

---

169 **it must be meet** that it *must* be fitting   172 **aediles** officers
attached to the tribunes   174 **Attach** arrest   176 **answer** (legal term
for "meeting a charge")   176 **goat** (the tribunes are evidently bearded;
cf. 2.1.89)   177 **surety** stand surety for

[*All.*] Tribunes!—Patricians!—Citizens!—What,
   ho!—   185
   Sicinius!—Brutus!—Coriolanus!—Citizens!—
   Peace, peace, peace!—Stay! Hold! Peace!

Menenius. What is about to be? I am out of breath.
   Confusion's° near. I cannot speak. You, tribunes
   To th' people! Coriolanus, patience!   190
   Speak, good Sicinius.

Sicinius.   Hear me, people; peace!

All [*Citizens*]. Let's hear our tribune. Peace!—Speak,
   speak, speak.

Sicinius. You are at point to lose° your liberties:
   Marcius would have all from you; Marcius,
   Whom late you have named for consul.

Menenius.   Fie, fie, fie! 195
   This is the way to kindle, not to quench.

First Senator. To unbuild the city, and to lay all flat.

Sicinius. What is the city but the people?

All [*Citizens*].   True,
   The people are the city.

Brutus. By the consent of all, we were established   200
   The people's magistrates.

All [*Citizens*].   You so remain.

Menenius. And so are like to do.

Cominius. That is the way to lay the city flat,
   To bring the roof to the foundation,
   And bury all which yet distinctly ranges,°   205
   In heaps and piles of ruin.

Sicinius.   This deserves death.

---

189 **Confusion** ruin (resulting from civil disorder, cf. line 110)   193 **at
point to lose** on point of losing   205 **distinctly ranges** extends in separate orderly rows (of buildings)

Brutus. Or° let us stand to° our authority,
Or let us lose it. We do here pronounce,
Upon the part o' th' people, in° whose power
210 We were elected theirs,° Marcius is worthy
Of present death.

Sicinius.   Therefore lay hold of him;
Bear him to th' rock Tarpeian,° and from thence
Into destruction cast him.

Brutus.   Aediles, seize him!

All [Citizens]. Yield, Marcius, yield!

Menenius.   Hear me one word;
215 Beseech you, tribunes, hear me but a word.

Aediles. Peace, peace!

Menenius. [*To Brutus*] Be that you seem, truly your
     country's friend,
And temp'rately proceed to what you would
Thus violently redress.

Brutus.   Sir, those cold ways,
220 That seem like prudent helps, are very poisonous
Where the disease is violent. Lay hands upon him,
And bear him to the rock.
                    Coriolanus draws his sword.

Coriolanus.   No, I'll die here.
There's some among you have beheld me fighting;
Come, try upon yourselves what you have seen me.

Menenius. Down with that sword! Tribunes, withdraw
225 awhile.

Brutus. Lay hands upon him.

Menenius.   Help Marcius, help,
You that be noble; help him, young and old!

207 **Or** either   207 **stand to** stand by   209 **in** by   210 **theirs** i.e.,
their representatives   212 **rock Tarpeian** (from which criminals were
thrown)

All [Citizens]. Down with him, down with him!
    In this mutiny,° *the Tribunes, the Aediles, and*
            the people are beat in.

Menenius. Go, get you to your house; begone, away!
 All will be naught° else.

Second Senator.   Get you gone.

Coriolanus.   Stand fast; *230*
 We have as many friends as enemies.

Menenius. Shall it be put to that?°

First Senator.   The gods forbid!
 I prithee, noble friend, home to thy house;
 Leave us to cure this cause.°

Menenius.   For 'tis a sore upon us
 You cannot tent° yourself. Begone, beseech you. *235*

Cominius. Come, sir, along with us.

Coriolanus. I would they were barbarians, as they are,
 Though in Rome littered; not Romans, as they are
  not,
 Though calved i' th' porch o' th' Capitol.°

Menenius.   Begone.
 Put not your worthy° rage into your tongue: *240*
 One time will owe another.°

Coriolanus.   On fair ground
 I could beat forty of them.

Menenius.   I could myself
 Take up a brace° o' th' best of them; yea, the two
  tribunes.

---

228 s.d. **mutiny** riot 229 **naught** ruined 232 **put to that** driven to
that extremity 234 **cause** dispute 235 **tent** treat (cf. 1.9.31) 239
porch o' th' Capitol (portico of the temple of Jupiter on the Capitoline
Hill) 240 **worthy** justifiable (?) noble (?) 241 **One time will owe
another** one time (the present, when the people are in revolt) will be
compensated by another (when the people are checked) 243 **Take up a
brace** take on a couple ("brace" often of dogs)

Cominius. But now 'tis odds beyond arithmetic;°
245   And manhood is called foolery when it stands
Against a falling fabric.° Will you hence
Before the tag° return? Whose rage doth rend
Like interrupted waters, and o'erbear°
What they are used to bear.

Menenius.   Pray you, begone.
250   I'll try whether my old wit be in request
With those that have but little. This must be patched
With cloth of any color.

Cominius.   Nay, come away.
              Exeunt Coriolanus and Cominius.

Patrician. This man has marred his fortune.

Menenius. His nature is too noble for the world:
255   He would not flatter Neptune for his trident,
Or Jove for's power to thunder. His heart's his mouth:
What his breast forges, that his tongue must vent;
And, being angry, does forget that ever
He heard the name of death.   *A noise within.*
Here's goodly work!

260 *Patrician.*   I would they were abed!

Menenius. I would they were in Tiber! What the vengeance!°
Could he not speak 'em fair?°

Enter Brutus and Sicinius, with the rabble again.

Sicinius.   Where is this viper
That would depopulate the city and
Be every man himself?

Menenius.   You worthy tribunes—

244 **beyond arithmetic** beyond number 246 **fabric** building 247 **tag** riffraff ("tag and rag") 248 **o'erbear** overcome 261 **What the vengeance** (an emphatic "What!"; cf. "What the devil!") 262 **speak 'em fair** talk civilly to them (and so flatter)

Sicinius. He shall be thrown down the Tarpeian rock   265
  With rigorous hands. He hath resisted law,
  And therefore law shall scorn him further trial
  Than the severity of the public power,°
  Which he so sets at nought.

First Citizen.   He shall well know
  The noble tribunes are the people's mouths,   270
  And we their hands.

All [*Citizens*]. He shall, sure on't.

Menenius.   Sir, sir—

Sicinius. Peace!

Menenius. Do not cry havoc,° where you should but
    hunt
  With modest warrant.°

Sicinius.   Sir, how comes't that you
  Have holp° to make this rescue?

Menenius.   Hear me speak: 275
  As I do know the consul's worthiness,
  So can I name his faults.

Sicinius.   Consul! What consul?

Menenius. The consul Coriolanus.

Brutus.   He consul!

All [*Citizens*]. No, no, no, no, no.

Menenius. If, by the tribunes' leave, and yours, good
    people,   280
  I may be heard, I would crave a word or two;
  The which shall turn you to no further harm
  Than so much loss of time.

Sicinius.   Speak briefly then;
  For we are peremptory° to dispatch

268 **the public power** i.e., the power derived from the people   273 **cry
havoc** call for general slaughter ("total war")   274 **With modest warrant** with moderate justification   275 **holp** helped   284 **peremptory**
resolved

285   This viperous traitor. To eject him hence
            Were but our danger,° and to keep him here
            Our certain death. Therefore it is decreed
            He dies tonight.

Menenius.   Now the good gods forbid
            That our renownèd Rome, whose gratitude
290   Towards her deservèd° children is enrolled
            In Jove's own book, like an unnatural dam
            Should now eat up her own!

Sicinius. He's a disease that must be cut away.

Menenius. O, he's a limb that has but a disease;
295   Mortal,° to cut it off; to cure it, easy.
            What has he done to Rome that's worthy death?
            Killing our enemies, the blood he hath lost—
            Which I dare vouch is more than that he hath
            By many an ounce—he dropped it for his country;
300   And what is left, to lose it by his country
            Were to us all that do't and suffer it
            A brand° to th' end o' th' world.

Sicinius.   This is clean kam.°

Brutus. Merely° awry. When he did love his country,
            It honored him.

Menenius.   The service of the foot
305   Being once gangrened, is not then respected
            For what before it was.

Brutus.   We'll hear no more.
            Pursue him to his house and pluck° him thence,
            Lest his infection, being of catching nature,
            Spread further.

Menenius.   One word more, one word!
310   This tiger-footed rage, when it shall find
            The harm of unscanned° swiftness, will, too late,

286 **but our danger** only the risk we now run   290 **deservèd**
deserving   295 **Mortal** deadly   302 **brand** mark of disgrace   302
clean kam completely wrong (literally *kam* = crooked)   303 **Merely**
absolutely   307 **pluck** take   311 **unscanned** thoughtless

Tie leaden pounds° to's° heels. Proceed by process;°
Lest parties (as he is beloved) break out,
And sack great Rome with Romans.

Brutus.   If it were so—

Sicinius. What° do ye talk?   *315*
 Have we not had a taste of his obedience?
 Our aediles smote? Ourselves resisted? Come!

Menenius. Consider this: he has been bred i' th' wars
 Since 'a could draw a sword, and is ill schooled
 In bolted° language; meal and bran together   *320*
 He throws without distinction. Give me leave,
 I'll go to him, and undertake to bring him
 Where he shall answer, by a lawful form,°
 In peace, to his utmost peril.°

First Senator.   Noble tribunes,
 It is the humane way. The other course   *325*
 Will prove too bloody, and the end of it
 Unknown to the beginning.

Sicinius.   Noble Menenius,
 Be you then as the people's officer.
 Masters, lay down your weapons.

Brutus.   Go not home.

Sicinius. Meet on the marketplace. We'll attend you
       there,   *330*
 Where, if you bring not Marcius, we'll proceed
 In our first way.

Menenius.   I'll bring him to you.
 [*To the Senators*] Let me desire your company. He
       must come,
 Or what is worst will follow.

Senators.   Pray you, let's to him.
                                    Exeunt omnes.°

312 **pounds** pound-weights   312 **to's** to his   312 **process** due process of
law   315 **What** why   320 **bolted** refined (literally, sifted)   323 **answer,
by a lawful form** meet the charges according to the forms of law   324 **to his
utmost peril** at the risk of the severest penalty   334 s.d. **omnes** all (Latin)

[Scene 2. *Rome. The house of Coriolanus.*]

Enter Coriolanus with Nobles.

Coriolanus. Let them pull all about mine ears; present
        me
        Death on the wheel° or at wild horses' heels;
        Or pile ten hills on the Tarpeian rock,
        That the precipitation° might down stretch
5   Below the beam of sight;° yet will I still
        Be thus to them.

A Noble.   You do the nobler.

Coriolanus. I muse° my mother
        Does not approve me further, who was wont
        To call them woolen vassals,° things created
10   To buy and sell with groats;° to show bare heads
        In congregations, to yawn, be still and wonder,
        When one but of my ordinance° stood up
        To speak of peace or war.

                        Enter Volumnia.

                                I talk of you:
        Why did you wish me milder—Would you have me
15   False to my nature? Rather say I play
        The man I am.

Volumnia.   O, sir, sir, sir,
        I would have had you put your power well on,
        Before you had worn it out.

3.2.2 **the wheel** (by being bound to a wheel and beaten to death; an Elizabethan, not Roman, penalty) 4 **precipitation** steepness 5 **Below
the beam of sight** i.e., beyond the range of sight (*beam* = a ray passing
from the object to the eye) 7 **muse** wonder 9 **woolen vassals** i.e.,
rough-dressed members of the lowest class 10 **groats** four-penny coins
12 **ordinance** rank

Coriolanus.   Let go.°

Volumnia. You might have been enough the man you
     are,
     With striving less to be so. Lesser had been   20
     The thwartings of your dispositions,° if
     You had not showed them how ye were disposed
     Ere they lacked power to cross you.

Coriolanus.   Let them hang.

Volumnia. Ay, and burn too.

          Enter Menenius with the Senators.

Menenius. Come, come, you have been too rough,
     something° too rough;   25
     You must return and mend it.

Senator.   There's no remedy,
     Unless, by not so doing, our good city
     Cleave in the midst° and perish.

Volumnia.   Pray be counseled;
     I have a heart as little apt° as yours,
     But yet a brain that leads my use of anger   30
     To better vantage.

Menenius.   Well said, noble woman!
     Before he should thus stoop to th' herd, but that
     The violent fit o' th' time craves it as physic°
     For the whole state, I would put mine armor on,
     Which I can scarcely bear.

Coriolanus.   What must I do?   35

Menenius. Return to th' tribunes.

Coriolanus.   Well, what then? What then?

Menenius. Repent what you have spoke.

18 **Let go** enough of that   21 **dispositions** inclinations   25 **something** somewhat   26–28 **There's . . . midst** there's no help for it; (you
must compromise;) else, because of your failure to do so, our good city
may be split in two   29 **apt** compliant   33 **physic** medical treatment

Coriolanus. For them! I cannot do it to the gods;
    Must I then do't to them?

Volumnia.   You are too absolute;
40   Though therein you can never be too noble
    But when extremities speak.° I have heard you say,
    Honor and policy, like unsevered° friends,
    I' th' war do grow together. Grant that, and tell me
    In peace what each of them by th' other lose
    That they combine not there.

Coriolanus.   Tush, tush!

45 *Menenius.*   A good demand.

Volumnia. If it be honor in your wars to seem
    The same you are not, which for your best ends
    You adopt° your policy, how is it less or worse
    That it° shall hold companionship in peace
50   With honor as in war; since that to both
    It stands in like request?°

Coriolanus.   Why force° you this?

Volumnia. Because that now it lies you on° to speak
    To th' people, not by your own instruction,
    Nor by th' matter which your heart prompts you,
55   But with such words that are but roted° in
    Your tongue, though but bastards and syllables
    Of no allowance to your bosom's truth.°
    Now, this no more dishonors you at all
    Than to take in° a town with gentle words,
60   Which else would put you to your fortune° and
    The hazard of much blood.
    I would dissemble with my nature, where
    My fortunes and my friends at stake required

---

41 **when extremities speak** when the most critical situations demand
(see Introduction, pp. lxxviii–lxxix)   42 **unsevered** inseparable   48
adopt adopt as   49 **it** (pretense, "to seem/The same you are not")   51
stands in like request is equally in demand   51 **force** urge   52 **it lies
you on** it is your duty   55 **roted** learned by rote   56–57 **but . . . truth**
only false expressions of your heart's true understanding wholly unac-
ceptable to it   59 **take in** capture   60 **put you to your fortune** force
you to take your chances (in war)

I should do so in honor.° I am in this°
Your wife, your son, these senators, the nobles;   65
And you will rather show our general° louts
How you can frown than spend a fawn upon 'em
For the inheritance° of their loves and safeguard
Of what that want° might ruin.

Menenius.   Noble lady!
Come, go with us; speak fair; you may salve so,   70
Not what is dangerous present, but the loss
Of what is past.

Volumnia.   I prithee now, my son,
Go to them with this bonnet in thy hand;
And thus far having stretched it (here be with
     them),
Thy knee bussing° the stones (for in such business   75
Action is eloquence, and the eyes of th' ignorant
More learnèd than the ears), waving° thy head,
Which° often thus correcting thy stout° heart,
Now humble as the ripest mulberry
That will not hold the handling; or° say to them,   80
Thou art their soldier, and being bred in broils
Hast not the soft way which, thou dost confess,
Were fit for thee to use, as they to claim,
In asking their good loves; but thou wilt frame
Thyself, forsooth,° hereafter theirs, so far   85
As thou hast power and person.

Menenius.   This but done,
Even as she speaks, why, their hearts were yours;
For they have pardons, being asked, as free°
As words to little purpose.

---

64 **in honor** in honor bound (*not* Coriolanus' understanding of "Honor")
64 **I am in this** I speak in this for (implying also, "I stand in place
of") 66 **general** common 68 **inheritance** possession 69 **that
want** (of their loves) 74–80 (the text may be corrupt) 75 **bussing**
kissing (touching) 77 **waving** bowing up and down 78 **Which** (subject of "correcting" in a nominative absolute; the sentence is urgent; the
syntax, sketchy) 78 **stout** proud 80 **or** (marks the turn from "action"
to "eloquence," line 76) 85 **forsooth** in truth 88 **free** liberal (to
grant)

Volumnia.   Prithee now,
   Go, and be ruled, although I know thou hadst
90   rather
   Follow thine enemy in a fiery gulf°
   Than flatter him in a bower.°

              Enter Cominius.

                    Here is Cominius.
Cominius. I have been i' th' marketplace;° and, sir,
   'tis fit
   You make strong party,° or defend yourself
95   By calmness or by absence. All's in anger.

Menenius. Only fair speech.

Cominius.   I think 'twill serve, if he
   Can thereto frame his spirit.

Volumnia.   He must, and will.
   Prithee now, say you will, and go about it.

Coriolanus. Must I go show them my unbarbed
   sconce?° Must I
100 With my base tongue give to my noble heart
   A lie that it must bear? Well, I will do't.
   Yet, were there but this single plot° to lose,
   This mold° of Marcius, they to dust should grind it,
   And throw't against the wind. To th' marketplace!
105 You have put me now to such a part° which never
   I shall discharge° to th' life.

Cominius.   Come, come, we'll prompt you.

Volumnia. I prithee now, sweet son, as thou hast said
   My praises made thee first a soldier, so,
   To have my praise for this, perform a part
   Thou hast not done before.
110 *Coriolanus.*   Well, I must do't.

91 **in a fiery gulf** into an abyss of flame   92 **bower** ladies' chamber
93 **marketplace** i.e., Forum of ancient Rome   94 **make strong party**
maintain your side strongly   99 **unbarbed sconce** unarmed head
("sconce" often used in comic contexts)   102 **plot** (of earth)   103
mold (both "frame" and "earth"; cf. 5.3.22)   105 **part** (in a play)   106
discharge perform

semi-soliloquy castrated

    Away, my disposition, and possess me
    Some harlot's° spirit! My throat of war be turned,
    Which quired° with my drum, into a pipe°
    Small as an eunuch or the virgin voice   *emasculating*
    That babies lulls asleep! The smiles of knaves *to him*   115
    Tent in my cheeks, and schoolboys' tears take up°
    The glasses of my sight!° A beggar's tongue
    Make motion through my lips, and my armed
        knees,
    Who bowed but in my stirrup, bend like his
    That hath received an alms! I will not do't;   120
    Lest I surcease° to honor mine own truth,   *won't*
    And by my body's action teach my mind
    A most inherent° baseness.

Volumnia.   At thy choice then.
    To beg of thee, it is my more dishonor
    Than thou of them. Come all to ruin! Let   125
    Thy mother rather feel thy pride than fear
    Thy dangerous stoutness,° for I mock at death
    With as big heart as thou. Do as thou list.°
    Thy valiantness was mine, thou suck'st it from me,
    But owe° thy pride thyself.

Coriolanus.   Pray, be content: 130
    Mother, I am going to the marketplace;
    Chide me no more. I'll mountebank° their loves,
    Cog° their hearts from them, and come home be-
        loved
    Of all the trades in Rome. Look, I am going.
    Commend me to my wife. I'll return consul;   135
    Or never trust to what my tongue can do
    I' th' way of flattery further.

---

112 **harlot** rascal (used of both sexes)   113 **quired** sang harmoniously
113 **pipe** i.e., voice   116 **take up** possess   117 **The glasses of my
sight** my eyeballs   121 **surcease** cease   123 **inherent** firmly settled
126–27 **feel ... stoutness** suffer the effects of thy pride, but not fear the
danger of it (*stoutness* = obstinacy, as in North, nearly equal to "pride";
cf. line 78)   128 **thou list** you please   130 **owe** own, have   132
mountebank win their loves by tricky actions (cf. a "mountebank," a
quack doctor, who puts on an act to sell his wares)   133 **Cog** cheat

Volumnia.   Do your will. *Exit Volumnia.*

Cominius. Away, the tribunes do attend you. Arm
    yourself
To answer mildly; for they are prepared
140 With accusations, as I hear, more strong
Than are upon you yet.

Coriolanus. The word° is "mildly." Pray you, let
    us go.
Let them accuse me by invention,° I
Will answer in° mine honor.

Menenius.   Ay, but mildly.

145 *Coriolanus.* Well, mildly be it then—mildly. *Exeunt.*

[Scene 3. *Rome. The Forum.*]

Enter Sicinius and Brutus.

Brutus. In this point charge him home,° that he
    affects°
Tyrannical power. If he evade us there,
Enforce him° with his envy° to the people,
And that the spoil got on° the Antiates
Was ne'er distributed.

Enter an Aedile.

5   What, will he come?

Aedile. He's coming.

Brutus.   How accompanied?

142 **word** password 143 **accuse me by invention** invent accusations
against me 144 **in** in a way consistent with 3.3.1 **charge him home**
press your accusations against him to the limit 1 **affects** aims at 3
Enforce him press him hard 3 **envy** ill-will 4 **got on** won from

Aedile. With old Menenius and those senators
  That always favored him.

Sicinius.   Have you a catalog
  Of all the voices that we have procured,
  Set down by th' poll?°

Aedile.   I have; 'tis ready.   10

Sicinius. Have you collected them by tribes?

Aedile.   I have.

Sicinius. Assemble presently° the people hither:
  And when they hear me say "It shall be so
  I' th' right and strength o' th' commons," be it
    either
  For death, for fine, or banishment, then let them,   15
  If I say "Fine," cry "Fine!"—if "Death," cry
    "Death!"
  Insisting on the old prerogative
  And power i' th' truth o' th' cause.°

Aedile.   I shall inform them.

Brutus. And when such time° they have begun to
  cry,
  Let them not cease, but with a din confused   20
  Enforce° the present execution
  Of what we chance to sentence.

Aedile.   Very well.

Sicinius. Make them be strong, and ready for this
  hint,°
  When we shall hap to give't them.

Brutus.   Go about it. [*Exit Aedile.*]
  Put him to° choler straight. He hath been used   25
  Ever to conquer and to have his worth°

---

10 **by th' poll** by counting heads   12 **presently** at once (cf. line 21)
18 **i' th' truth o' th' cause** resting in the justice of the case   19 **when
such time** at such time when   21 **Enforce** press for   23 **hint** opportunity   25 **Put him to** drive him to   26 **his worth** his pennyworth, i.e.,
his fill

Of contradiction. Being once chafed, he cannot
Be reined again to temperance; then he speaks
What's in his heart, and that is there which looks
With us° to break his neck:

Enter Coriolanus, Menenius, and Cominius,
with others.

30 *Sicinius.*   Well, here he comes.

Menenius. Calmly, I do beseech you.

Coriolanus. Ay, as an ostler, that for th' poorest piece°
    Will bear the knave by th' volume.° Th' honored
         gods
    Keep Rome in safety, and the chairs of justice
35 Supplied with worthy men! Plant love among's!
    Throng our large temples with the shows of peace,
    And not our streets with war!

First Senator.   Amen, amen.

Menenius. A noble wish.

Enter the Aedile, with the Plebeians.

Sicinius. Draw near, ye people.

Aedile. List to your tribunes. Audience!° peace, I
40   say!

Coriolanus. First, hear me speak.

Both Tribunes.   Well, say. Peace, ho!

Coriolanus. Shall I be charged no further than this
    present?°
    Must all determine° here?

Sicinius.   I do demand,°
    If you submit you to the people's voices,
45 Allow° their officers, and are content

29–30 **looks/With us** promises in harmony with our intent   32 **piece**
coin   33 **bear the knave by th' volume** endure being called knave
enough times to fill a book   40 **Audience** give ear   42 **this present**
this immediate occasion   43 **determine** reach a conclusion   43
demand ask   45 **Allow** acknowledge

To suffer lawful censure for such faults
As shall be proved upon you.

Coriolanus.   I am content.

Menenius. Lo, citizens, he says he is content.
    The warlike service he has done, consider; think
    Upon the wounds his body bears, which show   50
    Like graves i' th' holy churchyard.

Coriolanus.   Scratches with briers,
    Scars to move laughter only.

Menenius.   Consider further,
    That when he speaks not like a citizen,
    You find him like a soldier.° Do not take
    His rougher accents for malicious sounds,   55
    But, as I say, such as become a soldier
    Rather than envy° you.

Cominius.   Well, well, no more.

Coriolanus. What is the matter
    That, being passed for consul with full voice,
    I am so dishonored that the very hour   60
    You take it off again?

Sicinius.   Answer to us.

Coriolanus. Say, then. 'Tis true, I ought so.

Sicinius. We charge you, that you have contrived to
        take
    From Rome all seasoned° office, and to wind
    Yourself into° a power tyrannical,   65
    For which you are a traitor to the people.

Coriolanus. How! Traitor!

Menenius.   Nay, temperately! Your promise.

---

54 **like a soldier** (see Introduction, p. lxiv) 57 **envy** express malice
towards 64 **seasoned** established (or "moderate," "well moderated")
64–65 **wind/Yourself into** make your way by indirect and crooked
means

Coriolanus. The fires i' th' lowest hell fold in the
              people!
         Call me their traitor, thou injurious° tribune!
70   Within° thine eyes sat twenty thousand deaths,
         In thy hands clutched as many millions, in
         Thy lying tongue both numbers, I would say
         "Thou liest" unto thee with a voice as free°
         As I do pray the gods.

Sicinius.   Mark you this, people?

All [*Citizens*]. To th' rock, to th' rock with him!

75   *Sicinius.*   Peace!
         We need not put new matter to his charge.
         What you have seen him do and heard him speak,
         Beating your officers, cursing yourselves,
         Opposing laws with strokes, and here defying
80   Those whose great power must try him—even this,
         So criminal and in such capital° kind,
         Deserves th' extremest death.

Brutus.   But since he hath
         Served well for Rome—

Coriolanus.   What do you prate of service?

Brutus. I talk of that that know it.

85   *Coriolanus.* You!

Menenius. Is this the promise that you made your
              mother?

Cominius. Know, I pray you—

Coriolanus.   I'll know no further.
         Let them pronounce the steep Tarpeian death,°
         Vagabond exile, flaying, pent° to linger
90   But with a grain a day, I would not buy
         Their mercy at the price of one fair word,

69 **injurious** insulting   70 **Within** if within   73 **free** unrestrained
81 **capital** (defined by line 82)   88 **steep Tarpeian death** cf. line
103   89 **pent** i.e., "Let them pronounce" the sentence of being "pent,"
imprisoned

Nor check my courage° for what they can give,
To have't with saying "Good morrow."

Sicinius.   For that he has
(As much as in him lies°) from time to time
Envied against° the people, seeking means   95
To pluck away their power, as now° at last
Given hostile strokes, and that not° in the presence
Of dreaded justice, but on the ministers
That do distribute it—in the name o' th' people,
And in the power of us the tribunes, we,   100
Even from this instant, banish him our city,
In peril of precipitation
From off the rock Tarpeian, never more
To enter our Rome gates. I' th' people's name,
I say it shall be so.   105

All [*Citizens*]. It shall be so, it shall be so! Let him
    away!
He's banished, and it shall be so.

Cominius. Hear me, my masters and my common
    friends—

Sicinius. He's sentenced; no more hearing.

Cominius.   Let me speak.
I have been consul, and can show for Rome   110
Her enemies' marks upon me. I do love
My country's good with a respect more tender,
More holy and profound, than mine own life,
My dear wife's estimate,° her womb's increase
And treasure of my loins; then if I would   115
Speak that—

Sicinius.   We know your drift. Speak what?

Brutus. There's no more to be said, but he is banished
As enemy to the people and his country.
It shall be so.

92 **courage** spirit   94 **as in him lies** as lies in his power   95 **Envied against** shown malice towards   96 **as now** with respect to this occasion (or, "now," "as" being redundant)   97 **not** not only   114 **estimate** worth

All [Citizens]. It shall be so, it shall be so.

Coriolanus. You common cry° of curs, whose breath
120   I hate
        As reek° o' th' rotten fens, whose loves I prize
        As the dead carcasses of unburied men
        That do corrupt my air, I banish you.
        And here remain with your uncertainty!
125   Let every feeble rumor shake your hearts!
        Your enemies, with nodding of their plumes,
        Fan you into despair! Have the power still
        To banish your defenders, till at length
        Your ignorance (which finds not till it feels,°
130   Making but reservation of yourselves,°
        Still° your own foes) deliver you as most
        Abated° captives to some nation
        That won you without blows! Despising
        For you the city, thus I turn my back.
135   There is a world elsewhere.

                    Exeunt Coriolanus, Cominius, [Menenius,]
                              with the other Senators.

Aedile. The people's enemy is gone, is gone!

All [Citizens]. Our enemy is banished, he is gone!
        Hoo—oo!
                    They all shout, and throw up their caps.

Sicinius. Go see him out at gates, and follow him,
        As he hath followed you, with all despite;°
140   Give him deserved vexation.° Let a guard
        Attend us through the city.

All [Citizens]. Come, come, let's see him out at gates;
        come!
        The gods preserve our noble tribunes! Come.
                                              Exeunt.

---

120 **cry** pack   121 **reek** mist   129 **finds not till it feels** does not
understand until it suffers the consequences   130 **Making ... your-**
selves saving only yourselves   131 **Still** ever   132 **Abated** beaten
down   139 **despite** contempt   140 **Give him deserved vexation** tor-
ment him as he deserves

actions leading us to

ACT 4

[Scene 1. *Rome. Before a gate of the city.*]

*Enter Coriolanus, Volumnia, Virgilia, Menenius,
Cominius, with the young Nobility of Rome.*

Coriolanus. Come, leave your tears; a brief farewell.
    The beast
With many heads butts me away. Nay, mother,
Where is your ancient courage? You were used
To say extremities was° the trier of spirits;
That common chances common men could bear;   5
That when the sea was calm all boats alike
Showed mastership in floating; fortune's blows°
When most struck home, being gentle wounded
    craves
A noble cunning.° You were used to load me
With precepts that would make invincible   10
The heart that conned° them.

Virgilia. O heavens! O heavens!

Coriolanus.   Nay, I prithee, woman—

4.1.4 **extremities was** (plural subject permissible in Elizabethan usage)
7 **fortune's blows** (supply introductory "that") 7–9 **fortune's ...
cunning** (when fortune's blows strike hardest, to act the gentleman
though wounded demands a noble use of intelligence) 11 **conned**
studied

95

Volumnia. Now the red pestilence strike all trades in
        Rome,
    And occupations perish!

Coriolanus.   What, what, what!
15 I shall be loved when I am lacked. Nay, mother,
    Resume that spirit when you were wont to say,
    If you had been the wife of Hercules,
    Six of his labors you'd have done, and saved
    Your husband so much sweat. Cominius,
20 Droop not; adieu. Farewell, my wife, my mother.
    I'll do well yet. Thou old and true Menenius,
    Thy tears are salter than a younger man's,
    And venomous to thine eyes. My sometime°
        general,
    I have seen thee stern, and thou hast oft beheld
25 Heart-hard'ning spectacles; tell these sad women
    'Tis fond° to wail inevitable strokes,
    As 'tis to laugh at 'em. My mother, you wot° well
    My hazards still have been your solace,° and
    Believe't not lightly—though I go alone,
30 Like to a lonely dragon, that his fen
    Makes feared and talked of more than seen—your
        son
    Will or exceed the common° or be caught
    With cautelous° baits and practice.°

Volumnia.   My first son,
    Whither wilt thou go? Take good Cominius
35 With thee awhile. Determine on some course
    More than a wild exposture° to each chance
    That starts i' th' way before thee.

Coriolanus.   O the gods!

Cominius. I'll follow thee a month, devise with thee
    Where thou shalt rest, that thou mayst hear of us

---

23 **sometime** former 26 **fond** foolish 27 **wot** know 28 **solace**
interest 32 **or exceed the common** either surpass the usual achievements of men 33 **cautelous** crafty 33 **practice** treachery 36
exposture exposure

And we of thee. So, if the time thrust forth   40
A cause for thy repeal,° we shall not send
O'er the vast world to seek a single man,
And lose advantage,° which doth ever cool
I' th' absence of the needer.°

Coriolanus.   Fare ye well!
Thou hast years upon thee; and thou art too full   45
Of the wars' surfeits to go rove with one
That's yet unbruised. Bring° me but out at gate.
Come, my sweet wife, my dearest mother, and
My friends of noble touch;° when I am forth,
Bid me farewell, and smile. I pray you, come.   50
While I remain above the ground you shall
Hear from me still, and never of me aught
But what is like me formerly.

Menenius.   That's worthily
As any ear can hear. Come, let's not weep.
If I could shake off but one seven years   55
From these old arms and legs, by the good gods,
I'd° with thee every foot.

Coriolanus.   Give me thy hand.
Come.   *Exeunt.*

[Scene 2. *Rome. Near the gate.*]

*Enter the two Tribunes, Sicinius and Brutus,
with the Aedile.*

Sicinius. Bid them all° home; he's gone, and we'll no
   further.

41 **repeal** recall   43 **advantage** the opportune moment   44 **needer** (of
"advantage")   47 **Bring** conduct   49 **noble touch** tested nobility (cf.
"touchstone")   57 **I'd** would (go)   4.2.1 **them all** (the plebeians)

The nobility are vexed, whom we see have sided
In his behalf.

Brutus.   Now we have shown our power,
Let us seem humbler after it is done
Than when it was a-doing.

5 *Sicinius.*   Bid them home.
Say their great enemy is gone, and they
Stand in their ancient strength.

Brutus.   Dismiss them home.   [*Exit Aedile.*]
Here comes his mother.

     Enter Volumnia, Virgilia, and Menenius.

Sicinius.   Let's not meet her.

Brutus.   Why?

Sicinius. They say she's mad.

10 *Brutus.* They have ta'en note of us. Keep on your way.

Volumnia. O, y'are well met. Th' hoarded° plague o'
th' gods
Requite your love!

Menenius.   Peace, peace, be not so loud.

Volumnia. If that I could for weeping, you should
hear—
Nay, and you shall hear some. [*To Brutus*] Will
you be gone?

Virgilia. [*To Sicinius*] You shall stay too. I would I
15   had the power
To say so to my husband.

Sicinius.   Are you mankind?°

Volumnia. Ay, fool; is that a shame? Note but this,
fool.
Was not a man my father? Hadst thou foxship°

---

11 **hoarded** stored up (for punishment)   16 **mankind** mad, of man-
like violence (Sicinius' meaning; but Volumnia takes it in the sense of
"human")   18 **foxship** cunning

To banish him that struck more blows for Rome
Than thou hast spoken words? *deeds wrds*

Sicinius.   O blessed heavens!   20

Volumnia. Moe° noble blows than ever thou wise
    words;
  And for Rome's good. I'll tell thee what—yet go!
  Nay, but thou shalt stay too. I would my son
  Were in Arabia,° and thy tribe before him,
  His good sword in his hand.

Sicinius.   What then?

Virgilia.   What then!   25
  He'd make an end of thy posterity.

Volumnia. Bastards and all.
  Good man, the wounds that he does bear for Rome!

Menenius. Come, come, peace.

Sicinius. I would he had continued to his country   30
  As he began, and not unknit himself
  The noble knot he made.°

Brutus.   I would he had.

Volumnia. "I would he had!" 'Twas you incensed the
    rabble;
  Cats, that can judge as fitly of his worth
  As I can of those mysteries which heaven   35
  Will not have earth to know.

Brutus.   Pray, let's go.

Volumnia. Now, pray, sir, get you gone;
  You have done a brave deed. Ere you go, hear this:
  As far as doth the Capitol exceed
  The meanest house in Rome, so far my son—   40
  This lady's husband here, this, do you see?
  Whom you have banished—does exceed you all.

Brutus. Well, well, we'll leave you.

---

21 **Moe** more   24 **Arabia** a desert (outside Roman law and order)   32
noble knot he made (bond to Rome made by his heroic deeds)

Sicinius.   Why stay we to be baited
    With° one that wants her wits?   *Exit Tribunes.*

Volumnia.   Take my prayers with you.
45 I would the gods had nothing else to do
    But to confirm my curses! Could I meet 'em
    But once a day, it would unclog my heart
    Of what lies heavy to't.

Menenius.   You have told them home,°
    And by my troth you have cause. You'll sup with
    me?

50 *Volumnia.* Anger's my meat; I sup upon myself,
    And so shall starve with feeding. Come, let's go.
    Leave this faint puling,° and lament as I do,
    In anger, Juno-like. Come, come, come.
                 Exeunt [Volumnia and Virgilia].

Menenius. Fie, fie, fie!   *Exit.*

[Scene 3. *Between Rome and Antium.*]

Enter a Roman and a Volsce.

Roman. I know you well, sir, and you know me: your
    name, I think, is Adrian.

Volsce. It is so, sir. Truly, I have forgot you.

Roman. I am a Roman; and my services are, as you
5   are, against 'em.° Know you me yet?

Volsce. Nicanor? No!

Roman. The same, sir.

Volsce. You had more beard when I last saw you; but

44 **With** by   48 **told them home** ("hit them where it hurts")   52
puling whining   4.3.5 **'em** the Romans

your favor° is well appeared° by your tongue.
What's the news in Rome? I have a note° from the   10
Volscian state to find you out there. You have well
saved me a day's journey.

Roman. There hath been in Rome strange insurrec-
tions; the people against the senators, patricians,
and nobles.   15

Volsce. Hath been! Is it ended then? Our state thinks
not so; they are in a most warlike preparation, and
hope to come upon them in the heat of their
division.

Roman. The main blaze of it is past, but a small thing   20
would make it flame again; for the nobles receive°
so to heart the banishment of that worthy Coriolanus, that they are in a ripe aptness to take all
power from the people and to pluck from them
their tribunes forever. This lies glowing, I can tell   25
you, and is almost mature for the violent breaking
out.

Volsce. Coriolanus banished!

Roman. Banished, sir.

Volsce. You will be welcome with this intelligence,   30
Nicanor.

Roman. The day serves well for them° now. I have
heard it said the fittest time to corrupt a man's wife
is when she's fall'n out with her husband. Your
noble Tullus Aufidius will appear well in these   35
wars, his great opposer, Coriolanus, being now in
no request of° his country.

Volsce. He cannot choose.° I am most fortunate thus
accidentally to encounter you. You have ended my
business, and I will merrily accompany you home.   40

---

9 **favor** face   9 **appeared** made to appear   10 **a note** instructions
21 **receive** take   32 **them** (the Volscians)   36–37 **in no request of** in
no demand by   38 **cannot choose** (but appear well)

Roman. I shall, between this° and supper, tell you
most strange things from Rome, all tending to the
good of their adversaries. Have you an army ready,
say you?

45 *Volsce.* A most royal one; the centurions° and their
charges,° distinctly billeted,° already in th' entertainment,° and to be on foot at an hour's warning.

Roman. I am joyful to hear of their readiness, and am
the man, I think, that shall set them in present
50 action. So, sir, heartily well met, and most glad of
your company.

Volsce. You take my part from me, sir. I have the
most cause to be glad of yours.

Roman. Well, let us go together.   *Exeunt.*

[Scene 4. *Antium. Before Aufidius' house.*]

*Enter Coriolanus in mean apparel, disguised
and muffled.*

Coriolanus. A goodly city is this Antium. City,
'Tis I that made thy widows: many an heir
Of these fair edifices 'fore my wars°
Have I heard groan and drop. Then know me not,
5 Lest that thy wives with spits and boys with stones
In puny battle slay me.

Enter a Citizen.

Save you,° sir.

41 **this** this time   45 **centurions** commanders of smallest unit (century) of a Roman legion   46 **charges** men under them   46 **distinctly
billeted** separately enrolled   46–47 **in th' entertainment** in service
(maintained by the army)   4.4.3 **'fore my wars** before my attacks   6
Save you God save you

Citizen. And you.

Coriolanus.   Direct me, if it be your will,
  Where great Aufidius lies.° Is he in Antium?

Citizen. He is, and feasts the nobles of the state
  At his house this night.

Coriolanus.   Which is his house, beseech you?   *10*

Citizen. This here before you.

Coriolanus.   Thank you, sir: farewell.
                              Exit Citizen.
  O world, thy slippery turns! Friends now fast sworn,
  Whose double bosoms seems° to wear one heart,
  Whose hours, whose bed, whose meal and exercise
  Are still together, who twin, as 'twere, in love   *15*
  Unseparable, shall within this hour,
  On a dissension of a doit,° break out
  To bitterest enmity. So fellest° foes,
  Whose passions and whose plots have broke their
      sleep
  To take the one the other, by some chance,   *20*
  Some trick° not worth an egg, shall grow dear
      friends
  And interjoin their issues.° So with me:
  My birthplace hate I, and my love's upon
  This enemy town. I'll enter. If he slay me,
  He does fair justice; if he give me way,   *25*
  I'll do his country service.   *Exit.*

8 **lies** lives   13 **seems** (perhaps an old plural in -s)   17 **of a doit** worth
a doit (coin of little value; cf. 1.5.6)   18 **fellest** fiercest   21 **trick**
trifle   22 **interjoin their issues** let their children intermarry; become
close partners in action ("issues" in sense of "deeds"?)

[Scene 5. *Antium. A hall in Aufidius' house.*]

Music plays. Enter a Servingman.

First Servingman. Wine, wine, wine! What service is
here! I think our fellows are asleep.   [*Exit.*]

Enter another Servingman.

Second Servingman. Where's Cotus? My master calls
for him. Cotus!   *Exit.*

Enter Coriolanus.

Coriolanus. A goodly house. The feast smells well,
5   but I
Appear not like a guest.

Enter the First Servingman.

First Servingman. What would you have, friend?
Whence are you? Here's no place for you: pray go
to the door!°   *Exit.*

10 **Coriolanus.** I have deserved no better entertainment,
In being Coriolanus.

Enter Second Servingman.

Second Servingman. Whence are you, sir? Has the
porter his eyes in his head that he gives entrance to
such companions?° Pray get you out.

15 **Coriolanus.** Away!

Second Servingman. "Away!" Get you away.

Coriolanus. Now thou'rt troublesome.

4.5.9 **to the door** out of doors   14 **companions** fellows (in bad sense)

Second Servingman. Are you so brave?° I'll have you talked with anon.°

Enter Third Servingman; the first meets him.

Third Servingman. What fellow's this?   20

First Servingman. A strange one as ever I looked on! I cannot get him out o' th' house. Prithee call my master to him.

Third Servingman. What have you to do here, fellow? Pray you avoid° the house.   25

Coriolanus. Let me but stand; I will not hurt your hearth.

Third Servingman. What are you?

Coriolanus. A gentleman.

Third Servingman. A marv'lous° poor one.   30

Coriolanus. True, so I am.

Third Servingman. Pray you, poor gentleman, take up some other station; here's no place for you. Pray you avoid. Come.

Coriolanus. Follow your function,° go and batten° on   35
cold bits.

Pushes him away from him.

Third Servingman. What, you will not? Prithee, tell my master what a strange guest he has here.

Second Servingman. And I shall.

Exit Second Servingman.

Third Servingman. Where dwell'st thou?   40

Coriolanus. Under the canopy.°

Third Servingman. Under the canopy!

Coriolanus. Ay.

---

18 **brave** impudent   19 **anon** soon   25 **avoid** leave   30 **marv'lous** strangely   35 **Follow your function** do your regular work   35 **batten** grow fat   41 **canopy** sky (cf. "canopy" over a throne)

Third Servingman. Where's that?

45 *Coriolanus.* I' th' city of kites and crows.

Third Servingman. I' th' city of kites and crows! What
an ass it is! Then thou dwell'st with daws° too?

Coriolanus. No, I serve not thy master.

Third Servingman. How, sir! Do you meddle with my
50 master?

Coriolanus. Ay; 'tis an honester service than to meddle with thy mistress. Thou prat'st, and prat'st;
serve with thy trencher.° Hence!

                                    Beats him away.

Enter Aufidius with the [Second] Servingman.

Aufidius. Where is this fellow?

55 *Second Servingman.* Here, sir. I'd have beaten him
like a dog, but for disturbing the lords within.

Aufidius. Whence com'st thou? What wouldst thou?
    Thy name?
Why speak'st not? Speak, man. What's thy name?

Coriolanus. [*Unmuffling*]   If, Tullus,
Not yet thou know'st me, and, seeing me, dost not
60 Think me° for the man I am, necessity
Commands me name myself.

Aufidius.   What is thy name?

Coriolanus. A name unmusical to the Volscians' ears,
And harsh in sound to thine.

Aufidius.   Say, what's thy name?
Thou hast a grim appearance, and thy face
65 Bears a command° in't. Though thy tackle's torn,
Thou show'st° a noble vessel. What's thy name?

---

47 **daws** (foolish birds) 53 **trencher** wooden plate 60 **Think me**
i.e., take me 65 **a command** i.e., a look of authority 66 **show'st**
appear'st

Coriolanus. Prepare thy brow to frown. Know'st thou
    me yet?

Aufidius. I know thee not. Thy name!

Coriolanus. My name is Caius Marcius, who hath
    done
  To thee particularly, and to all the Volsces,   70
  Great hurt and mischief;° thereto witness may
  My surname, Coriolanus. The painful° service,
  The extreme dangers, and the drops of blood
  Shed for my thankless country, are requited
  But with that surname—a good memory°   75
  And witness of the malice and displeasure
  Which thou shouldst bear me. Only that name
    remains.
  The cruelty and envy° of the people,
  Permitted by our dastard nobles, who
  Have all forsook me, hath devoured the rest;   80
  And suffered me by th' voice of slaves to be
  Whooped out of Rome. Now, this extremity
  Hath brought me to thy hearth; not out of hope
  (Mistake me not) to save my life; for if
  I had feared death, of all the men i' th' world   85
  I would have 'voided thee; but in mere spite,
  To be full quit of° those my banishers,
  Stand I before thee here. Then if thou hast
  A heart of wreak° in thee, that wilt revenge
  Thine own particular wrongs and stop those maims 90
  Of shame° seen through thy country, speed thee
    straight
  And make my misery serve thy turn. So use it
  That my revengeful services may prove
  As benefits to thee; for I will fight
  Against my cank'red° country with the spleen°   95
  Of all the under fiends.° But if so be

---

71 **mischief** serious harm   72 **painful** laborious   75 **memory** memorial   78 **envy** ill-will   87 **full quit of** fully revenged on (cf. "quits with")   89 **heart of wreak** vengeful heart   90–91 **maims/Of shame** shameful wounds (e.g., the Roman occupation of Corioli)   95 **cank'red** corrupted (by ingratitude and envy)   95 **spleen** rage   96 **under fiends** devils in hell

Thou dar'st not this and that to prove more for-
        tunes°
Thou'rt tired, then, in a word, I also am
Longer to live most weary, and present
100 My throat to thee and to thy ancient malice;
Which not to cut would show thee but a fool,
Since I have ever followed thee with hate,
Drawn tuns° of blood out of thy country's breast,
And cannot live but to thy shame, unless
It be to do thee service.

105 *Aufidius.*   O Marcius, Marcius!
Each word thou hast spoke hath weeded from my
        heart
A root of ancient envy. If Jupiter
Should from yond cloud speak divine things,
And say " 'Tis true," I'd not believe them more
110 Than thee, all noble Marcius. Let me twine
Mine arms about that body, where against
My grainèd ash° an hundred times hath broke
And scarred the moon with splinters. Here I clip°
The anvil of my sword, and do contest
115 As hotly and as nobly with thy love
As ever in ambitious strength I did
Contend against thy valor. Know thou first,
I loved the maid I married; never man
Sighed truer breath. But that° I see thee here,
120 Thou noble thing, more dances my rapt° heart
Than when I first my wedded mistress saw
Bestride my threshold. Why, thou Mars, I tell thee,
We have a power on foot,° and I had purpose
Once more to hew thy target° from thy brawn,°
125 Or lose mine arm for't. Thou hast beat me out°
Twelve several times, and I have nightly since
Dreamt of encounters 'twixt thyself and me.
We have been down together in my sleep,

---

97 **prove more fortunes** try the chances of fortune further   103 **tuns**
casks   112 **grainèd ash** spear of ash, the grain showing   113 **clip**
embrace   119 **that** because   120 **rapt** enraptured   123 **power on
foot** force in the field   124 **target** shield   124 **brawn** brawny
arm   125 **out** completely

Unbuckling helms, fisting each other's throat,
And waked° half dead with nothing. Worthy
　Marcius,　　　　　　　　　　　　　　　　　　　*130*
Had we no other quarrel else to Rome but that
Thou art thence banished, we would muster all
From twelve to seventy, and pouring war
Into the bowels of ungrateful Rome,
Like a bold flood o'erbeat.° O, come, go in,　　　*135*
And take our friendly senators by th' hands,
Who now are here, taking their leaves of me
Who am prepared against your territories,
Though not for Rome itself.

Coriolanus.　　　　　　　　You bless me, gods!

Aufidius. Therefore, most absolute° sir, if thou wilt
　have　　　　　　　　　　　　　　　　　　　*140*
The leading of thine own revenges, take
Th' one half of my commission,° and set down°—
As best thou art experienced, since thou know'st
Thy country's strength and weakness—thine own
　ways,
Whether to knock against the gates of Rome,　　*145*
Or rudely visit them in parts remote
To fright them ere destroy. But come in.
Let me commend thee first to those that shall
Say yea to thy desires. A thousand welcomes!
And more a friend than e'er an enemy;　　　　　*150*
Yet, Marcius, that was much. Your hand:
　most welcome!　　　　　　　　　　　　*Exeunt.*

　　　　Enter° two of the Servingmen.

First Servingman. Here's a strange alteration!

Second Servingman. By my hand, I had thought to
　have strucken him with a cudgel; and yet my mind
　gave me° his clothes made a false report of him.　*155*

---

130 **waked** (I have) awakened　135 **o'erbeat** surge over (the
land)　140 **absolute** perfect　142 **my commission** the forces under
me　142 **set down** determine　151 s.d. **Enter** (perhaps they come forward from backstage, since neither has been assigned an "*Exit*")　154–55
my mind gave me I had an idea

First Servingman. What an arm he has! He turned me
about with his finger and his thumb, as one would
set up a top.

Second Servingman. Nay, I knew by his face that there
160   was something in him; he had, sir, a kind of face,
methought—I cannot tell how to term it.

First Servingman. He had so, looking as it were—
would I were hanged, but I thought there was more
in him than I could think.

165 *Second Servingman.* So did I, I'll be sworn. He is
simply the rarest man i' th' world.

First Servingman. I think he is; but a greater soldier
than he, you wot° one.

Second Servingman. Who, my master?

170 *First Servingman.* Nay, it's no matter for that.

Second Servingman. Worth six on him.

First Servingman. Nay, not so neither. But I take him
to be the greater soldier.

Second Servingman. Faith, look you, one cannot tell
175   how to say that. For the defense of a town our
general is excellent.

First Servingman. Ay, and for an assault too.

Enter the Third Servingman.

Third Servingman. O slaves, I can tell you news—
news, you rascals!

180 *Both* [*First and Second Servingmen*]. What, what,
what? Let's partake.

Third Servingman. I would not be a Roman, of all
nations; I had as lief° be a condemned man.

Both. Wherefore? Wherefore?

167–77 (the *First Servingman* is cautiously and cunningly vague in his
references to the "greater soldier")   168 **wot** know   183 **lief** willingly

Third Servingman. Why here's he that was wont to 185
thwack our general—Caius Marcius.

First Servingman. Why do you say "thwack our
general"?

Third Servingman. I do not say "thwack our general,"
but he was always good enough for him. 190

Second Servingman. Come, we are fellows° and
friends. He was ever too hard for him; I have heard
him say so himself.

First Servingman. He was too hard for him directly,°
to say the troth on't. Before Corioles he scotched° 195
him and notched him like a carbonado.°

Second Serviceman. And he had been cannibally
given, he might have boiled and eaten him too.

First Servingman. But more of thy news?

Third Servingman. Why, he is so made on° here 200
within as if he were son and heir to Mars; set at
upper end o' th' table; no question asked him by
any of the senators but they stand bald° before
him. Our general himself makes a mistress of him;
sanctifies himself with's hand,° and turns up the 205
white o' th' eye° to his discourse. But the bottom°
of the news is, our general is cut i' th' middle
and but one half of what he was yesterday, for the
other has half by the entreaty and grant of the
whole table.° He'll go, he says, and sowl° the 210
porter of Rome gates by th' ears. He will mow all
down before him, and leave his passage polled.°

191 **fellows** comrades 194 **directly** plainly 195 **scotched** slashed
196 **carbonado** meat scored with knife, for broiling 200 **so made
on** made so much of 203 **bald** bareheaded 205 **sanctifies himself
with's hand** touches his hand as if it were a holy relic 205–6 **turns up
the white o' th' eye** (in pious wonder) 206 **bottom** last (jokingly for
"the climax") 209–10 **has ... table** i.e., has half because all at the
table beg him to take it, and give it to him 210 **sowl** drag 212 **polled**
cleared (used of cutting hair)

Second Servingman. And he's as like to do't as any
man I can imagine.

215 *Third Servingman.* Do't! He will do't; for look you,
sir, he has as many friends as enemies; which
friends, sir, as it were, durst not (look you, sir)
show themselves (as we term it) his friends whilst
he's in directitude.°

220 *First Servingman.* Directitude! What's that?

Third Servingman. But when they shall see, sir, his
crest up° again and the man in blood,° they will
out of their burrows (like conies° after rain) and
revel all with him.

225 *First Servingman.* But when goes this forward?

Third Servingman. Tomorrow, today, presently.° You
shall have the drum struck up this afternoon. 'Tis
as it were a parcel° of their feast, and to be executed ere they wipe their lips.

230 *Second Servingman.* Why, then we shall have a stirring
world again. This peace is nothing but to rust iron,
increase tailors, and breed ballad-makers.

First Servingman. Let me have war, say I; it exceeds
peace as far as day does night; it's sprightly walk-
235 ing, audible,° and full of vent.° Peace is a very
apoplexy, lethargy; mulled,° deaf, sleepy, insensi-
ble; a getter of more bastard children than war's a
destroyer of men.

Second Servingman. 'Tis so; and as wars in some sort
240 may be said to be a ravisher, so it cannot be denied
but peace is a great maker of cuckolds.

First Servingman. Ay, and it makes men hate one
another.

219 **directitude** (comic mistake for "discredit"?)   222 **crest up** (like an
animal aroused)   222 **in blood** in top condition   223 **conies** rabbits   226
presently now   228 **parcel** part   235 **audible** of good hearing   235
full of vent with plenty of outlets for energy (?: cf. 1.1.226)   236 **mulled**
dulled (like wine sweetened and heated)

Third Servingman. Reason: because they then less
    need one another. The wars for my money. I hope 245
    to see Romans as cheap as Volscians. They are
    rising,° they are rising.

Both [First and Second Servingmen]. In, in, in, in!
                                                    Exeunt.

[Scene 6. *Rome. A public place.*]

Enter the two Tribunes, Sicinius and Brutus.

Sicinius. We hear not of him, neither need we fear
    him;
    His remedies are tame.° The present peace
    And quietness of the people, which before
    Were in wild hurry,° here do make his friends
    Blush that the world goes well; who rather had, 5
    Though they themselves did suffer by't, behold
    Dissentious numbers pest'ring° streets than see
    Our tradesmen singing in their shops, and going
    About their functions friendly.

Brutus. We stood to't° in good time. 10

                    Enter Menenius.

                                        Is this Menenius?

Sicinius. 'Tis he, 'tis he. O, he is grown most kind
    Of late. Hail, sir!

Menenius.   Hail to you both!

Sicinius. Your Coriolanus is not much missed

247 **rising** getting up from table 4.6.2 **His remedies are tame** his
attempts to "cure" the state are (now) harmless (cf. "dangerous physic,"
3.1.154) 4 **hurry** commotion 7 **pest'ring** filling with disturbance
10 **stood to't** made an issue of it

But with his friends. The commonwealth doth
stand,
15   And so would do, were he more angry at it.

Menenius. All's well; and might have been much
better, if
He could have temporized.

Sicinius.   Where is he, hear you?

Menenius. Nay, I hear nothing. His mother and his
wife
Hear nothing from him.

                Enter three or four Citizens.

All [Citizens]. The gods preserve you both!

20   *Sicinius.*   Good-e'en,° our neighbors.

Brutus. Good-e'en to you all, good-e'en to you all.

First Citizen. Ourselves, our wives, and children, on
our knees,
Are bound to pray for you both.

Sicinius.   Live, and thrive!

Brutus. Farewell, kind neighbors. We wished
Coriolanus
Had loved you as we did.

25   *All [Citizens].*   Now the gods keep you!

Both Tribunes. Farewell, farewell.

                        Exeunt Citizens.

Sicinius. This is a happier and more comely° time
Than when these fellows ran about the streets
Crying confusion.°

Brutus.   Caius Marcius was
30   A worthy officer i' th' war, but insolent,
O'ercome with pride, ambitious past all thinking,
Self-loving—

20 **Good-e'en** good evening 27 **comely** respectable 29 **Crying
confusion** calling for disorder

Sicinius.   And affecting° one sole throne,
    Without assistance.°

Menenius.   I think not so.

Sicinius. We should by this, to all our lamentation,
    If he had gone forth consul, found° it so.   35

Brutus. The gods have well prevented it, and Rome
    Sits safe and still without him.

                    Enter an Aedile.

Aedile.   Worthy tribunes,
    There is a slave, whom we have put in prison,
    Reports the Volsces with two several powers°
    Are ent'red in the Roman territories   40
    And with the deepest malice of the war
    Destroy what lies before 'em.

Menenius.   'Tis Aufidius,
    Who, hearing of our Marcius' banishment,
    Thrusts forth his horns° again into the world,
    Which were inshelled when Marcius stood for
        Rome,   45
    And durst not once peep out.

Sicinius.   Come, what talk you
    Of Marcius?

Brutus. Go see this rumorer whipped. It cannot be
    The Volsces dare break with us.

Menenius.   Cannot be!
    We have record that very well it can;   50
    And three examples of the like hath been
    Within my age. But reason with° the fellow,
    Before you punish him, where he heard this,
    Lest you shall chance to whip your information
    And beat the messenger who bids beware   55
    Of what is to be dreaded.

___

32 **affecting** aiming at   33 **Without assistance** not sharing his powers
with others   35 **found** have found   39 **several powers** separate forces
44 **horns** (like a snail)   52 **reason with** talk with

Sicinius.   Tell not me:
   I know this cannot be.

Brutus.   Not possible.

             Enter a Messenger.

Messenger. The nobles in great earnestness are going
   All to the Senate House. Some news is coming
60   That turns° their countenances.

Sicinius.   'Tis this slave—
   Go whip him 'fore the people's eyes—his raising,°
   Nothing but his report.

Messenger.   Yes, worthy sir,
   The slave's report is seconded;° and more,
   More fearful, is delivered.

Sicinius.   What more fearful?

65 *Messenger.* It is spoke freely out of many mouths,
   How probable I do not know, that Marcius,
   Joined with Aufidius, leads a power 'gainst Rome,
   And vows revenge as spacious as between
   The young'st and oldest thing.°

Sicinius.   This is most likely!

70 *Brutus.* Raised only that the weaker sort may wish
   Good Marcius home again.

Sicinius.   The very trick on't.

Menenius. This is unlikely:
   He and Aufidius can no more atone°
   Than violent'st contrariety.

       Enter [a second] Messenger.

75 *Second Messenger.* You are sent for to the Senate.
   A fearful army, led by Caius Marcius

  60 **turns** changes   61 **his raising** his starting (i.e., the rumor; note
comma and the following explanatory phrase)   63 **seconded** confirmed
(by further reports)   68–69 **as spacious ... thing** covering the span
between youngest and oldest, i.e., the whole population   73 **atone** be
reconciled

 Associated with Aufidius, rages
 Upon our territories, and have already
 O'erborne their way,° consumed with fire, and took
 What lay before them.   *80*

       Enter Cominius.

Cominius. O, you have made good work!

Menenius.   What news? What news?

Cominius. You have holp to ravish your own daugh-
  ters and
 To melt the city leads° upon your pates,
 To see your wives dishonored to° your noses—

Menenius. What's the news? What's the news? *85*

Cominius. Your temples burnèd in their cement, and
 Your franchises, whereon you stood,° confined
 Into an auger's bore.

Menenius.   Pray now, your news?—
 You have made fair work, I fear me.—Pray, your
  news?—
 If Marcius should be joined wi' th' Volscians—

Cominius.   If! *90*
 He is their god; he leads them like a thing
 Made by some other deity than Nature,
 That shapes man better; and they follow him
 Against us brats with no less confidence
 Than boys pursuing summer butterflies,   *95*
 Or butchers killing flies.

Menenius.   You have made good work,
 You and your apron-men;° you that stood so much
 Upon the voice of occupation° and
 The breath of garlic-eaters!

Cominius.   He'll shake
 Your Rome about your ears.

79 **O'erborne their way** (like a stream) overflowed everything in their
way 83 **leads** roofs 84 **to** before 87 **franchises, whereon you
stood** rights on which you insisted 97 **apron-men** artisans 98 **occupation** manual workers

100 Menenius.   As Hercules
    Did shake down mellow fruit. You have made fair
    work!

Brutus. But is this true, sir?

Cominius.   Ay; and you'll look pale
    Before you find it other. All the regions
    Do smilingly revolt, and who resists
105   Are mocked for valiant ignorance,
    And perish constant° fools. Who is't can blame
    him?
    Your enemies and his find something in him.

Menenius. We are all undone, unless
    The noble man have mercy.

Cominius.   Who shall ask it?
110   The tribunes cannot do't for shame; the people
    Deserve such pity of him as the wolf
    Does of the shepherds. For his best friends, if they
    Should say "Be good to Rome," they charged° him
    even
    As those should do that had deserved his hate,
    And therein showed° like enemies.

115 Menenius.   'Tis true:
    If he were putting to my house the brand
    That should consume it, I have not the face
    To say "Beseech you, cease." You have made fair
    hands,°
    You and your crafts! You have crafted fair!°

Cominius.   You have brought
120   A trembling upon Rome, such as was never
    S' incapable° of help.

Tribunes.   Say not we brought it.

---

106 **constant** loyal   113 **charged** would attack, urge (both senses relevant)   115 **showed** would show   118 **made fair hands** handled matters finely   119 **crafted fair** plied your trade (of cunning) beautifully
121 **S' incapable** so unsusceptible

Menenius. How! Was't we? We loved him, but, like
    beasts
  And cowardly nobles, gave way unto your clusters,°
  Who did hoot him out o' th' city.

Cominius.   But I fear
  They'll roar him in again. Tullus Aufidius,   *125*
  The second name of men,° obeys his points°
  As if he were his officer. Desperation
  Is all the policy, strength, and defense,
  That Rome can make against them.

        Enter a troop of Citizens.

Menenius.   Here come the clusters.
  And is Aufidius with him? You are they   *130*
  That made the air unwholesome when you cast
  Your stinking greasy caps in hooting at
  Coriolanus' exile. Now he's coming,
  And not a hair upon a soldier's head
  Which will not prove a whip. As many coxcombs° ·   *135*
  As you threw caps up will he tumble down,
  And pay you for your voices.° 'Tis no matter;
  If he could burn us all into one coal,°
  We have deserved it.

Omnes. Faith, we hear fearful news.

First Citizen.   For mine own part,   *140*
  When I said banish him, I said 'twas pity.

Second Citizen. And so did I.   *comedy*

Third Citizen. And so did I; and, to say the truth, so
  did very many of us. That we did, we did for the
  best; and though we willingly consented to his ban-   *145*
  ishment, yet it was against our will.

Cominius. Y'are goodly things, you voices!

Menenius.   You have made

123 **clusters** crowds   126 **second name of men** second in renown (to
Coriolanus)   126 **points** directions (?)   135 **coxcombs** fools' heads
(cf. costume of a fool)   137 **voices** votes   138 **coal** piece of burned
fuel (cf. charcoal)

    Good work, you and your cry!° Shall's° to the
      Capitol?

Cominius. O, ay, what else?   *Exeunt both.*

150 *Sicinius.* Go masters, get you home; be not dismayed;
    These are a side° that would be glad to have
    This true which they so seem to fear. Go home,
    And show no sign of fear.

First Citizen. The gods be good to us! Come, masters,
155 let's home. I ever said we were i' th' wrong when we
    banished him.

Second Citizen. So did we all. But come, let's home.
                       Exit Citizens.

Brutus. I do not like this news.

Sicinius. Nor I.

160 *Brutus.* Let's to the Capitol. Would half my wealth
    Would buy this for a lie!

Sicinius.   Pray, let's go.
                     Exeunt Tribunes.

[Scene 7. *A camp not far from Rome.*]

Enter Aufidius with his Lieutenant.

Aufidius. Do they still fly to th' Roman?

Lieutenant. I do not know what witchcraft's in him,
    but
    Your soldiers use him as the grace 'fore meat,
    Their talk at table and their thanks at end;
5   And you are dark'ned° in this action sir,
    Even by your own.°

148 **cry** pack   148 **Shall's** shall us (we)   151 **side** faction   4.7.5 **dark-'ned** put in the shade   6 **your own** your own men

Aufidius.   I cannot help it now,
Unless by using means° I lame the foot
Of our design. He bears himself more proudlier,
Even to my person, than I thought he would
When first I did embrace him; yet his nature   *10*
In that's no changeling,° and I must excuse
What cannot be amended.

Lieutenant.   Yet I wish, sir—
I mean for your particular°—you had not
Joined in commission° with him, but either
Have borne the action of yourself, or else   *15*
To him had left it solely.

Aufidius. I understand thee well; and be thou sure,
When he shall come to his account, he knows not
What I can urge against him. Although it seems,
And so he thinks, and is no less apparent   *20*
To th' vulgar eye, that he bears all things fairly,
And shows good husbandry° for the Volscian state,
Fights dragon-like, and does achieve as soon
As draw his sword. Yet he hath left undone
That which shall break his neck or hazard mine,   *25*
Whene'er we come to our account.

Lieutenant. Sir, I beseech you, think you he'll carry
Rome?

Aufidius. All places yields to him ere he sits down,°
And the nobility of Rome are his;
The senators and patricians love him too.   *30*
The tribunes are no soldiers, and their people
Will be as rash in the repeal, as hasty
To expel him thence. I think he'll be to Rome
As is the osprey° to the fish, who takes it
By sovereignty of nature.° First he was   *35*
A noble servant to them, but he could not

---

7 **using means** taking steps   11 **no changeling** i.e., he is the self-same
man   13 **your particular** your own sake   14 **Joined in commission**
shared the command   22 **husbandry** management   28 **sits down** lays
siege   34 **osprey** fish hawk   35 **By sovereignty of nature** (refers to
the osprey's supposed power of subduing its prey before touching it)

vice a virtue or virtue a vice depending on time

Carry his honors even.° Whether 'twas pride,
Which out of daily fortune ever taints°
The happy° man; whether defect of judgment,
40   To fail in the disposing of those chances
Which he was lord of; or whether nature,
Not to be other than one thing, not moving
From th' casque° to th' cushion,° but commanding peace
Even with the same austerity and garb
45   As he controlled the war; but one of these—
As he hath spices° of them all—not all,
For I dare so far free him—made him feared,
So hated, and so banished. But he has a merit
To choke it in the utt'rance.° So our virtues
50   Lie in th' interpretation of the time;°
And power, unto itself most commendable,
Hath not a tomb so evident as a chair°
T' extol what it hath done.
One fire drives out one fire; one nail, one nail;
55   [Rights by rights founder, strengths by strengths do
         fail.°]
Come, let's away. When, Caius, Rome is thine,
Thou art poor'st of all; then shortly art thou mine.

                                          Exeunt.

★ *Aufidius gives many reasons*
for what has happened to Coriolanus
speculation
assessment of character

37 **even** (and keep his balance) 38 **daily fortune ever taints** success coming day after day always infects 39 **happy** lucky 43 **casque** helmet, i.e., military life 43 **cushion** i.e., position of authority in civil life; cf. 3.1.101 46 **spices** flavors, i.e., traces 48–49 **a merit/To choke it in the utt'rance** a merit that is nullified in the very act of being expressed (because of faults inseparable from the particular virtues being praised) 50 **the time** the age (our contemporaries) 52 **chair** (of the speaker who praises the achievements made possible by "power," line 51; probably with reference to the Roman rostrum, or speakers' platform) 54–55 **One fire ... fail** (examples of the self-destructive process described in lines 48–53)

Complexity of human motivation

ACT 5

[Scene 1. *Rome. A public place.*]

*Enter Menenius, Cominius, Sicinius, Brutus,
the two Tribunes, with others.*

Menenius. No, I'll not go. You hear what he hath
said
Which was sometime° his general, who loved him
In a most dear particular.° He called me father;
But what o' that? Go you that banished him,
A mile before his tent fall down, and knee   5
The way° into his mercy. Nay, if he coyed°
To hear Cominius speak, I'll keep at home.

Cominius. He would not seem to know me.

Menenius.   Do you hear?

Cominius. Yet one time he did call me by my name.
I urged our old acquaintance, and the drops   10
That we have bled together. Coriolanus
He would not answer to; forbad all names;
He was a kind of nothing, titleless,
Till he had forged himself a name o' th' fire
Of burning Rome.

5.1.2 **sometime** formerly   3 **a most dear particular** a most precious
intimacy   5–6 **knee/The way** make your way on your knees   6 **coyed**
showed reluctance

123

15 *Menenius.*   Why, so! You have made good work!
      A pair of tribunes that have wracked° fair Rome
      To make coals° cheap! A noble memory!

   Cominius. I minded° him how royal 'twas to pardon
      When it was less expected; he replied,
20   It was a bare° petition of a state
      To one whom they had punished.

   Menenius.   Very well.
      Could he say less?

   Cominius. I offered° to awaken his regard
      For's private friends. His answer to me was,
25   He could not stay to pick them in a pile
      Of noisome musty chaff. He said 'twas folly,
      For one poor grain or two, to leave unburnt
      And still to nose th' offense.°

   Menenius.   For one poor grain or two!
      I am one of those; his mother, wife, his child,
30   And this brave fellow too, we are the grains;
      You are the musty chaff, and you are smelt
      Above the moon. We must be burnt for you.

   Sicinius. Nay, pray, be patient; if you refuse your aid
      In this so never-needed° help, yet do not
35   Upbraid's with our distress. But, sure, if you
      Would be your country's pleader, your good tongue,
      More than the instant army we can make,°
      Might stop our countryman.

   Menenius.   No, I'll not meddle.

   Sicinius. Pray you, go to him.

   Menenius.   What should I do?

40 *Brutus.* Only make trial what your love can do
      For Rome, towards° Marcius.

---

16 **wracked** ruined   17 **coals** charcoal   18 **minded** reminded   20
bare mere   23 **offered** tried   28 **nose th' offense** smell the offensive
stuff   34 **so never-needed** never so needed (as now)   37 **the instant
army we can make** the army we can raise at this time   41 **towards** in
relation to

Menenius.   Well, and say that Marcius
   Return me, as Cominius is returned,
   Unheard—what then?
   But as a discontented friend, grief-shot°
   With his unkindness? Say't be so?

Sicinius.   Yet your good will   45
   Must have that thanks from Rome after the measure
   As you intended well.°

Menenius.   I'll undertake't:
   I think he'll hear me. Yet to bite his lip
   And hum at good Cominius much unhearts° me.
   He was not taken well;° he had not dined.   50
   The veins unfilled, our blood is cold, and then
   We pout upon the morning, are unapt
   To give or to forgive; but when we have stuffed
   These pipes and these conveyances° of our blood
   With wine and feeding, we have suppler souls   55
   Than in our priestlike fasts. Therefore I'll watch
     him
   Till he be dieted to° my request,
   And then I'll set upon him.

Brutus. You know the very road into his kindness,
   And cannot lose your way.

Menenius.   Good faith, I'll prove° him,   60
   Speed° how it will. I shall ere long have knowledge
   Of my success.   *Exit.*

Cominius.   He'll never hear him.

Sicinius.   Not?

Cominius. I tell you he does sit in gold, his eye
   Red as 'twould burn Rome, and his injury°
   The jailer to his pity. I kneeled before him;   65

---

44 **grief-shot** struck by grief 46–47 **after the measure/As you
intended well** in proportion to your good intentions 49 **unhearts** dis-
courages 50 **taken well** approached at a good time 54 **conveyances**
channels 57 **dieted to** prepared for by feeding 60 **prove** make trial
of 61 **Speed** turn out 64 **injury** sense of the wrong done to him

'Twas very faintly he said "Rise"; dismissed me
Thus with his speechless hand. What he would do
He sent in writing after me, what he would not,
Bound with an oath to yield° to his conditions;
70 So that all hope is vain,°
Unless° his noble mother and his wife,
Who (as I hear) mean to solicit him
For mercy to his country. Therefore, let's hence,
And with our fair entreaties haste them on.

                                        Exeunt.

[Scene 2. *Entrance of the Volscian camp
before Rome.*]

Enter Menenius to the Watch on Guard.

First Watch. Stay. Whence are you?

Second Watch.   Stand, and go back.

Menenius. You guard like men, 'tis well; but, by your
        leave,
    I am an officer of state, and come
    To speak with Coriolanus.

First Watch.   From whence?

Menenius.   From Rome.

First Watch. You may not pass, you must return: our
5   general
    Will no more hear from thence.

67–69 **What ... yield** i.e., he sent a written message saying what he
would do and what he would not, all this (the statement of terms) being
bound with an oath that we should yield (text probably corrupt)   70
vain (because the conditions are ruinous)   71 **Unless** except for (or perhaps "solicit him," line 72, is to be understood: "unless his noble mother
and his wife solicit him")

Second Watch. You'll see your Rome embraced with
   fire, before
   You'll speak with Coriolanus.

Menenius.   Good my friends,
   If you have heard your general talk of Rome
   And of his friends there, it is lots to blanks°   10
   My name hath touched your ears: it is Menenius.

First Watch. Be it so; go back. The virtue of your
   name
   Is not here passable.°

Menenius.   I tell thee, fellow,
   Thy general is my lover. I have been
   The book of his good acts whence men have read   15
   His fame unparalleled—haply amplified;
   For I have ever verified° my friends
   (Of whom he's chief) with all the size that verity
   Would without lapsing° suffer. Nay, sometimes,
   Like to a bowl upon a subtle° ground,   20
   I have tumbled past the throw,° and in his praise
   Have almost stamped° the leasing.° Therefore,
      fellow,
   I must have leave to pass.

First Watch. Faith, sir, if you had told as many lies
   in his behalf as you have uttered words in your   25
   own, you should not pass here; no, though it were
   as virtuous to lie as to live chastely. Therefore go
   back.

Menenius. Prithee, fellow, remember my name is
   Menenius, always factionary° on the party of your   30
   general.

5.2.10 **lots to blanks** (more than an even chance; "lots" refers to tickets
in a lottery taking prizes; "blanks," to those not taking prizes)   13 **passable** current (of money, but with a pun on "password")   17 **verified** tes-
tified to the merit of   19 **lapsing** slipping (into error)   20 **subtle**
deceptive   21 **tumbled past the throw** rolled beyond the proper dis-
tance   22 **stamped** given currency to (cf. "stamp" a coin)   22 **leasing**
falsehood   30 **factionary** an active worker

Second Watch. Howsoever you have been his liar, as
you say you have, I am one that, telling true under
him, must say you cannot pass. Therefore go back.

35 *Menenius.* Has he dined, canst thou tell? For I would
not speak with him till after dinner.

First Watch. You are a Roman, are you?

Menenius. I am, as thy general is.

First Watch. Then you should hate Rome, as he does.
40 Can you, when you have pushed out your gates the
very defender of them, and in a violent popular
ignorance given your enemy your shield, think to
front° his revenges with the easy groans of old
women, the virginal palms of your daughters, or
45 with the palsied intercession of such a decayed
dotant° as you seem to be? Can you think to blow
out the intended fire your city is ready to flame in,
with such weak breath as this? No, you are deceived; therefore, back to Rome, and prepare for
50 your execution. You are condemned; our general
has sworn you out of reprieve and pardon.

Menenius. Sirrah, if thy captain knew I were here, he
would use me with estimation.°

First Watch. Come, my captain knows you not.

55 *Menenius.* I mean, thy general.

First Watch. My general cares not for you. Back, I
say; go, lest I let forth your half-pint of blood.
Back—that's the utmost of your having.° Back.

Menenius. Nay, but, fellow, fellow—

Enter Coriolanus with Aufidius.

60 *Coriolanus.* What's the matter?

Menenius. Now, you companion,° I'll say an errand°

43 **front** face   46 **dotant** dotard   53 **estimation** esteem   58 **of your
having** you can get   61 **companion** fellow   61 **say an errand** give a
message

for you; you shall know now that I am in estimation; you shall perceive that a Jack guardant° cannot office me° from my son Coriolanus. Guess but
by my entertainment° with him if thou stand'st not   65
i' th' state of hanging, or of some death more long
in spectatorship and crueller in suffering; behold
now presently, and swoon for what's to come upon
thee. [*To Coriolanus*] The glorious gods sit in
hourly synod about thy particular prosperity, and   70
love thee no worse than thy old father Menenius
does! O my son, my son! Thou art preparing fire
for us; look thee, here's water to quench it. I was
hardly° moved to come to thee; but being assured
none but myself could move thee, I have been   75
blown out of your° gates with sighs; and conjure
thee to pardon Rome and thy petitionary° countrymen. The good gods assuage thy wrath, and turn
the dregs of it upon this varlet here; this, who, like
a block,° hath denied my access to thee.   80

Coriolanus. Away!

Menenius. How! Away!

Coriolanus. Wife, mother, child, I know not. My
    affairs
Are servanted° to others. Though I owe
My revenge properly,° my remission° lies   85
In Volscian breasts. That we have been familiar,°
Ingrate forgetfulness° shall poison rather
Than pity note how much.° Therefore be gone.
Mine ears against your suits are stronger than
Your gates against my force. Yet, for° I loved thee,   90
Take this along; I writ it for thy sake,

63 **Jack guardant** wretch of a sentry   64 **office me** use his office to
keep me   65 **entertainment** reception   74 **hardly** with difficulty   76
your (of Rome)   77 **petitionary** who are asking for mercy   80 **block**
blockhead   84 **servanted** subject (servant-like)   84–85 **I owe/My
revenge properly** my revenge belongs to me alone   85 **remission**
power to pardon   86 **That we have been familiar** our intimacy in the
past   87 **Ingrate forgetfulness** my ungrateful forgetfulness   88 **how
much** (how much "we have been familiar," how great the intimacy was)
90 **for** because

And would have sent it. Another word, Menenius,
I will not hear thee speak. This man, Aufidius,
Was my beloved in Rome; yet thou behold'st.

95 *Aufidius.* You keep a constant° temper.

Exeunt [Coriolanus and Aufidius].
Manet the Guard and Menenius.

First Watch. Now, sir, is your name Menenius?

Second Watch. 'Tis a spell, you see, of much power.
You know the way home again.

First Watch. Do you hear how we are shent°
100   keeping your greatness back?

Second Watch. What cause, do you think, I have to
swoon?

Menenius. I neither care for th' world nor your general. For such things as you, I can scarce think
105   there's any, y'are so slight. He that hath a will to
die by himself° fears it not from another. Let your
general do his worst. For you, be that you are,
long; and your misery increase with your age! I
say to you, as I was said to, Away!   *Exit.*

110 *First Watch.* A noble fellow, I warrant him.

Second Watch. The worthy fellow is our general. He's
the rock, the oak not to be wind-shaken.

Exit Watch.

---

95 **constant** loyal, true   99 **shent** scolded   106 **by himself** by his
own hand

[Scene 3. *The tent of Coriolanus.*]

Enter Coriolanus and Aufidius [with others].

Coriolanus. We will before the walls of Rome to-
    morrow
    Set down° our host. My partner in this action,
    You must report to th' Volscian lords how plainly°
    I have borne° this business.

Aufidius.   Only their ends
    You have respected; stopped your ears against   5
    The general suit of Rome; never admitted
    A private whisper—no, not with such friends
    That thought them sure of you.

Coriolanus.   This last old man,
    Whom with a cracked heart I have sent to Rome,
    Loved me above the measure of a father,   10
    Nay, godded me° indeed. Their latest refuge°
    Was to send him; for whose old love I have
    (Though I showed° sourly to him) once more
        offered
    The first conditions, which they did refuse
    And cannot now accept; to grace° him only   15
    That thought he could do more, a very little
    I have yielded to. Fresh embassies and suits,
    Nor° from the state nor private friends, hereafter
    Will I lend ear to. (*Shout within*). Ha! What shout
    · is this?
    Shall I be tempted to infringe my vow   20
    In the same time 'tis made? I will not.

5.3.2 **Set down** i.e., in a siege 3 **plainly** openly 4 **borne** conducted
11 **godded me** made me a god 11 **latest refuge** last resource 13
showed appeared 15 **grace** honor 18 **Nor** neither

Transcendence but misguided – blindness

*Enter Virgilia, Volumnia, Valeria, young Marcius,
with Attendants.*

My wife comes foremost; then the honored mold°
Wherein this trunk° was framed, and in her hand
The grandchild to her blood. But out, affection!
25 All bond and privilege of nature, break!
Let it be virtuous to be obstinate.
What is that curtsy worth? Or those doves' eyes,
Which can make gods forsworn? I melt, and am not
Of stronger earth° than others. My mother bows,
30 As if Olympus° to a molehill should
In supplication nod; and my young boy
Hath an aspect of intercession which
Great Nature cries "Deny not." Let the Volsces
Plough Rome, and harrow Italy! I'll never
35 Be such a gosling to° obey instinct, but stand
As if a man were author of himself
And knew no other kin.

Virgilia.   My lord and husband!

Coriolanus. These eyes are not the same I wore in
Rome.

Virgilia. The sorrow that delivers° us thus changed
Makes you think so.

40 *Coriolanus.*   Like a dull actor now,
I have forgot my part and I am out,°
Even to a full disgrace.—Best of my flesh,
Forgive my tyranny;° but do not say,
For that, "Forgive our Romans." O, a kiss
45 Long as my exile, sweet as my revenge!
Now, by the jealous queen of heaven,° that kiss
I carried from thee, dear, and my true lip
Hath virgined it e'er since. You gods! I prate,°
And the most noble mother of the world

22–37 (See Introduction, p. lxxxi) **22 mold** form (also "earth") **23
trunk** body **28–29 not/Of stronger earth** cf. "our common clay" **30
Olympus** a mountain, home of the Greek gods **35 to** as to **39 delivers**
presents **41 out** speechless ("stuck") **43 tyranny** cruelty **46 queen
of heaven** Juno, guardian of marriage **48 prate** babble

Leave unsaluted. Sink, my knee, i' th' earth; *Kneels.* 50
Of thy deep duty° more impression° show
Than that of common sons.

Volumnia.   O, stand up blest!
  Whilst with no softer cushion than the flint
  I kneel before thee, and unproperly°
  Show duty, as mistaken all this while   55
  Between the child and parent.   [*Kneels.*]

Coriolanus.   What's this?
  Your knees to me? To your corrected° son?
  Then let the pebbles on the hungry° beach
  Fillip° the stars! Then let the mutinous winds
  Strike the proud cedars 'gainst the fiery sun,   60
  Murd'ring impossibility, to make
  What cannot be, slight work.

Volumnia.   Thou art my warrior;
  I holp to frame thee. Do you know this lady?

Coriolanus. The noble sister of Publicola,
  The moon of Rome, chaste as the icicle   65
  That's curdied° by the frost from purest snow
  And hangs on Dian's temple—dear Valeria!

Volumnia. This is a poor epitome° of yours,°
  Which by th' interpretation of full time°
  May show° like all yourself.

Coriolanus.   The god of soldiers,°   70
  With the consent of supreme Jove, inform°
  Thy thoughts with nobleness, that thou mayst
    prove
  To shame unvulnerable, and stick° i' th' wars

---

51 **duty** reverence 51 **impression** i.e., "i' th' earth" 54 **unproperly**
(defined by lines 55–56: in a way that does not belong to me, as though I
had always misunderstood the relation between child and parent) 57
corrected who is corrected (by your kneeling) 58 **hungry** barren 59
Fillip strike 66 **curdied** congealed 68 **epitome** brief but compre-
hensive version of a larger work 68 **of yours** belonging to you, of you
69 **time** ("time" is compared to a commentator on a text) 70 **show**
appear 70 **god of soldiers** Mars, Coriolanus' special divinity 71
inform imbue (give an inner form or character to) 73 **stick** stand out

Like a great sea-mark,° standing every flaw,°
And saving those that eye thee!

75 *Volumnia.*   Your knee, sirrah.°

Coriolanus. That's my brave boy!

Volumnia. Even he, your wife, this lady, and myself
Are suitors to you.

Coriolanus.   I beseech you, peace!
Or, if you'd ask, remember this before:
80 The thing I have forsworn° to grant may never
Be held by you denials.° Do not bid me
Dismiss my soldiers, or capitulate°
Again with Rome's mechanics.° Tell me not
Wherein I seem unnatural. Desire not
85 T' allay my rages and revenges with
Your colder reasons.

Volumnia.   O, no more, no more!
You have said you will not grant us anything;
For we have nothing else to ask but that
Which you deny already. Yet we will ask,
90 That, if you fail in° our request, the blame
May hang upon your hardness. Therefore hear us.

Coriolanus. Aufidius, and you Volsces, mark; for
we'll
Hear nought from Rome in private. Your request?

Volumnia. Should we be silent and not speak, our
raiment
95 And state of bodies would bewray° what life
We have led since thy exile. Think with thyself
How more unfortunate than all living women
Are we come hither; since that thy sight, which
should

---

74 **a great sea-mark** some prominent object that guides mariners (cf.
"landmark," the common modern term)   74 **flaw** gust of wind   75
sirrah sir (affectionately)   80 **forsworn** sworn not to   81 **denials** i.e.,
refusals to all of you (therefore, plural)   82 **capitulate** arrange terms
83 **mechanics** manual laborers   90 **fail in** fail to grant   95 **bewray**
reveal

Make our eyes flow with joy, hearts dance with
    comforts,
Constrains them weep and shake with fear and
    sorrow,   *100*
Making the mother, wife, and child, to see
The son, the husband, and the father, tearing
His country's bowels out. And to poor we°
Thine enmity's most capital:° thou barr'st us
Our prayers to the gods, which is a comfort   *105*
That all but we enjoy. For how can we,
Alas, how can we for our country pray,
Whereto we are bound, together with thy victory,
Whereto we are bound? Alack, or° we must lose
The country, our dear nurse, or else thy person, *110*
Our comfort in the country. We must find
An evident° calamity, though we had
Our wish, which side should win; for either thou
Must as a foreign recreant° be led
With manacles through our streets, or else   *115*
Triumphantly tread on thy country's ruin,
And bear the palm for having bravely shed
Thy wife and children's blood. For myself, son,
I purpose not to wait on fortune till
These wars determine.° If I can not persuade thee *120*
Rather to show a noble grace° to both parts°
Than seek the end of one, thou shalt no sooner
March to assault thy country than to tread
(Trust to't, thou shalt not) on thy mother's womb
That brought thee to this world.

Virgilia.   Ay, and mine,   *125*
That brought you forth this boy, to keep your name
Living to time.°

Boy.   'A° shall not tread on me;
I'll run away till I am bigger, but then I'll fight.

---

103 **we** (for "us")   104 **capital** deadly   109 **or** either   112 **evident**
certain   114 **recreant** traitor   120 **determine** come to an end   121
grace consideration, favor   121 **parts** sides (parties)   126–127 **keep
your name/Living to time** perpetuate your name (keep living as long as
time lasts)   127 **'A** he

Coriolanus. Not of a woman's tenderness to be,
130   Requires nor child nor woman's face to see.
        I have sat too long.

Volumnia.   Nay, go not from us thus.
                                        [*Rises.*]

        If it were so that our request did tend
        To save the Romans, thereby to destroy
        The Volsces whom you serve, you might condemn
        us,
135   As poisonous of your honor. No, our suit
        Is that you reconcile them; while the Volsces
        May say "This mercy we have showed," the
        Romans,
        "This we received"; and each in either side
        Give the all-hail to thee, and cry "Be blest
        For making up this peace!" Thou know'st, great
140   son,
        The end of war's uncertain; but this certain,
        That, if thou conquer Rome, the benefit
        Which thou shalt thereby reap is such a name
        Whose repetition will be dogged with curses,
145   Whose chronicle thus writ,° "The man was noble,
        But with his last attempt° he wiped it° out,
        Destroyed his country, and his name remains
        To th' ensuing age abhorred." Speak to me, son.
        Thou hast affected the fine strains° of honor,
150   To imitate the graces of the gods,°
        To tear with thunder the wide cheeks o' th' air,
        And yet to charge° thy sulphur° with a bolt
        That should but rive an oak. Why dost not speak?
        Think'st thou it honorable for a noble man
155   Still to remember wrongs? Daughter, speak you:
        He cares not for your weeping. Speak thou, boy:
        Perhaps thy childishness will move him more

---

145 **writ** will be written   146 **attempt** undertaking   146 **it** (his nobility)   149 **affected the fine strains** aimed at the refinements   150
graces of the gods (qualities that give the gods splendor and power; illustrated with irony, lines 151–53)   152 **charge** load (make heavy, or
"load," as of a gun)   152 **sulphur** lightning (see Introduction, p. lxxxiii)

appeal of mother
argument of honor

Than can our reasons. There's no man in the world
More bound to's mother, yet here he lets me prate
Like one i' th' stocks. Thou hast never in thy life   160
Showed thy dear mother any courtesy,
When she (poor hen) fond of° no second brood,
Has clocked° thee to the wars, and safely home
Loaden° with honor. Say my request's unjust,
And spurn me back. But if it be not so,   165
Thou art not honest,° and the gods will plague thee
That thou restrain'st from me the duty which
To a mother's part belongs. He turns away.
Down, ladies! Let us shame him with our knees.
To his surname Coriolanus 'longs more pride   170
Than pity to our prayers. Down! An end;
This is the last. So we will home to Rome,
And die among our neighbors. Nay, behold's!°
This boy, that cannot tell what he would have,
But kneels and holds up hands for fellowship,   175
Does reason° our petition with more strength
Than thou hast to deny't. Come, let us go.
This fellow had a Volscian to his mother;
His wife is in Corioles, and his child
Like him by chance. Yet give us our dispatch.°   180
I am hushed until our city be a-fire,
And then I'll speak a little.

                    Holds her by the hand, silent.

Coriolanus.   O mother, mother!
What have you done? Behold, the heavens do ope,
The gods look down, and this unnatural scene
They laugh at. O my mother, mother! O!   185
You have won a happy victory to Rome;
But, for your son—believe it, O, believe it!—
Most dangerously you have with him prevailed,
If not most mortal to° him. But let it come.
Aufidius, though I cannot make true wars,   190
I'll frame convenient° peace. Now, good Aufidius,

162 **fond of** eager for   163 **clocked** clucked   164 **Loaden** laden
166 **honest** honorable   173 **behold's** behold us   176 **reason** plead
for   180 **dispatch** dismissal   189 **mortal to** with deadly results for
191 **convenient** fitting

Were you in my stead, would you have heard
A mother less? Or granted less, Aufidius?

Aufidius. I was moved withal.°

Coriolanus. I dare be sworn you were!
195 And, sir, it is no little thing to make
Mine eyes to sweat compassion. But, good sir,
What peace you'll make, advise me. For my part,
I'll not to Rome, I'll back with you; and pray you
Stand to° me in this cause. O mother! Wife!

Aufidius. [*Aside*] I am glad thou hast set thy mercy
200 and thy honor
At difference in thee. Out of that I'll work
Myself a former fortune.°

Coriolanus. [*To Volumnia and Virgilia*] Ay, by and
by;
But we will drink together; and you shall bear
A better witness back than words, which° we
205 On like conditions will have countersealed.
Come, enter with us. Ladies, you deserve
To have a temple° built you. All the swords
In Italy, and her confederate arms,°
Could not have made this peace. *Exeunt.*

[*Scene 4. Rome. A public place.*]

Enter Menenius and Sicinius.

Menenius. See you yond coign° o' th' Capitol, yond
cornerstone?

194 **withal** by it (thereby) 199 **Stand to** stand by 201–2
work/Myself a former fortune regain my former position and
power 204 **which** i.e., the written document 207 **temple** (of the Fortune of Women; see Plutarch, p. 193) 208 **confederate arms** allied
powers 5.4.1 **coign** corner

Sicinius. Why, what of that?

Menenius. If it be possible for you to displace it with
your little finger, there is some hope the ladies of   5
Rome, especially his mother, may prevail with him.
But I say there is no hope in't; our throats are sentenced, and stay upon° execution.

Sicinius. Is't possible that so short a time can alter the
condition of a man?   10

Menenius. There is difference between a grub and a
butterfly; yet your butterfly was a grub. This Marcius is grown from man to dragon: he has wings;
he's more than a creeping thing.

Sicinius. He loved his mother dearly.   15

Menenius. So did he me; and he no more remembers
his mother now than an eight-year-old horse. The
tartness of his face sours ripe grapes. When he
walks, he moves like an engine° and the ground
shrinks before his treading. He is able to pierce a   20
corslet° with his eye, talks like a knell, and his
hum° is a battery.° He sits in his state° as a thing
made for Alexander.° What he bids be done is finished with his bidding. He wants nothing of a god
but eternity and a heaven to throne in.   25

Sicinius. Yes, mercy, if you report him truly.

Menenius. I paint him in the character. Mark what
mercy his mother shall bring from him. There is no
more mercy in him than there is milk in a male
tiger; that shall our poor city find. And all this is   30
'long of° you.

Sicinius. The gods be good unto us!

Menenius. No, in such a case the gods will not be

8 **stay upon** wait for   19 **engine** machine of war   21 **corslet** body
armor   21–22 **his hum** i.e., his saying "Hum!"   22 **battery** beating of
drums for an attack   22 **state** chair of state   22–23 **thing made for
Alexander** image of Alexander the Great   31 **'long of** along of,
because of

good unto us. When we banished him, we respected
35 not them; and, he returning to break our necks,
they respect not us.

Enter a Messenger.

Messenger. Sir, if you'd save your life, fly to your
house.
The plebeians have got your fellow-tribune,
And hale° him up and down; all swearing if
40 The Roman ladies bring not comfort home
They'll give him death by inches.

Enter another Messenger.

Sicinius.   What's the news?

Second Messenger. Good news, good news! The ladies
have prevailed,
The Volscians are dislodged,° and Marcius gone.
A merrier day did never yet greet Rome,
No, not th' expulsion of the Tarquins.

45 *Sicinius.*   Friend,
Art thou certain this is true? Is't most certain?

Second Messenger. As certain as I know the sun is
fire.
Where have you lurked,° that you make doubt
of it?
Ne'er through an arch so hurried the blown° tide,
As the recomforted through th' gates. Why, hark
50 you!
        Trumpets, hautboys;° drums beat; all together.
The trumpets, sackbuts,° psalteries,° and fifes,
Tabors° and cymbals, and the shouting Romans,
Make the sun dance. Hark you! (*A shout within.*)

Menenius.   This is good news.
I will go meet the ladies. This Volumnia

39 **hale** haul   43 **are dislodged** have broken up camp   48 **lurked**
been hiding   49 **blown** swollen (by wind)   50 s.d. **hautboy** (original
of the modern oboe)   51 **sackbuts** trombones   51 **psalteries** harplike
stringed instruments   52 **Tabors** small drums

Is worth of consuls, senators, patricians,   55
A city full; of tribunes such as you,
A sea and land full. You have prayed well today.
This morning for ten thousand of your throats
I'd not have given a doit. Hark, how they joy!
                    Sound still with the shouts.

Sicinius. First, the gods bless you for your tidings;
    next,   60
Accept my thankfulness.

Second Messenger.   Sir, we have all
Great cause to give great thanks.

Sicinius.   They are near the city!

Second Messenger. Almost at point to enter.

Sicinius.   We'll meet them,
And help the joy.   *Exeunt.*

[Scene 5. *Rome. Near the gate.*]

*Enter two Senators, with Ladies, passing over the
            Stage, with other Lords.*

First Senator. Behold our patroness, the life of Rome!
Call all your tribes together, praise the gods,
And make triumphant fires; strew flowers before
    them.
Unshout the noise that banished Marcius,
Repeal° him with the welcome of his mother.   5
Cry "Welcome, ladies, welcome!"

All.   Welcome, ladies,
Welcome!
            A flourish with drums and trumpets.

5.5.5 **Repeal** recall

[Scene 6. *Corioli. A public place.*]

Enter Tullus Aufidius, with Attendants.

Aufidius. Go tell the lords o' th' city I am here.
   Deliver them this paper. Having read it,
   Bid them repair to th' marketplace, where I,
   Even in theirs and in the commons' ears,
5 Will vouch the truth of it. Him° I accuse
   The city ports° by this hath entered, and
   Intends t' appear before the people, hoping
   To purge himself with words. Dispatch.

                              [*Exeunt Attendants.*]

Enter three or four Conspirators of Aufidius' faction.

   Most welcome!

First Conspirator. How is it with our general?

10 *Aufidius.*   Even so
   As with a man by his own alms empoisoned,°
   And with° his charity slain.

Second Conspirator.   Most noble sir,
   If you do hold the same intent wherein
   You wished us parties,° we'll deliver you
   Of your great danger.

15 *Aufidius.*   Sir, I cannot tell;
   We must proceed as we do find the people.

Third Conspirator. The people will remain uncertain
      whilst
   'Twixt you there's difference; but the fall of either
   Makes the survivor heir of all.

5.6.5 **Him** he whom   6 **ports** gates   11 **empoisoned** destroyed   12
with by   14 **parties** partisans

Aufidius.   I know it,
And my pretext to strike at him admits   20
A good construction. I raised him, and I pawned°
Mine honor for his truth;° who being so heightened,
He watered his new plants with dews of flattery,
Seducing so my friends; and, to this end,
He bowed his nature, never known before   25
But to be rough, unswayable, and free.

Third Conspirator. Sir, his stoutness°
When he did stand for consul, which he lost
By lack of stooping—

Aufidius.   That I would have spoke of.
Being banished for't, he came unto my hearth,   30
Presented to my knife his throat. I took him,
Made him joint-servant with me;° gave him way°
In all his own desires; nay, let him choose
Out of my files,° his projects to accomplish,
My best and freshest men; served his designments°   35
In mine own person; holp to reap the fame
Which he did end° all his; and took some pride
To do myself this wrong; till at the last
I seemed his follower, not partner; and
He waged me with his countenance,° as if   40
I had been mercenary.°

First Conspirator.   So he did, my lord.
The army marveled at it; and, in the last,°
When he had carried° Rome and that we looked
For no less spoil than glory—

Aufidius.   There was it;°
For which my sinews° shall be stretched upon° him.   45
At° a few drops of women's rheum,° which are

21 **pawned** staked   22 **truth** loyalty   27 **stoutness** proud obstinacy
32 **joint-servant with me** sharer of my service (to the state)   32 **gave
him way** humored him   34 **files** ranks   35 **designments** designs   37
end get in (of crops)   40 **waged me with his countenance** for wages
gave me patronizing looks   41 **mercenary** serving for pay   42 **in the
last** in the last place, finally   43 **carried** won   44 **There was it** that
was the crucial thing   45 **sinews** i.e., strength   45 **upon** against   46
At at the price of   46 **rheum** tears

As cheap as lies, he sold the blood and labor
Of our great action. Therefore shall he die,
And I'll renew me in his fall. But hark!

> *Drums and trumpets sounds, with great shouts*
> *of the people.*

First Conspirator. Your native town you entered like
50   a post,°
And had no welcomes home; but he returns,
Splitting the air with noise.

Second Conspirator.   And patient fools,
Whose children he hath slain, their base throats
      tear
With giving him glory.

Third Conspirator.   Therefore, at your vantage,°
55   Ere he express himself or move the people
With what he would say, let him feel your sword,
Which we will second.° When he lies along,°
After your way his tale pronounced° shall bury
His reasons with his body.

Aufidius.   Say no more:
60   Here come the lords.

> *Enter the Lords of the city.*

All Lords. You are most welcome home.

Aufidius.   I have not deserved it.
But, worthy lords, have you with heed perused
What I have written to you?

All [Lords].   We have.

First Lord.   And grieve to hear't.
What faults he made before the last, I think
65   Might have found easy fines;° but there to end
Where he was to begin, and give away

---

50 **post** messenger 54 **at your vantage** at a moment opportune for
you 57 **second** support (with our swords) 57 **along** stretched at full
length 58 **After your way his tale pronounced** his story told in your
version 65 **fines** penalties

The benefit of our levies,° answering us
With our own charge,° making a treaty where
There was a yielding—this admits no excuse.

Aufidius. He approaches. You shall hear him.   *70*

*Enter Coriolanus, marching with drum and colors,
        the commoners being with him.*

Coriolanus. Hail, lords! I am returned your soldier;
No more infected° with my country's love
Than when I parted° hence, but still subsisting°
Under your great command. You are to know
That prosperously I have attempted, and   *75*
With bloody passage° led your wars even to
The gates of Rome. Our spoils we have brought
    home
Doth more than counterpoise a full third part
The charges° of the action. We have made peace
With no less honor to the Antiates   *80*
Than shame to th' Romans; and we here deliver,
Subscribed° by th' consuls and patricians,
Together with the seal o' th' senate, what
We have compounded° on.

Aufidius.   Read it not, noble lords;
But tell the traitor in the highest degree   *85*
He hath abused your powers.

Coriolanus. Traitor! How now!

Aufidius.   Ay, traitor, Marcius!

Coriolanus.   Marcius!

Aufidius. Ay, Marcius, Caius Marcius! Dost thou
    think
I'll grace° thee with that robbery, thy stol'n name
Coriolanus, in Corioles?   *90*

67 **our levies** the armies we raised   67–68 **answering us/With our
own charge** paying us (only) with our own expenditure   72 **infected**
(see Introduction, p. lxxxiv)   73 **parted** departed   73 **subsisting**
remaining   76 **passage** action   78–79 **more ... charges** exceed the
costs by a whole third (cf. line 68)   82 **Subscribed** signed   84 **com-
pounded** agreed   89 **grace** honor

You lords and heads o' th' state, perfidiously
He has betrayed your business and given up,
For certain drops of salt, your city Rome,
I say "your city," to his wife and mother;
95   Breaking his oath and resolution, like
A twist° of rotten silk; never admitting
Counsel o' th' war; but at his nurse's tears
He whined and roared away your victory;
That° pages blushed at him, and men of heart°
Looked wond'ring each at others.

100 *Coriolanus.*   Hear'st thou, Mars?

Aufidius. Name not the god, thou boy of tears!

Coriolanus.   Ha!

Aufidius. No more.

Coriolanus. Measureless liar, thou hast made my
        heart
Too great for what contains it. "Boy"! O slave!
105   Pardon me, lords, 'tis the first time that ever
I was forced to scold. Your judgments, my grave
        lords,
Must give this cur the lie; and his own notion°—
Who wears my stripes impressed upon him, that
Must bear my beating to his grave—shall join
110   To thrust the lie unto him.

First Lord. Peace, both, and hear me speak.

Coriolanus. Cut me to pieces, Volsces, men and lads,
Stain all your edges on me. "Boy"! False hound!
If you have writ your annals true, 'tis there,°
115   That, like an eagle in a dovecote, I
Fluttered your Volscians in Corioles.
Alone I did it. "Boy"?

Aufidius.   Why, noble lords,

96 **twist** thread (made of more than one strand)   99 **That** so that   99
of heart of spirit   107 **notion** understanding   114 **there** (written)
there

Will you be put in mind of his blind fortune,°
Which was your shame, by this unholy braggart,
'Fore your own eyes and ears?

All Conspirators.　　　　　　　Let him die for't.　　120

All People. Tear him to pieces!—Do it presently!°—
He killed my son!—My daughter!—He killed my
cousin Marcius!—He killed my father!

Second Lord. Peace, ho! no outrage, peace!
The man is noble, and his fame folds in°　　125
This orb o' th' earth. His last offenses to us
Shall have judicious° hearing. Stand,° Aufidius,
And trouble not the peace.

Coriolanus.　　　　　　　O that I had him,
With six Aufidiuses or more—his tribe,
To use my lawful sword!

Aufidius.　　　　　　　Insolent villain!　　130

All Conspirators. Kill, kill, kill, kill, kill him!
　　Draw the Conspirators and kill Marcius, who falls.
　　　　　　　　Aufidius stands on him.

Lords.　　　　　　　Hold, hold, hold, hold!

Aufidius. My noble masters, hear me speak.

First Lord.　　　　　　　O Tullus!

Second Lord. Thou hast done a deed whereat valor
　　will weep.

Third Lord. Tread not upon him. Masters all, be
　　quiet;
Put up your swords.　　135

Aufidius. My lords, when you shall know—as in this
　　rage
Provoked by him, you cannot—the great danger
Which this man's life did owe you,° you'll rejoice

---

118 **blind fortune** mere good luck (Fortune is a blind goddess)　121
presently at once　125 **folds in** embraces　127 **judicious** judicial
127 **Stand** stop　138 **did owe you** held in payment for you

That he is thus cut off. Please it your honors
140 To call me to your senate, I'll deliver°
       Myself your loyal servant, or endure
       Your heaviest censure.°

     First Lord.   Bear from hence his body,
       And mourn you for him. Let him be regarded
       As the most noble corse° that ever herald
       Did follow to his urn.

145 *Second Lord.*   His own impatience
       Takes from Aufidius a great part of blame.
       Let's make the best of it.

     Aufidius.   My rage is gone,
       And I am struck with sorrow. Take him up.
       Help, three o' th' chiefest soldiers; I'll be one.
150 Beat thou the drum, that it speak mournfully;
       Trail your steel pikes. Though in this city he
       Hath widowed and unchilded many a one,
       Which to this hour bewail the injury,
       Yet he shall have a noble memory.°
155 Assist.

                    Exeunt bearing the body of Marcius.
                    A dead march sounded.

                    FINIS

___

140 **deliver** prove 142 **censure** sentence 144 **corse** corpse 154 **memory** memorial

Textual Note

The text of *Coriolanus* has survived only in the First Folio (1623), on which the present edition is based. There are no records of performances earlier than 1623, but there is a mocking imitation of the curious phrase, "lurched all swords of the garland" (2.2.102), in Ben Jonson's *Epicoene, or The Silent Woman* (1609). It is therefore almost certain that the play was written and performed not later than 1609. The use in Menenius' fable of the body and its members of expressions from William Camden's *Remains* of 1605 and the probable allusion to the Midlands revolt of 1607 point to a date of 1607 or later. (See "The Source of *Coriolanus*," p. 154.) There is also the possible reference to the Great Frost of 1607–08 in the phrase "the coal of fire upon the ice" (1.1.174). It seems safe to assume that *Coriolanus* was written after *Antony and Cleopatra,* somewhere between 1607 and 1609.

The Folio text of *Coriolanus* might be described, like that of *The Tempest,* as a distinguished one; it was prepared with great care and is especially remarkable for its elaborate stage directions. W. W. Greg's assertion that the text was printed from the author's manuscript is now widely accepted. The stage directions, presumably Shakespeare's own, are those of a man of the theater who has his eye on the stage and the actors. For example: *"Enter Marcius and Aufidius, at several doors"* (1.8); *"They all bustle about Coriolanus"* (3.1.184); and the most telling gesture of the play, *"Holds her by the hand, silent"* (5.3.182).

But though the text brings us so close to the practicing hand of the poet-playwright, it was edited and printed by mortal men. It has a fairly high number of errors, and emendations have been found necessary in at least twenty to twenty-five places. One line has been omitted (2.3.249), and in two passages the style is so cryptic as to seem almost surely corrupt (3.2.74–80; 5.1.67–69). The most disturbing defect of the Folio text of *Coriolanus* is the widespread mislineation. There are many lines that are either too short or too long, as measured by the usual blank-verse norm, and it is often very hard to determine where the line division should occur. Most of these abnormalities, it has been pointed out, come in short speeches, or at the end or beginning of speeches in rapid dialogue. There are a relatively few instances in which speeches are assigned to seemingly inappropriate speakers. There are also variations in the names of speakers, most of them of little significance, and usually in names of minor persons. The town that gives the hero his honorific title is usually called "Corioles," though "Coriolus" and "Corialus" also occur. There is considerable uncertainty as to how both "Corioles" and "Coriolanus" are to be accented. The common reader, like the learned editor, is free to follow his rhythmic sense in particular lines: "Coríoles" or "Coriŏles"? "Coriolânus" (the usual pronunciation) or "Coriŏlanus"?

The present edition follows the Folio text closely, but spelling and punctuation are modernized, abbreviations are amplified, names of speakers regularized, and some stage directions are moved slightly. The act divisions (translated from Latin) are those of the Folio; no scenes, except the first, are indicated in the Folio text. All other scene divisions printed here (in square brackets) are those of the Globe edition. The list of readings given in the following table includes only those words in the Folio that have been omitted or emended. The reading adopted in this edition is printed in italics, followed by the original reading in roman.

1.1.7 *Marcius* Martius (throughout the play)   16 *on* one   28 *First Citizen* All   35 *Second Citizen* All   58 *First Citizen* 2 Cit. (throughout the rest of Scene 1)   93 *stale't* scale't   111 *tauntingly* taintingly   215 *Shouting* Shooting   219 *unroofed* vnroo'st   227 s.d. *Junius* Annius   240 *Lartius* Lucius

1.2.s.d. *Corioles* Coriolus   4 *on* one   30 *They've* Th'haue

1.3.39 *that's* that   46 *sword, contemning. Tell* sword. Contenning, tell   85 *Virgilia* Vlug.   87 *yarn* yearne   88 *Ithaca* Athica   102 *whom* who

1.4.s.d., 12s.d. *Corioles* Corialus   31 *herd of—boils* Heard of Byles   42 *trenches. Follow's* Trenches followes   45s.d. *Enters the gates* Enter the Gati   57 *Were* Weare   58 *Cato's* Calues

1.6.21 *Who's* Whose   22 *flayed* Flead   53 *Antiates* Antients   70 *Lesser* Lessen

1.8.7 *Holloa* hollow

1.9.46 *coverture* Ouerture   50 *shout* shoot   65 *Caius Marcius* Marcus Caius (in this order throughout)

1.10.30 *cypress* Cyprus

2.1.24 *how are* ho ware   58 *cannot* can   63 *you* you you   66 *bisson* beesome   171 *Coriolanus* Martius Caius Coriolanus   184 *wear* were   186 *Coriolanus* Com.   192 *you* yon   210s.d. *Brutus* Enter Brutus   219 *flamens* Plamins   240 *napless* Naples   261 *touch* teach

2.2.26 *ascent* assent   51 *state's* states   82 *one on's* on ones   92 *chin* Shinne   93 *bristled* brizled

2.3.29 *wedged* wadg'd   44 *all together* altogether   71 *Ay, not I,* but   119 *hire* higher   120 *toge* tongue   249 *And Censorinus that was so surnamed* [F omits. This line, invented by N. Delius in his edition of 1872, is indebted to Plutarch. See below, p. 159]   260 *Citizens* All

3.1.33 *herd* Heard   48 *Coriolanus* Com.   91 *good* God!   92 *reckless* wreaklesse   126 *Their* There   143 *Where one* Whereon   185 *All* [F has no speech prefix here, but gives "All" before line 187]   214 *All* [*Citizens*] All Ple.   228 *him!* him. Exeunt.   229 *your* our   230 *Coriolanus* Com.   236 *Cominius* Corio.   237 *Coriolanus* Mene. [speech assigned to Menenius through line 241]   239 *Menenius* [see preceding note]   286 *our* one   322 *bring him* bring him in peace

3.2.21 *thwartings* things   32 *herd* heart   55 *roted* roated   115 *lulls* lull

3.3.32 *for th'* fourth   36 *Throng* Through   55 *accents* Actions   89 *flaying* Fleaing   99 *do* doth   110 *for* from   135s.d. *The other Senators* Cumalijs

4.1.24 *thee* the   34 *Whither wilt* Whether will

4.3.35 *will* well

4.4.23 *hate* haue

4.5.3 *master* M.   82 *Whooped* Hoop'd   98 *Thou'rt* Th'art   113 *clip* cleep   183 *lief* liue   236 *sleepy* sleepe

4.6.4 *do* do we   34 *lamentation* Lamention   90 *wi' th'* with   138 *one* oue

4.7.34 *osprey* Aspray   37 *'twas* 'was   39 *defect* detect   49 *virtues* Vertue   55 *founder* fouler

5.1.16 *wracked fair* wrack'd for

5.2.s.d. *on* or   16 *haply* happely   61 *errand* arrant   64–65 *but by my* but my   102 *swoon* swoond

5.3.48 *prate* pray   63 *holp* hope   104 *enmity's* enmities   141 *war's* Warres

149 *fine* fiue   152 *charge* change   169 *him with* him with him with   192 *stead* steed

5.4.50 s.d. *all together* altogether

5.5.4 *Unshout* Vnshoot

5.6.116 *Fluttered* Flatter'd   131 s.d. *the Conspirators* both the Conspirators

The Source of
Coriolanus

The main source used by Shakespeare in writing *Coriolanus* is the *Life of Coriolanus* in Sir Thomas North's translation of Plutarch's *Lives of the Noble Grecians and Romans* (first published in 1579). Comparison of the play with the *Life* will remind us that both "source" and "use" are misleading terms for describing what happens when a writer of the first rank makes a new work out of an old one. In writing *Coriolanus*, Shakespeare was not merely borrowing discrete items from Plutarch; he was engaged in a total imaginative act, seeking to satisfy his inner measure of what was right for his own sensibility, for his sense of the hero's character, and for his complex "feel" of the dramatic world that was coming into being as he wrote. Our certainty that the play is one of Shakespeare's "most assured artistic successes," as T. S. Eliot has said, is strengthened when we discover what he accepted and what he rejected, and particularly when we see how he adapted his borrowings to his vision of Coriolanus and the tragedy as a whole.

Shakespeare's vision—though for all time—was not timeless in origin, but shaped in part by the social and literary culture in which he lived and by the audience for which he produced his plays. We have seen in the Introduction (pp. lxvii–lxxiii) how the Greco-Roman heroic ideal in its Renaissance form had an effect on *Coriolanus* and on its meaning for contemporary and succeeding audiences. Shakespeare's treatment of civil disorders in Republican Rome was almost certainly affected also by popular protests and uprisings in England during the early 1600's, disturbances brought on by the enclosure of farm lands and by the lack of grain and the consequent "dearth." That Shakespeare takes the famine as the principal cause for the plebeians' complaints, rather than as in Plutarch "the sore oppression of usurers," is almost certainly traceable to the unrest in England, and, more

153

especially, to the Midlands revolt of 1607. The extensive emphasis in the play—as compared with the *Life*—on the body-state metaphor is probably to be explained in part by the contemporary concern with the dangers of insurrection. Shakespeare also elaborated on Plutarch's brief tale of the body and its members by drawing on Sidney's *Apology for Poetry,* Livy's *Roman History,* both in the original and in the translation of Philemon Holland (1600), and William Camden's *Remains of a Greater Work Concerning Britain* (1605).

The main events of Shakespeare's play, including the important scenes of Coriolanus' attack on the tribuneship (3.1), his banishment and his joining Aufidius (4.1.5), and the climactic scene with his mother (5.3), are all based on Plutarch. The principal features that Shakespeare stresses in his portrayal of Coriolanus have their origin, at least in an elementary form, in the pages of the *Life.* But Shakespeare has given even greater importance than Plutarch to Corio-lanus' pride and uncontrollable temper and especially to the close emotional bond to his mother. (See also Introduction, pp. lxxiv–lxxvi.) Some critics have seen in the prominent role of Menenius, of which there is only the slightest hint in Plutarch (pp. 163-64), Shakespeare's intention of mini-mizing the social isolation that Plutarch ascribes to his hero, his unfitness for association with other men. But Menenius spends much of his time warning Coriolanus of these defi-ciencies, and of the likely consequences of his heroically simple and inept behavior. It also should be noted that in spite of his temperamental aloneness, Plutarch's hero, like Shakespeare's, has strong political supporters among the patricians. Where Shakespeare departs, and significantly, is in eliminating all references to political maneuvering by Coriolanus, of which there are fairly many instances in the *Life.* Other critics have noted that Plutarch attributes a repu-tation for eloquence to Coriolanus, whereas Shakespeare seems to stress his lack of ability as a speaker and debater. But the point surely is that Shakespeare, as Menenius explains, endows Coriolanus with the eloquence of a soldier—violent and powerful, though often tactless, utter-ance. He has but one style, and hence his calls for the defense of the state sound strangely like his calls to battle. (Compare 3.1.149–57 and 1.6.67–75.)

A survey of the principal scenes that are wholly or largely invented by Shakespeare will give some idea of how thoroughly he adapted Plutarch's moral history to fit his peculiar dramatic subject of the Achillean hero exposed to the complexities and necessary compromises of the Roman-Jacobean political world. First, there are all the episodes in which Menenius figures prominently, with the exception of that part of the first scene in which he tells his fable. The occasion for this moral lesson, the retreat to the Sacred Mount, is passed over by Shakespeare, though Plutarch's narrative of it contains his sole mention of Menenius (p. 164). In Livy's *History,* Menenius dies soon after this event takes place. All the other scenes in which Menenius does so much to defend Coriolanus against his enemies, or enhance his noble exploits, or to temper his wrath, are entirely of Shakespeare's making. In 2.1, there is the bitterly comic telling-off of the tribunes, followed by the joyous welcome of the returning hero; in 2.3, the dialogue with Coriolanus and with the tribunes during the election scene; and the further exchanges with the tribunes in 3.1, after Coriolanus has been accused of being a traitor. Although in some of these earlier scenes Shakespeare is using Menenius to voice arguments advanced by the more politic patricians of the *Life,* he had little basis in Plutarch for the prominent part taken by Menenius in a number of the scenes that follow Coriolanus' banishment. As often in this play, Shakespeare telescopes two or three Plutarchan scenes into one, centering the action on one of his more important characters. The scene in which Menenius begs Coriolanus to spare Rome is—like Cominius' report of his own attempt—a substitution for one of several embassies from Rome described in Plutarch's narrative.

Shakespeare has invented all of the scenes in which Volumnia figures, with the exception of the women's embassy of 5.3. The scene that introduces Volumnia, Virgilia, and Valeria (1.3), in which Volumnia shows that she had indeed made Coriolanus after her own image of "valiantness," grows from a single remark in the *Life* about the "joy his mother did take of him." The later scene in which she and Menenius urge Coriolanus to act "mildly" in answering the tribunes (3.2) is a brilliant piece of dramatic foreshadowing, preparing for the final submission of son to mother in Act 5. (One characteristic of the play is the number of scenes that have close parallels, in which Coriolanus goes through the same routines but under changed circumstances, which he alone seems not to notice. Hence the odd *déjà vu,* almost nightmarish quality of much of the action in the latter part of the play.) Shakespeare also introduces a number of other scenes or episodes in which Volumnia has an important part, such as her rejoicing over her son's return from war (2.1), her farewell at the gate and her railing afterward (4.1.2), and her triumphant return from the final embassy (5.5). The speeches and scenes in which Shakespeare builds up the ambiguous hate-love relationship between Aufidius and Coriolanus in anticipation of their meeting in 4.5. grow from a single reference to their rivalry in the *Life* (pp. 180–81).

But no listing of inventions or parallels between *Coriolanus* and Plutarch's narrative can give a true impression of how wonderfully Shakespeare has transformed the Plutarchan original, even when seeming to follow it closely. The most obvious example, Volumnia's great appeal (5.3.19–209), offers the most telling proof of the art with which Shakespeare adapted North's language to suit the immediate context while keeping in view the larger dramatic and poetic design of the play. A few instances may suggest what can be learned by comparing the scene with the original in North's translation (pp. 190–92). Where Plutarch's Coriolanus is "overcome with natural affection" even before his mother speaks, Shakespeare's hero is caught in a violently shifting debate between the claims of nature, great and small, a conflict expressed in direct speech wholly invented by Shakespeare (lines 22–37). As we have seen (Introduction, pp. lxxiv–lxxv), the debate is not limited to this speech but runs deeply through the play. In the play, in which the bond with the mother is so central to the hero's character, the son kneels first to the mother, and in the wholly new passages between Coriolanus and his son, we are reminded of the parallel to Hector (in a domestic and "natural" moment

Coriolanus becomes less Achillean); we are reminded too of the early scene in which the boy-killer of butterflies is Coriolanus in miniature. The image he invokes of "a great seamark" is rooted in the imagery of natural forces and "things" so characteristic of Shakespeare's awesome and nonhuman hero. An example of where the verbal parallels are closest will indicate the remarkable depth and consistency of Shakespeare's dramatic and poetic art:

> *Volumnia.*   thou shalt no sooner
> March to assault thy country than to tread
> (Trust to't, thou shalt not) on thy mother's womb
> That brought thee to this world.   (122–25)

> . . . thou shalt see, my son, and trust unto it, thou shalt no sooner march forward to assault thy country, but thy foot shall tread upon thy mother's womb that brought thee first into this world.
>
> (Plutarch's *Life of Coriolanus*, p. 191)

Shakespeare has closely imitated in his verse the climactic form of North's sentence, with its skillful suspension through well-placed pauses and the repeated "thou shalt"; but by building the whole speech to end at this point, he has exploited the emotional climax much more fully than North, who has Volumnia go straight on with "And I may not defer to see the day. . . ." More important, Shakespeare anticipates the image earlier in the speech in a way to make inescapable the identification of the mother's physical self with "mother Rome." North has Volumnia say earlier, "making myself to see my son, and my daughter here her husband, besieging the walls of his native country" (p. 191). Shakespeare brings this triple allegiance home and focuses it in a metaphor of such violence that even Coriolanus must feel the unnaturalness of his behavior and recognize in advance the implication of the final image:

> Making the mother, wife, and child, to see
> The son, the husband, and the father, tearing
> His country's bowels out.   (101–3)

The identity of "mothers," human and national, is quietly underlined a moment later in Volumnia's passing reference to "The country, our dear nurse" (110). Compare with this North's relatively aloof and cold "the nurse of their native country" (p. 191). But the full impact of the appeal would be lost if we did not feel back of these physical mother-and-country images the recurring metaphors of the body politic and the large dramatic and philosophic premise they express. The personal and the patriotic appeals, which Shakespeare found in Plutarch, have been fused with a local intensity of feeling and with a far-reaching reference to Shakespeare's view, both of his individual characters and of the society in which they act. Dryden once spoke of Shakespeare as having "all the images of Nature . . . present to him" as he wrote. In comparing Volumnia's speech with its "source," we see Shakespeare writing *Coriolanus* with one eye on North, to be sure, but with all the images of the play and all their dramatic values present to his plastic imagination.

PLUTARCH

From The Lives of the Noble Grecians and Romans

The Life of Caius Martius Coriolanus

The house of the Martians at Rome was of the number of
the patricians, out of the which have sprung many noble personages, whereof Ancus Martius was one, King Numa's
daughter's son, who was King of Rome after Tullus Hostilius. Of the same house were Publius and Quintus, who
brought to Rome their best water they had, by conduits. Censorinus also came of that family, that was so surnamed
because the people had chosen him Censor twice. Through
whose persuasion they made a law, that no man from thenceforth might require or enjoy the Censorship twice.

Caius Martius, whose life we intend now to write, being
left an orphan by his father, was brought up under his mother
a widow; who taught us by experience, that orphanage
bringeth many discommodities to a child, but doth not
hinder him to become an honest man, and to excel in virtue
above the common sort; as they that are meanly born wrong-
fully do complain, that it is the occasion of their casting

In printing the following selections from North's version of the *Life of
Coriolanus*, most passages have been omitted that have no observable relation
to Shakespeare's play. The text reprinted here is that of W. W. Skeat: *Shakespeare's Plutarch* (1895), with some further modernization of spelling and
punctuation; and further division of the text into paragraphs. North's translation was first published in a folio of 1579. New editions also appeared in 1595
and in 1603. Variations among the three editions in the text of the *Life of
Coriolanus* are slight, though minor misprints of the 1579 text have often been
corrected in the text of 1595 (and some new errors have been introduced).
There are occasional improvements in the text of 1603. Skeat used an edition
of 1612, which is a reproduction of the edition of 1603. Which of the three earlier editions Shakespeare used in writing *Coriolanus* has not been determined.

159

away, for that no man in their youth taketh any care of them to see them well brought up and taught that were meet. This man also is a good proof to confirm some men's opinions, that a rare and excellent wit, untaught, doth bring forth many good and evil things together; as a fat soil that lieth unmanured bringeth forth both herbs and weeds. For this Martius' natural wit and great heart did marvelously stir up his courage to do and attempt notable acts. But on the other side, for lack of education, he was so choleric and impatient, that he would yield to no living creature, which made him churlish, uncivil, and altogether unfit for any man's conversation. Yet men marveling much at his constancy, that he was never overcome with pleasure nor money and how he would endure easily all manner of pains and travails, thereupon they well liked and commended his stoutness and temperancy. But for all that, they could not be acquainted with him, as one citizen useth to be with another in the city. His behavior was so unpleasant to them by reason of a certain insolent and stern manner he had, which, because he was too lordly, was disliked. And to say truly, the greatest benefit that learning bringeth unto men is this: that it teacheth men that be rude and rough of nature, by compass and rule of reason, to be civil and courteous, and to like better the mean state than the higher. Now in those days, valiantness was honored in Rome above all other virtues, which they call *virtus*, by the name of virtue itself, as including in that general name all other special virtues besides. So that *virtus* in the Latin was as much as valiantness.

But Martius, being more inclined to the wars than any other gentleman of his time, began from his childhood to give himself to handle weapons, and daily did exercise himself therein; and he esteemed outward armor to no purpose, unless one were naturally armed within. Moreover he did so exercise his body to hardness and all kind of activity, that he was very swift in running, strong in wrestling, and mighty in griping, so that no man could ever cast him. Insomuch as those that would try masteries with him for strength and nimbleness would say when they were overcome, that all was by reason of his natural strength and hardness of ward, that never yielded to any pain or toil he took upon him.

The first time he went to the wars, being but a stripling,

was when Tarquin, surnamed the proud (that had been King of Rome and was driven out for his pride, after many attempts made by sundry battles to come in again, wherein he was ever overcome), did come to Rome with all the aid of the Latins, and many other people of Italy; even as it were to set up his whole rest upon a battle by them, who with a great and mighty army had undertaken to put him into his kingdom again, not so much to pleasure him, as to overthrow the power of the Romans, whose greatness they both feared and envied. In this battle, wherein were many hot and sharp encounters of either party, Martius valiantly fought in the sight of the Dictator; and a Roman soldier being thrown to the ground even hard by him, Martius straight bestrid him and slew the enemy with his own hands, that had before overthrown the Roman. Hereupon, after the battle was won, the Dictator did not forget so noble an act, and therefore first of all he crowned Martius with a garland of oaken boughs. For whosoever saveth the life of a Roman, it is a manner among them, to honor him with such a garland.

Moreover, it is daily seen that honor and reputation lighting on young men before their time, and before they have any great courage by nature, the desire to win more dieth straight in them, which easily happeneth, the same having no deep root in them before. Where contrariwise, the first honor that valiant minds do come unto doth quicken up their appetite, hasting them forward, as with force of wind, to enterprise things of high-deserving praise. For they esteem not to receive reward for service done, but rather take it for a remembrance and encouragement, to make them do better in time to come, and be ashamed also to cast their honor at their heels, not seeking to increase it still by like desert of worthy valiant deeds. This desire being bred in Martius, he strained still to pass himself in manliness; and being desirous to show a daily increase of his valiantness, his noble service did still advance his fame, bringing in spoils upon spoils from the enemies. Whereupon, the captains that came afterwards (for envy of them that went before) did contend who should most honor him, and who should bear most honorable testimony of his valiantness. Insomuch as the Romans having many wars and battles in those days, Coriolanus was at them all; and there was not a battle fought from whence he returned not with some reward of honor.

And as for other, the only respect that made them valiant was that they hoped to have honor; but touching Martius, the only thing that made him to love honor was the joy he saw his mother did take of him. For he thought nothing made him so happy and honorable, as that his mother might hear everybody praise and commend him, that she might always see him return with a crown upon his head, and that she might still embrace him with tears running down her cheeks for joy. Which desire they say Epaminondas did avow and confess to have been in him, as to think himself a most happy and blessed man, that his father and mother in their lifetime had seen the victory he won in the plain of Leuctres. Now as for Epaminondas, he had this good hap, to have his father and mother living, to be partakers of his joy and prosperity. But Martius, thinking all due to his mother that had been also due to his father if he had lived, did not only content himself to rejoice and honor her, but at her desire took a wife also, by whom he had two young children, and yet never left his mother's house therefore.

Now he being grown to great credit and authority in Rome for his valiantness, it fortuned there grew sedition in the city, because the Senate did favor the rich against the people, who did complain of the sore oppression of usurers, of whom they borrowed money. For those that had little were yet spoiled of that little they had by their creditors, for lack of ability to pay the usury, who offered their goods to be sold to them that would give most. And such as had nothing left, their bodies were laid hold on, and they were made their bondmen, notwithstanding all the wounds and cuts they showed, which they had received in many battles, fighting for defense of their country and commonwealth. Of the which, the last war they made was against the Sabines, wherein they fought upon the promise the rich men had made them, that from thenceforth they would intreat them more gently, and also upon the word of Marcus Valerius, chief of the Senate, who, by authority of the council, and in the behalf of the rich, said they should perform that they had promised. But after that they had faithfully served in this last battle of all, where they overcame their enemies, seeing they were never a whit the better, nor more gently intreated, and that the Senate would give no ear to them but made as though they had forgotten the former promise, and suffered them to be made slaves and bondmen to their creditors, and besides, to be turned out of all that ever they had, they fell then even to flat rebellion and mutiny, and to stir up dangerous tumults within the city.

The Romans' enemies, hearing of this rebellion, did straight enter the territories of Rome with a marvelous great power, spoiling and burning all as they came. Whereupon the Senate immediately made open proclamation, by sound of trumpet, that all those that were of lawful age to carry weapon should come and enter their names into the muster-master's book, to go to the wars; but no man obeyed their commandment. Whereupon their chief magistrates and many of the Senate began to be of divers opinions among themselves. For some thought it was reason they should somewhat yield to the poor people's request, and that they should a little qualify the severity of the law. Other held hard against that opinion, and that was Martius for one. For he alleged that the creditors' losing their money they had lent was not the worst thing that was herein, but that the lenity that was favored was a beginning of disobedience, and that the proud attempt of the communalty was to abolish law and to bring all to confusion. Therefore, he said, if the Senate were wise, they should betimes prevent and quench this ill-favored and worse-meant beginning. The Senate met many days in consultation about it; but in the end they concluded nothing.

The poor common people, seeing no redress, gathered themselves one day together; and one encouraging another, they all forsook the city and encamped themselves upon a hill, called at that day the Holy Hill, along the river of Tiber, offering no creature any hurt or violence, or making any show of actual rebellion, saving that they cried as they went up and down that the rich men had driven them out of the city, and that throughout all Italy they might find air, water, and ground to bury them in. Moreover, they said, to dwell at Rome was nothing else but to be slain, or hurt with continual wars and fighting for defense of the rich men's goods.

The Senate, being afraid of their departure, did send unto

them certain of the pleasantest old men, and the most acceptable to the people among them. Of those Menenius Agrippa was he who was sent for chief man of the message from the Senate. He, after many good persuasions and gentle requests made to the people on the behalf of the Senate, knit up his oration in the end with a notable tale, in this manner: that on a time all the members of man's body did rebel against the belly, complaining of it that it only remained in the midst of the body without doing anything, neither did bear any labor to the maintenance of the rest; whereas all other parts and members did labor painfully, and were they careful to satisfy the appetites and desires of the body. And so the belly, all this notwithstanding, laughed at their folly and said, "It is true, I first receive all meats that nourish man's body; but afterwards I send it again to the nourishment of other parts of the same." "Even so," quoth he, "O you, my masters, and citizens of Rome, the reason is alike between the Senate and you. For matters being well digested, and their counsels thoroughly examined, touching the benefit of the commonwealth, the senators are cause of the common commodity that cometh unto every one of you."

These persuasions pacified the people conditionally, that the Senate would grant there should be yearly chosen five magistrates, which they now call *Tribuni plebis,* whose office should be to defend the poor people from violence and oppression. So Junius Brutus and Sicinius Vellutus were the first tribunes of the people that were chosen, who had only been the causers and procurers of this sedition. Hereupon, the city being grown again to good quiet and unity, the people immediately went to the wars, showing that they had a good will to do better than ever they did, and to be very willing to obey the magistrates in that they would command concerning the wars.

Martius also, though it liked him nothing to see the greatness of the people thus increased, considering it was to the prejudice and imbasing of the nobility, and also saw that other noble patricians were troubled as well as himself, he did persuade the patricians to show themselves no less forward and willing to fight for their country than the common people were, and to let them know by their deeds and acts, that they did not so much pass the people in power and riches as they did exceed them in true nobility and valiantness.

In the country of the Volsces, against whom the Romans made war at that time, there was a principal city and of most fame, that was called Corioles, before the which the consul Cominius did lay siege. Wherefore all the other Volsces, fearing lest that city should be taken by assault, they came from all parts of the country to save it, intending to give the Romans battle before the city, and to give an onset on them in two several places. The consul Cominius understanding this, divided his army also into two parts; and taking the one part with himself, he marched towards them that were drawing to the city out of the country; and the other part of his army he left in the camp with Titus Lartius (one of the valiantest men the Romans had at that time) to resist those that would make any sally out of the city upon them.

So the Coriolans, making small account of them that lay in camp before the city, made a sally out upon them, in the which at the first the Coriolans had the better, and drave the Romans back again into the trenches of their camp. But Martius being there at that time, running out of the camp with a few men with him, he slew the first enemies he met withal, and made the rest of them stay upon the sudden, crying out to the Romans that had turned their backs, and calling them again to fight with a loud voice. For he was even such another, as Cato would have a soldier and a captain to be, not only terrible and fierce to lay about him, but to make the enemy afeared with the sound of his voice and grimness of his countenance. Then there flocked about him immediately a great number of Romans; whereat the enemies were so afeared that they gave back presently. But Martius, not staying so, did chase and follow them to their own gates that fled for life. And there perceiving that the Romans retired back, for the great number of darts and arrows which flew about their ears from the walls of the city, and that there was not one man amongst them that durst venture himself to follow the flying enemies into their city, for that it was full of men of war very well armed and appointed, he did encourage his fellows with words and deeds, crying out to them that fortune had opened the gates of the city, more for the followers than the fliers. But all this notwithstanding, few had the hearts to follow him.

Howbeit Martius, being in the throng amongst the enemies,

thrust himself into the gates of the city and entered the same among them that fled, without that any one of them durst at the first turn their face upon him or offer to stay him. But he, looking about him, and seeing he was entered the city with very few men to help him, and perceiving he was environed by his enemies that gathered round about to set upon him, did things, as it is written, wonderful and incredible, as well for the force of his hand, as also for the agility of his body. And with a wonderful courage and valiantness he made a lane through the midst of them and overthrew also those he laid at; that some he made run to the furthest part of the city, and other for fear he made yield themselves, and to let fall their weapons before him. By this means Martius, that was gotten out, had some leisure to bring the Romans with more safety into the city.

The city being taken in this sort, the most part of the soldiers began incontinently to spoil, to carry away, and to look up the booty they had won. But Martius was marvelous angry with them, and cried out on them that it was no time now to look after spoil and to run straggling here and there to enrich themselves, whilst the other consul and their fellow-citizens peradventure were fighting with their enemies, and how that, leaving the spoil, they should seek to wind themselves out of danger and peril. Howbeit, cry and say to them what he could, very few of them would hearken to him. Wherefore taking those that willingly offered themselves to follow him, he went out of the city and took his way toward that part where he understood the rest of the army was, exhorting and entreating them by the way that followed him not to be fainthearted; and oft holding up his hands to heaven, he besought the gods to be gracious and favorable unto him, that he might come in time to the battle, and in a good hour to hazard his life in defense of his countrymen. . . .

When they saw him at his first coming, all bloody and in a sweat, and but with a few men following him, some thereupon began to be afeared. But soon after, when they saw him run with a lively cheer to the Consul and to take him by the hand, declaring how he had taken the city of Corioles, and that they saw the consul Cominius also kiss and embrace him, then there was not a man but took heart again to him and began to be of good courage; some hearing him report, from point to point, the happy success of this exploit, and other also conjecturing it by seeing their gestures afar off. Then they all began to call upon the Consul to march forward and to delay no longer, but to give charge upon the enemy. Martius asked him how the order of their enemy's battle was and on which side they had placed their best fighting men. The Consul made him answer that he thought the bands which were in the vaward of their battle were those of the Antiates, whom they esteemed to be the warlikest men, and which, for valiant courage, would give no place to any of the host of their enemies. Then prayed Martius to be set directly against them. The Consul granted him, greatly praising his courage.

Then Martius, when both armies came almost to join, advanced himself a good space before his company and went so fiercely to give charge on the vaward that came right against him, that they could stand no longer in his hands: he made such a lane through them, and opened a passage into the battle of the enemies. But the two wings of either side turned one to the other, to compass him in between them; which the consul Cominius perceiving, he sent thither straight of the best soldiers he had about him. So the battle was marvelous bloody about Martius, and in a very short space many were slain in the place. But in the end the Romans were so strong that they distressed the enemies and brake their array, and scattering them, made them fly. Then they prayed Martius that he would retire to the camp, because they saw he was able to do no more, he was already so wearied with the great pain he had taken and so faint with the great wounds he had upon him. But Martius answered them, that it was not for conquerors to yield, nor to be fainthearted; and thereupon began afresh to chase those that fled, until such time as the army of the enemies was utterly overthrown, and numbers of them slain and taken prisoners.

The next morning betimes Martius went to the Consul and the other Romans with him. There the consul Cominius, going up to his chair of state in the presence of the whole army, gave thanks to the gods for so great, glorious, and prosperous a victory. Then he spake to Martius, whose valiantness he commended beyond the moon, both for that he himself saw him do with his eyes, as also for that Martius had reported unto him. So in the end he willed Martius that he should choose out of all the horses they had taken of their enemies, and of all their goods they had won (whereof there was great store) ten of every sort which he liked best, before any distribution should be made to other. Besides this great honorable offer he had made him, he gave him, in testimony that he had won that day the price of prowess above all other, a goodly horse with a caparison, and all furniture to him; which the whole army beholding, did marvelously praise and commend. But Martius, stepping forth, told the Consul he most thankfully accepted the gift of his horse, and was a glad man besides that his service had deserved his general's commendation. And as for his other offer, which was rather a mercenary reward than a honorable recompense, he would have none of it, but was contented to have his equal part with the other soldiers. "Only, this grace," said he, "I crave and beseech you to grant me. Among the Volsces there is an old friend and host of mine, an honest wealthy man, and now a prisoner; who, living before in great wealth in his own country, liveth now a poor prisoner in the hands of his enemies. And yet notwithstanding all this his misery and misfortune, it would do me great pleasure if I could save him from this one danger, to keep him from being sold as a slave."

The soldiers, hearing Martius' words, made a marvelous great shout among them, and there were more that wondered at his great contentation and abstinence when they saw so little covetousness in him, than they were that highly praised and extolled his valiantness. For even they themselves that did somewhat malice and envy his glory, to see him thus honored and passingly praised, did think him so much the more worthy of an honorable recompense for his valiant service, as the more carelessly he refused the great offer made unto him for his profit; and they esteemed more the virtue that was in him that made him refuse such rewards, than that which made them to be offered to him, as unto a worthy person. For it is far more commendable to use riches well than to be valiant; and yet it is better not to desire them than to use them well.

After this shout and noise of the assembly was somewhat

appeased, the consul Cominius began to speak in this sort: "We cannot compel Martius to take these gifts we offer him if he will not receive them, but we will give him such a reward for the noble service he hath done as he cannot refuse. Therefore we do order and decree that henceforth he be called Coriolanus, unless his valiant acts have won him that name before our nomination." And so ever since, he still bare the third name of Coriolanus. And thereby it appeareth that the first name the Romans have, as Caius, was as our Christian name now. The second, as Martius, was the name of the house and family they came of. The third was some addition given, either for some act or notable service, or for some mark on their face, or·of some shape of their body, or else for some special virtue they had. Even so did the Grecians in old time give additions to princes by reason of some notable act worthy memory. As when they have called some "Soter" and "Callinicos," as much to say as "savior" and "conqueror." . . .

Now when this war was ended, the flatterers of the people began to stir up sedition again, without any new occasion or just matter offered of complaint. For they did ground this second insurrection against the nobility and patricians upon the people's misery and misfortune that could not but fall out, by reason of the former discord and sedition between them and the nobility. Because the most part of the arable land within the territory of Rome was become heathy and barren for lack of plowing, for that they had no time nor mean to cause corn to be brought them out of other countries to sow, by reason of their wars; which made the extreme dearth they had among them. Now those busy prattlers that sought the people's goodwill by such flattering words, perceiving great scarcity of corn to be within the city—and though there had been plenty enough, yet the common people had no money to buy it—they spread abroad false tales and rumors against the nobility, that they, in revenge of the people, had practiced and procured the extreme dearth among them.

Furthermore, in the midst of this stir, there came ambassadors to Rome from the city of Velitres, that offered up their city to the Romans and prayed them they would send new inhabitants to replenish the same, because the plague had been so extreme among them and had killed such a number of them, as there was not left alive the tenth person of the people that had been there before. So the wise men of Rome began to think that the necessity of the Velitrians fell out in a most happy hour; and how, by this occasion, it was very meet, in so great a scarcity of victuals, to disburden Rome of a great number of citizens; and by this means as well to take away this new sedition and utterly to rid it out of the city, as also to clear the same of many mutinous and seditious persons, being the superfluous ill humors that grievously fed this disease. Hereupon the Consuls pricked out all those by a bill, whom they intended to send to Velitres, to go dwell there as in form of a colony. And they levied out all the rest that remained in the city of Rome a great number to go against the Volsces, hoping, by the mean of foreign war, to pacify their sedition at home. Moreover, they imagined, when the poor with the rich, and the mean sort with the nobility, should by this device be abroad in the wars and in one camp, and in one service, and in one like danger, that then they would be more quiet and loving together.

But Sicinius and Brutus, two seditious tribunes, spake against either of these devices and cried out upon the noblemen that under the gentle name of a colony they would cloak and color the most cruel and unnatural fact as might be: because they sent their poor citizens into a sore infected city and pestilent air, full of dead bodies unburied, and there also to dwell under the tuition of a strange god that had so cruelly persecuted his people. "This were," said they, "even as much as if the Senate should headlong cast down the people into a most bottomless pit; and are not yet contented to have famished some of the poor citizens heretofore to death, and to put other of them even to the mercy of the plague; but afresh they have procured a voluntary war, to the end they would leave behind no kind of misery and ill wherewith the poor silly people should not be plagued, and only because they are weary to serve the rich." The common people, being set on a broil and bravery with these words, would not appear when the Consuls called their names by a bill, to prest them for the wars, neither would they be sent out to this new colony; insomuch as the Senate knew not well what to say or to do in the matter.

Martius then, who was now grown to great credit, and a stout man besides, and of great reputation with the noblest men of Rome, rose up and openly spake against these flattering Tribunes. And for the replenishing of the city of Velitres, he did compel those that were chosen to go thither and to depart the city, upon great penalties to him that should disobey. But to the wars the people by no means would be brought or constrained. So Martius, taking his friends and followers with him, and such as he could by fair words entreat to go with him, did run certain forays into the dominion of the Antiates, where he met with great plenty of corn and had a marvelous great spoil, as well of cattle as of men he had taken prisoners, whom he brought away with him, and reserved nothing for himself. Afterwards, having brought back again all his men that went out with him, safe and sound to Rome, and every man rich and loaden with spoil, then the home-tarriers and house-doves that kept Rome still began to repent them that it was not their hap to go with him, and so envied both them that had sped so well in this journey. And also, of malice to Martius, they spited to see his credit and estimation increase still more and more, because they accounted him to be a great hinderer of the people.

Shortly after this, Martius stood for the consulship; and the common people favored his suit, thinking it would be a shame to them to deny and refuse the chiefest nobleman of blood, and most worthy person of Rome, and specially him that had done so great service and good to the commonwealth. For the custom of Rome was at that time that such as did sue for any office should for certain days before be in the marketplace, only with a poor gown on their backs, and without any coat underneath, to pray the citizens to remember them at the day of election. Which was thus devised, either to move the people the more, by requesting them in such mean apparel, or else because they might show them their wounds they had gotten in the wars in the service of the commonwealth, as manifest marks and testimonies of their valiantness. . . .

Now Martius, following this custom, showed many wounds and cuts upon his body, which he had received in seventeen years' service at the wars, and in many sundry battles, being ever the foremost man that did set out feet to fight. So that there was not a man among the people but was ashamed of himself, to refuse so valiant a man: and one of them said to another, "We must needs choose him consul, there is no remedy." But when the day of election was come, and that Martius came to the marketplace with great pomp, accompanied with all the Senate and the whole nobility of the city about him, who sought to make him consul with the greatest instance and entreaty they could, or ever attempted for any man or matter, then the love and goodwill of the common people turned straight to an hate and envy toward him, fearing to put this office of sovereign authority into his hands, being a man somewhat partial towards the nobility, and of great credit and authority amongst the patricians, and as one they might doubt would take away altogether the liberty from the people. Whereupon, for these considerations, they refused Martius in the end, and made two other that were suitors, consuls.

The Senate, being marvelously offended with the people, did account the shame of this refusal rather to redound to themselves than to Martius; but Martius took it in far worse part than the Senate, and was out of all patience. For he was a man too full of passion and choler, and too much given over to self-will and opinion, as one of a high mind and great courage that lacked the gravity and affability that is gotten with judgment of learning and reason, which only is to be looked for in a governor of state; and that remembered not how willfulness is the thing of the world, which a governor of a commonwealth, for pleasing should shun, being that which Plato called "solitariness," as in the end, all men that are willfully given to a self-opinion and obstinate mind, and who will never yield to others' reason but to their own, remain without company and forsaken of all men. For a man that will live in the world must needs have patience, which lusty bloods make but a mock at. So Martius, being a stout man of nature, that never yielded in any respect, as one thinking that to overcome always and to have the upper hand in all matters, was a token of magnanimity and of no base and faint courage—which spitteth out anger from the most weak and passioned part of the heart, much like the matter of an impostume—went home to his house, full freighted with spite and malice against the people, being accompanied with all the lustiest young gentlemen, whose minds were nobly bent, as those that came of noble race, and commonly used for to follow and honor him. But then specially they flocked about him, and kept him company to his much harm, for they did but kindle and inflame his choler more and more, being sorry with him for the injury the people offered him; because he was their captain and leader to the wars, that taught them all martial discipline and stirred up in them a noble emulation of honor and valiantness, and yet, without envy praising them that deserved best.

In the mean season there came great plenty of corn to Rome that had been bought, part in Italy, and part was sent out of Sicily, as given by Gelon the tyrant of Syracusa; so that many stood in great hope that the dearth of victuals being holpen, the civil dissension would also cease. The Senate sat in council upon it immediately; the common people stood also about the palace where the council was kept, gaping what resolution would fall out; persuading themselves that the corn they had bought should be sold good cheap, and that which was given should be divided by the poll, without paying any penny; and the rather, because certain of the senators amongst them did so wish and persuade the same.

But Martius, standing upon his feet, did somewhat sharply take up those who went about to gratify the people therein, and called them people-pleasers and traitors to the nobility. "Moreover," he said, "they nourished against themselves the naughty seed and cockle of insolence and sedition, which had been sowed and scattered abroad amongst the people, which they should have cut off, if they had been wise, in their growth; and not (to their own destruction) have suffered the people to establish a magistrate for themselves of so great power and authority as that man had to whom they had granted it. Who was also to be feared, because he obtained what he would and did nothing but what he listed, neither passed for any obedience to the consuls but lived in all liberty, acknowledging no superior to command him, saving the only heads and authors of their faction, whom he called his magistrates. Therefore," said he, "they that gave counsel and persuaded that the corn should be

given out to the common people *gratis,* as they used to do in
the cities of Greece, where the people had more absolute
power, did but only nourish their disobedience, which would
break out in the end to the utter ruin and overthrow of the
whole state. For they will not think it is done in recompense
of their service past, sithence they know well enough they
have so oft refused to go to the wars when they were commanded; neither for their mutinies when they went with us,
whereby they have rebelled and forsaken their country; neither for their accusations which their flatterers have preferred unto them, and they have received, and made good
against the Senate. But they will rather judge, we give and
grant them this as abasing ourselves and standing in fear of
them, and glad to flatter them every way. By this means their
disobedience will still grow worse and worse; and they will
never leave to practice new sedition and uproars. Therefore
it were a great folly for us, methinks, to do it. Yea, shall I say
more? We should, if we were wise, take from them their tribuneship, which most manifestly is the embasing of the consulship, and the cause of the division of the city. The state
whereof, as it standeth, is not now as it was wont to be, but
becometh dismembered in two factions, which maintains
always civil dissension and discord between us, and will
never suffer us again to be united into one body."

Martius, dilating the matter with many such like reasons,
won all the young men and almost all the rich men to his
opinion; insomuch, as they rang it out, that he was the only
man and alone in the city who stood out against the people
and never flattered them. There were only a few old men that
spake against him, fearing lest some mischief might fall out
upon it, as indeed there followed no great good afterward.
For the tribunes of the people, being present at this consultation of the Senate, when they saw that the opinion of Martius was confirmed with the more voices, they left the Senate
and went down to the people, crying out for help, and that
they would assemble to save their tribunes.

Hereupon the people ran on head in tumult together,
before whom the words that Martius spake in the Senate
were openly reported; which the people so stomached that
even in that fury they were ready to fly upon the whole
Senate. But the tribunes laid all the fault and burthen wholly

upon Martius, and sent their sergeants forthwith to arrest him, presently to appear in person before the people to answer the words he had spoken in the Senate. Martius stoutly withstood these officers that came to arrest him. Then the tribunes in their own persons, accompanied with the aediles, went to fetch him by force, and so laid violent hands upon him. Howbeit, the noble patricians, gathering together about him, made the tribunes give back, and laid sore upon the aediles; so for that time the night parted them, and the tumult appeased.

The next morning betimes, the Consuls, seeing the people in an uproar, running to the marketplace out of all parts of the city, they were afraid lest all the city would together by the ears. Wherefore assembling the Senate in all haste, they declared how it stood them upon to appease the fury of the people with some gentle words or grateful decrees in their favor; and moreover, like wise men, they should consider it was now no time to stand at defense and in contention, nor yet to fight for honor against the commonalty, they being fallen to so great an extremity and offering such imminent danger. Wherefore they were to consider temperately of things, and to deliver some present and gentle pacification. The most part of the senators that were present at this council thought this opinion best, and gave their consents unto it.

Whereupon the Consuls, rising out of council, went to speak unto the people as gently as they could, and they did pacify their fury and anger, purging the Senate of all the unjust accusations laid upon them, and used great modesty in persuading them and also in reproving the faults they had committed. And as for the rest, that touched the sale of corn, they promised there should be no disliking offered them in the price. So the most part of the people being pacified, and appearing so plainly, by the great silence that was among them, as yielding to the Consuls and liking well of their words, the tribunes then of the people rose out of their seats, and said: "Forasmuch as the Senate yielded unto reason, the people also for their part, as became them, did likewise give place unto them; but notwithstanding, they would that Martius should come in person to answer to the articles they had devised. First, whether he had not solicited and procured the

Senate to change the present state of the commonweal, and to take the sovereign authority out of the people's hands? Next, when he was sent for by authority of their officers, why he did contemptuously resist and disobey? Lastly, seeing he had driven and beaten the aediles into the marketplace before all the world, if, in doing this, he had not done as much as in him lay to raise civil wars and to set one citizen against another?"

All this was spoken to one of these two ends: either that Martius, against his nature, should be constrained to humble himself and to abase his haughty and fierce mind; or else, if he continued still in his stoutness, he should incur the people's displeasure and ill will so far that he should never possibly win them again. Which they hoped would rather fall out so than otherwise; as indeed, they guessed unhappily, considering Martius' nature and disposition.

So Martius came and presented himself to answer their accusations against him, and the people held their peace and gave attentive ear to hear what he would say. But where they thought to have heard very humble and lowly words come from him, he began not only to use his wonted boldness of speaking (which of itself was very rough and unpleasant, and did more aggravate his accusation than purge his innocency) but also gave himself in his words to thunder, and look therewithal so grimly, as though he made no reckoning of the matter. This stirred coals among the people, who were in wonderful fury at it, and their hate and malice grew so toward him that they could hold no longer, bear, nor endure his bravery and careless boldness. Whereupon Sicinius, the cruelest and stoutest of the tribunes, after he had whispered a little with his companions, did openly pronounce, in the face of all the people, Martius as condemned by the tribunes to die. Then presently he commanded the aediles to apprehend him and carry him straight to the rock Tarpeian and to cast him headlong down the same.

When the aediles came to lay hands upon Martius to do that they were commanded, divers of the people themselves thought it too cruel and violent a deed. The noblemen, being much troubled to see so much force and rigor used, began to cry aloud, "Help Martius." So those that laid hands on him being repulsed, they compassed him in round among themselves, and some of them, holding up their hands to the people, besought them not to handle him thus cruelly. But neither their words nor crying out could aught prevail; the tumult and hurly-burly was so great, until such time as the tribunes' own friends and kinsmen, weighing with themselves the impossibleness to convey Martius to execution without great slaughter and murder of the nobility, did persuade and advise not to proceed in so violent and extraordinary a sort as to put such a man to death without lawful process in law, but that they should refer the sentence of his death to the free voice of the people.

Then Sicinius, bethinking himself a little, did ask the patricians for what cause they took Martius out of the officers' hands that went to do execution? The patricians asked him again why they would of themselves so cruelly and wickedly put to death so noble and valiant a Roman as Martius was, and that without law and justice? "Well then," said Sicinius, "if that be the matter, let there be no quarrel or dissension against the people; for they do grant your demand, that his cause shall be heard according to the law. Therefore," said he to Martius, "we do will and charge you to appear before the people, the third day of our next sitting and assembly here, to make your purgation for such articles as shall be objected against you, that by free voice the people may give sentence upon you as shall please them." The noblemen were glad then of the adjournment, and were much pleased they had gotten Martius out of this danger.

In the mean space before the third day of their next session came about, the same being kept every ninth day continually at Rome (whereupon they call it now in Latin *Nundinae*), there fell out war against the Antiates, which gave some hope to the nobility that this adjournment would come to little effect, thinking that this war would hold them so long, as that the fury of the people against him would be well suaged or utterly forgotten, by reason of the trouble of the wars. But contrary to expectation, the peace was concluded presently with the Antiates, and the people returned again to Rome.

Then the patricians assembled oftentimes together, to consult how they might stand to Martius and keep the tribunes from occasion to cause the people to mutine again and rise against the nobility. And there Appius Claudius (one that was taken ever as an heavy enemy to the people) did avow and protest that they would utterly abase the authority of the Senate and destroy the commonweal if they would suffer the common people to have authority by voices to give judgment against the nobility. On the other side again, the most ancient senators, and such as were given to favor the common people, said that when the people should see they had authority of life and death in their hands, they would not be so cruel and fierce, but gentle and civil. More also, that it was not for contempt of nobility or the Senate that they sought to have the authority of justice in their hands, as a preeminence and prerogative of honor, but because they feared that themselves should be contemned and hated of the nobility. So as they were persuaded, that so soon as they gave them authority to judge by voices, they would leave all envy and malice to condemn any.

Martius, seeing the Senate in great doubt how to resolve, partly for the love and goodwill the nobility did bear him, and partly for the fear they stood in of the people, asked aloud of the tribunes what matter they would burden him with? The tribunes answered him that they would show how he did aspire to be king, and would prove that all his actions tended to usurp tyrannical power over Rome. Martius, with that, rising upon his feet, said that thereupon he did willingly offer himself to the people, to be tried upon that accusation; and that if it were proved by him he had so much as once thought of any such matter, that he would then refuse no kind of punishment they would offer him—"conditionally," quoth he, "that you charge me with nothing else beside, and that ye do not also abuse the Senate." They promised they would not. Under these conditions the judgment was agreed upon, and the people assembled.

And first of all the tribunes would in any case (whatsoever became of it) that the people should proceed to give their voices by tribes, and not by hundreds. For by this means the multitude of the poor needy people (and all such rabble as had nothing to lose, and had less regard of honesty before their eyes) came to be of greater force (because their voices were numbered by the poll) than the noble honest citizens, whose persons and purse did dutifully serve the commonwealth in their wars. And then, when the tribunes saw they could not prove he went about to make himself king, they began to broach afresh the former words that Martius had spoken in the Senate in hindering the distribution of the corn at mean price unto the common people and persuading also to take the office of tribuneship from them. And for the third, they charged him anew that he had not made the common distribution of the spoil he had gotten in the invading the territories of the Antiates, but had of his own authority divided it among them who were with him in that journey.

But this matter was most strange of all to Martius, looking least to have been burdened with that as with any matter of offense. Whereupon being burdened on the sudden, and having no ready excuse to make even at that instant, he began to fall a praising of the soldiers that had served with him in that journey. But those that were not with him, being the greater number, cried out so loud and made such a noise that he could not be heard. To conclude, when they came to tell the voices of the tribes, there were three voices odd, which condemned him to be banished for ever. After declaration of the sentence, the people made such joy as they never rejoiced more for any battle they had won upon their enemies, they were so brave and lively and went home so jocundly from the assembly, for triumph of this sentence.

The Senate again, in contrary manner, were as sad and heavy, repenting themselves beyond measure that they had not rather determined to have done and suffered anything whatsoever before the common people should so arrogantly and outrageously have abused their authority. There needed no difference of garments, I warrant you, nor outward shows, to know a plebeian from a patrician, for they were easily discerned by their looks. For he that was on the people's side looked cheerfully on the matter. But he that was sad and hung down his head, he was sure of the noblemen's side, saving Martius alone, who neither in his countenance nor in his gait did ever show himself abashed, or once let fall his great courage. But he only, of all other gentlemen that were angry at his fortune, did outwardly show no manner of passion, nor care at all of himself. Not that he did patiently bear and temper his evil hap in respect of any reason he had, or by his quiet condition; but because he was so carried away with the vehemency of anger and desire of revenge, that he had no sense nor feeling of the hard state he was in; which the common people judge not to be sorrow, although indeed it be the very same. For when sorrow (as you would say) is set on fire, then it is converted into spite and malice, and driveth away for that time all faintness of heart and natural fear. And this is the cause why the choleric man is so altered and mad in his actions, as a man set on fire with a burning ague; for when a man's heart is troubled within, his pulse will beat marvelous strongly.

Now that Martius was even in that taking, it appeared true soon after by his doings. For when he was come home to his house again, and had taken his leave of his mother and wife, finding them weeping and shrieking out for sorrow, and had also comforted and persuaded them to be content with his chance, he went immediately to the gate of the city, accompanied with a great number of patricians that brought him thither. From whence he went on his way with three or four of his friends only, taking nothing with him nor requesting anything of any man. So he remained a few days in the country at his houses, turmoiled with sundry sorts and kinds of thoughts such as the fire of his choler did stir up.

In the end, seeing he could resolve no way to take a profitable or honorable course, but only was pricked forward still to be revenged of the Romans, he thought to raise up some great wars against them, by their nearest neighbors. Whereupon he thought it his best way first to stir up the Volsces against them, knowing they were yet able enough in strength and riches to encounter them, notwithstanding their former losses they had received not long before, and that their power was not so much impaired as their malice and desire was increased to be revenged of the Romans. Now in the city of Antium there was one called Tullus Aufidius, who, for his riches as also for his nobility and valiantness, was honored among the Volsces as a king. Martius knew very well that Tullus did more malice and envy him than he did all the Romans besides, because that many times, in battles where they met, they were ever at the encounter one against another, like lusty courageous youths striving in all emulation of honor, and had encountered many times together. Insomuch as, besides the common quarrel between them, there was bred a marvelous private hate, one against another.

Yet notwithstanding, considering that Tullus Aufidius was a man of a great mind, and that he above all other of the Volsces most desired revenge of the Romans for the injuries they had done unto them, he did an act that confirmed the words of an ancient poet to be true, who said:

> It is a thing full hard, man's anger to withstand,
> If it be stiffly bent to take an enterprise in hand.
> For then most men will have the thing that they desire,
> Although it cost their lives therefore, such force hath wicked ire.

And so did he. For he disguised himself in such array and attire, as he thought no man could ever have known him for the person he was, seeing him in that apparel he had upon his back; and as Homer said of Ulysses:

> So did he enter into the enemies' town.

It was even twilight when he entered the city of Antium, and many people met him in the streets, but no man knew him. So he went directly to Tullus Aufidius' house, and when he came thither, he got him up straight to the chimney hearth and sat him down, and spake not a word to any man, his face all muffled over. They of the house spying him wondered what he should be, and yet they durst not bid him rise. For ill-favoredly muffled and disguised as he was, yet there appeared a certain majesty in his countenance and in his silence. Whereupon they went to Tullus, who was at supper, to tell him of the strange disguising of this man.

Tullus rose presently from the board, and coming towards him, asked him what he was and wherefore he came. Then Martius unmuffled himself, and after he had paused awhile, making no answer, he said unto him: "If thou knowest me not yet, Tullus, and, seeing me, dost not perhaps believe me to be the man I am indeed, I must of necessity bewray myself to be that I am. I am Caius Martius, who hath done to thyself particularly, and to all the Volsces generally, great hurt and mischief, which I cannot deny for my surname of Coriolanus that I bear. For I never had other benefit nor recompense of the true and painful service I have done, and the extreme dangers I have been in, but this only surname—a good memory and witness of the malice and displeasure thou shouldest bear me. Indeed the name only remaineth with me; for the rest the envy and cruelty of the people of Rome have taken from me, by the sufferance of the dastardly nobility and magistrates, who have forsaken me, and let me be banished by the people. This extremity hath now driven me to come as a poor suitor to take thy chimney hearth, not of any hope I have to save my life thereby. For if I had feared death, I would not have come hither to have put myself in hazard, but pricked forward with desire to be revenged of them that thus have banished me; which now I do begin, in putting my person into the hands of their enemies. Wherefore, if thou hast any heart to be wrecked of the injuries thy enemies have done thee, speed thee now, and let my misery serve thy turn, and so use it as my service may be a benefit to the Volsces, promising thee that I will fight with better goodwill for all you than I did when I was against you, knowing that they fight more valiantly who know the force of the enemy than such as have never proved it. And if it be so that thou dare not and that thou art weary to prove fortune any more, then am I also weary to live any longer. And it were no wisdom in thee, to save the life of him who hath been heretofore thy mortal enemy, and whose service now can nothing help nor pleasure thee."

Tullus, hearing what he said, was a marvelous glad man, and taking him by the hand, he said unto him: "Stand up, O Martius, and be of good cheer, for in proffering thyself unto us thou doest us great honor; and by this means thou mayest hope also of greater things at all the Volsces' hands." So he feasted him for that time and entertained him in the honorablest manner he could, talking with him of no other matter at that present. But within few days after, they fell to consultation together in what sort they should begin their wars.

Now on the other side, the city of Rome was in marvelous uproar and discord, the nobility against the commonalty, and chiefly for Martius' condemnation and banishment. Moreover, the priests, the soothsayers, and private men also came and declared to the Senate certain sights and wonders in the air, which they had seen and were to be considered of. . . .

Tullus and Martius had secret conference with the greatest personages of the city of Antium, declaring unto them that now they had good time offered them to make war with the Romans, while they were in dissension one with another. They answered them, they were ashamed to break the league, considering that they were sworn to keep peace for two years. Howbeit, shortly after, the Romans gave them great occasion to make war with them. For on a holy day, common plays being kept in Rome, upon some suspicion or false report, they made proclamation by sound of trumpet that all the Volsces should avoid out of Rome before sunset. Some think this was a craft and deceit of Martius, who sent one to Rome to the Consuls to accuse the Volsces falsely, advertising them how they had made a conspiracy to set upon them while they were busy in seeing these games, and also to set their city on fire.

This open proclamation made all the Volsces more offended with the Romans than ever they were before. And Tullus, aggravating the matter, did so inflame the Volsces against them that in the end they sent their ambassadors to Rome, to summon them to deliver their lands and towns again, which they had taken from them in times past, or to look for present wars. The Romans, hearing this, were marvelously nettled and made no other answer but this: "If the Volsces be the first that begin war, the Romans will be the last that will end it." Incontinently upon return of the Volsces' ambassadors and delivery of the Romans' answer, Tullus caused an assembly general to be made of the Volsces, and concluded to make war upon the Romans. This done, Tullus did counsel them to take Martius into their service, and not to mistrust him for the remembrance of anything past, but boldly to trust him in any matter to come; for he would do them more service in fighting for them than ever he did them displeasure in fighting against them. So Martius was called forth, who spake so excellently in the presence of them all that he was thought no less eloquent in tongue than warlike in show, and declared himself both expert in wars and wise with valiantness.

Thus he was joined in commission with Tullus as general of the Volsces, having absolute authority between them to follow and pursue the wars. But Martius, fearing lest tract of time to bring this army together with all the munition and furniture of the Volsces would rob him of the mean he had to execute his purpose and intent, left order with the rulers and chief of the city to assemble the rest of their power and to prepare all necessary provision for the camp. Then he, with the lightest soldiers he had and that were willing to follow him, stole away upon the sudden, and marched with all speed, and entered the territories of Rome before the Romans heard any news of his coming. Insomuch as the Volsces found such spoil in the fields, as they had more than they could spend in their camp and were weary to drive and carry away that they had.

Howbeit, the gain of the spoil and the hurt they did to the Romans in this invasion was the least part of his intent. For his chiefest purpose was to increase still the malice and dissension between the nobility and the commonalty. And to draw that on, he was very careful to keep the noblemen's lands and goods safe from harm and burning, but spoiled all the whole country besides, and would suffer no man to take or hurt anything of the noblemen's. This made greater stir and broil between the nobility and the people than was before. For the noblemen fell out with the people because they had so unjustly banished a man of so great valor and power. The people, on the other side, accused the nobility; how they had procured Martius to make these wars to be revenged of them—because it pleased them to see their goods burnt and spoiled before their eyes, whilst themselves were well at ease and did behold the people's losses and misfortunes, knowing their own goods safe and out of danger—and how the war was not made against the noblemen, that had the enemy abroad to keep that they had in safety. Now Martius, having done his first exploit (which made the Volsces bolder and less fearful of the Romans), brought home all the army again without loss of any man.

After their whole army (which was marvelous great and very forward to service) was assembled in one camp, they agreed to leave part of it for garrison in the country about, and the other part should go on and make the war upon the Romans. So Martius bade Tullus choose and take which of the two charges he liked best. Tullus made him answer; he knew by experience that Martius was no less valiant than himself, and how he ever had better fortune and good hap in all battles than himself had. Therefore he thought it best for him to have the leading of those that would make the wars abroad, and himself would keep home, to provide for the safety of the cities of his country and to furnish the camp also of all necessary provision abroad. . . .

In this while, all went still to wrack at Rome. For, to come into the field to fight with the enemy, they could not abide to hear of it, they were one so much against another, and full of seditious words, the nobility against the people, and the people against the nobility. Until they had intelligence at the length that the enemies had laid siege to the city of Lavinium, in the which were all the temples and images of their gods their protectors, and from whence came first their ancient original, for that Aeneas at his first arrival into Italy did build that city. Then fell there out a marvelous sudden change of mind among the people, and far more strange and contrary in the nobility. For the people thought it good to repeal the condemnation and exile of Martius. The Senate, assembled upon it, would in no case yield to that—who either did it of a self-will to be contrary to the people's desire, or because Martius should not return through the grace and favor of the people. Or else, because they were thoroughly angry and offended with him that he would set upon the whole, being offended but by a few, and in his doings would show himself an open enemy besides unto his country. Notwithstanding, the most part of them took the wrong they had done him in marvelous ill part, and as if the injury had been done unto themselves. Report being made of the Senate's resolution, the people found themselves in a straight; for they could authorize and confirm nothing by their voices, unless it had been first propounded and ordained by the Senate.

But Martius, hearing this stir about him, was in a greater rage with them than before; inasmuch as he raised his siege incontinently before the city of Lavinium, and going towards Rome, lodged his camp within forty furlong of the city, at the ditches called Cluiliae. His encamping so near Rome did put all the whole city in a wonderful fear. Howbeit, for the present time it appeased the sedition and dissension betwixt the nobility and the people. For there was no consul, senator, nor magistrate that durst once contrary the opinion of the people for the calling home again of Martius.

When they saw the women in a marvelous fear, running up and down the city, the temples of the gods full of old people weeping bitterly in their prayers to the gods, and finally, not a man either wise or hardy to provide for their safety, then they were all of opinion that the people had reason to call home Martius again to reconcile themselves to him, and that the Senate, on the contrary part, were in marvelous great fault to be angry and in choler with him, when it stood them upon rather to have gone out and entreated him. So they all agreed together to send ambassadors unto him, to let him understand how his countrymen did call him home again, and restored him to all his goods, and besought him to deliver them from this war.

The ambassadors that were sent were Martius' familiar friends and acquaintance, who looked at the least for a courteous welcome of him, as of their familiar friend and kinsman. Howbeit they found nothing less; for at their coming they were brought through the camp to the place where he was set in his chair of state, with a marvelous and an unspeakable majesty, having the chiefest men of the Volsces about him. So he commanded them to declare openly the cause of their coming. Which they delivered in the most humble and lowly words they possibly could devise, and with all modest countenance and behavior agreeable to the same. When they had done their message for the injury they had done him, he answered them very hotly and in great choler. But as general of the Volsces he willed them to restore unto the Volsces all their lands and cities they had taken from them in former wars, and moreover, that they should give them the like honor and freedom of Rome as they had before given to the Latins. For otherwise they had no other means to end this war, if they did not grant these honest and just conditions of peace. Thereupon he gave them thirty days respite to make him answer.

So the ambassadors returned straight to Rome, and Martius forthwith departed with his army out of the territories of the Romans. This was the first matter wherewith the Volsces (that most envied Martius' glory and authority) did charge Martius with. Among those, Tullus was chief, who though he had received no private injury or displeasure of Martius, yet the common fault and imperfection of man's nature wrought in him, and it grieved him to see his own reputation blemished through Martius' great fame and honor, and so himself to be less esteemed of the Volsces than he was before. This fell out the more, because every man honored Martius, and thought he only could do all, and that all other governors and captains must be content with such credit and authority as he would please to countenance them with. From hence they derived all their first accusations and secret murmurings against Martius. For private captains, conspiring against him, were very angry with him and gave it out that the removing of the camp was a manifest treason, not of the towns, nor forts, nor of arms, but of time and occasion, which was a loss of great importance, because it was that which in reason might both loose and bind all, and preserve the whole. . . .

Now all the city was full of tumult, fear, and marvelous doubt what would happen, until at the length there fell out such a like matter, as Homer oftimes said they would least have thought of. For in great matters that happen seldom, Homer saith, and crieth out in this sort:

The goddess Pallas she, with her fair glistering eyes,
Did put into his mind such thoughts, and made him so devise.

And in another place:

But sure some god hath tane out of the people's mind
Both wit and understanding eke, and have therewith assigned
Some other simple spirit, instead thereof to bide,
That so they might their doings all, for lack of wit, misguide.

And in another place:

The people of themselves did either it consider,
Or else some god instructed them, and so they join'd together.

Many reckon not of Homer, as referring matters unpossible and fables of no likelihood or troth unto man's reason, free will, or judgment, which indeed is not his meaning. But things true and likely he maketh to depend of our own free will and reason. For he oft speaketh these words:

I have thought it in my noble heart.

And in another place:

> Achilles angry was, and sorry for to hear
> Him so to say, his heavy breast was fraught with pensive fear.

And in another place:

> Bellerophon (she) could not move with her fair tongue,
> So honest and so virtuous he was, the rest among.

But in wondrous and extraordinary things, which are done by secret inspirations and motions, he doth not say that God taketh away from man his choice and freedom of will, but that he doth move it; neither that he doth work desire in us, but objecteth to our minds certain imaginations whereby we are led to desire, and thereby doth not make this our action forced, but openeth the way to our will and addeth thereto courage and hope of success. For either we must say that the gods meddle not with the causes and beginnings of our actions; or else what other means have they to help and further men? It is apparent that they handle not our bodies nor move not our feet and hands when there is occasion to use them, but that part of our mind from which these motions proceed is induced thereto, or carried away by such objects and reasons, as God offereth unto it.

Now the Roman ladies and gentlewomen did visit all the temples and gods of the same, to make their prayers unto them. But the greatest ladies (and more part of them) were continually about the altar of Jupiter Capitolin, among which troup by name was Valeria, Publicola's own sister—the self-same Publicola who did such notable services to the Romans, both in peace and wars, and was dead also certain years before, as we have declared in his life. His sister Valeria was greatly honored and reverenced among all the Romans, and did so modestly and wisely behave herself that she did not shame nor dishonor the house she came of. So she suddenly fell into such a fancy as we have rehearsed before, and had (by some god, as I think) taken hold of a noble device.

Whereupon she rose and the other ladies with her, and they all together went straight to the house of Volumnia, Martius' mother, and coming in to her, found her and Martius' wife, her daughter-in-law, set together and having her husband Martius' young children in her lap. Now all the train of these ladies sitting in a ring round about her, Valeria first began to speak in this sort unto her: "We ladies are come to visit you ladies (my lady Volumnia and Virgilia) by no direction from the Senate, nor commandment of other magistrate, but through the inspiration (as I take it) of some god above; who, having taken compassion and pity of our prayers, hath moved us to come unto you, to entreat you in a matter as well beneficial for us as also for the whole citizens in general, but to yourselves in special (if it please you to credit me), and shall redound to your more fame and glory than the daughters of the Sabines obtained in former age, when they procured loving peace instead of hateful war between their fathers and their husbands. Come on, good ladies, and let us go all together unto Martius, to entreat him to take pity upon us, and also to report the truth unto him, how much you are bound unto the citizens; who notwithstanding they have sustained great hurt and losses by him, yet they have not hitherto sought revenge upon your persons by any discourteous usage, neither ever conceived any such thought or intent against you, but to deliver you safe into his hands, though thereby they look for no better grace or clemency from him." When Valeria had spoken this unto them, all the other ladies together, with one voice, confirmed that she had said.

Then Volumnia in this sort did answer her: "My good ladies, we are partakers with you of the common misery and calamity of our country, and yet our grief exceedeth yours the more, by reason of our particular misfortune, to feel the loss of my son Martius' former valiancy and glory, and to see his person environed now with our enemies in arms, rather to see him forthcoming and safe kept than of any love to defend his person. But yet the greatest grief of our heaped mishaps is to see our poor country brought to such extremity that all the hope of the safety and preservation thereof is now unfortunately cast upon us simple women; because we know not what account he will make of us, since he hath cast from him all care of his natural country and commonweal, which heretofore he hath holden more dear and precious than either his mother, wife, or children. Notwithstanding, if ye think we can do good, we will willingly do what you will have us; bring us to him, I pray you. For if we cannot prevail, we may yet die at his feet, as humble suitors for the safety of our country."

Her answer ended, she took her daughter-in-law and Martius' children with her, and being accompanied with all the other Roman ladies, they went in troup together unto the Volsces' camp; whom when they saw, they of themselves did both pity and reverence her, and there was not a man among them that once durst say a word unto her. Now was Martius set then in his chair of state, with all the honors of a general, and when he had spied the women coming afar off, he marveled what the matter meant. But afterwards knowing his wife, which came foremost, he determined at the first to persist in his obstinate and inflexible rancor. But overcome in the end with natural affection and being altogether altered to see them, his heart would not serve him to tarry their coming to his chair, but coming down in haste he went to meet them, and first he kissed his mother and embraced her a pretty while, then his wife and little children. And nature so wrought with him that the tears fell from his eyes, and he could not keep himself from making much of them but yielded to the affection of his blood, as if he had been violently carried with the fury of a most swift running stream.

After he had thus lovingly received them, and perceiving that his mother Volumnia would begin to speak to him, he called the chiefest of the council of the Volsces to hear what she would say. Then she spake in this sort: "If we held our peace, my son, and determined not to speak, the state of our poor bodies, and present sight of our raiment, would easily bewray to thee what life we have led at home since thy exile and abode abroad. But think now with thyself, how much more unfortunate than all the women living we are come hither, considering that the sight which should be most pleasant to all other to behold, spiteful fortune had made most fearful to us, making myself to see my son, and my daughter here her husband, besieging the walls of his native country; so as that which is the only comfort to all other in their adversity and misery, to pray unto the gods and to call to them for aid, is the only thing which plungeth us into most deep perplexity. For we cannot, alas, together pray both for victory to our country and for safety of thy life also: but a world of grievous curses, yea, more than any mortal enemy can heap upon us, are forcibly wrapt up in our prayers. For the bitter sop of most hard choice is offered thy wife and children, to forgo one of the two: either to lose the person of thyself or the nurse of their native country.

"For myself, my son, I am determined not to tarry till fortune, in my lifetime, do make an end of this war. For if I cannot persuade thee rather to do good unto both parties than to overthrow and destroy the one, preferring love and nature before the malice and calamity of wars, thou shalt see, my son, and trust unto it, thou shalt no sooner march forward to assault thy country, but thy foot shall tread upon thy mother's womb that brought thee first into this world. And I may not defer to see the day, either that my son be led prisoner in triumph by his natural countrymen, or that he himself do triumph of them, and of his natural country.

"For if it were so, that my request tended to save thy country, in destroying the Volsces, I must confess, thou wouldest hardly and doubtfully resolve on that. For as to destroy thy natural country, it is altogether unmeet and unlawful, so were it not just and less honorable to betray those that put their trust in thee. But my only demand consisteth to make a jail-delivery of all evils, which delivereth equal benefit and safety both to the one and the other, but most honorable for the Volsces. For it shall appear that, having victory in their hands, they have of special favor granted us singular graces, peace, and amity, albeit themselves have no less part of both than we. Of which good, if so it came to pass, thyself is the only author, and so hast thou the only honor. But if it fail and fall out contrary, thyself alone deservedly shalt carry the shameful reproach and burthen of either party.

"So, though the end of war be uncertain, yet this notwithstanding is most certain: that, if it be thy chance to conquer, this benefit shalt thou reap of thy goodly conquest, to be chronicled the plague and destroyer of thy country. And if fortune overthrow thee, then the world will say that through desire to revenge thy private injuries, thou hast forever undone thy good friends, who did most lovingly and courteously receive thee."

Martius gave good ear unto his mother's words, without interrupting her speech at all, and after she had said what she would, he held his peace a pretty while and answered not a word. Hereupon she began again to speak unto him, and said: "My son, why dost thou not answer me? Dost thou think it good altogether to give place unto thy choler and desire of revenge, and thinkest thou it not honesty for thee to grant thy mother's request in so weighty a cause? Dost thou take it honorable for a noble man to remember the wrongs and injuries done him, and dost not in like case think it an honest noble man's part, to be thankful for the goodness that parents do show to their children, acknowledging the duty and reverence they ought to bear unto them? No man living is more bound to show himself thankful in all parts and respects than thyself; who so unnaturally showest all ingratitude. Moreover (my son) thou hast sorely taken of thy country, exacting grievous payments upon them, in revenge of the injuries offered thee; besides, thou hast not hitherto showed thy poor mother any courtesy. And therefore it is not only honest, but due unto me, that without compulsion I should obtain my so just and reasonable request of thee. But since by reason I cannot persuade thee to it, to what purpose do I defer my last hope?" And with these words, herself, his wife and children fell down upon their knees before him.

Martius, seeing that, could refrain no longer, but went straight and lift her up, crying out, "Oh, Mother, what have you done to me?" And holding her hard by the right hand, "Oh, Mother," said he, "you have won a happy victory for your country, but mortal and unhappy for your son; for I see myself vanquished by you alone." These words being spoken openly, he spake a little apart with his mother and wife, and then let them return again to Rome, for so they did request him.

And so remaining in camp that night, the next morning he dislodged and marched homeward into the Volsces' country again, who were not all of one mind nor all alike contented. For some misliked him and that he had done; other, being well pleased that peace should be made, said that neither the one nor the other deserved blame nor reproach. Other, though they misliked that was done, did not think him an ill man for that he did, but said he was not to be blamed, though he yielded to such a forcible extremity. Howbeit, no man contraried his departure, but all obeyed his commandment, more for respect of his worthiness and valiancy than for fear of his authority.

Now the citizens of Rome plainly showed in what fear and danger their city stood of this war, when they were delivered. For so soon as the watch upon the walls of the city perceived the Volsces' camp to remove, there was not a temple in the city but was presently set open and full of men wearing garlands of flowers upon their heads, sacrificing to the gods, as they were wont to do upon the news of some great obtained victory. And this common joy was yet more manifestly showed by the honorable courtesies the whole Senate and people did bestow on their ladies. For they were all thoroughly persuaded and did certainly believe that the ladies only were cause of the saving of the city and delivering themselves from the instant danger of the war.

Whereupon the Senate ordained that the magistrates, to gratify and honor these ladies, should grant them all that they would require. And they only requested that they would build a temple of Fortune for the women, unto the building whereof they offered, themselves, to defray the whole charge of the sacrifices and other ceremonies belonging to the service of the gods. Nevertheless, the Senate, commending their goodwill and forwardness, ordained that the temple and image should be made at the common charge of the city. Notwithstanding that, the ladies gathered money among them and made with the same a second image of Fortune, which the Romans say did speak as they offered her up in the temple and did set her in her place; and they affirm that she spake these words: "Ladies, ye have devoutly offered me up." Moreover, that she spake that twice together, making us to believe things that never were and are not to be credited. . . .

Now when Martius was returned again into the city of Antium from his voyage, Tullus, that hated and could no longer abide him for the fear he had of his authority, sought diverse means to make him away, thinking if he let slip that present time, he should never recover the like and fit occasion again. Wherefore Tullus, having procured many other of his confederacy, required Martius might be deposed from his estate to render up account to the Volsces of his charge and government. Martius, fearing to become a private man again under Tullus being general (whose authority was greater otherwise than any other among all the Volsces), answered; he was willing to give up his charge and would resign it into the hands of the lords of the Volsces, if they did all command him, as by all their commandment he received it. And moreover, that he would not refuse even at that present to give up an account unto the people, if they would tarry the hearing of it.

The people hereupon called a common council, in which assembly there were certain orators appointed that stirred up the common people against him; and when they had told their tales, Martius rose up to make them answer. Now, notwithstanding the mutinous people made a marvelous great noise, yet when they saw him, for the reverence they bare unto his valiantness, they quieted themselves and gave him audience to allege with leisure what he could for his purgation. Moreover, the honestest men of the Antiates, and who most rejoiced in peace, showed by their countenance that they would hear him willingly and judge also according to their conscience.

Whereupon Tullus, fearing that if he did let him speak, he would prove his innocency to the people, because amongst other things he had an eloquent tongue; besides that the first good service he had done to the people of the Volsces did win him more favor than these last accusations could purchase him displeasure; and furthermore, the offense they laid to his charge was a testimony of the goodwill they ought him; for they would never have thought he had done them wrong for that they took not the city of Rome, if they had not been very near taking of it by means of his approach and conduction. For these causes Tullus thought he might no longer delay his pretense and enterprise, neither to tarry for the mutining and rising of the common people against him. Wherefore those that were of the conspiracy began to cry out that he was not to be heard, and that they would not suffer a traitor to usurp tyrannical power over the tribe of the

Volsces, who would not yield up his state and authority. And in saying these words, they all fell upon him and killed him in the marketplace, none of the people once offering to rescue him.

Howbeit, it is a clear case that this murder was not generally consented unto of the most part of the Volsces. For men came out of all parts to honor his body, and did honorably bury him, setting out his tomb with great store of armor and spoils, as the tomb of a worthy person and great captain. The Romans, understanding of his death, showed no other honor or malice, saving that they granted the ladies their request they made, that they might mourn ten months for him. And that was the full time they used to wear blacks for the death of their fathers, brethren, or husbands, according to Numa Pompilius' order who established the same, as we have enlarged more amply in the description of his life.

Now Martius being dead, the whole state of the Volsces heartily wished him alive again. For, first of all, they fell out with the Aeques (who were their friends and confederates) touching preeminence and place; and this quarrel grew on so far between them that frays and murders fell out upon it, one with another. After that, the Romans overcame them in battle, in which Tullus was slain in the field, and the flower of all their force was put to the sword; so that they were compelled to accept most shameful conditions of peace, in yielding themselves subject unto the conquerors and promising to be obedient at their commandment.

Commentaries

A. C. BRADLEY

Coriolanus

BRITISH ACADEMY SHAKESPEARE
LECTURE, 1912

Coriolanus[1] is beyond doubt among the latest of Shakespeare's tragedies: there is some reason for thinking it the last. Like all those that succeeded *Hamlet,* it is a tragedy of vehement passion; and in none of them are more striking revolutions of fortune displayed. It is full of power, and almost every one feels it to be a noble work. We may say of it, as its hero that, if not one of Shakespeare's greatest creations, it is certainly one of his biggest.

---

[1]Shakespeare's treatment of his subject is often best understood through comparison with his authority, Plutarch's *Life of Coriolanus* in North's translation, a translation most conveniently read in the volume edited by Prof. Skeat and entitled *Shakespeare's Plutarch.* For a full development of the comparison, and, generally, for a discussion of the play much more complete than mine could be, see Prof. MacCallum's book, *Shakespeare's Roman Plays and their Background* (1910), which is admirable both for its thoroughness and for the insight and justice of its criticism. I should perhaps add that, though I read the greater part of Prof. MacCallum's book when it appeared, I was prevented from going on to the chapters on *Coriolanus,* and did so only after writing my lecture. I left untouched in the lecture the many observations which this reading confirmed, but on one or two doubtful points I have added a Postscript.

From *A Miscellany* by A. C. Bradley (London: Macmillan and Co. Ltd., 1929). Reprinted by permission of Macmillan & Co. Ltd.

Nevertheless, it is scarcely popular. It is seldom acted, and perhaps no reader ever called it his favorite play. Indeed, except for educational purposes, it is probably, after *Timon*, the least generally read of the tragedies.

Even the critic who feels bound to rank it above *Romeo and Juliet*, and even above *Julius Caesar*, may add that he prefers those dramas all the same; and if he ignores his personal preferences, still we do not find him asking whether it is not the equal of the four great tragedies. He may feel his doubt as to *Antony and Cleopatra*, but not as to *Coriolanus*.

The question why this should be so will at once tell us something about the drama. We cannot say that it shows any decline in Shakespeare's powers, though in parts it may show slackness in their use. It has defects, some of which are due to the historical material; but all the tragedies have defects, and the material of *Antony and Cleopatra* was even more troublesome. There is no love-story; but then there is none in *Macbeth*, and next to none in *King Lear*. Thanks in part to the badness of the Folio text, the reader is impeded by obscurities of language and irritated by the mangling of Shakespeare's meter; yet these annoyances would not much diminish the effect of *Othello*. It may seem a more serious obstacle that the hero's faults are repellent and chill our sympathy; but Macbeth, to say nothing of his murders, is a much less noble being than Coriolanus. All this doubtless goes for something; yet there must be some further reason why this drama stands apart from the four great tragedies and *Antony and Cleopatra*. And one main reason seems to be this. Shakespeare could construe the story he found only by conceiving the hero's character in a certain way; and he had to set the whole drama in tune with that conception. In this he was, no doubt, perfectly right; but he closed the door on certain effects, in the absence of which his whole power in tragedy could not be displayed. He had to be content with something less, or rather with something else; and so have we.

Most of the great tragedies leave a certain imaginative impression of the highest value, which I describe in terms intended merely to recall it. What we witness is not the passion and doom of mere individuals. The forces that meet in the tragedy stretch far beyond the little group of figures and the tiny tract of space and time in which they appear. The darkness that covers the scene, and the light that strikes across it, are more than our common night and day. The hero's fate is, in one sense, intelligible, for it follows from his character and the conditions in which he is placed; and yet everything, character, conditions, and issue, is mystery. Now of this effect there is very little in *Coriolanus*. No doubt the story has a universal meaning, since the contending forces are permanent constituents of human nature; but that peculiar *imaginative* effect or atmosphere is hardly felt. And, thinking of the play, we notice that the means by which it is produced elsewhere are almost absent here. One of these means is the use of the supernatural; another a treatment of nature which makes her appear not merely as a background, nor even merely as a conscious witness of human feelings, sufferings, and deeds, but as a vaster fellow-actor and fellow-sufferer. Remove in fancy from *Hamlet, Lear,* and *Macbeth* all that appeals to imagination through these means, and you find them utterly changed, but brought nearer to *Coriolanus*. Here Shakespeare has deliberately withdrawn his hand from those engines. He found, of course, in Plutarch allusions to the gods, and some of these he used; but he does not make us feel that the gods take part in the story. He found also wonders in the firmament, portents, a strange vision seen by a slave, a statue that spoke. He found that the Romans in their extremity sent the priests, augurs, and soothsayers to plead with Coriolanus; and that the embassy of the women which saved Rome was due to a thought which came suddenly to Valeria, which she herself regarded as a divine inspiration, and on the nature of which Plutarch speculates. But the whole of this Shakespeare ignored. Nor would he use that other instrument I spoke of. Coriolanus was not the man to be terrified by twilight, or to feel that the stars or the wind took part against or with him. If Lear's thunderstorm had beat upon his head, he would merely have set his teeth. And not only is the mystery of nature absent; she is scarcely present even as a background. The hero's grim description of his abode in exile as "the city of kites and crows" (it is not in Plutarch) is almost all we have. In short, *Coriolanus* has scarcely more atmosphere, either supernatural or natural, than the average serious prose drama of today.

In Shakespeare's greatest tragedies there is a second source—in one or two the chief source—of supreme imaginative appeal, the exhibition of inward conflict, or of the outburst of one or another passion, terrible, heartrending, or glorious to witness. At these moments the speaker becomes the greatest of poets; and yet, the dramatic convention admitted, he speaks in character. The hero in *Coriolanus* is never thus the greatest of poets, and he could not be so without a breach of more than dramatic convention. His nature is large, simple, passionate; but (except in one point, to which I will return, as it is irrelevant here) his nature is not, in any marked degree, imaginative. He feels all the rapture, but not, like Othello, all the poetry, of war. He covets honor no less than Hotspur, but he has not Hotspur's vision of honor. He meets with ingratitude, like Timon, but it does not transfigure all mankind for him. He is very eloquent, but his only free eloquence is that of vituperation and scorn. It is sometimes more than eloquence, it is splendid poetry; but it is never such magical poetry as we hear in the four greatest tragedies. Then, too, it lies in his nature that his deepest and most sacred feeling, that for his mother, is almost dumb. It governs his life and leads him uncomplaining towards death, but it cannot speak. And, finally, his inward conflicts are veiled from us. The change that came when he found himself alone and homeless in exile is not exhibited. The result is partly seen in the one soliloquy of this drama, but the process is hidden. Of the passion that possesses him when his triumph seems at hand we get a far more vivid idea from the words of Cominius than from any words of his own:

> I tell you he does sit in gold, his eye
> Red as 'twould burn Rome.

In the most famous scene, when his fate is being decided, only one short sentence reveals the gradual loosening of his purpose during his mother's speech. The actor's face and hands and bearing must show it, not the hero's voice; and his submission is announced in a few quiet words, deeply moving and impressive, but destitute of the effect we know elsewhere of a lightning flash that rends the darkness and discloses every cranny of the speaker's soul. All this we can see to be as it should be, but it does set limits to the flight of Shakespeare's imagination.

I have spoken of something that we miss in *Coriolanus*. Unfortunately there is something which a good many readers find, or think they find, and which makes it distasteful to them. A political conflict is never the center of interest in Shakespeare's plays, but in the historical plays it is an element more or less essential, and in this one it is very prominent. Here, too, since it may be plausibly described as a conflict between people and nobles, or democracy and aristocracy, the issue is felt to be still alive. And Shakespeare, it is thought, shows an animus, and sides against the people. A hundred years ago Hazlitt, dealing with this tragedy, wrote: "Shakespeare himself seems to have had a leaning to the arbitrary side of the question, perhaps from some feeling of contempt for his own origin; and to have spared no occasion of baiting the rabble. What he says of them is very true; what he says of their betters is also very true, though he dwells less upon it." This language is very tentative and mild compared with that of some later writers. According to one, Shakespeare "loathed the common Englishman." He was a neuropath who could not endure the greasy aprons and noisome breath of mechanics, and "a snob of the purest English water." According to another, he was probably afflicted for some years with an "enormous self-esteem." A hero similarly afflicted, and a nauseous mob—behold the play!

I do not propose to join this dance, or even to ask whether any reasonable conjecture as to Shakespeare's political views and feelings could be formed from the study of this play and of others. But it may be worthwhile to mention certain questions which should be weighed by anyone who makes the adventure. Are not the chief weaknesses and vices shown by the populace, or attributed to it by speakers, in these plays, those with which it had been habitually charged in antiquity and the Middle Ages; and did not Shakespeare find this common form, if nowhere else, in Plutarch? Again, if these traits and charges are heightened in his dramas, what else do we expect in drama, and especially in that of the Elizabethans? Granted, next, that in Shakespeare the people play a sorry political part, is that played by English nobles and Roman patricians much more glorious or beneficent? And if, in Hazlitt's phrase, Shakespeare says more of the faults of the people than those of their betters, would we have him give to humble unlettered persons the powers of invective of lordly orators? Further, is abuse of the people ever dramatically inappropriate in Shakespeare; and is it given to Henry the Fifth, or Brutus (who had some cause for it), or, in short, to any of the most attractive characters? Is there not, besides, a great difference between his picture of the people taken as individuals, even when they talk politics, and his picture of them as a crowd or mob? Is not the former, however humorously critical, always kindly; and is a personal bias really needed to account for the latter? And, to end a catalogue easy to prolong, might not that talk, which is scarcely peculiar to Shakespeare, about greasy caps and offensive odors, have some other origin than his artistic nerves? He had, after all, some little gift of observation, and, when first he mixed with a class above his own, might he not resemble a son of the people now who, coming among his betters, observes with amusement the place held in their decalogue by the morning bath? I do not for a moment suggest that, by weighing such questions as these, we should be led to imagine Shakespeare as any more inclined to champion the populace than Spenser or Hooker or Bacon; but I think we should feel it extremely hazardous to ascribe to him any political feelings at all, and ridiculous to pretend to certainty on the subject.

Let us turn to the play. The representation of the people, whatever else it may be, is part of a dramatic design. This design is based on the main facts of the story, and these imply a certain character in the people and the hero. Since the issue is tragic, the conflict between them must be felt to be unavoidable and well-nigh hopeless. The necessity for dramatic sympathy with both sides demands that on both there should be some right and some wrong, both virtues and failings; and if the hero's monstrous purpose of destroying his native city is not to extinguish our sympathy, the provocation he receives must be great. This being so, the picture of the people is, surely, no darker than it had to be; the desired result would have been more easily secured by making it darker still. And one must go further. As regards the political situation, the total effect of the drama, it appears to me, is this. The conflict of hero and people is hopeless; but it is he alone who makes the conflict of patricians and plebeians, I do not say hopeless, but in any high degree dangerous. The people have bad faults, but no such fault as, in his absence, would prevent a constitutional development in their favor.

I will not try to describe their character, but I will illustrate this statement by comparing two accusations of their opponents with the facts shown; for these we must accept, but the accusations we must judge for ourselves. In the first scene the people are called cowards, both by the hero and by their friendly critic, Menenius. Now there is no sign that they possess the kind of courage expected of gentlemen, or feel the corresponding shame if their courage fails. But if they were cowards, how could Rome be standing where we see it stand? They are the common soldiers of Rome. And when we see them in war, what do we find? One division, under Cominius, meets the Volscians in the field; the other, under Coriolanus, assaults Corioli. Both are beaten back. This is what Cominius says to his men:

> Breathe you, my friends: well fought: we are come off
> Like Romans, neither foolish in our stands,
> Nor cowardly in retire.

Nothing hints that the other division has not fought well or was cowardly in retire; but it was encouraged beforehand with threats, and, on its failure, with a torrent of curses and abuse. Nevertheless it advances again and forces the enemy to the gates, which Coriolanus enters, calling on his men to follow him.

> *First Sol.* Foolhardiness; not I.
> *Second Sol.* Nor I.
> *First Sol.* See, they have shut him in.
> *All.* To the pot, I warrant him.

Disgusting, no doubt; but the answer to threats and curses. They would not have served Cominius so; and indeed, when Lartius comes up and merely suggests to them to "fetch off" the reappearing hero, they respond at once and take the city. These men are not cowards; but their conduct depends on their leaders. The same thing is seen when Coriolanus himself appeals to the other division for volunteers to serve in the van. For once he appeals nobly, and the whole division volunteers.

Another charge he brings against the people is that they can neither rule nor be ruled. On this his policy of "thorough" is based. Now, judging from the drama, one would certainly say that they could not rule alone—that a pure democracy would lead to anarchy, and perhaps to foreign subjection. And one would say also that they probably could not be ruled by the patricians if all political rights were denied them. But to rule them, while granting them a place in the constitution, would seem quite feasible. They are, in fact, only too easy to guide. No doubt, collected into a mob, led by demagogues, and maddened by resentment and fear, they become wild and cruel. It is true, also, that, when their acts bear bitter fruit, they disclaim responsibility and turn on their leaders: "that we did, we did for the best; and though we willingly consented to his banishment, yet it was against our will." But they not only follow their tribunes like sheep; they receive abuse and direction submissively from anyone who shows goodwill. They are fundamentally good-natured, like the Englishmen they are, and have a humorous consciousness of their own weaknesses. They are, beyond doubt, mutable, and in that sense untrustworthy; but they are not by nature ungrateful, or slow to admire their bitterest enemy. False charges and mean imputations come from their leaders, not from them. If one of them blames Coriolanus for being proud, another says he cannot help his pride. They insist on the bare form of their right to name him consul, but all they want is the form, and not the whole even of that. When he asks one of them, "Well then, I pray, your price of the consulship?" the answer, "The price is to ask it kindly," ought to have melted him at once; yet when he asks it contemptuously it is still granted. Even later, when the arts of the tribunes have provoked him to such a storm of defiant

and revolutionary speech that both the consulship and his
life are in danger, one feels that another man might save both
with no great trouble. Menenius tells him that the people

> have pardons, being ask'd, as free
> As words to little purpose.

His mother and friends urge him to deceive the people with
false promises. But neither false promises nor apologies are
needed; only a little humanity and some acknowledgment
that the people are part of the state. He is capable of neither,
and so the conflict is hopeless. But it is not so because the
people, or even the tribunes, are what they are, but because
he is what we call an "impossible" person.

The result is that all the force and nobility of Rome's
greatest man have to be thrown away and wasted. That is
tragic; and it is doubly so because it is not only his faults that
make him impossible. There is bound up with them a nobleness of nature in which he surpasses everyone around him.

We see this if we consider, what is not always clear to the
reader, his political position. It is not shared by any of the
other patricians who appear in the drama. Critics have called
him a Tory or an ultra-Tory; but the tribune who calls him a
"traitorous innovator" is quite as near the mark. The people
have been granted tribunes. The tribunate is a part of the
constitution, and it is accepted, with whatever reluctance, by
the other patricians. But Coriolanus would abolish it, and
that not by law but by the sword. Nor would this content
him. The right of the people to control the election of the
consul is no new thing; it is an old traditional right; but it,
too, he says, might well be taken away. The only constitution tolerable in his eyes is one where the patricians are the
state, and the people a mere instrument to feed it and fight
for it. It is this conviction that makes it so dangerous to
appoint him consul, and also makes it impossible for him to
give way. Even if he could ask pardon for his abuse of the
people, he could not honestly promise to acknowledge their
political rights.

Now the nobleness of his nature is at work here. He is not
tyrannical; the charge brought against him of aiming at a

tyranny is silly. He is an aristocrat. And Shakespeare has put decisively aside the statement of Plutarch that he was "churlish, uncivil, and altogether unfit for any man's conversation." Shakespeare's hero, though he feels his superiority to his fellow-patricians, always treats them as equals. He is never rude or overbearing. He speaks to them with the simple directness or the bluff familiarity of a comrade. He does not resent their advice, criticism, or reproof. He shows no trace of envy or jealousy, or even of satisfaction at having surpassed them. The suggestion of the tribunes that he is willing to serve under Cominius because failure in war will be credited to Cominius, and success in war to himself, shows only the littleness of their own minds. The patricians are his fellows in a community of virtue—of a courage, fidelity, and honor, which cannot fail them because they are "true-bred," though the bright ideal of such virtue become perfect still urges them on. But the plebeians, in his eyes, are destitute of this virtue, and therefore have no place in this community. All they care for is food in peace, looting in war, flattery from their demagogues; and they will not even clean their teeth. To ask anything of them is to insult not merely himself but the virtues that he worships. To give them a real share in citizenship is treason to Rome; for Rome means these virtues. They are not Romans, they are the rats of Rome.

He is very unjust to them, and his ideal, though high, is also narrow. But he is magnificently true to it, and even when he most repels us we feel this and glory in him. He is never more true to it than when he tries to be false; and this is the scene where his superiority in nobleness is most apparent. He, who had said of his enemy, "I hate him worse than a promise-breaker," is urged to save himself and his friends by promises that he means to break. To his mother's argument that he ought no more to mind deceiving the people than outwitting an enemy in war, he cannot give the obvious answer, for he does not really count the people his fellow-countrymen; but the proposal that *he* should descend to lying or flattering astounds him. He feels that if he does so he will never be himself again; that his mind will have taken on an inherent baseness and no mere simulated one. And he is sure, as we are, that he simply cannot do what is required

of him. When at last he consents to try, it is solely because
his mother bids him and he cannot resist her chiding. Often
he reminds us of a huge boy; and here he acts like a boy
whose sense of honor is finer than his mother's, but who is
too simple and too noble to frame the thought.

Unfortunately he is altogether too simple and too ignorant
of himself. Though he is the proudest man in Shakespeare,
he seems to be unaware of his pride, and is hurt when his
mother mentions it. It does not prevent him from being
genuinely modest, for he never dreams that he has attained
the ideal he worships; yet the sense of his own greatness is
twisted round every strand of this worship. In almost all his
words and deeds we are conscious of the tangle. I take a
single illustration. He cannot endure to be praised. Even his
mother, who has a charter to extol her blood, grieves him
when she praises him. As for others,

> I had rather have one scratch my head i' the sun
> When the alarum were struck, than idly sit
> To hear my nothings monster'd.

His answer to the roar of the army hailing him "Coriolanus"
is, "I will go wash." His wounds are "scratches with briars."
In Plutarch he shows them to the people without demur; in
Shakespeare he would rather lose the consulship. There is a
greatness in all this that makes us exult. But who can assign
the proportions of the elements that compose this impatience
of praise: the feeling (which we are surprised to hear him
express) that he, like hundreds more, has simply done what
he could; the sense that it is nothing to what might be done;
the want of human sympathy (for has not Shelley truly said
that fame is love disguised?); the pride which makes him
feel that he needs no recognition, that after all he himself
could do ten times as much, and that to praise his achievement implies a limit to his power? If any one could solve this
problem, Coriolanus certainly could not. To adapt a phrase
in the play, he has no more introspection in him than a tiger.
So he thinks that his loathing of the people is all disgust at
worthlessness, and his resentment in exile all a just indignation. So too he fancies that he can stand

> As if a man were author of himself
> And knew no other kin,

while in fact public honor and home affections are the breath of his nostrils, and there is not a drop of stoic blood in his veins.

What follows on his exile depends on this self-ignorance. When he bids farewell to his mother and wife and friends he is still excited and exalted by conflict. He comforts them: he will take no companion; he will be loved when he is lacked, or at least he will be feared; while he remains alive, they shall always hear from him, and never aught but what is like him formerly. But the days go by, and no one, not even his mother, hears a word. When we see him next, he is entering Antium to offer his services against his country. If they are accepted, he knows what he will do; he will burn Rome.

As I have already remarked, Shakespeare does not exhibit to us the change of mind which issues in this frightful purpose; but from what we see and hear later we can tell how he imagined it; and the key lies in that idea of *burning* Rome. As time passes, and no suggestion of recall reaches Coriolanus, and he learns what it is to be a solitary homeless exile, his heart hardens, his pride swells to a mountainous bulk, and the wound in it becomes a fire. The fellow-patricians from whom he parted lovingly now appear to him ingrates and dastards, scarcely better than the loathsome mob. Somehow, he knows not how, even his mother and wife have deserted him. He has become nothing to Rome, and Rome shall hear nothing from him. Here in solitude he can find no relief in a storm of words; but gradually the blind intolerable chaos of resentment conceives and gives birth to a vision, not merely of battle and indiscriminate slaughter, but of the whole city one tower of flame. To see that with his bodily eyes would satisfy his soul; and the way to the sight is through the Volscians. If he is killed the moment they recognize him, he cares little: better a dead nothing than the living nothing Rome thinks him. But if he lives, she shall know what he is. He bears himself among the Volscians with something that resembles self-control: but what controls him is the vision that never leaves him and never changes, and his eye is red with its glare when he sits in his state before the doomed city.[2]

This is Shakespeare's idea, not Plutarch's. In Plutarch there is not a syllable about the burning of Rome. Coriolanus (to simplify a complicated story) intends to humiliate his country by forcing on it disgraceful terms of peace. And this, apart from its moral quality, is a reasonable design. The Romans, rather than yield to fear, decline to treat unless peace is first restored; and therefore it will be necessary to assault the city. In the play we find a single vague allusion to some unnamed conditions which, Coriolanus knows, cannot now be accepted; but everywhere, among both Romans and Volscians, we hear of the burning of Rome, and in the city there is no hope of successful resistance. What Shakespeare wanted was a simpler and more appalling situation than he found in Plutarch, and a hero enslaved by his passion and driven blindly forward. How blindly, we may judge, if we ask the questions: what will happen to the hero if he disappoints the expectation he has raised among the Volscians, when their leader is preparing to accuse him even if he fulfills it: and, if the hero executes his purpose, what will happen to his mother, wife, and child: and how can it be executed by a man whom we know in his home as the most human of men, a husband who is still the lover of his wife, and a son who regards his mother not merely with devoted affection but with something like religious awe? Very likely the audience in the theatre was not expected to ask these questions, but it *was* expected to see in the hero a man totally ignorant of himself, and stumbling to the destruction either of his life or of his soul.

In speaking of the famous scene where he is confronted with Volumnia and Valeria, Virgilia and her boy, and the issue is decided, I am obliged to repeat what I have said elsewhere in print;[3] and I must speak in the first person because I do not know how far others share my view. To me the scene is one in which the tragic feelings of fear and pity have little place. Such anxiety as I feel is not for the fate of the hero or of anyone else: it is, to use religious language, for the safety

[2]See Postscript, p. 215.
[3]*Shakespearean Tragedy*, p. 84.

of his soul. And when he yields, though I know, as he divines, that his life is lost, the emotion I feel is not pity: he is above pity and above life. And the anxiety itself is but slight: it bears no resemblance to the hopes and fears that agitate us as we approach the end in *Othello* or *King Lear*. The whole scene affects me, to exaggerate a little, more as a majestic picture of stationary figures than as the fateful climax of an action speeding to its close. And the structure of the drama seems to confirm this view. Almost throughout the first three acts— that is, up to the banishment—we have incessant motion, excited and resounding speech, a violent oscillation of fortunes. But, after this, the dramatic tension is suddenly relaxed, and, though it increases again, it is never allowed to approach its previous height. If Shakespeare had wished it to do so in this scene, he had only to make us wait in dread of some interposition from Aufidius, at which the hero's passion might have burst into a fury fatal even to the influence of Volumnia. But our minds are crossed by no shadow of such dread. From the moment when he catches sight of the advancing figures, and the voice of nature—what he himself calls "great nature"—begins to speak in his heart long before it speaks aloud to his ear, we know the end. And all that is in harmony with that characteristic of the drama which we noticed at first—we feel but faintly, if at all, the presence of any mysterious or fateful agency. We are witnessing only the conquest of passion by simple human feelings, and *Coriolanus* is as much a drama of reconciliation as a tragedy. That is no defect in it, but it is a reason why it cannot leave the same impression as the supreme tragedies, and should be judged by its own standard.

A tragedy it is, for the passion is gigantic, and it leads to the hero's death. But the catastrophe scarcely diminishes the influence of the great scene. Since we know that his nature, though the good in it has conquered, remains unchanged, and since his rival's plan is concerted before our eyes, we wait with little suspense, almost indeed with tranquility, the certain end. As it approaches it is felt to be the more inevitable because the steps which lead to it are made to repeat as exactly as possible the steps which lead to his exile. His task, as then, is to excuse himself, a task the most repugnant to his pride. Aufidius, like the tribunes then, knows how to render its fulfillment impossible. He hears a word of insult, the same that he heard then—"traitor." It is followed by a sneer at the most sacred tears he ever shed, and a lying description of their effect on the bystanders; and his pride, and his loathing of falsehood and meanness, explode, as before, in furious speech. For a moment he tries to check himself and appeals to the senators; but the effort seems only to treble his rage. Though no man, since Aufidius spoke, has said a word against him, he defies the whole nation, recalling the day of its shame and his own triumph, when alone, like an eagle, he fluttered the dovecotes in Corioli. The people, who had accompanied him to the marketplace, splitting the air with the noise of their enthusiasm, remember their kinsfolk whom he slaughtered, change sides, and clamor for his death. As he turns on Aufidius, the conspirators rush upon him, and in a moment, before the vision of his glory has faded from his brain, he lies dead. The instantaneous cessation of enormous energy (which is like nothing else in Shakespeare) strikes us with awe, but not with pity. As I said, the effect of the preceding scene, where he conquered something stronger than all the Volscians and escaped something worse than death, is not reversed; it is only heightened by a renewed joy in his greatness. Roman and Volscian will have peace now, and in his native city patrician and plebeian will move along the way he barred. And they are in life, and he is not. But life has suddenly shrunk and dwindled, and become a home for pygmies and not for him.[4]

Dr. Johnson observed that "the tragedy of *Coriolanus* is one of the most amusing of our author's performances." By

[4]I have tried to indicate the effect at which Shakespeare's imagination seems to have aimed. I do not say that the execution is altogether adequate. And some readers, I know, would like Coriolanus to die fighting. Shakespeare's idea is probably to be gathered from the hero's appeal to the senators to judge between Aufidius and him, and from the word "lawful" in the last speech:

> O that I had him,
> With six Aufidiuses, or more, his tribe,
> To use my lawful sword!

He is not before the people only, but before the senators, his fellow-patricians, though of another city. Besides—if I may so put it—if Coriolanus were allowed to fight at all, he would have to annihilate the whole assembly.

"amusing" he did not mean "mirth-provoking"; he meant that in *Coriolanus* a lively interest is excited and sustained by the variety of the events and characters; and this is true. But we may add that the play contains a good deal that is amusing in the current sense of the word—more of this, it has been observed, than do the other Roman tragedies. When the people appear as individuals they are frequently more or less comical. Shakespeare always enjoyed the inconsequence of the uneducated mind, and its tendency to express a sound meaning in an absurd form. Again, the talk of the servants with one another and with the muffled hero, and the conversation of the sentinels with Menenius, are amusing. There is a touch of comedy in the contrast between Volumnia and Virgilia when we see them on occasions not too serious. And then, not only at the beginning, as in Plutarch, but throughout the story, we meet with that pleasant and wise old gentleman, Menenius, whose humor tells him how to keep the peace while he gains his point, and to say without offense what the hero cannot say without raising a storm. Perhaps no one else in the play is regarded from beginning to end with such unmingled approval, and this is not lessened when the failure of his embassy to Coriolanus makes him the subject as well as the author of mirth. If we regard the drama from this point of view we find that it differs from almost all the tragedies, though it has a certain likeness to *Antony and Cleopatra*. What is amusing in it is, for the most part, simply amusing, and has no tragic tinge. It is not like the gibes of Hamlet at Polonius, or the jokes of the clown who, we remember, is digging Ophelia's grave, or that humor of Iago which for us is full of menace; and who could dream of comparing it with the jesting of Lear's fool? Even that Shakespearean audacity, the interruption of Volumnia's speech by the hero's little son, makes one laugh almost without reserve. And all this helps to produce the characteristic tone of this tragedy.

The drawing of the character of Aufidius seems to me by far the weakest spot in the drama. At one place, where Aufidius moralizes on the banishment of the hero, Shakespeare, it appears to some critics, is himself delivering a speech which tells the audience nothing essential and ends in desperate obscurity.[5] Two other speeches have been criticized. In the first, Aufidius, after his defeat in the field, declares that, since he cannot overcome his rival in fair fight, he will do it in any way open to him, however dishonorable. The other is his lyrical cry of rapture when Coriolanus discloses himself in the house at Antium. The intention in both cases is clear. Aufidius is contrasted with the hero as a man of much slighter and less noble nature, whose lively impulses, good and bad, quickly give way before a new influence, and whose action is in the end determined by the permanent pressure of ambition and rivalry. But he is a man of straw. He was wanted merely for the plot, and in reading some passages in his talk, we seem to see Shakespeare yawning as he wrote. Besides, the unspeakable baseness of his sneer at the hero's tears is an injury to the final effect. Such an emotion as mere disgust is out of place in a tragic close; but I confess I feel nothing but disgust as Aufidius speaks the last words, except some indignation with the poet who allowed him to speak them, and an unregenerate desire to see the head and body of the speaker lying on opposite sides of the stage.

Though this play is by no means a drama of destiny, we might almost say that Volumnia is responsible for the hero's life and death. She trained him from the first to aim at honor in arms, to despise pain, and to

> forget that ever
> He heard the name of death;

to strive constantly to surpass himself, and to regard the populace with inhuman disdain as

> things created
> To buy and sell with groats.

Thus she led him to glory and to banishment. And it was she who, in the hour of trial, brought him to sacrifice his pride and his life.

Her sense of personal honor, we saw, was less keen than

---

[5]But Prof. MacCallum's defense of this passage is perhaps successful.

his; but she was much more patriotic. We feel this superiority even in the scene that reveals the defect; in her last scene we feel it alone. She has idolized her son; but, whatever motive she may appeal to in her effort to move him, it is not of him she thinks; her eyes look past him and are set on Rome. When, in yielding, he tells her that she has won a happy victory for her country, but a victory most dangerous, if not most mortal, to her son, she answers nothing. And her silence is sublime.

These last words would be true of Plutarch's Volumnia. But in Plutarch, though we hear of the son's devotion, and how he did great deeds to delight his mother, neither his early passion for war nor his attitude to the people is attributed to her influence, and she has no place in the action until she goes to plead with him. Hence she appears only in majesty, while Shakespeare's Volumnia has a more varied part to play. She cannot be majestic when we see her hurrying through the streets in wild exultation at the news of his triumph; and where, angrily conquering her tears, she rails at the authors of his banishment, she can hardly be called even dignified. What Shakespeare gains by her animation and vehemence in these scenes is not confined to them. He prepares for the final scene a sense of contrast which makes it doubly moving and impressive.

In Volumnia's great speech he is much indebted to Plutarch, and it is, on the whole, in the majestic parts that he keeps most close to his authority. The open appeal to affection is his own; and so are the touches of familiar language. It is his Volumnia who exclaims, "here he lets me prate like one i' the stocks," and who compares herself, as she once was, to a hen that clucks her chicken home. But then the conclusion, too, is pure Shakespeare; and if it has not majesty, it has something dramatically even more potent. Volumnia, abandoning or feigning to abandon hope, turns to her companions with the words:

> Come, let us go:
> This fellow had a Volscian to his mother;
> His wife is in Corioli, and his child
> Like him by chance. Yet give us our dispatch:

I am hush'd until our city be a-fire,
And then I'll speak a little.[6]

Her son's resolution has long been tottering, but now it falls
at once. Throughout, it is not the substance of her appeals
that moves him, but the bare fact that she appeals. And the
culmination is that she ceases to appeal, and defies him. This
has been observed by more than one critic. I do not know if
it has been noticed[7] that on a lower level exactly the same
thing happens when she tries to persuade him to go and
deceive the people. The moment she stops, and says, in
effect, "Well, then, follow your own will," his will gives
way. Deliberately to set it against hers is beyond his power.

Ruskin, whose terms of praise and blame were never
overcautious, wrote of Virgilia as "perhaps the loveliest of
Shakespeare's female characters." Others have described
her as a shrinking submissive being, afraid of the very name
of a wound, and much given to tears. This description is true;
and, I may remark in passing, it is pleasant to remember that
the hero's letter to his mother contained a full account of his
wounds, while his letter to his wife did not mention them at
all. But the description of these critics can hardly be the
whole truth about a woman who inflexibly rejects the
repeated invitations of her formidable mother-in-law and
her charming friend to leave her house; who later does what
she can to rival Volumnia in rating the tribunes; and who at
last quietly seconds Volumnia's assurance that Coriolanus
shall only enter Rome over her body. Still these added traits
do not account for the indefinable impression which Ruskin
received (if he did not rightly interpret it), and which thousands of readers share. It comes in part from that kind of
muteness in which Virgilia resembles Cordelia, and which is
made to suggest a world of feeling in reserve. And in part it
comes from the words of her husband. His greeting when he
returns from the war, and she stands speechless before him:

My gracious silence, hail!
Wouldst thou have laugh'd had I come coffin'd home,
That weep'st to see me triumph? Ah, my dear,

[6]What she will utter, I imagine, is a mother's dying curse.
[7]Yes, it is noticed by Prof. MacCallum.

> Such eyes the widows in Corioli wear,
> And mothers that lack sons:

his exclamation when he sees her approaching at their last meeting and speaks first of her and not of Volumnia:

> What is that curtsy worth, or those doves' eyes
> Which can make gods forsworn? I melt, and am not
> Of stronger earth than others;

these words envelop Virgilia in a radiance which is reflected back upon himself. And this is true also of his praise of Valeria in the lines perhaps most often quoted from this drama:

> The noble sister of Publicola,
> The moon of Rome, chaste as the icicle
> That's curdied by the frost from purest snow,
> And hangs on Dian's temple: dear Valeria!

I said that at one point the hero's nature *was* in a high degree imaginative; and it is here. In his huge violent heart there was a store, not only of tender affection, but of delicate and chivalrous poetry. And though Virgilia and Valeria evoke its expression we cannot limit its range. It extends to the widows and mothers in Corioli; and we feel that, however he might loathe and execrate the people, he was no more capable of injury or insult to a daughter of the people than Othello, or Chaucer's Knight, or Don Quixote himself.

POSTSCRIPT

Professor Case, in the Introduction to his admirable Arden edition of *Coriolanus,* while approving the interpretation suggested in this paragraph of the change in the hero's mind, withholds his assent to the stress laid in the paragraph on the particular idea of the *burning* of Rome. Instead of arguing the question I will simply describe the way in which the emphasis on that particular idea came to impress me.

When I was studying the play afresh with a view to this lecture, I noticed that, as the action approached its climax, the image of fire, not present to me before, became increasingly present, persistent and vivid; and at last, when Cominius, reporting his futile embassy to the hero, exclaims,

> I tell you he does sit in gold, his eye
> Red as 'twould burn Rome,

I said to myself, "Yes, *that* image of vengeance is what came to him in the solitude of his exile and has now become a possession." And, if I could have doubted this, doubt would have vanished when I reached Volumnia's speech (5.3.131), and read the words, its *final* words,

> Yet give us our dispatch:
> I am hushed until our city be a-fire,
> And then I'll speak a little.

The "possession" is shattered, and the catastrophe sure—and welcome.

Dismissing imagination, I have now made a research, and some readers may be interested in the result.

Throughout the greater part of the play, though there is plenty of fighting and Corioles is taken, we hear, I think, nothing of any burning of towns or cities. There is a mention of fire at 2.1.263–65, but it is the fire of contention between the hero and the people; and the "burning" and "fires" of 3.2.24 and 3.3.68 are those of hell; and even at 4.3.20–25, where the image of fire is decidedly more vivid, this fire is that of the anger of the two parties in Rome. But in 4.6.79, 83, 86, 116, 138, we have crowded and vivid references to the burning of the Roman territory by the army of Coriolanus, and to the prospect of his burning the city. And then, after a short scene, comes, at 5.1.14, 17, 27, 32 (where Cominius makes the report of his interview and repeats the words of Coriolanus) fire-image after fire-image, the series culminating at 64 in that of the "eye red as 'twould burn Rome." In the next scene (7, 47, 72) the series, naturally, continues; but in 5.3. where Volumnia is to appear, it ceases (for the hero is inwardly beginning to yield), until it reappears in her final words. And, after that, we have only the reference (5.5.3) to the "triumphant fires" in the saved city.

WYNDHAM LEWIS

From The Lion and the Fox

Troilus and Cressida, Professor Schelling says, is "the only play in which we feel that his [Shakespeare's] clarity and equanimity for the moment failed him and turned to bitterness and cynicism." That is a statement that appears to me typically sentimentalist and untrue. For is it not possible to match out of *Lear, Timon, Hamlet, Macbeth,* the "bitterest" that can be found in *Troilus*? The *cynical railer, altofronto* type, is one to which Shakespeare, far from being averse, seems particularly partial. Hamlet or Jaques provides incessant and deeply "bitter" examples. It seems beyond all contradiction that, however that statement affects your opinion of this gigantic poet, the *altofronto* mood was a permanent and characteristic one with him. That (accepting it, as best you can) you have to reconcile it with the "heroism" of his Antonys, Hectors and Othellos. No more than you can get a unity of time and place with Shakespeare can you get a unity of soul.

Before going further into this I will repeat the judgments at which I have arrived. In a sense, perhaps, Falstaff was Shakespeare's knight, as Don Quixote was the knight of Cervantes. For in the sphere of comedy, of tragicomedy, that is the natural parallel. And Sir John is the antithesis of Don Quixote. But Shakespeare had another, and almost a separate, department; and that was full of quixotic shapes. Timon, Coriolanus, Brutus, Hamlet, *are all Quixotes.* Only he sees them all, except perhaps Othello, more coldly than Cervantes saw his *hijo seco,* save when something like a sexual excitement seems to take possession of him, and he

From *The Lion and the Fox* by Wyndham Lewis (London: Methuen & Co. Ltd., 1951; New York: Hillary House, Inc., 1955). Reprinted by permission of Methuen & Co. Ltd.

begins caressing and adoring his hero as though he were a woman—like another Antonio in front of a Sebastian, in *Twelfth Night*.

To take only one of these—and I will choose the one that introduces naturally the next point that we shall have to take up—Coriolanus. That is the great creation that establishes Shakespeare—for those who want to see him as such—as "the feudal poet." Coriolanus is the demented "aristocrat," the incarnation of violent snobbery. In that, as in most Elizabethan plays, you get the invective against the "multitude." The spirit of Marston is found in it in full force; though there is nowhere in it as convinced an "aristocratism" as terminates the following lines from *Antonio and Mellida:*

O rotten props of the craz'd multitude,
How you still double, falter, under the lightest chance
That strains your veins! Alas, one battle lost,
Your whorish love, your drunken healths—your houts and
    shouts,
Your smooth God save's, and all your devil's last
That tempts our quiet to your hell of throngs!

But Coriolanus, as a figure, is of course the super-snob. Of all Shakespeare's heroes he is the coldest, and the one that Shakespeare himself seems to have felt most coldly towards. He was the child of Volumnia, not of Shakespeare, and one that never became anything but a schoolboy, crazed with notions of privilege and social distinction, incapable of thinking (not differing in that from the rest of Shakespeare's nursery of colossi), but also congealed into a kind of machine of unintelligent pride. He is like a Nietzschean, artificial "aristocrat," with little nobility in the sense that Don Quixote caricaturally embodied the noble, but possessing only a maniacal intolerance and stiffness.

There is a hollowness in the "heroics" in Coriolanus. But no hero could ever expect to be quite safe with the author of *Troilus and Cressida*. The following description, for instance, of the behavior of the little son of Coriolanus by a friend of the family is "true to life," but too true not to have been observed with a mind detached from any infatuation with the speakers. It is impossible that this picture of a little

Coriolanus growing up "just like his father" is not meant to illuminate Coriolanus for us:

> *Valeria.* O' my word, the father's son; I'll swear, 'tis a very pretty boy. O' my troth, I looked upon him o' Wednesday half an hour together; has such a confirmed countenance. I saw him run after a gilded butterfly; and when he caught it, he let it go again; and after it again; and over and over he comes, and up again; catched it again: or whether his fall enraged him, or how 'twas, he did so set his teeth; and tear it. O, I warrant, how he mammocked it!
>
> *Volumnia.* One on's father's moods.
>
> *Valeria.* Indeed, la, 'tis a noble child.
>
> *Virgilia.* A crack, madam.

"Indeed, la, 'tis a noble child" is a remark that would certainly not pass the censorship in a despotic super-feudal state, or recommend its author to a Nietzschean. And had Shakespeare wished to engage the sympathy of almost any audience with this fine little fellow, he certainly would not have chosen such a pretty and also flimsy thing as a butterfly to show him wracking one of his "father's moods" on.

It would appear that Shakespeare means at this point to show us the true Coriolanus, a cruel and stupid child, and to show him to us through the eyes of what he conceived to be a typical member of this early Roman society, Valeria, "dear Valeria"—"as chaste as an icicle," of the same composition as Volumnia. So it would appear, and why should we not accept that as Shakespeare's intention? But there are, of course, many reasons why such things should be bowdlerized, as it were, by the critic. But Shakespeare is full of scandalous matter that has to be hushed up. When the critic arrives at certain passages in *Lear* or *Macbeth* (as regards *Troilus and Cressida* he ignores the whole thing as far as possible) he will refer in a sober voice to this little "lapse from sanity" of Shakespeare, and then hurry on. Edgar's remark about his father's blindness in the fifth act of *King Lear* is one of these:

> The gods are just, and of our pleasant vices
> Make instruments to plague us:

> The dark and vicious place where thee he got,
> Cost him his eyes.

That is one of Shakespeare's more notorious "lapses." *Troilus and Cressida* is one vast "lapse," and *Timon* is almost another. But, in spite of these disturbing phenomena, the improper nature of much that is spread everywhere through all the plays is denied or ignored. And so in process of time whole plays, like *Coriolanus,* have received an interpretation that is contradicted everywhere in the play itself. Sir James Robertson, for instance, in writing of *Coriolanus,* treats Valeria and the chip-off-the-old-block episode as follows:

"It was probably a circumstantial accident that gave us, in addition to those incomparable portraits of women, yet a third, that of Valeria, who . . . has strictly nothing to do with the action of the play save to suggest anew, by her account of the boy Marcius, how even admirable women may miseducate children. Shakespeare is careful to insist on her nobility and charm by putting a warm eulogium of her in the mouth of Coriolanus; but had before introduced her as enjoying the episode of the child rending a butterfly in pieces."

He had indeed "before introduced her" in the act of enjoying the spectacle of this promising young chief engaged in a characteristic Roman sport, and preparing himself for the martial preoccupations of the life that awaited him. But we are not to suppose that Shakespeare meant her to be anything less than noble, and possessed of the greatest charm. Indeed, has he not been "careful to insist on" this in a "warm eulogium of her in the mouth of Coriolanus"? (The "warm eulogium" referred to is, of course, when Coriolanus later describes her as "an icicle.")

Now this in manner and in matter is very typical of English Shakespearian criticism. If the play is read with any interest and attention, this version of Sir James Robertson's of a charming "lady of great nobility," in the case of Valeria, will be seen as what it is—the deferential euphuism of a highly respectable upper-servant of the old English school. That large class of able middle-class men, domiciled in universities, of the type of the correct and snobbish family solicitor, usually ending life with a few irrelevant honors, is responsible as a rule for Shakespeare criticism. Sir James Robertson is better than that, but still is of that genus of critics. Shakespeare, both in the circumstances of a rough and bitter life, and in the vigor and recklessness of his mind, will not fit that social framework. So, as we have said, most Shakespeare criticism comes to be a mild adaptation and bowdlerization, the sort of meaningless respectability of the English professional man smeared over everything that looks too stark, or that would seem to make it difficult to describe Shakespeare subsequently as "with a kindly twinkle in his eye," or as "a gentleman": "gentle" alone ("gentle Shakespeare") would not be regarded as possessing any particular relevance.

So the Valeria episode is explained by Sir James Robertson as showing how "even admirable women may miseducate children." And there is an end of it: it means nothing more than that: it is an unfortunate episode, undoubtedly—it leaves an unfortunate impression: but it is introduced by the poet after one of those incessant readings of Montaigne (in which he seems to have spent most of his time), and is a little burst of educationalist enthusiasm—nothing more! The picture is paradoxically put into the mouth of *a most charming and well-bred woman;* which again may have been intended by this most ingenious of poets to show how strong *custom* is, and how it may induce even the most gracious of gentle-women to let slip a few remarks that might be misunderstood by someone not familiar—ahem!—with the *natural kindliness* that is such a characteristic of the nobility and gentry—ahem—of any land or period of history!

This episode of the little budding Coriolanus is, however, with the utmost consistency, typical of the play and Shakespeare's treatment of Coriolanus from beginning to end. It is an astonishingly close picture of a particularly cheerless and unattractive snob, such as must have pullulated in the court of Elizabeth, and such as the English public-school and university system has produced ever since. He is a fearless and efficient leader in war, with every opportunity of training, and the stimulus of self-interest, to be such—and nothing else. In every other respect he is a glum, vain and extremely peevish dog, always abusing a crowd of supers for not incessantly

flattering him, and furthering his interests and those of
Volumnia; with exhortations to deeds of matchless heroism,
for which, if they performed them, they would receive nothing but further abuse, bearing largely on the respective diet
of the carefully kept dog in the fine marble kennel and the ill-
kept dog in the mud one. Both these species have their faults,
and Coriolanus is allowed to hit off those of the rabble with
sufficient force; as when he chides them:

> He that depends
> Upon your favors swims with fins of lead
> And hews down oaks with rushes. Trust ye? Hang ye!
> With every minute ye do change your mind,
> And call him noble that was now your hate,
> Him vile that was your garland.

But since his own small senatorial crowd prove themselves equally undependable, and are separated by almost as
wide a trench from his demented ideal of authority, this
abuse remains a Timon-like outpouring of unreason from
the point of view of life's realities. Menenius Agrippa,
Cominius or Titus Lartius are the real workaday "aristocrats," and are as much strangers to an ideal of inflexible
authority as are the people themselves: and naturally veer to
the popular side when this quixotic doctrinaire pushes them
to uphold the letter of their superiority.

In war the "thunder-like percussion" of his "sounds" is a
martial rhetoric Shakespeare was very capable of mea-
suring. And therewith Aufidius sounds the Machiavellian
note—which caused Coleridge so much embarrassment:
when the Volscian leader says that as he is unable to beat
him fairly, as "man to man," he must "potch at him some
way," a Volscian soldier remarks, "He's the devil!" referring to Coriolanus; and Aufidius replies:

> Bolder, though not so subtle. My valor's poison'd
> With only suffering stain by him,

and we then get the Achilles-Hector situation, with the same
frantic and luscious sensuality of strife that is reproduced in

the battlefield rivalries of the Greek and Trojan captains, and in the case of Hotspur and Prince Hal.

The confrontation of Coriolanus and his mother, Volumnia, in 3.2, is the most characteristic of the piece, and gives the true interpretation of Coriolanus. He is shown there as the child, drilled into a second nature which goes on mechanically obeying. His mother—whose ultra-Roman despotism has been shown in other scenes—has coached and formed him into the madman he is. Then, when he comes fresh from acting on her teaching, to his own undoing, he is suddenly, with a naïve confusion, confronted with his mother's disapproval. And the obedient schoolboy, rebuked for doing what he has been taught to do, turns with baffled reproach on his teacher:

> *Coriolanus.* I muse my mother
> Does not approve me further, who was wont
> To call them woolen vassals; things created
> To buy and sell with groats, to show bare heads
> In congregations, to yawn, be still, and wonder,
> When one but of my ordinance stood up
> To speak of peace or war.
>   *[Enter* VOLUMNIA]
>   I talk of you:
> Why did you wish me milder? Would you have me
> False to my nature? Rather say I play
> The man I am.
>   *Volumnia.* O, sir, sir, sir,
> I would have had you put your power well on,
> Before you had worn it out.
>   *Cor.* Let go.
>   *Vol.* You might have been enough the man you are,
> With striving less to be so.

This scene between Coriolanus and his mother is the key to the play: it shows Coriolanus as the rigid and hypnotized schoolboy influenced in his most susceptible years by a snobbish and violent parent, and urged into a course of destruction, which, the machine of an idea, he mesmerically pursues: it is now too late even for the mastermind to pull him up.

The scene to which this critical confrontation of the

mother and son should be compared is the last scene of all, when he is killed by Aufidius and his followers. The word with which he is dismissed from the scene of this world is "Boy," and he is shown as resenting it very much indeed.

> *Aufidius.* He has betray'd your business, and given up,
> For certain drops of salt, your city Rome
> (I say "your city") to his wife and mother;
> Breaking his oath and resolution, like
> A twist of rotten silk; never admitting
> Counsel o' the war; but, at his nurse's tears,
> He whin'd and roar'd away your victory;
> That pages blush'd at him, and men of heart
> Look'd wondering at each other.
>   *Cor.* Hear'st thou, Mars?
>   *Auf.* Name not the god, thou boy of tears!
>   *Cor.* Ha!
>   *Auf.* No more.
>   *Cor.* Measureless liar, thou hast made my heart
> Too great for what contains it. Boy! O slave!—
> Pardon me, lords, 'tis the first time that ever
> I was forc'd to scold.

But during the ensuing lines he goes on repeating "Boy!"—which epithet appears to have entirely overpowered him:

> *Cor.* Cut me to pieces, Volsces; men and lads,
> Stain all your edges on me.—Boy! false hound!
> If you have writ your annals true, 'tis there,
> That, like an eagle in a dovecote, I
> Flutter'd your Volscians in Corioli:
> Alone I did it.—Boy!

"Boy" is almost the last word of Coriolanus. The action of his little son as described by Valeria is one of the things that anyone would chiefly remember in the play, and is the thing in it to which the critics naturally turn, and which they have to explain away to fit their substituted picture. And the child-parent situation is the mechanism of the piece in any case. Since we possess a great deal of evidence as to what Shake-

speare thought of military glory and martial events, we have
no reason to suppose that the military heroics in *Coriolanus*
are of a different order to what they are elsewhere. There is
the curious demented sensuality that he is fond of attributing
to military rivals, but which is not an element calculated to
increase the atmosphere of respect at their feats of daring: it
even makes them—the Hotspurs, Achilles, Hals and so
forth—a little ridiculous. As to this feudal poet's courtly
leanings, I do not think they are proved. He is quite ready to
support his characters when the moment arrives for them to
abuse the "many-headed multitude" (which was the usual
term—"we have been called so of many," the Citizen in
2.3 says). Shakespeare no doubt agreed with all the abuse his
puppet Coriolanus was called upon to hurl at the Roman
crowd. It would very nearly describe what Shakespeare
probably felt about the London crowd of his time, and especially as he came in contact with it at the theatre. But from
this to supposing that he had discriminated between this
crowd and that other smaller crowd to which Coriolanus
belonged—the crowd that thronged the more expensive
seats of the Bankside theatres—is a long step of snobbish
unreason and self-deception that we have no right to assume
Shakespeare at all likely to have taken. For him *l'un vaudrait
l'autre*, I expect. For it was human nature about which
Shakespeare wrote, and he did not write on a tone of morals,
nor on one of class prejudice or class illusion.

Coriolanus is no more a play to exhibit the virtues and
destinies of the aristocrat (with a strong propaganda for a
severe oligarchical form of government, and a strong snobbish illusion about the graceful advantages of the aristocratic
life) than it is a play of educationist propaganda, whether for
or against a certain type of training. It is a play about a conventional military hero, existing as the characteristic ornament of a strong aristocratic system. Shakespeare was
neither for or against him, on propagandist, feudal or non-
feudal grounds. He was quite ready to curse the crowd with
him: and he was equally ready to examine with as little pleasure the child of a harsh practical system, abusing his many
advantages, and showing to perfection how the top, as likewise the under, dog is unsatisfactory and foolish, the one
very nearly worthy of the other—the violent, dull, conceited

leader, and the resentful but cowardly slave. Meantime the play is charged with a magnificent rhetoric, as wherever any character utters Shakespeare's blank verse. Coriolanus speaks frequently like a god; also the *altofronto* tone is adopted by him from time to time, as by most Shakespeare heroes—his banter and bitterness being often just the same as that of Hamlet, Timon or Lear. But that is Shakespeare's own voice and manner that you hear, the central surge, that, wherever the music he is making excites him, comes out and is heard. What belongs properly to Coriolanus is not meant by Shakespeare to be attractive: he shows none of the sympathy for him that he does for Othello, Antony or Timon. Yet he is cast for the lion part; and Shakespeare gives him, as remarked above, his portion of magnificent music. Also he has to the full one of the great requisites of the Shakespearian *lion;* he is completely helpless, childlike, truthful and unfortunate. So it is the rôle, rather than the figure filling it, that would set the tragic organ playing.

The *fox* is there too; the tribunes Sicinius and Brutus supply the Iago element very adequately, except that no unpopularity is concentrated on them.

D. A. TRAVERSI

From An Approach to Shakespeare

Coriolanus has rarely satisfied the critics. Most of them have found it frigid and have even suggested that Shakespeare's interest flagged in the writing of it; on the other hand, an important minority—including T. S. Eliot and J. Middleton Murry—have been considerably attracted by the play, and have even found an important place for it in the development of their own experience.[1] The only point upon which there seems to be agreement is that *Coriolanus* is difficult and that its artistic quality is peculiar. Even sympathetic critics must account for the fact that the figure of the hero is harsh and at times grotesque, while Aufidius' behavior is puzzling and inconsistent. It is the task of a critical interpretation of the play to decide whether these contradictions are part of the stuff of the author's experience, or whether they are only the odds and ends left over by imperfect assimilation.

The mastery displayed in the verse of *Coriolanus* does not suggest declining powers or lack of interest. There is an interesting example of this in the very first verse speech of the play, when Menenius rebukes the citizens for their mutterings:

> For your wants,
> Your suffering in this dearth, you may as well
> Strike at the heaven with your staves as lift them

[1]See J. Middleton Murry's essay on "A Neglected Heroine of Shakespeare," *Countries of the Mind* (London, 1922) and, for T. S. Eliot, the essay on *Hamlet* (*Selected Essays*) and the two poems entitled "Coriolan."

From *An Approach to Shakespeare* by D. A. Traversi (London: Sands & Co. [Publishers] Ltd., 1938). Reprinted by permission of Sands & Co. (Publishers) Ltd.

> Against the Roman state; whose course will on
> The way it takes, cracking ten thousand curbs
> Of more strong link asunder than can ever
> Appear in your impediment. For the dearth,
> The gods, not the patricians, make it, and
> Your knees to them, not arms, must help.   (1.1)

It is impossible not to feel that this is an example of the unique, free mastery of Shakespeare's later verse. We should be aware of the conciseness of the last sentence, of the way in which the "not arms" parenthesis enables us to grasp the essential contrast without the distraction that would result from a full statement of the alternatives; it is a telescoping of language that follows the movement of living thought. More important is the way in which the rhythm of the earlier lines serves to develop a nervous power in the words, expressing the irresistible motion of tremendous and unfeeling force. Once more, the force is not only stated but given concrete embodiment in the movement of the verse. The division of "cracking" and "asunder," both words which carry with them strong feelings of physical separation, bear the reader over the intervening words so that this experience partakes of the irresistible movement of the Roman state. The emotional impetus thus created is then brought to a sudden curb by the ending of the sentence in the middle of the familiar blank verse unit of the line, an ending prepared for and emphasized by the decisive Latin word "impediment." The movement of the verse, in fact, is that of a poet who is in complete mastery of his medium, which has become a pliant instrument to express the subtle movement of his consciousness. It is sufficient to suggest that *Coriolanus* is a great play.

I have quoted the passage, however, less to establish Shakespeare's powers of versification than to introduce the issues with which the play deals. The central feeling of the speech is clearly that suggested by the phrase "strike at the heaven with your staves," and emphasized in the nervous strength of the passage as a whole. To be certain of this, we may reinforce the impression of "staves" by referring to Menenius' talk of the citizens' "bats and clubs" just above, echoed once more by "stiff bats and clubs" in the course of the same argument. Professor Wilson Knight, in *The Imperial Theme,*[2] acutely pointed out that these phrases, and others of the same kind, give a peculiar sensation of hardness and ruthless impenetrability to the play. In other words, the sense of social stiffness and utter incompatibility is woven by Shakespeare into the emotional texture of his work, and gives a peculiar tone to the political and social study which underlies it. The "bats and clubs" of the contending parties strike at one another in a closed universe; the "heavens," with all their associations of light and "grace," remain rigid and impenetrable, so that we can almost hear the "stiff" weapons clang when raised against them. This sense of hard hostility is essential to *Coriolanus,* and is repeated, as we shall see, in the play's attitude toward war and in the character of the hero himself. For the present, we shall merely note the vividness of Shakespeare's political study of Roman conditions, the sense of a social order hardened into insensibility on the one hand and unworthiness on the other, the patricians and the people utterly out of contact with one another, hard, hostile, exclusive in their attitude. The patricians have no contact with the people; Menenius' speech stresses their merciless lack of feeling and responsibility, and Coriolanus himself caricatures his warlike valor in the following speech:

> Would the nobility lay aside their ruth,
> And let me use my sword, I'd make a quarry,
> With thousands of these quartered slaves, as high
> As I could pick my lance. (1.1)

This perversion of the traditional speech of warlike heroes is a masterpiece of irony. On the other hand, the people are weak, worthless, and brutal, easily led astray by the scheming tribunes, and quite incapable of seeing beyond the selfish ends of the moment.

All this is more or less apparent. Much more important is the image under which Shakespeare develops this discord and gives it significance. The theme is a variation of that of "degree," so prominent in *Troilus and Cressida,* but here

[2]London, 1932.

less "metaphysically" and more socially conceived. The
verse of *Troilus*, however, even that given to Ulysses, is not
equal to that of *Coriolanus* in the precision which denotes
mastery of experience; the comparative lack of organization
which accompanies the extraordinary complexity of the language in the earlier play indicates, as we have seen, a mind
overwhelmed by a superabundance of new conceptions—
conceptions which will need to be worked out in the devel-
oping pattern of the tragedies. As in *Troilus*, however, the
essential image which Shakespeare chose to give point to his
study is that of the functioning of the human body. As usual,
it appears almost at once in order to set clearly the tone of the
play. Menenius develops it fully in his fable to the citizens:

> There was a time when all the body's members
> Rebell'd against the belly; thus accused it:
> That only like a gulf it did remain
> I' the midst of the body, idle and unactive,
> Still cupboarding the viand, never bearing
> Like labor with the rest; where the other instruments
> Did see and hear, devise, instruct, walk, feel,
> And, mutually participate, did minister
> Unto the appetite and affection common
> Of the whole body.   (1.1)

Now this speech and the discussion which follows are based
on North's Plutarch, but are there stated in the abstract
manner of the moralist, occupying only a few lines and in no
way suggesting the individuality of Shakespeare's version.
Upon this basis the poet created a fundamental criticism of
Roman society—fundamental precisely because it was not
merely political, but based upon a sensation of fine living
developed through the whole pattern of the tragedies. The
speech has been so worded, in short, as to invest a political
commonplace with Shakespeare's own sense of poetic
significance.

The first point to notice concerns the quality of feeling
conveyed by the verse. The prevailing tone is one of idle-
ness, of stagnation, of a general obstruction of everything
that suggests life and activity. We note before everything the
unhealthy heaviness of "idle and unactive," and the direct

coarseness implied by the vernacular of "cupboarding."
Then we find this contrasted with the very noticeable
livening of the verse when Menenius comes to speak of "the
other instruments," the senses and active parts of the body.
This balance of two contrasted elements, the keenness of the
senses carrying with it a related feeling of sluggishness and
physical repulsion, is already evident in the earlier plays.
Here, too, this intensity of feeling is connected with the contrasted baseness and satiation of lust. The feeling of the
speech is given another subtle turn by the reference to "the
appetite and affection common." "Appetite" has behind it
associations with the "universal wolf" of Ulysses' great
speech, as well as with frequent Elizabethan references to
incontinence; the latter are further strengthened by the word
"common," so often used by Shakespeare's contemporaries
to indicate promiscuity. The fable conveys then a feeling,
very like that of *Troilus,* of a social organism in disorder and
decay, an impression further strengthened by the promi-
nence given to the idea of food and the process of digestion.
Greed and satiety are the main images by which we are prepared for the tragedy of *Coriolanus.*

So far, in substance if not in detail, we have most of the
critics with us. It is generally recognized that there are elements of disorder and decadence in the Rome presented in
this play. But there is also a feeling that the author's sympa-
thies were with the patricians. This view, however, immediately lands us in the perplexities already indicated, on the
strength of which this tragedy has so often been condemned
as a failure. If Coriolanus is really the "hero," and the patricians on the whole an admirable class, why is his behavior
so inconsistent, not to say degrading? A moment's consideration of this same speech will show us that the scope of
Shakespeare's political analysis is much more ample than
many of his critics would have us believe. For the patricians
are presented to us in the likeness of the "belly," with the
result that there is an essential contrast between their stagnation and their indispensability. Menenius criticizes justly
the failure of the populace to play a proper part in the social
organism; but the figure he chooses to elaborate his point
turns the argument equally against his own position. Though
the belly was indispensable to the proper working of the

body, it was also "idle and unactive," self-satisfied in the security of its position; in this connection we should note that brilliant stroke:

> With a kind of smile,
> Which ne'er came from the lungs, but even thus . . .   (1.1)

with its fine balance between the comic and the complacent. Shakespeare goes even further. He gives to the First Citizen some of the most bitter and penetrating words in the whole discussion. There is no hiding the force with which the "cormorant belly" and "the sink o' the body" cut through the complacent assumption of superiority recorded by Menenius. Lastly, we should not pass over Shakespeare's ambiguous attitude toward the belly as distributor of food to the whole body; if it gives life to the rest of the body, it is also the receptacle of the worthless bran.

The result of this speech then is a very acute apprehension of the condition of a social organism, as revealed through the power of a living and penetrating sensibility. We are shown a populace incapable of discerning its own good, vicious and vulgar, and needing the leadership of a class superior to itself. On the other hand, we are also shown a patrician class who have forfeited their right to superiority by showing a complete selfishness and lack of responsibility. They are, in fact, merely subsisting on a position gained in the more or less distant past. Both these factions are set in an iron social framework which permits no contact, no community of interests, nothing but repression on one side and animal discontent on the other. That is the full intention of the inflexible quality of Menenius' first speech.

Having provided as a background such a many-sided social study, Shakespeare was not likely to place in the foreground a hero whom he regarded as a simple and romantic warrior struck down by the worthless and ungrateful people. Even those who have tended to this view have always been baffled by the way in which the play stresses both Coriolanus' proud obstinacy and his unnatural lack of feeling for the whole setting of his past life. It is more hopeful to approach him through the feeling expressed in the war poetry of the play, and more particularly by Cominius in his eulogy at the Capitol:

> His pupil age
> Man-enter'd thus, he waxed like a sea;
> And, in the brunt of seventeen battles since,
> He lurch'd all swords of the garland. . . .
>   . . . as weeds before
> A vessel under sail, so men obey'd,
> And fell below his stern: his sword, death's stamp,
> Where it did mark, it took; from face to foot
> He was a thing of blood, whose every motion
> Was timed with dying cries: alone he enter'd
> The mortal gate of the city, which he painted
> With shunless destiny; aidless came off,
> And with a sudden reinforcement struck
> Corioli like a planet: now all's his:
> When, by and by, the din of war 'gan pierce
> His ready sense; then straight his doubled spirit
> Requicken'd what in flesh was fatigate,
> And to the battle came he; where he did
> Run reeking o'er the lives of men, as if
> 'Twere a perpetual spoil; and till we call'd
> Both field and city ours, he never stood
> To ease his breast with panting.   (2.2)

It is impossible not to feel at once that this is Shakespeare at his mature best; who else would have used that bold comparison "man-enter'd," in which explicitness is waived in favor of speed and immediacy of expression? The verse moves with the utmost ease and freedom, a perfectly plastic medium for catching shifts of feeling; such a shift is recorded in the emphasized contrast between the splendor of "he waxed like a sea" and the leaden reality of "lurch'd" and "brunt." These things are conveyed easily to a reader who is prepared for them; the voice is carried irresistibly by rhythms which are always based on living speech to the proper emphasis, the delicately felt pause by which Shakespeare so often converts the statement of a fact into its apprehension by a completely sensitive response. The line

> And with a sudden reinforcement struck
> Corioli . . . ,

with its telling isolation of "struck" at the end of the line, is an outstanding example; it produces the sense of weighty and fatal pressure which is so essential to the impression aimed at.

So we come to the feeling of the speech. In it Shakespeare is using his unique capacity for compressing the feelings that underlie his exploration of a situation into the unity of a single utterance, whose central images are conversely radiated out into the surrounding matter, of which they serve at once as a concentration and a point of departure. It is in this sense that the mature plays could be described, from the point of view of their poetic structure, as organic, the product of a sensibility whose life was not only diffused through a play but concentrated into every part of it. The speech gives us a peculiar impression of Coriolanus as a warrior. It stresses at once his energy, his splendid and superabundant life, and his heaviness, his cruelty, almost his fantastic absurdity; and the two are part of the same man. The first of these qualities is expressed not only in the rich, splendid image we have already noted—"he waxed like a sea"—but it is also given a definite living quality, a fine nervous delicacy in:

> . . . the din of war 'gan pierce
> His ready sense; then straight his doubled spirit
> Requicken'd what in flesh was fatigate . . .

This superb sensitive response to "the din of war" is not new in *Coriolanus*. We are carried back to Othello's reaction to "the spirit-stirring drum, the ear-piercing fife," which gives the same impression of the senses at work at the confines of their intensity. War gives rise here to a fine keenness of feeling that is only paralleled by Shakespeare's reaction to love in certain scenes of *Antony and Cleopatra*. It is, indeed, worth remembering that the two plays were written at the same period, for we shall see that there is some association between their respective treatment of love and war.

All this does not mean, of course, that Shakespeare was a

crude and ignorant enthusiast for war. He had already, in his earlier period, made a thorough study of the political implications of patriotism in *Henry V* and, if certain aspects of the character of Coriolanus recall Othello, they also suggest how the related strength and weakness of the tragic hero is here used to add mature depth to the treatment of a political theme. The greatness of this speech depends, indeed, upon the manner in which there is intertwined with the sense of superb vitality a dead heaviness, which culminates in an almost grotesque insensibility. That is the reason why the munificence of "he waxed like a sea" is immediately qualified by the ponderous impact of "brunt" and "lurch'd." It should be seen, further, that these lines deal with Coriolanus' growth into manhood. They suggest perfectly the double process which Shakespeare saw and conveyed in his verse in the history of the great soldier. On the one hand, Coriolanus grew into the full development of his powers, the complete expression of his maturity. On the other, his new power converted itself more and more, with success, into heaviness and indifference to life, into an exclusion of the very qualities of sensitivity which maturity should have crowned. So we pass through the splendid and ruthless image of the "vessel under sail" to the description of the sword as "death's stamp," a description which gives it the destructive weight and inflexibility of a battering ram. These things prepare us for the entry of a mechanical warrior, a man turned into an instrument of war, grotesquely indifferent to the suffering he has caused:

> ... from face to foot
> He was a thing of blood, whose every motion
> Was timed with dying cries.   (2.2)

This impression is further reinforced by the suggestion of an irresistible impact behind "planet," which helps to make him no longer a mere warrior, but an "instrument" (the word is significant in view of what we have already said about the battering ram) "of shunless destiny" against "the mortal gates of the city." In the word "mortal" is contained not only an expression of helplessness but a protest on the part of

downtrodden life against this insentient minister of fate.
Then, to balance the argument, comes that remarkable
quickening of the machine which we have already noted, a
quickening followed, however, by the renewed grotesque
callousness of:

> ... he did
> Run reeking o'er the lives of men, as if
> 'Twere a perpetual spoil,   (2.2)

and we are left with Coriolanus "panting" like a hot-blooded
bull after his orgy of destruction. In this way, right through
Cominius' eulogy, a balance is held which is essential to a
proper reading of the play.

In case it should be thought that too much stress has been
laid on a single passage, it can easily be shown how this balance is preserved throughout the play and is, indeed, an inte-
gral part of its structure. There is the feeling of the iron
mechanical warrior in the earliest scenes, as when Titus Lartius speaks of:

> ... thy grim looks and
> The thunder-like percussion of thy sounds;   (1.4)

and, at the end, when Coriolanus seems to be on the point of
taking his revenge on Rome, we have a very remarkable
prose passage from Menenius:

MENENIUS: The tartness of his face sours ripe grapes: when he
walks, he moves like an engine, and the ground shrinks
before his treading: he is able to pierce a corslet with his
eye; talks like a knell, and his hum is a battery. He sits in his
state, as a thing made for Alexander. What he bids to be
done is finished with his bidding. He wants nothing of a god
but eternity and a heaven to throne in.

SICINIUS: Yes, mercy, if you report him truly.

MENENIUS: I paint him in the character. Mark what mercy his
mother shall bring from him; there is no more mercy in him
than there is milk in a male tiger.

(5.4)

This is a fine example of the prose of Shakespeare's late period, prose which is not content to develop the facts of a situation, but is informed with the same continual consciousness of the emotional unity of the play as that which is reflected in the verse. Passing by that fine enlistment of the palate in the opening image, we come once more to a description of the human war-machine, this time absolutely explicit. The later part of the speech suggests not only the grotesque lack of human feeling in this machine but also the futility of this artificial insensibility. This comparison of Coriolanus' pretensions with a state of divinity was clearly Shakespeare's expression of a fundamental criticism, for he had already put it once into the mouth of the tribunes. Brutus had said:

> You speak of the people,
> As if you were a god to punish, not
> A man of their infirmity.   (3.1)

On a great many accounts of the play it would be very hard to explain the wisdom of these utterances given to the otherwise detestable tribunes. But, as we have suggested, Shakespeare's insight was keener than that of his critics, and so the tribunes are allowed to throw the clearest light of all upon the futility which is undeniably part of Coriolanus' character. This vanity, moreover, is brought home to us by a further stroke of irony, for we know, as Menenius does not, that this supposedly inflexible warrior has not only self-consciously paraded his firmness before Aufidius—

> Shall I be tempted to infringe my vow,
> In the same time 'tis made? I will not . . .
>
> Aufidius, and you Volsces, mark; for we'll
> Hear naught from Rome in private. Your request?—
>   (5.3)

but has capitulated at the very moment of his posing. As Aufidius says, with a bitter cynicism which is part of the spirit of this play:

> At a few drops of women's rheum, which are
> As cheap as lies, he sold the blood and labor
> Of our great action . . .   (5.6)

That, at least, is one aspect of Coriolanus' career as a warrior.

The other aspect, however, as we have already suggested in discussing Cominius' speech, is equally present. There is no question that this play connects the action of war with a sense of splendid and living ecstasy. The most obvious example is to be found in the scene where Coriolanus first meets Aufidius, after his exile, and the Volscian general addresses him in the following terms:

> Let me twine
> Mine arms about that body, where against
> My grainèd ash an hundred times hath broke,
> And scarr'd the moon with splinters: here I clip
> The anvil of my sword, and do contest
> As hotly and as nobly with thy love
> As ever in ambitious strength I did
> Contend against thy valor. Know thou first,
> I loved the maid I married; never man
> Sigh'd truer breath; but that I see thee here,
> Thou noble thing! more dances my rapt heart
> Than when I first my wedded mistress saw
> Bestride my threshold.   (4.5)

The note of exaltation reminds us once more of *Antony and Cleopatra*. Here too the life that expresses itself in war is communicated in terms of love. From Aufidius' behavior in this play, we should not have expected him to express ecstasy (if, indeed, such a word were within the compass of his experience) in terms of his own emotions in love. But the justification, of course, is less in character than in the emotional makeup of the play. In character the discrepancy between poetry and behavior helps to emphasize the dual nature of Aufidius, poised strangely between heroism and treachery prompted by jealous selfishness, just as Coriolanus, in Cominius' speech, is poised between divinity and insensibility. But these divergences of personal principle are only products of the disharmony to be found in the social analysis of the play, and this analysis is in turn a projection of the original poetic mood. The martial exaltation of Coriolanus and Aufidius is counterbalanced by their respective brutality and treachery, in the same way that the superior keenness and vividness of the senses in Menenius' opening parable is necessarily attached to the grossness of the "cormorant belly" from which they try in vain to free themselves.

A type of poetry identical in quality with that which we have just discussed in Aufidius is also to be found in Coriolanus himself, as we shall see if we consider some of the speeches, which are among his finest, made when he returns to his family after his triumph at Corioli. Outstanding among them, perhaps, is:

> My gracious silence, hail!
> Would'st thou have laugh'd had I come coffin'd home,
> That weep'st to see me triumph?[3]   (2.1)

The experience with which the critic of *Coriolanus* has to establish contact is one that, while forming a single emotional whole, has to include the divergence between this and the warrior who "moves like an engine" over the corpses he has battered to death. That is the central contradiction, to which those in Aufidius' behavior are merely subsidiary. There is a split at the heart of Shakespeare's experience which introduces a division into the fabric of his play, both at Rome and Corioli. That split, already to be observed in the dramatist's presentation of the related strength and weakness of his tragic heroes and in the attitude which these heroes adopt towards themselves, is related to a political study of the type originally presented in the English historical plays and here taken up in the light of the intervening tragic development. The sensation of life expressed in terms of passion, worked out so triumphantly at certain moments in Antony, is here studied, at the same period, in its relationship to war; and war is seen as a product of the same life,

---

[3]This passage and others like it in the play have been admirably discussed by J. Middleton Murry in his essay above mentioned [i.e., in "A Neglected Heroine of Shakespeare," *Countries of the Mind*].

but one which tends to the death which is its opposite. *Coriolanus,* in fact, is at once the complement of *Antony and Cleopatra* and its reversal. In the latter play defeat in war becomes, in some sense and for the duration of certain scenes, the prelude to a triumph in the vitality of love; in *Coriolanus* victory in war is accompanied by a callous hardening of feeling, which only reasserts itself to give an ironic note to the hero's fate.

It is worthwhile, at this point, to refer a little more fully to the irony of the play, which gives it a note not easily squared with its usual definition as a tragedy; this fact helps, perhaps more than any other, to account for the prevalent critical uneasiness. This irony is, as in all Shakespeare's political plays, a critical irony; that is, it springs out of a vigilant hostility to unsustained pretensions and unexamined enthusiasms. Perhaps its most successful expression is that exposure of the characters of Volumnia and Valeria (1.3), which shows the lack of human feeling in Coriolanus to be rooted in the outlook of his family, and so, in turn, in the general social maladjustments we have already discussed. In this way the scene has an important structural position, for it serves to connect the personal tragedy of Coriolanus with the wider social study. The scene is an invention of Shakespeare's; one cannot imagine that Plutarch would have thought of Valeria speaking of Coriolanus' son in this way:

> O' my word, the father's son; I'll swear, 'tis a very pretty boy. O' my troth, I looked upon him o' Wednesday half an hour together; he has such a confirmed countenance. I saw him run after a gilded butterfly; and when he caught it, he let it go again; and after it again; and over and over he comes, and up again; catched it again: or whether his fall enraged him, or how 'twas, he did so set his teeth and tear it; O, I warrant, how he mammocked it!

(1.3)

The whole passage is a sufficient exposure of the deadly lack of feeling which surrounds Coriolanus, and of which he partakes; indeed, it is emphasized that the boy is "the father's son." To complete the impression, we need only the crushing irony implicit in Valeria's comment: "Indeed, la, 'tis a noble child." The author of this scene was the same who had once written Falstaff's penetrating remarks on "honor" in the assured balance of a spirit that was not less artistic for being truly critical. Instead of Sir Walter Blunt's "grinning honor" we have Volumnia's ideal:

> . . . had I a dozen sons . . . I had rather eleven die nobly for their country than one voluptuously surfeit out of action.

But in *Coriolanus* the clear-sighted outlook of *Henry IV* is reinforced by the experience gained in the whole body of the tragedies, so that it becomes part of an emotional whole more complex than itself. A good deal in the study of the hero was taken from traditional sources: Plutarch, according to North, had already suggested that Coriolanus was "so cholericke and impacient, that he would yeeld to no liuing creature: which made him churlishe, unciuill, and altogether unfit for any man's conuersation." It is also true that there was a substantial precedent in traditional farce for the refusal to accept a great classical warrior at the most heroic estimate; Shakespeare had done this himself in *Troilus and Cressida*. When the Roman soldiers refuse to follow Coriolanus into the gates of the besieged city (1,4), and when he scolds them with most unheroic vituperation in the same scene, his behavior was not strange to an Elizabethan mind. Only the scholars might be shocked.

When all this has been conceded, however, there remains the essence of Shakespeare's achievement to be accounted for. As we have suggested, the greatness and uniqueness of this play are due to the fact that Shakespeare judged the political situation in Rome in the light of his own experience developed in the tragedies. The failure of Coriolanus is a failure in sensitivity, a failure in living; and it represents a failure on the part of a whole society. The hero is shown always in relation to that society, and conditioned by it; it explains him, and his tragedy illuminates it. Perhaps the fundamental quality of the verse reflects the sense of a continual clash between a certain fineness of sensibility and an iron rigidity which accompanies and contrasts with it. Some of

these contrasts are expressed by incidental comparisons that
have a magnificent tactual immediacy; such are:

> When steel grows soft as the parasite's silk,   (1.9)

and:

>   . . . nature,
> Not to be other than one thing, not moving
> From the casque to the cushion, but commanding peace
> Even with the same austerity and garb
> As he controll'd the war . . .   (4.7)

where the first gives an immediate impression of different
and opposed textures in the closest contact, and where the
second emphasizes the contrast between the casques and the
cushion by the rigid strength given in "austerity and garb."
Such passages indicate the quality of this play. In it we find
a sensation of life expressed in terms of a transcendent passion, but continually chafing against the iron of an unnatural
rigidity, which is reflected in a stiffness in family relations
and in a hardened social order. Coriolanus' great lyric passages are not continual and spontaneous, like those of
Antony at his best moments. They seem rather to burst out
against a perpetual restraint, to be produced by a continual
friction against the iron insensibility which he has inherited.
Coriolanus is hopelessly divided between his unnatural discipline of "honor" and his natural, but incompletely mature,
humanity. That is the real source of the play's irony, and the
reason why he never carries any course of action to its complete fulfillment. His "honor" is turned by his class and
family into a willingness, if only temporary, to gain power
at any price. There are few things in Shakespeare more
ironic than the way Coriolanus has to use his wounds to gain
election to the consulship; but, having debased himself, his
natural pride intervenes, and he falls. But, precisely because
he is divided, his reaction does not reinstate him as a heroic
character, but expresses itself in petulant and ridiculous
curses against "the common cry of curs," "the reek o' the
rotten fens," the people whom he has just courted to gain
power. The same contradiction is seen in his last exploits.

Egoism has always prompted him to his wars; we are told in the opening dialogue that his prowess was due to his desire "to please his mother, and to be partly proud." It drives him to neglect all natural feeling and to return at the head of his former enemies to sack Rome. Such a change, after his sworn hatred of Aufidius, is in itself ironic. But this inhuman project cannot overcome the other part of his nature—what should have been in a harmonious personality normal feeling but is in his divided state weakness—so that he gives up his idea in the very moment of success. Such division and paralysis can only end in his rather absurd and ironic death. Shakespeare makes him die indignant at being called "Boy!" by those whom he had once beaten, in a mixture of "scolding" (by his own confession) and an attempt to justify himself in the light of his past exploits. This justification is felt to be the final proof of the tragic futility of his career.

JOYCE VAN DYKE

Making a Scene: Language and Gesture in *Coriolanus*

Coriolanus does not have much of a sense of play. We have very few glimpses of him when he is not in the thick of very serious matters, but we do get one early in the play which warns us of his habitual earnestness. Coriolanus and Lartius are with the troops before Corioli, watching a messenger arrive. They wager their horses on what the news will be, and Coriolanus loses.

> *Lartius.* So, the good horse is mine.
> *Marcius.*   I'll buy him of you.
> *Lartius.*
>   No, I'll nor sell nor give him; lend you him I will
>   For half a hundred years.   (1. 4. 5–7)

Even a wager made to pass time before battle Coriolanus takes completely seriously; for him, the wager is literal, a bond with material consequences, whereas Lartius's banter emphasizes its insubstantial nature. Coriolanus only engages in wordplay when he is in disguise, wearing the gown of humility or the "mean apparel" he appears in at Aufidius's house. In both cases he begins to speak ironically, mocking himself and his audience, making plays on words, all in all behaving most uncharacteristically. This wittiness is an indication of his own discomfort; and its apparently compulsive nature suggests, to adapt Coriolanus's phrase, that the body's action is teaching the mind a most inherent

We reprint Part II of an essay with this title, originally published in *Shakespeare Survey* 30 (1977). Reprinted with permission of Cambridge University Press.

ironic attitude. Under the constraint of unnatural appearance and action, his language assumes strange disguises and facetious appearances as well.

Coriolanus, under ordinary circumstances, is playing the man he is (3.2.15–16), by which I think he means that he is behaving naturally, being true to himself, but also that he is quite conscious that this is what he is doing. We have noted how responsive the public is to Coriolanus's appearance. He too seems frequently aware of the impression he is making, especially when he thinks that that impression might be misleading. He draws attention to any divergence between his being and seeming, and attempts to reconcile them: though I seem to be thus, I am really thus and so. There are numerous examples of this situation. When Coriolanus meets Aufidius at Corioli, battle-weary and covered with blood, he hastens to represent himself as a threatening opponent:

> Within these hours, Tullus,
> Alone I fought in your Corioles walls,
> And made what work I pleased. 'Tis not my blood
> Wherein thou seest me mask'd.   (1.8.7–10)

He tells the citizens, when they ask why he is standing for their voices, that his "desert" not, as they may suppose, his "desire" has brought him there (2.3.69–71). In his farewell to his mother, he assures her that he is still her son: she will hear nothing "But what is like me formerly" (4.1.53),

> ——though I go alone,
> Like to a lonely dragon, that his fen
> Makes feared and talked of more than seen—
>   (29–31)

Conscious of the mean disguise in which he seeks Aufidius's hospitality, he says,

> A goodly house. The feast smells well, but I
> Appear not like a guest.   (4.5.5–6)

And as he is about to name himself, to assume his true form, he prompts Aufidius to make a consistent response: "Prepare

thy brow to frown" (67). Coriolanus reports to the Volscians
that for Menenius's

> old love I have
> (Though I showed sourly to him) once more offered
> The first conditions. (5.3.12–14)

The same discomfiture which provokes such remarks is in
little that which provokes his violent outbursts at being
called traitor or boy. He is enraged at the possibility that he
could seem to be a boy when in fact (even in the annals) he
is a hero; he insists upon seeming what he is.

It is not surprising then that some of the most notable
scenes Coriolanus makes concern just this situation. Menenius asks him, just as Valeria requested Virgilia, to perform
a normal, customary act, and Coriolanus responds just as his
wife had responded:

> I do beseech you
> Let me o'erleap that custom, for I cannot
> Put on the gown. (2.2.136–38)

To Menenius, the protest is nonsense or petulance, but to
Coriolanus it is an occasion on which he fully expects that to
the people he will seem what he is not; he will show them his
scars which they will perceive

> As if I had received them for the hire
> Of their breath only! (150–51)

He not only anticipates the event as playing a part, he anticipates gesture, words, and audience response, all the trappings
of a role. When the approach of the citizens is imminent, he
stands in the gown of humility "rehearsing" what he must
perform:

> What must I say?
> "I pray, sir"—Plague upon't! I cannot bring
> My tongue to such a pace. "Look, sir, my wounds!
> I got them in my country's service, when

Some certain of your brethren roared and ran
From th' noise of our own drums." (2.3.53–58)

The rehearsal quickly modulates from prescription to an ironic undercutting of his "lines," and the tone he achieves here is sustained during his encounter with the people.

Throughout, Coriolanus attempts to withdraw as far as possible from the part he is constrained to play. His language sophistically suggests to the people that he is playing up to them when he is clearly demonstrating his disdain, "I have here the customary gown" (90–91), he says, as though he were holding it at arm's length. He holds the people at arm's length too; instead of performing his ritual obligations and instead of ingratiating himself, he says he *will* do so, conjuring up a degraded future image of himself: "since the wisdom of their choice is rather to have my hat than my heart, I will practice the insinuating nod, and be off to them most counterfeitly" (102–5). As one of the citizens says, "But this is something odd" (86). Quite probably, as Coriolanus is promising to take his hat off to them in this ingratiating fashion, the citizens are perceiving that what he is actually doing is waving it in scorn, as one complains later on.

The ritual act of wearing the gown of humility dictates what Coriolanus must do here, and he is not inherently opposed to custom and ceremony; he is proud to wear the oaken garland, and to receive the name Coriolanus. But his next role is harder to accept, and it is dictated only by policy. The mutiny in the marketplace which he aroused in part by playing the man he is, is now to be appeased by his assumption of an artificial role. Everyone recognizes the "lawful form" Menenius has requested as an occasion for acting. Volumnia, backed up by Menenius and Cominius, becomes a prompter and director.

Volumnia's argument is essentially that performing a part is not difficult or perverted but easy and quite natural. We have just heard Menenius say "His heart's his mouth" (3.1.256) but Volumnia strives to separate the two. His heart is what "prompts" his tongue; Coriolanus normally speaks "by [his] own instruction" (3.2.53–54). Even natural speech thus is described as a response to prompting, to rehearsal, as opposed to Coriolanus's automatic responses. It is not much different in operation then from false-speaking, in which the tongue is also instructed, but by another agent.

Volumnia's rhetoric dismembers heart and mouth, but when Coriolanus decides to take the part, he views it as a total fracturing of identity, the destruction of "This mold of Marcius" (3.2.103). Just as before, he anticipates himself in the role, and responding to his mother's general directions, anticipates or rehearses what he must do. (Volumnia's directions call for a gesticulating, flattering, puppet-like Coriolanus perilously like the one he conjured up to mock the citizens.)

> Well, I must do't.
> Away, my disposition, and possess me
> Some harlot's spirit! My throat of war be turned,
> Which quired with my drum, into a pipe
> Small as an eunuch or the virgin voice
> That babies lulls asleep! The smiles of knaves
> Tent in my cheeks, and schoolboys' tears take up
> The glasses of my sight! A beggar's tongue
> Make motion through my lips, and my armed knees,
> Who bowed but in my stirrup, bend like his
> That hath received an alms!   (110–20)

This catalogue of disjunct entities—harlot, eunuch, virgin, knaves, schoolboys, beggar—demonstrates the complete confusion of identity which acting entails for him. (The confusion of identity is no longer even human when Coriolanus next assumes disguise: like an asocial animal, he dwells under the canopy in the country of kites and crows.) It is a grotesque vision, and so eloquently grotesque that in speaking it, Coriolanus persuades himself that he cannot go through with the part. The speech is virtually a string of curses, and by the end of it he indeed realizes that to accept such a role would be to accomplish his own damnation.

If we have seen in these scenes that Coriolanus considers acting and disguise to be fearful and self-destructive, what then must be the effect of his entry in 4.4 *"in mean apparel, disguised and muffled"*? (The disguise is in Plutarch, but the prior emphasis on Coriolanus's attitude to disguise is not.)

Surely this voluntary assumption of a beggar-like disguise is a potent visual suggestion that something in the man himself, not just in his circumstances, has changed. His own explanation that the disguise is expedient is rather remarkable in light of the fact that we have just watched him allow himself to be banished, rather than speak one expedient fair word. And the irony is that here there is no need to be expedient. There is a comic pathos in the very idea of the hero making allowance for the "wives with spits and boys with stones" (5) who would try to slay him, and in his certainty that disguise is necessary to avoid recognition, since it becomes absurdly clear from his treatment by the servants and Aufidius that no one has the faintest idea who he is. If hitherto Coriolanus insisted he could not perform a part without destroying or degrading himself, are we to understand that now he can assume a disguise because he has been destroyed?

Part of the difficulty in assessing Coriolanus's response to banishment is that he offers such scant assessment of the situation himself. When Antony flees at Actium, he recognizes that his dishonourable act has in some sense destroyed him, and although he rallies, as he does from the actual suicide blow, he repeatedly returns to the realization of the present difficulty or impossibility of being Antony. Now the great hero must

> To the young man send humble treaties, dodge
> And palter in the shifts of lowness,
>
> *(Ant. & Cleo.,* 3.11.62–63)

This is exactly what we see Coriolanus doing and yet his own verbal responses seem grossly inadequate to his circumstances. Look at his analysis of what has happened. In soliloquy he discusses the revolutions of fortune: inseparable friends "On a dissension of a doit" become enemies, while enemies "by some chance,/Some trick not worth an egg" (20–21) become allied. The generalization clearly refers to his own situation, yet there is a curious depreciation or suppression of the cause of change, as if there were no real connection between one state and another. Here we see again Coriolanus's disjunctive habit of perception, but in this case the transition he deprecates happens to be the most violent and earth-shaking experience of his life. His lack of response seems to reveal a deadness of feeling which is not mitigated by the violence of his statement to Aufidius when he has unmuffled, for he offers to fight against Rome or to present his throat to Aufidius's knife as equal alternatives (and it is one of the ironies fulfilled by the play that in fact they are identical choices). His banishment from Rome, his loss of the political and familiar orders which defined him, have mortally stricken Coriolanus, and though he may not speak of his wounds, his altered behaviour reveals them.

This incident is not his only voluntary assumption of a disguise or role subsequent to banishment. He also deliberately "shows sourly" to Menenius: he pretends to be divorced from his family, though he fails "Like a dull actor" (5.3.40); he enters Corioli greeting the lords of the city as a triumphant hero even though he has confessed to Aufidius that he has been forced to compromise. Laurence Kitchin's very interesting review of a Memorial Theatre production with Laurence Olivier suggests that Coriolanus can very plausibly be played along the lines that his beggarly disguise initially suggests, and that this scene shows us the beginning of his disintegration.[1]

The behavior of Aufidius's servants to him recapitulates Coriolanus's banishment from Rome; as he notices,

> I have deserved no better entertainment
> In being Coriolanus.   (4.5.10–11)

The servants keep trying to rid the house of a nuisance, while he echoes their words and gestures of banishment, once pushing and once beating them away. Subsequent to his banishment from Rome, we can see Coriolanus's behaviour as

---

[1]Laurence Kitchin, *Mid-Century Drama* (1960), p. 144: "There was no doubt at all where the play's climax comes. It is on the sealing of their pact, or so I shall always believe after Olivier's extraordinary handshake. He had been very quiet during the scene. There was a deathly, premonitory misgiving in the way he eventually shook hands; and his eyes were glazed. Whatever integration the character of Marcius had possessed fell apart at that moment. The rest was crumble, detonation and collapse, with part of him fatalistically detached."

one long reactive series, pushing away the servants, dismissing Cominius, saying "Away!" (5.2.81) to Menenius as well, physically turning away from Rome even as he had first turned his back.

In their last confrontation, Coriolanus attempts to face Volumnia

As if a man were author of himself
And knew no other kin. (5.3.36–37)

He is performing a part, in other words, and this time it is Volumnia's task to persuade him to be a natural man again, to be Coriolanus, her son, a Roman. He is also, however, in performing this part, being true to himself, to the vow he has made and his sworn loyalty to the Volscians. He is hopelessly divided against himself: witness the fact that now it is not playacting which he thinks would make him effeminate and childlike, but natural behaviour, obedience to instinct, which would make him a "gosling" (35) or "of a woman's tenderness" (129).

Previously, Coriolanus has proved himself a most unable actor, particularly in the matter of gesticulation, since gesture is for him the mode of expression least susceptible to corruption by the will or intellect. Volumnia (and her party), arguing for the natural man, has all the influence of this potent form of expression on her side, while Coriolanus has only his verbal and intellectual resolve to counter it with. It is their physical presence and gestures which move him; Coriolanus melts, in fact, before a word has been exchanged, at the sight of Virgilia, his mother's bow, his son's "aspect of intercession" (32). The instinct he swears he will not obey has been throughout the overriding motive for all his conduct, including his turn against Rome, and it cannot now be wilfully ignored.

The scene begins with a series of ceremonially heightened gestures: Coriolanus's embrace of Virgilia; his salute to his mother by kneeling; Volumnia's reciprocation of that gesture; Coriolanus's lyric apostrophe to Valeria; his benediction of his son; and the boy's genuflection in response. Once Coriolanus has turned to her, it is Volumnia who orchestrates these exchanges, confirming relationships. Her first

long plea is full of bodily and gestural images of the sort
which must impress themselves on Coriolanus's imagination: she offers him the alternative images of himself led
manacled through Rome or treading triumphantly on his
mother's womb. Then, when she finds she must yet intensify
her plea, she does so by emphasizing the immediate, their
physical presence, their actions as pleaders, and finally by
acting, directing and interpreting dramatic gesture for
Coriolanus who is the unwilling audience:

> He turns away.
> Down, ladies! Let us shame him with our knees.
> To his surname Coriolanus 'longs more pride
> Than pity to our prayers. Down! An end;
> This is the last. So we will home to Rome,
> And die among our neighbors. Nay, behold's!
> This boy, that cannot tell what he would have,
> But kneels and holds up hands for fellowship,
> Does reason our petition with more strength
> Than thou hast to deny't. Come, let us go.   (168–77)

The impact of such a reversal must be breathtaking to
Coriolanus. After insisting by word and gesture during the
entire course of the scene on the physical and emotional
bonds between him and themselves, and at this climactic
moment of unified gestural appeal, Volumnia rises, snaps
the bond, and denies the existence of any relationship
whatsoever:

> This fellow had a Volscian to his mother;
> His wife is in Corioles, and his child
> Like him by chance.   (178–80)

It is that denial and withdrawal which finally provokes
Coriolanus's instinctive response; his hand binds her to him.
    Though we see Coriolanus fail "like a dull actor" in the
face of his family's appeal, his inability to act is no longer
the converse, as it once was, of the absolute integrity of his
character. If there is no longer such a strain between playing
a role and playing the man he is, it is because the man is no
longer a clearly definable entity. Certainly he is no longer

the singular incomparable hero, for after he has conceded to Volumnia, he asks,

> Were you in my stead, would you have heard
> A mother less? Or granted less, Aufidius?
>
> (192–93)

With its appeal for emotional support, and its implication that he is behaving as any other man would have behaved, such a question is startlingly new for Coriolanus.

His failure to act the solitary hero has led to an admission of his common humanity. As an ordinary man, no longer exalted by a proud idealistic integrity, he is groping towards the ordinary man's refuge: the capacity to pose, to act, to be politic. After his banishment Coriolanus can no longer play the man he is, but because of this very loss of integrity he can play a role; and the role he plays upon re-entering Corioli is that of the man he once was.

He enters Corioli with fanfare and the public adulation which previously had been repugnant to him. Here, he offers no such response; the stage direction reads that "the Commoners [are] with him." Coriolanus's speech to the lords of the city rings unbearably hollow: it poses as a tale of the triumphs Coriolanus used to tell, or rather which he heard told of him. But there is no triumph involved; there is instead political rhetoric:

> You are to know
> That prosperously I have attempted, and
> With bloody passage led your wars even to
> The gates of Rome. Our spoils we have brought home
> Doth more than counterpoise a full third part
> The charges of the action. We have made peace
> With no less honor to the Antiates
> Than shame to th' Romans;
>
> (5.6.74–81)

His real glory and real triumph lie in the past, when he *was* Coriolanus, and it is to this he reverts when he is insulted. The oaths, exclamations, acts, all of the last scene which Coriolanus makes, must be seen as the shadow of his earlier scenes, for his furious indignation is no longer pure self-defense or pure self-expression. At the last, crying out to use his sword, it is what is written in the annals, the historically recorded Coriolanus, which his gesture would defend.

BRUCE R. SMITH

Sexual Politics in *Coriolanus*°

Two particular moments in *Coriolanus* are likely to give
pause to readers and audiences who think of "heterosexual,"
"homosexual," and "bisexual" as natural categories for dis-
tinguishing one person from another. The first moment
comes early in the play, when Martius, fresh from his victory over Corioles and covered with blood, embraces the
Roman general Cominius. "O, let me clip [i.e. embrace] ye/
In arms as sound as when I wooed," Martius exclaims, "in
heart/ As merry as when our nuptial day was done,/ And
tapers burned to bedward" (1.6.29–32).[1] Cominius's reply is
understated but just as extravagant: "Flower of warriors!"
(32). He turns immediately to the business at hand and asks
about the other general in charge of the campaign, Titus Lartius. Later in the play, Aufidius sounds an uncanny echo of
Martius's speech when he welcomes the disguised Coriolanus to the Volscian camp:

> Let me twine
> Mine arms about that body, where against
> My grainèd ash an hundred times hath broke
> And scarred the moon with splinters. Here I clip
> The anvil of my sword, and do contest
> As hotly and as nobly with thy love
> As ever in ambitious strength I did
> Contend against thy valor. Know thou first,
> I loved the maid I married; never man
> Sighed truer breath. But that I see thee here,
> Thou noble thing, more dances my rapt heart

°Written especially for the revised Signet Classic Shakespeare, and used
with the kind permission of the author.

255

Than when I first my wedded mistress saw
Bestride my threshold.   (4.5.110–22)

Coriolanus's reply is just as understated, but just as passionate as Cominius's: "You bless me, gods" (139). What
are we to make of such speeches? Readers and audiences
today cannot help noticing the eroticism in both cases:
the physical embracement, the comparison with marriage,
the suggestion of sexual consummation in tapers lighting
the way to bed and the "wedded mistress" crossing the
bridegroom's threshold. The frank physicality of the
speeches is all the more surprising in a society that understood sodomy to be a felony, indeed an offense punishable
by death.[2]

Our cue for understanding the speeches of Martius and
Aufidius is provided by Aufidius's servants a few minutes
later in 4.5. The servants first gossip about how powerful the
disguised Coriolanus was when he refused their commands
to leave Aufidius's quarters. "What an arm he has!" says
one. "He turned me about with his finger and his thumb, as
one would set up a top" (156–58). Be that as it may, another
servant observes that Aufidius is treating the Roman refugee
like a woman. Not only that, Aufidius is himself behaving
like a woman, blessing himself and rolling his eyes when
Coriolanus speaks: "Our general himself makes a mistress
of him; sanctifies himself with's hand, and turns up the white
o' th' eye to his discourse" (204–6). To be a "mistress," in
the English of 1608, was to be either a female person who
wielded power by refusing a male suitor's advances (as
ladies were presumed to do in sonnets) or a female person
who yielded power by giving in to the suitor's sexual
desires.[3] In just which sense Coriolanus is playing the mistress is left ambiguous when we compare his reception as
Aufidius's figurative bride with the power he seems to have,
once ensconced in the Volscian camp, to emasculate the
bridegroom who has welcomed him so effusively.

"Emasculate" is the key concept here. Alan Bray has
called attention to an ambiguity in the "signs of male friendship" in early modern England: The embracements, the
kisses, and the rhetorical turns that betokened male friendship could also be read as signs of sodomy, producing poten-

tial anxiety over confusion between the two.[4] That is not, however, what Aufidius's servants are worried about. They are concerned not about the slippage between friendship and sodomy, but about the slippage between male and female modes of desire.[5] In effect, they invite us to view the play's conclusion as Aufidius's recovery of his temporarily abandoned manhood. That, indeed, seems to be on Aufidius's mind when he casts off Coriolanus in the play's last scene. Aufidius berates Coriolanus for having given in to the pleas of his mother and his wife to spare Rome: "[A]t his nurse's tears/ He whined," Aufidius tells the Volscians, "and roared away your victory" (5.6.97–98). When Coriolanus exclaims, "Hear'st thou, Mars?" Aufidius sneers, "Name not the god, thou boy of tears" (100–1).

What is at issue here is not whether Coriolanus and Aufidius sexually desire one another but whether in doing so they maintain their manhood, each in and through the other. The sexual energy that charges their speeches reinforces that consolidation of male power precisely because both speakers are men and, more to the point, men who are equals. In his *Nicomachean Ethics*, Aristotle affirms that friendship between men who "are good, and similar in their goodness" is the highest of human bonds: "It is those who desire the good of their friends, because each loves the other for what he is, and not for any incidental quality. Accordingly the friendship of such men lasts so long as they remain good; and goodness is an enduring quality."[6] Cicero's treatise "Of Friendship" (*De Amicitia*) advances the same opinion. Sir William Cornwallis is clearly thinking of Aristotle and Cicero when he proclaims in his essay "Of Love" (1600), "That which comes nearest to love is this, man with man agreeing in sex: I cannot think it is so between men and women, for it gives opportunity to lust, which the pureness of love will not endure."[7] Distribution of power in the sexual politics of Shakespeare's England was determined by the sex of the desiring person, not by the sex of the person desired. Hence there were no "homosexuals" or "bisexuals" in Shakespeare's England, nor "heterosexuals" either. All three terms are coinages from the late-nineteenth century. All three presume that the sex of the bodies one desires is more important than the sex of one's own body. It is the sexual politics of Shakespeare's England that dictates the extremely marginal position of women in *Coriolanus*. Volumnia, Virgilia, Valeria, and an attendant gentlewoman share the play with no fewer than forty-two male characters. Volumnia's attempt to assume male power over her son needs to be understood within this hypermasculine context.

So, too, does the behavior between Coriolanus and Aufidius that the Volscian's servants read as mistress to mistress. John Earle's characterization of "A lascivious man" in his character book *Microcosmography* (1628) portrays every indulgence of lust, regardless of the sex of the beloved, as a loss of manhood: "A lascivious man is the servant he says of many mistresses, but all are but his lust, to which only he is faithful, and none besides, and spends his best blood and spirits in the service. His soul is the bawd to his body. . . ."[8] Earle seems to be invoking both meanings of the word "mistress," by voicing his anxiety that lust puts the female on top, so to speak. Social class is at issue as well, since lust turns the lascivious man, whatever his actual status, into a servant. The erotic imagery in the speeches Martius exchanges with Cominius early in the play and Aufidius with Coriolanus toward the end are thus highly volatile. On the one hand, they celebrate male friendship as the highest of human bonds; on the other, they suggest that in the ardor of their mutual admiration Aufidius and Coriolanus run the risk of losing their masculinity. The sexual energy in those speeches can either affirm patriarchal power or else undermine it. The terms of that potential undermining have to do with the sex of the man who feels desire, not with the bodies of the persons he happens to desire.

It was in the early eighteenth century, according to Randolph Trumbach, that men who desire other men were first recognized as a social type and were ostracized by being gendered female. "Mollies" of the eighteenth century anticipated in some repects "homosexuals" of the nineteenth century.[9] The production history of *Coriolanus* reflects this paradigm shift. Nahum Tate's adaptation of the play, *The Ingratitude of a Commonwealth, or The Fall of Caius Martius Coriolanus* (first acted 1681), introduced all sorts of cuts and additions aimed at turning Coriolanus into a model family man, devoted to his wife and son, but Aufidius's lines

"Let me twine/ Mine arms about that body . . ." were retained intact. No contradiction seems to have been perceived between Coriolanus's domestic virtue and his physical attractiveness to Aufidius.[10] A hundred years later, however, those lines had become an embarrassment. The neoclassical version of *Coriolanus* acted by John Philip Kemble between 1789–97 and 1811–17 diffuses any hint of homoeroticism in the play's speeches.[11] It was in the very years of Kemble's career that a crisis arose with respect to Shakespeare's sonnets. When editors like George Steevens and Edmund Malone returned to the original 1609 quarto of the sonnets, they could not help but notice that many of Shakespeare's most famous love poems were addressed to a young man. Sonnet 20 ("A woman's face with nature's own hand painted/ Hast thou, the master-mistress of my passion") presented a particular problem. Steevens's comment on the poem, quoted in Malone's 1780 edition, could hardly be more explicit: "It is impossible to read the fulsome panegyric, addressed to a male object, without an equal mixture of disgust and indignation."[12] Kemble's successor in the role of Coriolanus, Edmund Kean, transformed the neoclassical hero of the eighteenth century into an impetuous Romantic hero out of the pages of Byron. Like his predecessor, however, Kean avoided any intimations of homoeroticism.[13] As well he might. The early nineteenth century witnessed a sudden rise in the number of prosecutions for sodomy.[14]

When directors, actors, and audiences were finally ready to confront the implications of Martius's and Aufidius's speeches in productions mounted during the second half of the twentieth century, they did so with Sigmund Freud, not Aristotle, as their guide. Two productions of the 1960s, Michael Langham's for the Stratford, Ontario, festival in 1961 and Tyrone Guthrie's for the Nottingham Playhouse in 1963, diagnosed Coriolanus as a case of arrested development, the victim of a dominating mother. "Male narcissism and aggression caused by infantile deprivation" in Paul Scofield's interpretation of the role in the Stratford, Ontario, production took a specifically homosexual turn in John Neville's interpretation, opposite Ian McKellen, in the Nottingham Playhouse production.[15] Since the 1969 Stonewall rebellion launched the gay liberation movement, productions of the play have tended to jettison Freud for what Alan Sinfield has called "metropolitan gay culture," in which "gay" figures, above all else, as a "life style."[16] Thus Terry Hands's direction of Alan Howard in the title role for the Royal Shakespeare Company in 1979 featured a leather-and-chains mise-en-scène that might have been transported from an East End after-hours club. Ten years later the same director, again working with the RSC, this time in collaboration with John Barton, presented Coriolanus as an object of bisexual fascination in the person of Charles Dance, whose bare-chested image beckoned from posters in London's Underground stations. Greater psychological subtlety characterized David Thacker's RSC production of 1993–94, in which the mature Aufidius's sexual fervor met with icy detachment on the part of Toby Stephens's conspicuously young and callow Coriolanus.

As sexual mores change, so will productions of *Coriolanus*. A queer Coriolanus waits in the wings. So does a postqueer Coriolanus. All such productions, like those since the eighteenth century, will operate within a sexual politics very different from the original staging of 1608–09, when the fundamental anxiety involved, not the sex of the protagonist's erotic objects, but the loss of the protagonist's manhood.

Notes

1. All quotations from *Coriolanus* are taken from the revised Signet Classic text, ed. Reuben Brower (New York: New American Library, 2002).

2. On the legal record concerning sodomy see Bruce R. Smith, *Homosexual Desire in Shakespeare's England: A Cultural Poetics* (Chicago: University of Chicago Press, 1991), 41–53.

3. Compare *Oxford English Dictionary*, 2nd ed. (Oxford: Oxford University Press, 1989), "mistress," 10a ("A woman who has command over a man's heart," with references from 1509) and 11 ("A woman who illicitly occupies the place of a wife," with most references datable to after 1600).

4. Alan Bray, "Homosexuality and the Signs of Male Friendship in Elizabethan England," in *Queering the Renaissance*, ed. Jonathan Goldberg (Durham, NC: Duke University Press, 1994), 40–61.

5. Bray, 81–112.

6. Aristotle, *The Ethics of Aristotle*, trans. J. A. K. Thomson (London: Penguin, 1976), 263.

7. William Cornwallis, *Essays* (London: William Mattes, 1600), sig. D8.

8. John Earle, *Microcosmography*, in *Character Writings of the Seventeenth Century*, ed. Henry Morley (London: Routledge, 1891), 29.

9. Randolph Trumbach, *Sex and the Gender Revolution* (Chicago: University of Chicago Press, 1998), 3–8.

10. On Tate's changes see Bruce R. Smith, *Shakespeare and Masculinity* (Oxford: Oxford University Press, 2000), 152–53.

11. John Ripley, *Coriolanus on Stage in England and America, 1609–1994* (Madison, NJ: Fairleigh Dickinson University Press, 1998), 122. See also Barbara Puschmann-Nalenz, "Using Shakespeare? The Appropriation of *Coriolanus* and *King Henry V* in John Philip Kemble's 1789 Production," in *Shakespeare and France*, ed. Hodges Klein and Jean-Marie Maguin (Lewiston, NY: Mellen, 1995), 219–32.

12. Quoted in Joseph Pequigney, *Such Is My Love: A Study of Shakespeare's Sonnets* (Chicago: University of Chicago Press, 1988), 30–31. See also Peter Stallybrass, "Editing as Cultural Formation: The Sexing of Shakespeare's Sonnets," in *Shakespeare's Sonnets: Critical Essays*, ed. James Schiffer (New York: Garland, 1998; rpt. London: Routledge, 2000), 75–88.

13. Ripley, 157.

14. Louis Crompton, *Byron and Greek Love: Homophobia in Nineteenth-century England* (Berkeley: University of California Press, 1985), 12–62.

15. Ripley, 304.

16. Alan Sinfield, *Gay and After* (London: Serpent's Tail, 1998), 1–17.

S. SCHOENBAUM

Coriolanus on Stage and Screen

In its own day *Coriolanus* was sufficiently familiar in production for Ben Jonson to be able, in 1609–10, to allude jestingly in *Epicoene, or The Silent Woman,* to a phrase from the tragedy. Cominius's apostrophe to Coriolanus's exploits in battle, "He lurch'd"—that is, robbed all other contenders—"all Swords of the garland," becomes, in the last speech of Jonson's comedy, the gallant Truewit's "You have lurch'd your friends of the better half of the garland." Yet no record of performance of *Coriolanus* exists before the Civil War in 1640 pulled down the curtain on professional stage representations in England for two decades.

When we do first hear of *Coriolanus* on the boards, it is not of Shakespeare's text, but of Nahum Tate's "improved" post-Restoration version, *The Ingratitude of a Commonwealth, or The Fall of Coriolanus,* printed in 1682 as it was acted at London's Theatre-Royal. Cuts are expectedly numerous, and there are also amplifications in keeping with the taste of the new age. Thus Tate abridges the part of Menenius Agrippa, but for mirth expands the part of Virgilia's friend Valeria, who in Shakespeare has only 14 speeches—41 lines (fewer than 350 words all told)—characterizing her as "an affected, talkative, fantastical Lady." A newly invented character is Nigridius, a cashiered Roman officer who, chafing under his "foul disgrace," throws in his lot with Aufidius.

An Irishman educated at Trinity College, Dublin, Tate (1652–1715) had migrated to London, where he enjoyed the patronage of the Tory minister, Lord Dorset—patronage which he repaid with suitable political obsequiousness. "Faction is a monster," Tate declared in his Dedication, "that often makes the slaughter 'twas designed for; and as often turns its fury on those that hatched it; the moral, therefore of these scenes being to recommend submission and adherence to established lawful power, which, in a word, is *loyalty*." Mainly Tate follows the plot of his original for the first four acts, but his concluding scene (5.2) becomes a Senecan farrago of violence and attempted pathos as the conspirators help Aufidius to wound Coriolanus, "who kills some, and hurts Aufidius." The latter threatens to rape Virgilia before Coriolanus's eyes but instead dies when Virgilia, self-wounded, is brought in to expire with her "chaste treasure" intact. Nigridius, we learn, has "Mangled,/Gashed, wracked, distorted" young Marcius, Coriolanus's son, and then thrown the "tortured brat, with ribs all broke" into Volumnia's arms. Coriolanus's mother comes on stage "distracted," and seizing a spear from one of the guards, runs Nigridius through, then hurriedly exits, leaving the elder Marcius to fly to "Death's calm Region" grasping his dying son in one arm and his dead wife in the other.

About Tate's adaptation the Prologue writer (Sir George Raynsford) boasts, "He [Tate] only ventures to make gold from ore, And turn to money, what lay dead before." But the money turned out to be only fool's gold, and "this tale of horror" folded very shortly after its first presentation. Tate had much better fortune with his upbeat travesty of *King Lear* (produced the same year), which held the stage for 150 years.

In 1718 Shakespeare's uncommingled *Tragedy of Coriolanus* was apparently performed in the rival house at Lincoln's Inn Fields, as restored to the boards by John Rich, the theater manager and pantomimist best known for his production of John Gay's *The Beggar's Opera*, an endeavor which (as a contemporary put it) made "Gay rich, and Rich gay." The next year another adaptation, this one by John Dennis (satirized as Appius in Pope's *Essay on Criticism*), and entitled *The Invader of His Country Or, The Fatal Resentment*, had its debut at Drury Lane in November. Debut was also finale, for the house rebuffed this *Invader*, leaving the disgruntled adaptor to point out to readers, in the preface to the printed edition, resemblances between the Roman rabble's treatment of Coriolanus and the indignities Dennis—and, consequently, his patron, the Duke of Newcastle—had suffered at the hands of the "insolent players" who allowed the work no more than three performances. The same month the rival house, Lincoln's Inn Fields, competed with a play with the same title as Dennis's but in the playbill announced as "written by Shakespeare." The following year the company did the honest thing and billed its offering as *Coriolanus*. James Quin, who had established his reputation as Richard III, and would go on to play many Shakespearean tragic leads, including Brutus and Macbeth, was a notable Coriolanus. Dennis attempted to give the play topical relevance: he had in mind the sectarian strife stirred by the 1715 rising of the Jacobites, as adherents of the exiled James II were termed. In his Prologue, Dennis claimed to have reduced—so far as was possible—the "wild confusion" of his original: this he accomplished by rewriting much of Shakespeare's verse, introducing infusions of his own, scanting Menenius's humor, and giving the talkative Valeria only one silent appearance.

The *Coriolanus* presented at Covent Garden in 1749 was neither Shakespeare's nor an adaptation but an original blank-verse drama—one of a sequence—by James Thomson, best known for his enormously popular and influential poem *The Seasons*. For his historical source Thomson turned not to Plutarch but to the somewhat different account of Coriolanus by the rhetorician Dionysius of Halicarnassus, who flourished during the reign of Augustus, and to whom Plutarch himself on occasion turned. In Dionysius, conspirators, not Aufidius (here called Attius Tullus), bear responsibility for Coriolanus's assassination.

In 1754 David Garrick, manager of Drury Lane and the greatest actor of his day, restored Shakespeare's unalloyed *Coriolanus* to Drury Lane, but he did not act in the play himself, nor did he ever essay the part. Henry Mossop won plaudits as the hero, and Hannah Pritchard—whose acting style accented articulation—played Volumnia. For a time the conflation of Shakespeare and Thomson enjoyed some popularity in both England and the United States. This hybrid was probably put together by Thomas Sheridan, the Irish actor-manager who would sire a more famous son, the playwright Richard Brinsley Sheridan, who delighted (and still delights) audiences everywhere with *The Rivals* and *The School for Scandal*. In the hybrid *Coriolanus,* Sheridan

senior took the part of Coriolanus; Lacy Ryan, of croaking
voice and damaged features (the result of a jaw injury), was
Aufidius. Apart from some sixteen lines of Shakespeare, the
last act trusted to Thomson.

The *Coriolanus* of John Philip Kemble (1757–1823), suc-
cessively manager of London's two premier theaters, Drury
Lane and Covent Garden, formed the crowning achievement
of a distinguished acting career. In 1789 *Coriolanus, as
Altered from Shakespeare and Thomson,* was first performed at Drury Lane, three months after Kemble had
become manager. For this version, which relies mainly on
Sheridan, Kemble—while not especially mindful, as were
his predecessors, of topical resonances—*was* responsive to
the Roman context, and (as his contemporary biographer
James Boaden remarks) based his interpretation on the
awareness that "the high patrician pride of that hero leads
him to venture everything for the Roman NAME." Indeed,
when audiences for weeks besieged Covent Garden,
Kemble became Coriolanus. That did not stop him from
taking liberties, more than he ever had taken before, with the
play that Shakespeare wrote. Gone from the first scene was
Menenius's fable of the belly, gone too most of Volumnia's
climactic pleadings with her son. Still, Kemble's Coriolanus
was esteemed by audiences—and by Kemble himself—as
his masterpiece. He would play the part often and choose it
for his valedictory performances in 1817. Kemble prided
himself on introducing historically accurate costumes and
settings into his Shakespearean revivals, drawing inspiration
from period paintings and engravings—a far cry from the
miserable pairs of flats producers used previously to clap
together.

Kemble's most famous Volumnia was his incomparable
sister Sarah Siddons, most celebrated for her Lady Macbeth.
Of Siddons the critic William Hazlitt—who had seen her
perform many times—wrote that she was "not less than a
goddess, or than a prophetess inspired by the gods." As
Volumnia, Siddons was the formidable Roman matron, yet
she could converse with Virgilia and Valeria with easy
familiarity. When her son returned in triumph from Corioli,
wearing his oaken garland, no fewer than 240 supers
marched in stately procession across the stage. Volumnia

marched too, with head erect, flashing eyes, proud smile, and hands pressed against her bosom, rolling—almost reeling—across the stage, recollecting that she was no longer Sarah Siddons but "the proud mother of a proud son, and conquering hero. . . . She towered above all around her, and yet became so true to nature, so picturesque, and so descriptive, that pit and gallery sprang to their feet electrified by the transcendent execution of the conception." So Julian Charles Young recalled long afterward, in 1871.

The great Edmund Kean attempted *Coriolanus* only once, in 1820 at Drury Lane, in one of the earliest productions of the play as Shakespeare wrote it, with omissions only. But the revival mustered only four performances before shutting down. Kean's unimpressive stature, ill suited to heroic parts, probably contributed to the failure. When his Coriolanus was banished from Rome, his contempt for the plebs ("I banish you") was redolent only of (as Hazlitt put it) "virulence of execration and rage of impotent despair." William Charles Macready, who three months earlier had mounted *Coriolanus* successfully at Covent Garden just after his triumphal *Richard III,* would return to *Coriolanus* fifteen times in five seasons with diminishing applause. The 1838 revival, however, was especially splendid scenically: on the backdrop appeared the Capitoline hill, citadel and temples, and—along the sloping side—clutches of thatched huts, while in the Senate a multitude of patricians sat in state in triple rows. At the siege of Rome soldiers propelled battering rams. In the streets a disorderly rabble rioted with rude weapons, while at Antium the port and lighthouse glowed in starlight.

Coriolanus was infrequently revived during the Victorian age. However, Samuel Phelps (1804–78), the actor who, with his perfect elocution, made it his mission to bring Shakespeare to the Sadler's Wells Theatre in London's Islington—a little removed from the West End theatrical hub—produced *Coriolanus* on no fewer than four occasions during his long career, first in 1848, when he won "overwhelming applause" from a full house. Henry Morley caught Phelps's 1860 production and in an article for the *Examiner* that September observed how the hero's attempt to flatter the mob was "really intense torture" for this man of "heroic pride." When in his final spasm of rage in the last scene Coriolanus declares

> That, like an eagle in a dovecote, I
> Fluttered your Volscians in Corioles.
> Alone I did it, (5.6.115–17)

Phelps would pause before "fluttered"; then, "lifting his arm to its full height above his head, he shook his head to and fro, as in the act of startling a flock of doves." With this gesture Phelps set his seal upon *Coriolanus.* Sir Henry Irving—the first English actor to be knighted—chose *Coriolanus* for his swan song at the Lyceum in April 1901. Ellen Terry, with Irving an inseparable acting partner, played Volumnia. Both gifted players were unsuited to their parts: the reflective, ruminative Irving called upon to play the man of action; Terry, famous for her beauty, voice, and charm, called upon to be the fierce warrior's fierce mother. The production folded after only thirty-four nights; audiences then anyway preferred light musical comedies at the Gaiety.

Frank Benson, whose provincial troupes were a mainstay of Shakespearean production in England for over thirty years, revived *Coriolanus* more than once (*Titus Andronicus* and *Troilus and Cressida* were the only plays he failed to do), including two stagings at Stratford-upon-Avon (1893 and 1898) and one at the Comedy Theatre in London (1901). Mrs. Benson often played Virgilia, and was hailed by Coriolanus as—fairly enough—"My gracious silence" (2.1.180). Sir Frank—he had been dubbed two nights previously in the theater, the first actor ever to be knighted in such a setting, by King George V—along with Lady Benson, performed in a tableau of a single scene in a tercentenary matinee special of scenes from nine Shakespeare plays in the spring of 1916, while across the Channel all was not quiet on the Western front during the Great War.

On another Shakespeare birthday, this time in 1926, William Bridges-Adams offered *Coriolanus* as the Birthday Play at Stratford-upon-Avon and again, seven years later, at the lately rebuilt Shakespeare Memorial Theatre, as the resident house was then called. Bridges-Adams had embarked on his tenure at the Memorial with the avowed policy, then revolutionary, of presenting full texts: unabridged-Adams, he was facetiously called. In time he became himself a fierce cutter, and the play that suffered most from his depradations was *Coriolanus,* which he produced spectacularly with the massive gates of Corioli being smashed in, with full-throated supers jostling onto the stage from the orchestra pit, and with Coriolanus at the end falling among conspiratorial swords with fierce laughter: after its own fashion, Epic Theater. The innovative William Poel (1854–1923) also cut ruthlessly when, at seventy-eight, he offered the play one morning in 1931 at London's Chelsea Palace Theatre on a platform stage appended to the proscenium arch; a stage on which actors could be viewed from three sides and thus (such was Poel's program) approximated Elizabethan the-atrical conditions. The whole performance took only an hour and a half.

In Stratford, *Coriolanus* was directed by Ben Iden Payne as the last play of the 1939 season with Alec Clunes as Coriolanus and Dorothy Green as Volumnia. War clouds were rapidly gathering, conscription had begun in Britain, Hitler's troops were about to invade Poland. Yet *Corio-lanus,* so powerfully suggestive politically in the midst of a divided Europe, was in this production distanced from such contemporary realities. The Romans performed in Eliza-bethan costumes while the opposing Volscians resembled (in one historian's words) "refugees from a Turkish harem." That was in May. September would extinguish the hopes—in the poet Auden's words—of "a low dishonest decade."

In 1938, at London's Old Vic, Laurence Olivier—still in his early thirties (he had recently acted Romeo)—acted Mar-cius as an arrogantly youthful patrician; Sybil Thorndike was his formidable mother. Since the war, *Coriolanus* has retained a secure place in the Shakespearean repertory, espe-cially in the United Kingdom. The 1948 Old Vic produc-tion was memorable mainly for Alec Guinness's subtle, humorous, yet always human Menenius Agrippa. At Strat-ford in 1952 Anthony Quayle's rasping Coriolanus, a tough yet boyish soldier, was, in the words of one reviewer, "wearing his wounds aggressively as badges of rank." Richard Burton took the lead at the Old Vic in 1954, with Fay Compton and Claire Bloom as, respectively, Volumnia and Virgilia. Olivier again played an arrogant, but now older, Coriolanus in a production staged by the youthful Peter Hall, still in his twenties, for the Memorial Theatre's centenary season in 1959. But Olivier's daring fall to his death at the end was something new: impaled by a multitude of spears, he toppled forward from an elevated stage promontory, to be caught, dangling, by the ankles. Edith Evans was the mother exercising powerful maternal dominion over her "boy"-son. The staircase-set invented by Boris Aronson, as it turned out, was an abrasive presence. Tyrone Guthrie's revival in Nottingham in 1963 put the Romans in Victorian dress and found pseudo-Freudian homosexual anticipations in the relationship between Marcius (John Neville) and Aufidius (Ian McKellen). At Stratford, in 1967, Ian Richardson was an uncharismatic Coriolanus in John Barton's production, in which the plebs and the patricians contested the territorial imperative unideologically on equal terms, and the battle scenes were played for all they were worth, which is a good deal.

Trevor Nunn at Stratford in 1972 (with directorial assistance from Buzz Goodfellow and Evan Smith) came up with a thematic season of Shakespeare's four Roman plays: *Coriolanus, Julius Caesar, Antony and Cleopatra,* and *Titus Andronicus* (in that order), presented under the omnibus title *The Romans:* a Stratford first. On a newly installed stage, permitting technological wizardry, directorial gimmicks— such as elaborate processional opening scenes unspecified by the texts—underscored cyclic and thematic links as Rome moved from repressive authoritarianism to end-of-empire decadence. Ian Hogg was Coriolanus, and when the production moved to London the next season, Nicol Williamson assumed the title role, capturing at once Marcius's propelling power and his capitulation, as his mother knelt before him, to filial emotion, his eyes being moved to "sweat compassion."

Alan Howard was this generation's most memorable— and, eventually, also most familiar—Coriolanus in Terry Hands's RSC production, which debuted in Stratford in 1977. Previously he had played Prince Hal and Henry V in Hands's presentation of the English history cycle. Hands choreographed the storming of Corioli as Coriolanus, in black leather and covered with blood, encountered Aufidius (Julian Glover) in the identical costume: Marcius's mirror image. This was physical warfare celebrated. Maxine Audley was a formidable Volumnia.

For Richard Digby Day's revival at Nottingham in 1983, Rome was England on the eve of the outbreak of Civil War, c. 1635: the patricians became Royalists; the plebeians, Puritans. This Coriolanus prefigured Charles I, who would—quite literally—lose his head. On the other hand, Sir Peter Hall's 1984 revival at the National Theatre, with Ian McKellen (sometimes in a flashy blazer, sometimes in military garb, sometimes stripped and blood-smeared), opted for modernity: Plebs were London audience members pressed onto the stage. Sicinius Brutus, the Tribune, became a gray-suited trade-union official, briefcase in hand. Thatcherism had triumphed in ancient Rome, mid-1980s-style. But modern dress, as one reviewer observed, failed to satisfy the thematic expectations of political urgency aroused by production technique. Irene Worth, however, excelled as Volumnia, responding to the tensions in her relationship with her son.

In the United States, until the advent of modern Shakespeare summer festivals, Coriolanus has been infrequently played. Of John Vandenhoff's rendition in 1837 at the National Theater one critic remarked that "supercilious disdain was never more powerfully expressed." But Edwin Forrest (1806–72) was the foremost American to take the part in the nineteenth century. Forrest first played Coriolanus in 1831, and thereafter kept the role—performed as an arrogant, albeit virile patrician—in repertory. Of Coriolanus's assassination in a Broadway production in 1855, a newspaper commented, "The crowd rush upon him, cover him from the view of the audience, and in the melee he is slain, but the manner of his death is left to the imagination." At Niblo's Garden in 1863 (also with Forrest), at the end a tableau depicted the hero's incineration on a funeral pyre.

On the Continent, on the eve of the Second World War, in the spring of 1934, the Action Française and other antirepublican groups in Paris agitating for a revolution (which—it was hoped—would overthrow a weak and decadent democracy waiting to be toppled) persuaded the

Comedie Française to mount a reworking of *Coriolanus* by Rene-Louis Piachaud (a Swiss national), admittedly freely translated and adapted to the conditions of the French stage. Intended as a devastating criticism of democratic processes, the production succeeded in provoking uproars in the theater and Fascist and monarchist riots in the streets, but did not—as was hoped—usher in a revolution. It did, however, lead M. Daladier, the French premier, to dismiss the director and appoint in his place the police commissioner, no theatrical hand.

Other voices, other versions; left as well as right. The Marxist playwright Bertolt Brecht (1898–1956) in East Berlin directed the celebrated, state-supported Berliner Ensemble. His last work, *Coriolanus,* was an unfinished adaptation of Shakespeare's tragedy, and an example of Brechtian Epic Theater. Brecht's citizens play their humorless roles in the class struggle; the Tribunes, no longer devious, speak for the People; even a few patricians join the poor folk of Rome in their efforts to rid society of a dictatorial warrior-hero. The Berliner Ensemble produced *Coriolan* in London in 1965. The RSC did not touch down in East Berlin when it toured the Continent with Terry Hands's *Coriolanus.*

"There is a world elsewhere," Coriolanus tells the throng of citizens in the Forum as he turns his back forever on Rome. The RSC too would discover a world elsewhere as Hands—after triumphing with *Coriolanus* in Stratford, Newcastle, and London in 1979—took his production on a continental tour, the itinerary for which included a week in Paris, followed by short stopovers in Vienna, Amsterdam, Brussels, Hamburg, West Berlin, Munich, and Zurich. The house lights dimmed, four huge stage walls moved like doors or became giant gates; drums beat, tympani and brass sounded, swords crossed; *Coriolanus* was performed, and rapt audiences were left at once exhilarated and exhausted.

Alan Howard also re-created his role for the BBC Television Shakespeare *Coriolanus* (1984) directed by Elijah Moshinsky and boasting a fine cast, which included Mike Gwilym as Aufidius and Irene Worth as a Volumnia who perforce knelt before her warrior son (5.3) yet took evident maternal pride in his achievements, however ferocious. The telecast version was severely cut, coming to only two and one half hours (an hour less than Terry Hands's almost complete RSC revival). Gone was the Upstairs-Downstairs interplay among the servingmen in Aufidius's house at Antium (4.5). When the two commanders met one another in this scene, Aufidius grasped his uninvited and unrecognized guest by the throat, then—seeing who he was— embraced him. A love-hate relationship was emphasized throughout; these two mortal adversaries were locked together as they fought on the battlefield, and, at the end, Aufidius and Coriolanus together grasped a single sword, which descended upon Coriolanus as both men cried, "Kill, kill." The conspirators were absent from this version. Nor were there togas in Rome in the Senate house or on the streets in this version, which opted for a late Renaissance contemporaneity of setting: dark blue velvet mantles for the men. The constraints of the modest budget did not rule out cinematic techniques; there was abundant cross-cutting; Coriolanus in battle (1.4) appeared on horseback and delivered his lines in voice-over.

Coriolanus has not otherwise been filmed for either the small or large screen, apart from an abbreviated one-hour BBC version (for a series of nine plays in 1963, dramatizing Shakespeare's Rome, called *The Spread of the Eagle*) and a 1972 Irish Television broadcast of *Coriolanus* with Frank Barry in the title role.

Postscript from the Twenty-First Century

The late Sam Schoenbaum's stage history covered productions up through 1984—Peter Hall's production at the National with Ian McKellen and Irene Worth, and Elijah Moshinsky's BBC television version with Alan Howard and Irene Worth. We can now comment briefly on the chief later productions, and then glance back at the stage history of *Coriolanus* in the second half of the twentieth century.

In 1988 Steven Berkoff directed a modern-dress *Coriolanus* at the New York Shakespeare Festival. The Citizens wore black leather pants and black shirts; the tribunes wore the pinstripes associated with mobsters; Coriolanus wore a long black leather coat, a black silk shirt and black trousers, evoking thoughts both of Nazism and of high fashion; and Tullus Aufidius wore a black jumpsuit and boots. The highly praised battle scenes were enacted without visible weapons. Coriolanus delivered uppercuts to the air, and his foes fell. (Berkoff later did somewhat similar productions in Munich [1991] and London [1996]).) Also in 1988, John Hirsch directed a production at the Old Globe Theatre in San Diego. This was the year of Irangate, when Congressional hearings were held to examine the clandestine sale of arms by the United States Army to Iran, in order to channel support to the right-wing Contras, who sought to overthrow the Socialist Sandinista government in Nicaragua. Hirsch saw Oliver North, a Marine Corps colonel who was the hero or the villain (depending on one's politics) of this investigation, as a kind of equivalent to Coriolanus. In Hirsch's view, America had an ambiguous attitude toward North— widespread admiration for a good-looking upright guy who put himself above the law in order to assist what he took to be a good cause. He cast Byron Jenning—passable as a North look-alike—in the role, giving him North's marine uniform, crew cut hairstyle, and sunglasses. The Volscians, chiefly Hispanic and African-American actors, looked appropriately Central American. Further contemporary references were included: Menenius was a Southern Democrat in a white suit; Virgilia, looking rather like Joan Kennedy, was given a drinking problem; Volumnia, based on Rose Kennedy, used her wheelchair as a weapon. Lest the relevance to the times be missed, the play, set in Washington and Nicaragua, began with a fifteen-minute prologue during which clips of the Congressional hearings—along with clips of activists such as Jane Fonda—were shown on sixteen television monitors at the sides of the stage. These images were then replaced by images of the actors on the stage, then a blackout, shots, red lights, policemen, looters, and persons bearing placards "Down with the Rich" and "Food not Talk." Coriolanus's entrance, recorded by a live TV crew on the stage, was also seen in close-ups on the TV screens. Throughout the play the monitors showed a mixture of what was taking place on the stage and what was taking place in America and elsewhere—for instance, shots of angry confrontations around the world. When Coriolanus set out for Rome, it was via helicopter. The text was fairly heavily cut, the diction of some of the surviving passages was simplified, and words like "amigo" and various obscenities were added. On the whole, a good time was had by all.

In 1992 the Renaissance Theatre Company, directed by Tim Supple, performed the play in England at the Chichester Festival, with Kenneth Branagh as Coriolanus and Judi Dench as Volumnia. The set, almost bare except for a red steel wall at the rear, with built-in stairs and ladders, suggested some sort of joyless, repressive place, but there was no explicit contemporary political connection. The reviews suggest that Branagh, in tight black leather breeches, steel breastplate, boots, and gloves, was a highly unsympathetic figure—that is, even more unsympathetic than in most productions. More attractive, in every way, was the handsome, athletic Coriolanus of Toby Stephens in the 1994 Royal Shakespeare Company production at the small Swan Theatre in Stratford, directed by David Thacker, and staged the next year at the larger Barbican Theatre in London. Costumes evoked the French Revolution and the first decade of the nineteenth century—the tribunes wore knee breeches, and the women wore gowns that were more or less of the Empire period. Spectators saw a broken brick wall revealing a sketchy blow-up of Delacroix's *Liberty Leading the People* (1830), a picture commemorating revolutionary idealism. This overt political symbol leads us to the Big Question: Can the play be effectively staged as something relevant to our own political issues?

By its use of Delacroix's painting, the 1994 RSC production suggested that the play is not about Roman times and not about Shakespeare's Jacobean times, but about revolutionary times. However, it did not go further and offer some sort of clear political interpretation. In this, it was somewhat like Paul Barry's 1973 production at the New Jersey Shakespeare Festival, set in Italy during World War II, in which the Volscians were costumed as Nazis, the Roman patricians were American officers and soldiers, and Coriolanus looked like General Patton—or rather, like George C. Scott, who had played Patton in a movie. Viewers gathered that the play had some sort of relevance to later times, but the relevance was not clear. Indeed, it seems characteristic of most productions that they are not political commentaries, even if they offer modern dress and televised images of current political happenings. There probably are two reasons for this curious presence of political imagery but absence of strong political interpretation. The first is that the play, despite all of its local politics, and despite its presentation of class struggle, essentially is (like Shakespeare's other tragedies) a play about personal issues, not political issues such as the demerits of democracy. Of course there *have* been some highly political interpretations, especially with a Marxist slant, for instance a once-famous production in Moscow at the Maly Theatre in 1934, which showed Coriolanus as a Western-style individualist who has betrayed the common people. Or consider Nahum Tate's adaptation (1682), whose moral we quoted at the beginning of this essay: "The moral," Tate said, is "to recommend submission and adherence to established lawful power." Still, and again, whether one reads or sees the play, one ends with the feeling that it finally is about personal relationships, not political ones.

A second reason, perhaps, for the lack of strong political readings, at least in the last thirty years or so, is the triumph of postmodernism, with its emphasis on "indecipherability," multiple meanings, or ultimately, meaninglessness. Among the characteristics of postmodernism are the use of a variety of styles, a tendency toward pastiche and parody, a sense of alienation, and a belief that literature is its own reality rather than is an imitation of life. Postmodern directors, even in an age of director's theater, can hardly bring themselves to believe that the play has a coherent political meaning and that the meaning is relevant to our lives.

Finally, there is one other aspect of the play that has not been touched on, but that has sometimes been brought out in productions of the last few decades, and this is the possible erotic relationship between Aufidius and Coriolanus. The chief evidence is one of Aufidius's speeches to Coriolanus:

> Let me twine
> Mine arms about that body, where against
> My grainèd ash an hundred times hath broke
> And scarred the moon with splinters. Here I clip [i.e. embrace]

The anvil of my sword, and do contest
As hotly and as nobly with thy love
As ever in ambitious strength I did
Contend against thy valor. Know thou first,
I loved the maid I married, never man
Sighed truer breath. But that I see thee here,
Thou noble thing, more dances my rapt heart
Than when I first my wedded mistress saw
Bestride my threshold.   (4.5.110–22)

Some productions—John Barton's 1963 RSC production has already been mentioned—have fairly clearly indicated that Aufidius is sexually attracted to Coriolanus (in the 1994 RSC production, Menenius, too, was interested in a conspicuously attractive Coriolanus), including the 1983 BBC TV version and a 1991 production at the Folger Library. Interestingly, Coriolanus uses somewhat similar language when he greets Cominius:

O, let me clip ye
In arms as sound as when I wooed; in heart
As merry as when our nuptial day was done,
And tapers burned to bedward!   (1.6.29–32)

In Plutarch, Shakespeare's source, at this point Cominius embraces and kisses Coriolanus, a conventional expression of bonding in a military culture. But the comparison to a nuptial night is Shakespeare's addition. The issue, then, is whether such speeches are the homosocial expression of a warrior society or are something else, namely homoerotic expressions. The latter view gains some support from other speeches, notably Aufidius's assertion to Coriolanus that he nightly dreamed of "encounters 'twixt thyself and me." (4.5.127). But even productions that included a homoerotic slant did not allow it to dominate the interpretation.

Bibliographic Note: The editions of *Coriolanus* by Philip Brockbank (1976), R. B. Parker (1994), and Lee Bliss (2000) contain brief but useful stage histories, but the fullest account is John Ripley, *"Coriolanus" on Stage in England and America 1609–1994* (Madison, N.J.: Fairleigh Dickinson University Press, 1998). Ralph Berry's *Changing Styles In Shakespeare* (London: Allen and Unwin, 1981) has a perceptive chapter on "The Metamorphoses of *Coriolanus*" (pp. 18–36). David Daniell, in *"Coriolanus" in Europe* (London: Athlone, 1981), furnishes a detailed account of the 1980 RSC continental tour of Terry Hands's production. Kristinia Bedford, in *"Coriolanus" at the National* (Selinsgrove: Susquehanna University Press, 1992), documents Peter Hall's 1984 National Theatre production (Ian McKellen played Coriolanus, Irene Worth played Volumnia); Bedford more or less condenses the book into an essay in David Wheeler's collection of essays on the play, cited below.

For other relevant titles, see below, Section 4, Shakespeare on Stage and Screen. For reviews of current productions, see *Shakespeare Quarterly, Shakespeare Survey,* and especially *Shakespeare Bulletin.*

—SYLVAN BARNET

Suggested References

The number of possible references is vast and grows alarmingly. (The *Shakespeare Quarterly* devotes one issue each year to a list of the previous year's work, and *Shakespeare Survey*—an annual publication—includes a substantial review of biographical, critical, and textual studies, as well as a survey of performances.) The vast bibliography is best approached through James Harner, *The World Shakespeare Bibliography on CD-Rom: 1900–Present.* The first release, in 1996, included more than 12,000 annotated items from 1990–93, plus references to several thousand book reviews, productions, films, and audio recordings. The plan is to update the publication annually, moving forward one year and backward three years. Thus, the second issue (1997), with 24,700 entries, and another 35,000 or so references to reviews, newspaper pieces, and so on, covered 1987–94.

Though no works are indispensable, those listed below have been found especially helpful. The arrangement is as follows:

1. Shakespeare's Times
2. Shakespeare's Life
3. Shakespeare's Theater
4. Shakespeare on Stage and Screen
5. Miscellaneous Reference Works
6. Shakespeare's Plays: General Studies
7. The Comedies
8. The Romances
9. The Tragedies
10. The Histories
11. *The Tragedy of Coriolanus*

The titles in the first five sections are accompanied by brief explanatory annotations.

1. Shakespeare's Times

Andrews, John F., ed. *William Shakespeare: His World, His Work, His Influence,* 3 vols. (1985). Sixty articles, dealing not only with such subjects as "The State," "The Church," "Law," "Science, Magic, and Folklore," but also with the plays and poems themselves and Shakespeare's influence (e.g., translations, films, reputation).

Byrne, Muriel St. Clare. *Elizabethan Life in Town and Country* (8th ed., 1970). Chapters on manners, beliefs, education, etc., with illustrations.

Dollimore, John, and Alan Sinfield, eds. *Political Shakespeare: New Essays in Cultural Materialism* (1985). Essays on such topics as the subordination of women and colonialism, presented in connection with some of Shakespeare's plays.

Greenblatt, Stephen. *Representing the English Renaissance* (1988). New Historicist essays, especially on connections between political and aesthetic matters, statecraft and stagecraft.

Joseph, B. L. *Shakespeare's Eden: the Commonwealth of England 1558–1629* (1971). An account of the social, political, economic, and cultural life of England.

Kernan, Alvin. *Shakespeare, the King's Playwright: Theater in the Stuart Court 1603–1613* (1995). The social setting and the politics of the court of James I, in relation to *Hamlet, Measure for Measure, Macbeth, King Lear, Antony and Cleopatra, Coriolanus,* and *The Tempest.*

Montrose, Louis. *The Purpose of Playing: Shakespeare and the Cultural Politics of the Elizabethan Theatre* (1996). A poststructuralist view, discussing the professional theater "within the ideological and material frameworks of Elizabethan culture and society," with an extended analysis of *A Midsummer Night's Dream.*

Mullaney, Steven. *The Place of the Stage: License, Play, and Power in Renaissance England* (1988). New Historicist analysis, arguing that popular drama became a cultural institution "only by . . . taking up a place on the margins of society."

Schoenbaum, S. *Shakespeare: The Globe and the World*

(1979). A readable, abundantly illustrated introductory book on the world of the Elizabethans.

Shakespeare's England, 2 vols. (1916). A large collection of scholarly essays on a wide variety of topics, e.g., astrology, costume, gardening, horsemanship, with special attention to Shakespeare's references to these topics.

2. Shakespeare's Life

Andrews, John F., ed. *William Shakespeare: His World, His Work, His Influence,* 3 vols. (1985). See the description above.

Bentley, Gerald E. *Shakespeare: A Biographical Handbook* (1961). The facts about Shakespeare, with virtually no conjecture intermingled.

Chambers, E. K. *William Shakespeare: A Study of Facts and Problems,* 2 vols. (1930). The fullest collection of data.

Fraser, Russell. *Young Shakespeare* (1988). A highly readable account that simultaneously considers Shakespeare's life and Shakespeare's art.

————. *Shakespeare: The Later Years* (1992).

Schoenbaum, S. *Shakespeare's Lives* (1970). A review of the evidence and an examination of many biographies, including those of Baconians and other heretics.

————. *William Shakespeare: A Compact Documentary Life* (1977). An abbreviated version, in a smaller format, of the next title. The compact version reproduces some fifty documents in reduced form. A readable presentation of all that the documents tell us about Shakespeare.

————. *William Shakespeare: A Documentary Life* (1975). A large-format book setting forth the biography with facsimiles of more than two hundred documents, and with transcriptions and commentaries.

3. Shakespeare's Theater

Astington, John H., ed. *The Development of Shakespeare's Theater* (1992). Eight specialized essays on theatrical companies, playing spaces, and performance.

Beckerman, Bernard. *Shakespeare at the Globe, 1599–1609* (1962). On the playhouse and on Elizabethan dramaturgy, acting, and staging.

Bentley, Gerald E. *The Profession of Dramatist in Shakespeare's Time* (1971). An account of the dramatist's status in the Elizabethan period.

———. *The Profession of Player in Shakespeare's Time, 1590–1642* (1984). An account of the status of members of London companies (sharers, hired men, apprentices, managers) and a discussion of conditions when they toured.

Berry, Herbert. *Shakespeare's Playhouses* (1987). Usefully emphasizes how little we know about the construction of Elizabethan theaters.

Brown, John Russell. *Shakespeare's Plays in Performance* (1966). A speculative and practical analysis relevant to all of the plays, but with emphasis on *The Merchant of Venice*, *Richard II*, *Hamlet*, *Romeo and Juliet*, and *Twelfth Night*.

———. *William Shakespeare: Writing for Performance* (1996). A discussion aimed at helping readers to develop theatrically conscious habits of reading.

Chambers, E. K. *The Elizabethan Stage*, 4 vols. (1945). A major reference work on theaters, theatrical companies, and staging at court.

Cook, Ann Jennalie. *The Privileged Playgoers of Shakespeare's London, 1576–1642* (1981). Sees Shakespeare's audience as wealthier, more middle-class, and more intellectual than Harbage (below) does.

Dessen, Alan C. *Elizabethan Drama and the Viewer's Eye* (1977). On how certain scenes may have looked to spectators in an Elizabethan theater.

Gurr, Andrew. *Playgoing in Shakespeare's London* (1987). Something of a middle ground between Cook (above) and Harbage (below).

———. *The Shakespearean Stage, 1579–1642* (2nd ed., 1980). On the acting companies, the actors, the playhouses, the stages, and the audiences.

Harbage, Alfred. *Shakespeare's Audience* (1941). A study of the size and nature of the theatrical public, emphasizing the representativeness of its working class and middle-class audience.

Hodges, C. Walter. *The Globe Restored* (1968). A conjectural restoration, with lucid drawings.

Hosley, Richard. "The Playhouses," in *The Revels History of Drama in English*, vol. 3, general editors Clifford Leech and T. W. Craik (1975). An essay of a hundred pages on the physical aspects of the playhouses.

Howard, Jane E. "Crossdressing, the Theatre, and Gender Struggle in Early Modern England," *Shakespeare Quarterly* 39 (1988): 418–40. Judicious comments on the effects of boys playing female roles.

Orrell, John. *The Human Stage: English Theatre Design, 1567–1640* (1988). Argues that the public, private, and court playhouses are less indebted to popular structures (e.g., innyards and bear-baiting pits) than to banqueting halls and to Renaissance conceptions of Roman amphitheaters.

Slater, Ann Pasternak. *Shakespeare the Director* (1982). An analysis of theatrical effects (e.g., kissing, kneeling) in stage directions and dialogue.

Styan, J. L. *Shakespeare's Stagecraft* (1967). An introduction to Shakespeare's visual and aural stagecraft, with chapters on such topics as acting conventions, stage groupings, and speech.

Thompson, Peter. *Shakespeare's Professional Career* (1992). An examination of patronage and related theatrical conditions.

———. *Shakespeare's Theatre* (1983). A discussion of how plays were staged in Shakespeare's time.

4. Shakespeare on Stage and Screen

Bate, Jonathan, and Russell Jackson, eds. *Shakespeare: An Illustrated Stage History* (1996). Highly readable essays on stage productions from the Renaissance to the present.

Berry, Ralph. *Changing Styles in Shakespeare* (1981). Discusses productions of six plays (*Coriolanus*, *Hamlet*, *Henry V*, *Measure for Measure*, *The Tempest*, and *Twelfth Night*) on the English stage, chiefly 1950–1980.

————. *On Directing Shakespeare: Interviews with Contemporary Directors* (1989). An enlarged edition of a book first published in 1977, this version includes the seven interviews from the early 1970s and adds five interviews conducted in 1988.

Brockbank, Philip, ed. *Players of Shakespeare: Essays in Shakespearean Performance* (1985). Comments by twelve actors, reporting their experiences with roles. See also the entry for Russell Jackson (below).

Bulman, J. C., and H. R. Coursen, eds. *Shakespeare on Television* (1988). An anthology of general and theoretical essays, essays on individual productions, and shorter reviews, with a bibliography and a videography listing cassettes that may be rented.

Coursen, H. P. *Watching Shakespeare on Television* (1993). Analyses not only of TV versions but also of films and videotapes of stage presentations that are shown on television.

Davies, Anthony, and Stanley Wells, eds. *Shakespeare and the Moving Image: The Plays on Film and Television* (1994). General essays (e.g., on the comedies) as well as essays devoted entirely to *Hamlet*, *King Lear*, and *Macbeth*.

Dawson, Anthony B. *Watching Shakespeare: A Playgoer's Guide* (1988). About half of the plays are discussed, chiefly in terms of decisions that actors and directors make in putting the works onto the stage.

Dessen, Alan. *Elizabethan Stage Conventions and Modern Interpretations* (1984). On interpreting conventions such as the representation of light and darkness and stage violence (duels, battles).

Donaldson, Peter. *Shakespearean Films/Shakespearean Directors* (1990). Postmodernist analyses, drawing on Freudianism, Feminism, Deconstruction, and Queer Theory.

Jackson, Russell, and Robert Smallwood, eds. *Players of Shakespeare 2: Further Essays in Shakespearean Performance by Players with the Royal Shakespeare Company* (1988). Fourteen actors discuss their roles in productions between 1982 and 1987.

————. *Players of Shakespeare 3: Further Essays in Shake-

spearean Performance by Players with the Royal Shakespeare Company (1993). Comments by thirteen performers.

Jorgens, Jack. *Shakespeare on Film* (1977). Fairly detailed studies of eighteen films, preceded by an introductory chapter addressing such issues as music, and whether to "open" the play by including scenes of landscape.

Kennedy, Dennis. *Looking at Shakespeare: A Visual History of Twentieth-Century Performance* (1993). Lucid descriptions (with 170 photographs) of European, British, and American performances.

Leiter, Samuel L. *Shakespeare Around the Globe: A Guide to Notable Postwar Revivals* (1986). For each play there are about two pages of introductory comments, then discussions (about five hundred words per production) of ten or so productions, and finally bibliographic references.

McMurty, Jo. *Shakespeare Films in the Classroom* (1994). Useful evaluations of the chief films most likely to be shown in undergraduate courses.

Rothwell, Kenneth, and Annabelle Henkin Melzer. *Shakespeare on Screen: An International Filmography and Videography* (1990). A reference guide to several hundred films and videos produced between 1899 and 1989, including spinoffs such as musicals and dance versions.

Sprague, Arthur Colby. *Shakespeare and the Actors* (1944). Detailed discussions of stage business (gestures, etc.) over the years.

Willis, Susan. *The BBC Shakespeare Plays: Making the Televised Canon* (1991). A history of the series, with interviews and production diaries for some plays.

5. Miscellaneous Reference Works

Abbott, E. A. *A Shakespearean Grammar* (new edition, 1877). An examination of differences between Elizabethan and modern grammar.

Allen, Michael J. B., and Kenneth Muir, eds. *Shakespeare's Plays in Quarto* (1981). One volume containing facsimiles of the plays issued in small format before they were collected in the First Folio of 1623.

Bevington, David. *Shakespeare* (1978). A short guide to hundreds of important writings on the subject.

Blake, Norman. *Shakespeare's Language: An Introduction* (1983). On vocabulary, parts of speech, and word order.

Bullough, Geoffrey. *Narrative and Dramatic Sources of Shakespeare*, 8 vols. (1957–75). A collection of many of the books Shakespeare drew on, with judicious comments.

Campbell, Oscar James, and Edward G. Quinn, eds. *The Reader's Encyclopedia of Shakespeare* (1966). Old, but still the most useful single reference work on Shakespeare.

Cercignani, Fausto. *Shakespeare's Works and Elizabethan Pronunciation* (1981). Considered the best work on the topic, but remains controversial.

Dent, R. W. *Shakespeare's Proverbial Language: An Index* (1981). An index of proverbs, with an introduction concerning a form Shakespeare frequently drew on.

Greg, W. W. *The Shakespeare First Folio* (1955). A detailed yet readable history of the first collection (1623) of Shakespeare's plays.

Harner, James. *The World Shakespeare Bibliography*. See headnote to Suggested References.

Hosley, Richard. *Shakespeare's Holinshed* (1968). Valuable presentation of one of Shakespeare's major sources.

Kökeritz, Helge. *Shakespeare's Names* (1959), A guide to pronouncing some 1,800 names appearing in Shakespeare.

———. *Shakespeare's Pronunciation* (1953). Contains much information about puns and rhymes, but see Cercignani (above).

Muir, Kenneth. *The Sources of Shakespeare's Plays* (1978). An account of Shakespeare's use of his reading. It covers all the plays, in chronological order.

Miriam Joseph, Sister. *Shakespeare's Use of the Arts of Language* (1947). A study of Shakespeare's use of rhetorical devices, reprinted in part as *Rhetoric in Shakespeare's Time* (1962).

The Norton Facsimile: The First Folio of Shakespeare's Plays (1968). A handsome and accurate facsimile of the first collection (1623) of Shakespeare's plays, with a valuable introduction by Charlton Hinman.

Onions, C. T. *A Shakespeare Glossary*, rev. and enlarged by

R. D. Eagleson (1986). Definitions of words (or senses of words) now-obsolete.

Partridge, Eric. *Shakespeare's Bawdy*, rev. ed. (1955). Relatively brief dictionary of bawdy words; useful, but see Williams, below.

Shakespeare Quarterly. See headnote to Suggested References.

Shakespeare Survey. See headnote to Suggested References.

Spevack, Marvin. *The Harvard Concordance to Shakespeare* (1973). An index to Shakespeare's words.

Vickers, Brian. *Appropriating Shakespeare: Contemporary Critical Quarrels* (1993). A survey—chiefly hostile—of recent schools of criticism.

Wells, Stanley, ed. *Shakespeare: A Bibliographical Guide* (new edition, 1990). Nineteen chapters (some devoted to single plays, others to groups of related plays) on recent scholarship on the life and all of the works.

Williams, Gordon. *A Dictionary of Sexual Language and Imagery in Shakespearean and Stuart Literature*, 3 vols. (1994). Extended discussions of words and passages; much fuller than Partridge, cited above.

6. Shakespeare's Plays: General Studies

Bamber, Linda. *Comic Women, Tragic Men: A Study of Gender and Genre in Shakespeare* (1982).

Barnet, Sylvan. *A Short Guide to Shakespeare* (1974).

Callaghan, Dympna, Lorraine Helms, and Jyotsna Singh. *The Weyward Sisters: Shakespeare and Feminist Politics* (1994).

Clemen, Wolfgang H. *The Development of Shakespeare's Imagery* (1951).

Cook, Ann Jennalie. *Making a Match: Courtship in Shakespeare and His Society* (1991).

Dollimore, Jonathan, and Alan Sinfield. *Political Shakespeare: New Essays in Cultural Materialism* (1985).

Dusinberre, Juliet. *Shakespeare and the Nature of Women* (1975).

Granville-Barker, Harley. *Prefaces to Shakespeare*, 2 vols. (1946–47; volume 1 contains essays on *Hamlet, King*

Lear, Merchant of Venice, Antony and Cleopatra, and *Cymbeline*; volume 2 contains essays on *Othello, Coriolanus, Julius Caesar, Romeo and Juliet, Love's Labor's Lost*).

———. *More Prefaces to Shakespeare* (1974; essays on *Twelfth Night, A Midsummer Night's Dream, The Winter's Tale, Macbeth*).

Harbage, Alfred. *William Shakespeare: A Reader's Guide* (1963).

Howard, Jean E. *Shakespeare's Art of Orchestration: Stage Technique and Audience Response* (1984).

Jones, Emrys. *Scenic Form in Shakespeare* (1971).

Lenz, Carolyn Ruth Swift, Gayle Greene, and Carol Thomas Neely, eds. *The Woman's Part: Feminist Criticism of Shakespeare* (1980).

Novy, Marianne. *Love's Argument: Gender Relations in Shakespeare* (1984).

Rose, Mark. *Shakespearean Design* (1972).

Scragg, Leah. *Discovering Shakespeare's Meaning* (1994).

———. *Shakespeare's "Mouldy Tales": Recurrent Plot Motifs in Shakespearean Drama* (1992).

Traub, Valerie. *Desire and Anxiety: Circulations of Sexuality in Shakespearean Drama* (1992).

Traversi, D. A. *An Approach to Shakespeare,* 2 vols. (3rd rev. ed, 1968–69).

Vickers, Brian. *The Artistry of Shakespeare's Prose* (1968).

Wells, Stanley. *Shakespeare: A Dramatic Life* (1994).

Wright, George T. *Shakespeare's Metrical Art* (1988).

7. The Comedies

Barber, C. L. *Shakespeare's Festive Comedy* (1959; discusses *Love's Labor's Lost, A Midsummer Night's Dream, The Merchant of Venice, As You Like It, Twelfth Night*).

Barton, Anne. *The Names of Comedy* (1990).

Berry, Ralph. *Shakespeare's Comedy: Explorations in Form* (1972).

Bradbury, Malcolm, and David Palmer, eds. *Shakespearean Comedy* (1972).

Bryant, J. A., Jr. *Shakespeare and the Uses of Comedy* (1986).

Carroll, William. *The Metamorphoses of Shakespearean Comedy* (1985).

Champion, Larry S. *The Evolution of Shakespeare's Comedy* (1970).

Evans, Bertrand. *Shakespeare's Comedies* (1960).

Frye, Northrop. *Shakespearean Comedy and Romance* (1965).

Leggatt, Alexander. *Shakespeare's Comedy of Love* (1974).

Miola, Robert S. *Shakespeare and Classical Comedy: The Influence of Plautus and Terence* (1994).

Nevo, Ruth. *Comic Transformations in Shakespeare* (1980).

Ornstein, Robert. *Shakespeare's Comedies: From Roman Farce to Romantic Mystery* (1986).

Richman, David. *Laughter, Pain, and Wonder: Shakespeare's Comedies and the Audience in the Theater* (1990).

Salingar, Leo. *Shakespeare and the Traditions of Comedy* (1974).

Slights, Camille Wells. *Shakespeare's Comic Commonwealths* (1993).

Waller, Gary, ed. *Shakespeare's Comedies* (1991).

Westlund, Joseph. *Shakespeare's Reparative Comedies: A Psychoanalytic View of the Middle Plays* (1984).

Williamson, Marilyn. *The Patriarchy of Shakespeare's Comedies* (1986).

8. The Romances (*Pericles, Cymbeline, The Winter's Tale, The Tempest, The Two Noble Kinsmen*)

Adams, Robert M. *Shakespeare: The Four Romances* (1989).

Felperin, Howard. *Shakespearean Romance* (1972).

Frye, Northrop. *A Natural Perspective: The Development of Shakespearean Comedy and Romance* (1965).

Mowat, Barbara. *The Dramaturgy of Shakespeare's Romances* (1976).

Warren, Roger. *Staging Shakespeare's Late Plays* (1990).

Young, David. *The Heart's Forest: A Study of Shakespeare's Pastoral Plays* (1972).

9. The Tragedies

Bradley, A. C. *Shakespearean Tragedy* (1904).
Brooke, Nicholas. *Shakespeare's Early Tragedies* (1968).
Champion, Larry. *Shakespeare's Tragic Perspective* (1976).
Drakakis, John, ed. *Shakespearean Tragedy* (1992).
Evans, Bertrand. *Shakespeare's Tragic Practice* (1979).
Everett, Barbara. *Young Hamlet: Essays on Shakespeare's Tragedies* (1989).
Foakes, R. A. *Hamlet versus Lear: Cultural Politics and Shakespeare's Art* (1993).
Frye, Northrop. *Fools of Time: Studies in Shakespearean Tragedy* (1967).
Harbage, Alfred, ed. *Shakespeare: The Tragedies* (1964).
Mack, Maynard. *Everybody's Shakespeare: Reflections Chiefly on the Tragedies* (1993).
McAlindon, T. *Shakespeare's Tragic Cosmos* (1991).
Miola, Robert S. *Shakespeare and Classical Tragedy: The Influence of Seneca* (1992).
———. *Shakespeare's Rome* (1983).
Nevo, Ruth. *Tragic Form in Shakespeare* (1972).
Rackin, Phyllis. *Shakespeare's Tragedies* (1978).
Rose, Mark, ed. *Shakespeare's Early Tragedies: A Collection of Critical Essays* (1995).
Rosen, William. *Shakespeare and the Craft of Tragedy* (1960).
Snyder, Susan. *The Comic Matrix of Shakespeare's Tragedies* (1979).
Wofford, Susanne. *Shakespeare's Late Tragedies: A Collection of Critical Essays* (1996).
Young, David. *The Action to the Word: Structure and Style in Shakespearean Tragedy* (1990).
———. *Shakespeare's Middle Tragedies: A Collection of Critical Essays* (1993).

10. The Histories

Blanpied, John W. *Time and the Artist in Shakespeare's English Histories* (1983).

Campbell, Lily B. *Shakespeare's "Histories": Mirrors of Elizabethan Policy* (1947).

Champion, Larry S. *Perspective in Shakespeare's English Histories* (1980).

Hodgdon, Barbara. *The End Crowns All: Closure and Contradiction in Shakespeare's History* (1991).

Holderness, Graham. *Shakespeare Recycled: The Making of Historical Drama* (1992).

———, ed. *Shakespeare's History Plays: "Richard II" to "Henry V"* (1992).

Leggatt, Alexander. *Shakespeare's Political Drama: The History Plays and the Roman Plays* (1988).

Ornstein, Robert. *A Kingdom for a Stage: The Achievement of Shakespeare's History Plays* (1972).

Rackin, Phyllis. *Stages of History: Shakespeare's English Chronicles* (1990).

Saccio, Peter. *Shakespeare's English Kings: History, Chronicle, and Drama* (1977).

Tillyard, E. M. W. *Shakespeare's History Plays* (1944).

Velz, John W., ed. *Shakespeare's English Histories: A Quest for Form and Genre* (1996).

11. *The Tragedy of Coriolanus*

In addition to the titles mentioned in *Coriolanus* on Stage and Screen (p. 277) and those mentioned in Section 9, The Tragedies, the following are recommended.

For detailed information concerning dating, textual problems, glosses, and so forth, the edition by Lee Bliss (2000) is highly recommended. Other useful editions are by Philip Brockbank (1976) and by R. B. Parker (1994).

Brockman, B. A. *Shakespeare's "Coriolanus": A Casebook* (1979).

Farnham, Willard. *Shakespeare's Tragic Frontier* (1950).

George, David. "Plutarch, Insurrection, and Death in *Coriolanus*." *Shakespeare Survey* 53 (2000): 60–72.

Goldman, Michael. *Shakespeare and the Energies of Drama* (1972).

Gordon, D. J. "Name and Fame: Shakespeare's Coriolanus."

In *Papers Mainly Shakespearian,* ed. G. L. Duthie. (1964), pp. 40–57.

Honigmann, E. A. J. *Shakespeare: Seven Tragedies* (1976).

Kitto, H. D. F. *Poesis: Structure and Thought* (1966).

Knight, G. Wilson. *The Imperial Theme: Further Interpretations of Shakespeare's Tragedies Including the Roman Plays,* 3rd ed. (1951).

Knights, L. C. *Some Shakespearean Themes* (1959).

MacCallum, M. W. *Shakespeare's Roman Plays and their Background* (1910).

McAlindon, T. M. "*Coriolanus:* An Essentialist Tragedy," *RES* 44 (1993): 502–20.

Miola, Robert S. *Shakespeare's Rome* (1983).

Sicherman, Carol. "Coriolanus: The Failure of Words," *ELH* 39 (1972): 189–207.

Traversi, D. A. *Shakespeare: The Roman Plays* (1963).

Waith, Eugene. *The Herculean Hero* (1962).

Wheeler, David, ed. "*Coriolanus*": *Critical Essays* (1995).